MAJOR FARRAN'S HAT

MAJOR FARRAN'S HAT

The Untold Story of the Struggle
to Establish the Jewish State

David Cesarani

DA CAPO PRESS
A Member of the Perseus Books Group

Printed in the United States of America. For information, address
Da Capo Press, 11 Cambridge Center, Cambridge, MA 02142.

Set in Goudy by Palimpsest Book Production Limited, Grangemouth,
Stirlingshire Map of Palestine 1945-46 (p. xi) and map of Jerusalem 1947
(p. xii) by ML Design, London, www.ml-design.co.uk

Cataloging-in-Publication data for this book
is available from the Library of Congress
ISBN: 978-0-306-81845-5

First Da Capo Press edition 2009
Reprinted by arrangement with William Heinemann,
a division of The Random House Group, Limited

Published by Da Capo Press
A Member of the Perseus Books Group
www.dacapopress.com

Da Capo Press books are available at special
discounts for bulk purchases in the U.S. by corporations,
institutions, and other organizations. For more information,
please contact the Special Markets Department at the Perseus Books
Group, 2300 Chestnut Street, Suite 200, Philadelphia, PA
19103, or call (800) 810-4145, extension 5000 or
e-mail special.markets@perseusbooks.com

10 9 8 7 6 5 4 3 2 1

Contents

Preface

This is the story of a murder and a cover-up that took place in Palestine during 1947, the last year in which Britain ruled that troubled land under a mandate from the League of Nations. The murder and the scandal it provoked were direct consequences of Britain's war against Jewish insurgents, militant Zionists, who were trying to bring the mandate to an end and create a Jewish state. The British response to this challenge exposed the lengths to which imperial warriors would go in the last-ditch defence of the empire.

This book explores the character and the intentions of the courageous young men who fought that bitter rearguard and shows that, ultimately, they were pawns in a fierce contest between British civilian and military leaders, victims of a profound disagreement over the best strategy and tactics for imperial defence. It explains why Britain lost the mandate for Palestine; why its counter-insurgency strategy was at odds with its diplomacy; and why the tactics of both the police force and the army were ill-judged, poorly conducted and futile. These errors culminated in a scandal that helped to strip British rule of whatever legitimacy it still had in the eyes of the Jewish inhabitants of Palestine and to many more people around the world. Behind the public scandal, though, lay a deeper one that has remained hidden until today. Revealed here, for the first time, is evidence that officials at the highest levels of the security forces and the government conspired to pervert the course of justice. As a result an innocent boy who was murdered never had the justice for which his family begged, while the men who killed him and those who conspired to hide his crime were garlanded with honours.

The facts laid out here challenge the widely held belief that Britain surrendered its empire gracefully and with dignity. On the contrary, this book argues that the conflict between the British and the Jews in Palestine created a poisonous legacy which infected the British response to subsequent anti-colonial movements that posed a threat to imperial rule. Yet the actions of the men described here were only a small part of a counter-insurgency war and the measures taken against the first modern international terrorist campaign. This book also reveals previously unknown details of Jewish terrorist operations in Europe and a succession of strikes against the British mainland. It shows that although Britain failed to cope with the insurgency in Palestine the security forces were more successful (and also lucky) in homeland defence, preventing or deterring Jewish terrorists from triggering a major incident on the British mainland. *Major Farran's Hat* is not, however, a comprehensive history of how Israel came into existence and it does not touch on the conflict between Jews and Arabs in Palestine. For the most part the Arabs were bystanders to the struggle between the Jews and the British between mid 1945 and November 1947. Its outcome, though, did have a profound and terrible impact on Palestinian Arab society.

Britain's decision to hand Palestine to the United Nations was a direct result of the failure of its counter-insurgency campaign and the loss of political will to keep up the fight; the UN's decision to end the mandate and to partition Palestine into a Jewish state and an Arab state reflected Britain's loss of legitimacy, exemplified by the revelation that elements in the British regime had resorted to brutal and illegal methods in order to hang on; and, finally, Britain's decision to withdraw without enforcing the settlement prescribed by the UN was a direct consequence of military exhaustion brought on by three years of grinding and ultimately futile anti-terrorist warfare. As a result of this concatenation of events, British forces remained neutral in the communal warfare between Jews and Arabs that erupted between November 1947 and May 1948. During this period the Jewish forces gained the upper hand and conquered several cities, triggering the exodus of their Arab inhabitants, while hundreds of Arab villages were captured, destroyed, and their populations expelled. To that extent the Palestinian Arabs, too, were indirectly victims of the scandalous events covered in this narrative.

Many of the sources on which the book is based have only recently become available. In the wake of the scandal key documents belonging to the Palestine government, including records of the Palestine Police Force that contained evidence of an unsolved crime, were wilfully destroyed. But much material was transmitted to London where it survived, by sheer chance, unnoticed and unweeded in the files of the Colonial Office. Enough, at least, to reconstruct the events that occurred sixty years ago. These files have now been made available by The National Archives: Public Record Office at Kew, London. The papers held there add essential detail to the records in the archives of the Jewish underground movements in the Jabotinsky Institute in Tel Aviv, and the records of the Jewish Agency, held at the Central Zionist Archive in Jerusalem. The bigger, strategic picture has been available since the 1970s thanks to the papers of the last British high commissioner for Palestine, Sir Alan Cunningham, held at the Middle East Centre, St Antony's College, Oxford, and the diaries of his bête noire, the Chief of the Imperial General Staff Field Marshal Viscount Montgomery of Alamein, held at the Imperial War Museum. The addition of the new records finally shows the disastrous mismatch between strategy and tactics.

It was simply not possible to reveal the extent of the Jewish terrorist effort in Europe and the UK until the relevant files of the security services were declassified and opened to researchers in May 2004. Agents of the Jewish underground had previously written 'memoirs' and even given interviews to journalists or historians, but these were inevitably wary if not downright misleading. The declassified files make it feasible to reconstruct the Jewish terrorist networks in Britain in 1946–8 and evaluate how MI5, MI6 and Special Branch handled the threat they posed. When placed alongside the files of the Foreign Office dealing with Jewish terrorist operations in Europe (with support from sympathisers in the United States) and Colonial

Office documents on the font of these activities in Palestine, the records of the security services enable us to grasp for the first time the full extent and ambition of Jewish terrorism in the late 1940s.

David Cesarani
Royal Holloway, University of London
June 2008

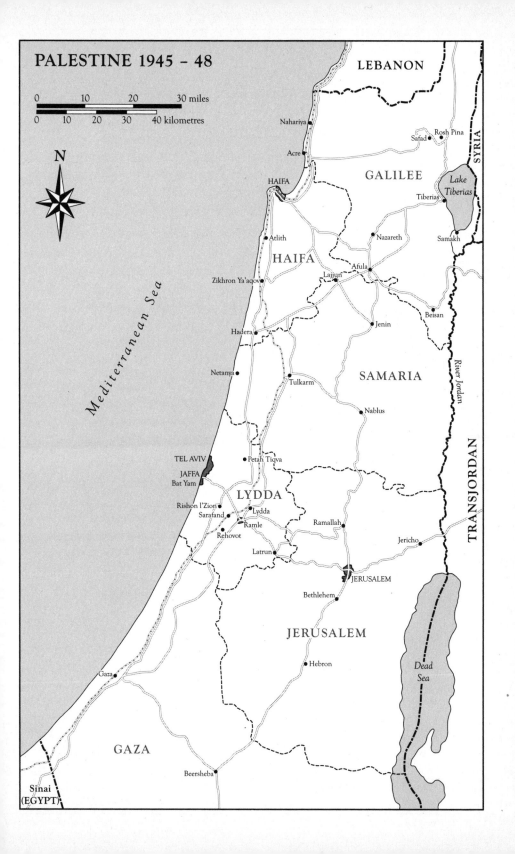

PALESTINE 1945 – 48

LEBANON

0   10   20   30 miles

0 10 20 30 40 kilometres

N

Mediterranean Sea

SYRIA

Nahariya

Safad   Rosh Pina

Acre

HAIFA

GALILEE

Lake Tiberias

Tiberias

Atlith

Nazareth

Samakh

HAIFA

Zikhron Ya'aqov

Lajjun   Afula

Hadera

Beisan

Jenin

Netanya

SAMARIA

Tulkarm

Nablus

TEL AVIV
JAFFA
Bat Yam

Petah Tiqva

River Jordan

TRANSJORDAN

LYDDA

Rishon l'Zion
Sarafand   Lydda
Ramle
Rehovot
Latrun

Ramallah

Jericho

JERUSALEM

Bethlehem

JERUSALEM

Gaza

Hebron

Dead Sea

GAZA

Beersheba

Sinai
(EGYPT)

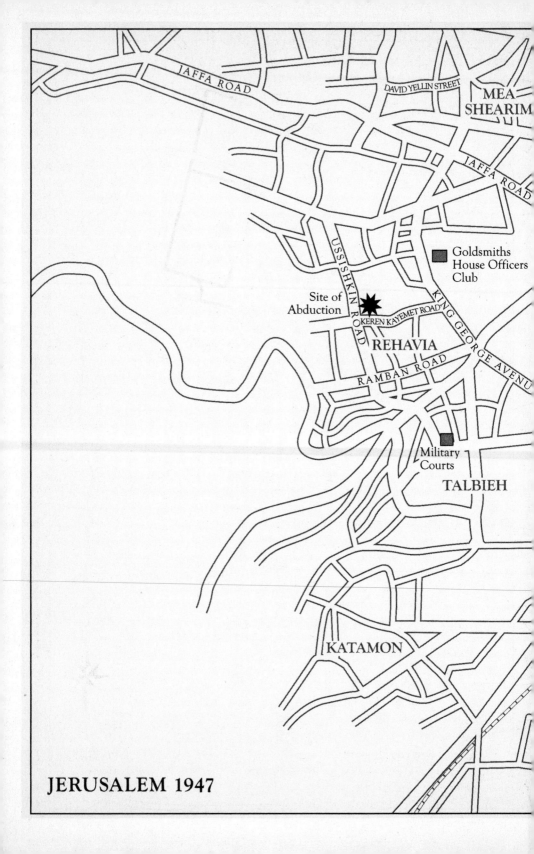

JAFFA ROAD

DAVID YELLIN STREET

MEA SHEARIM

JAFFA ROAD

USSISHKIN ROAD

Goldsmiths House Officers Club

Site of Abduction

KEREN KAYEMET ROAD

KING GEORGE AVENUE

REHAVIA

RAMBAN ROAD

Military Courts

TALBIEH

KATAMON

JERUSALEM 1947

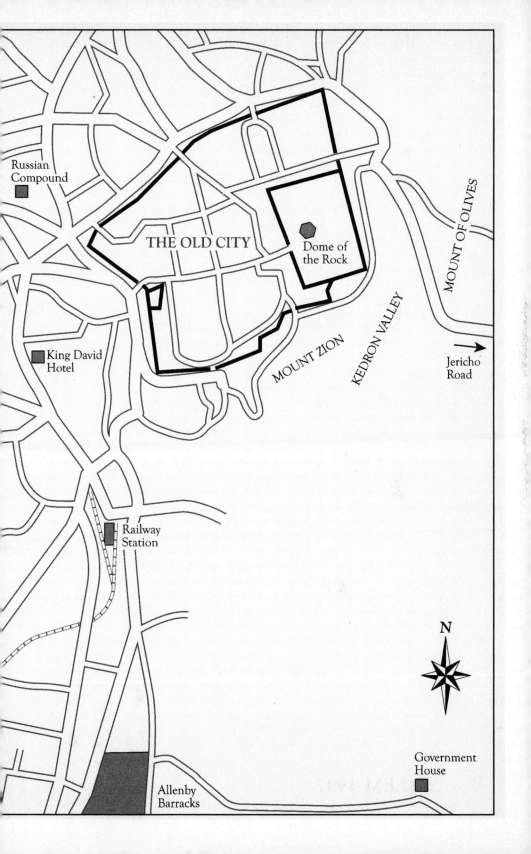

Russian
Compound

THE OLD CITY

Dome of
the Rock

King David
Hotel

MOUNT ZION

KEDRON VALLEY

MOUNT OF OLIVES

Jericho
Road

Railway
Station

N

Government
House

Allenby
Barracks

Prologue

Abduction in Jerusalem

At six-thirty on the evening of Tuesday 6 May 1947, Alexander Rubowitz left his home at 22 David Yellin Street in Mea Shearim, a Jewish suburb on the northern edge of Jerusalem. Although he was only sixteen years old, Alexander was setting out on a mission for the Lohamei HaHerut b'Yisrael, the Fighters for the Freedom of Israel. Known by their Hebrew acronym as LEHI they were more familiar, not to say notorious, to the rest of the world as the Stern Gang – a ferociously effective and murderous terrorist group fighting to end British rule in Palestine and establish a Jewish state. Alexander was tall and slim, with dark hair and dark eyes that gave him a rather dreamy look. He was a quiet boy, but his placid demeanour concealed a fanatical temperament that fitted him perfectly for the war that the Jewish underground was waging against the British.[1]

Alexander lived at home with his parents, two older brothers and a younger sister. The family were Orthodox Jews and, rather unusually, could trace their roots in Jerusalem back at least one generation. Alexander's father, Yedidya, was the son of a rabbi who had emigrated from Eastern Europe to Palestine in the 1850s. At that time it took pioneering spirit as well as religious fervour for a Jew to settle in Jerusalem. Yedidya was also something of a pioneer. He became a pharmacist at the Rothschild Hospital in Jerusalem and opened a chemist's shop that was one of the first of its kind in Palestine. Alexander's mother, Miriam, was a sickly woman and was housebound for much of the time. But she was a fierce Zionist and though she knew that Alexander was putting himself in danger she declined to play the part of an ailing matriarch reining in her children.[2]

For the past year and a half Alexander had belonged to the Brit Hashmonaim, the Covenant of the Hasmoneans, a religious youth group that was also a front organisation for LEHI. It had about 150 members in Jerusalem, of whom some thirty were engaged in covert activity. LEHI routinely used teenagers for distributing propaganda, as couriers, and even for moving arms around the city. They were more expendable than experienced fighters and faced less severe punishment if they were caught. Youths were especially useful for putting up wall posters. This was important work because LEHI had lost its clandestine radio station in a police raid in February 1946 and had no regular party newspaper to trumpet its ideology. Wall posters were essential for getting its message across and telling the Jewish public what it was doing. Every few days bundles of the crudely produced news poster called *HaMa'as* (the *Deed*) and the news-sheet *HeChazit* (the *Front*) were sent up from Tel Aviv by taxi and stashed in secret locations by militants. They passed them on to the youthful volunteers for distribution, but it was risky work. The teenagers were vulnerable to police patrols and were frequently caught.[3]

Although the Rubowitz family sympathised with militant Jewish nationalism they apparently had little idea of what Alexander was up to until his parents were summoned to Ma'aleh High School, where Alexander was a student, to see the headmaster. Because Miriam was ill and Yedidya was looking after her, Alexander's elder brother Ya'acov went. He was taken aback when the headmaster told him that Alexander had been seen putting up posters for the Jewish underground. Ya'acov tried to defend his kid brother by pointing out that he was hard-working and smart, while what he did outside of school hours was his own business. But the headmaster complained that Alexander was working for the underground inside the school, too, recruiting youngsters for the cause. Although there was no proof that he was engaged in violence, he had written an essay entitled 'Our Path to Independence' which justified the use of terrorist methods. 'And,' said the headmaster, 'that's enough for me.' Alexander was brought into the head's office and asked if it was true that he had joined the 'dissidents', the Jewish underground groups that refused to accept the authority of the official Jewish leadership in Palestine. Alexander admitted that it was true. When the headmaster asked him to give up this activity Alexander said he had sworn an oath of loyalty and refused. So he was expelled.[4]

Alexander enrolled in a second school, but it was not long before his militancy came to the notice of the authorities there as well. The official leadership of the Jewish community in Palestine, the Jewish Agency, was so afraid that terrorism would provoke a severe backlash from the British that it periodically co-operated with the security forces or used its own militia to suppress the 'dissidents'. Consequently, Alexander's avowed membership of LEHI painted him as a 'traitor'. He was harassed by students and teachers until, finally, he was again thrown out.[5] Afraid of the strain that Alexander's misadventures might place on their mother's health, his brothers tried to talk him into leaving LEHI. Ya'acov even contacted the leader of the Brit Hashmonaim, Yael Ben-Dov, and pleaded with her to cut him loose. As a last throw Yedidya told Miriam what was going on, but she would not lend herself to emotional blackmail. Instead, according to Ya'acov, she told her sons 'he has to go. They're all going now. Do you want him to lie under a bed? Does it matter where he goes? They're all going now. He has to go and succeed.'[6]

With this blessing from his mother Alexander abandoned any thought of schooling and looked for work that would allow him to continue his underground activity. After a while he found a job at the Jerusalem office of the *Ha'aretz* newspaper, Palestine's leading Hebrew daily. But *Ha'aretz* firmly supported the Jewish Agency and when someone snitched to the management about Alexander's allegiances he was promptly sacked. Undeterred he continued to get up before dawn day after day, met with the nine other boys in his group, and set out to plaster messages from LEHI all over town. When the struggle between the British and the Jewish resistance intensified during spring 1947 the work became all-consuming. Ezra Yakim, one of Alexander's companions in the underground, recalled that the boys 'gave up any ideas of a life of ease and tranquillity'.

They were surrounded by 'constant danger'. Like true militants they gradually slipped out of the ambit of friends and family, and eventually detached from society as a whole. 'The cell was now their family.' The intensity of comradeship compensated for their alienation and the nerve-wracking possibility of capture. In Yakim's vivid words they lived in a 'blur of anonymity'.[7]

Under the *nom de guerre* Haim, Alexander emerged as the leader in his ten-strong cell. 'Whenever we met', Yakim remembered many years later, 'he would speak of his desire to confront the enemy of his people with gun in hand. His attitude to the British, a combination of derision and fury, was contagious.' Alexander envied Yakim for being older because this meant that if the British caught him, he might be sentenced to death. According to Yakim, Alexander announced that 'To go to the gallows is a very great privilege, for every hanging brings us closer to salvation. Every hanging widens the chasm between them and our people. They have always hated us and always will, but if it will make our nation rise up against them, then we must suffer, sacrifice our lives, go to the gallows . . .' Whether the sixteen-year-old Alexander Rubowitz really said this, or whether these patriotic sentiments were attributed to him in the light of what subsequently happened, it was not long before wishful thinking became a gruesome reality.[8]

Having left his home in the Mea Shearim district, Alexander headed south and crossed the busy Jaffa Road. The sun was setting on a hot and humid day as he threaded his way through the crowded streets of the Mahane Yehuda quarter, home to a sprawling food market, and entered the spacious and leafy suburb of Rehavia. En route he may have picked up some clandestine material because he was not noticed in Rehavia until around 8 p.m. It was then that a young woman standing on the balcony of her flat noticed a teenage boy running down Haran (today Aharon) Street. Despite the twilight gloom Mrs Sherlin had a good view from her vantage point and clearly saw a youth, who she later identified as Alexander Rubowitz, being chased by a burly, fair-haired man wearing tennis shoes, slacks and 'an army-style shirt'. Alexander fled from Haran Street into Ussishkin Street, but his pursuer was more powerful and athletic. Near the junction of Ussishkin Street and Keren Kayemet

L'Yisrael Street he grabbed Alexander and wrestled him to a stand-still. Two thirteen-year-old boys, Moshe Khesin and Jacob Jacobson, who were on some waste ground collecting wood for a bonfire party to mark the minor Jewish festival of Lag B'omer, then saw the man force Alexander into a waiting motor car. He struggled so furiously that it took the assistance of a second man, who emerged from the six-seater saloon, to finally bundle him into the back.[9]

At this point Meir Cohen, a fifteen-year-old who had also been observing the struggle, plucked up the courage to intervene. Meir went over to the car and asked who they were and what they were doing. The man who was still outside replied in perfect English that he was a police officer. To underline his words he produced a document that Cohen recognised as a Police Identification Certificate. He then brandished a revolver and threatened to shoot the lad if he didn't clear off. But Meir, stood his ground long enough to hear a Hebrew-speaker shouting from inside the car, 'I'm from the Rubowitz family.' He also glimpsed the unwilling occupant of the back seat being hit repeatedly across the head. The doors slammed shut and Cohen watched helplessly as the big saloon began to pull away from the kerb. As it accelerated up the long, straight road heading north several of the onlookers were able to read the number plate: 993. Some later claimed they heard shouts from inside the car as it disappeared down a dip in the road and was finally lost from sight.[10]

However, scenes like this were not unfamiliar on the streets of Jerusalem at this time. The Jewish underground frequently kidnapped British civilians, policemen and soldiers to use as hostages against the lives of captured terrorists. During the episodic struggles between the official Jewish militia, the Hagana, and the 'dissidents', it was not unknown for one faction to seize dozens of activists from another. Samuel Katz, an activist in the 'dissident' underground group Irgun Zvai Leumi, recalled that during the periodic 'hunting seasons' when the Jewish Agency and its paramilitary arms co-operated with the British, or for their own purposes tried to suppress the 'dissidents', 'kidnappings, beatings, torture, direct denunciations to the British became the sole occupation of the action-hungry soldiers of the Hagana'. The *Palestine Post* reported four unsolved kidnappings, three involving teenagers, in May 1947 alone. In one instance, a fourteen-year-old-boy was abducted from the hospital where he was being treated for a bullet wound inflicted while he was fleeing a police patrol which discovered him putting up Stern Gang posters.[11]

So once the commotion had subsided Moshe Khesin and Jacob Jacobson went back to their games in the street. It was then they noticed a grey felt hat lying in the road. The grey trilby had been knocked off the head of one of the men involved in the tussle beside the car. They picked it up and fooled around with it before taking the hat with them to the nearby Shaarei Hessed synagogue. Their sport was interrupted when an irritated Torah student confiscated the trilby and placed it out of reach on top of a cupboard. The fun over, Moshe and Jacob wandered off and forgot about it.

But Alexander did not return home that night. Naturally, by the next morning his family were frantic with worry. His brothers Ya'acov and Nehamiah walked the short distance from their apartment to Mustashfa police station in Mahane Yehuda and reported his disappearance to the duty officer. Because they knew that Alexander was working for the underground they thought it was more than possible that he had been picked up by the police or the British Army. If so, they anticipated that the officers at the police station would quickly find out where he was being held. However, routine enquiries revealed nothing.[12]

The next day the Rubowitz family arranged for descriptions of the missing teenager to be published in the Hebrew press. They had an immediate effect. On 9 May *Ha'aretz* ran a small piece about the disappearance headlined 'Abducted or Arrested?' The article gave the details of what Alexander was wearing when last seen by his family and a brief account of the incident taken from an unnamed passer-by. It also reported that enquiries had revealed Alexander was not in police custody, although the family knew that this was not conclusive proof of anything because it was quite likely that he would have given a false name if he had been picked up.[13]

On Monday 12 May the family published a photograph of Alexander in the Hebrew dailies. The picture jogged memories. The next day Moshe Khesin and Jacob Jacobson reported to the police that they had seen a youth resembling Alexander being taken away by 'blond' men in a car with the number plate M993. They also remembered that after the scuffle by the car they had found a hat in the street. When Ya'acov and Nehamiah heard that the boys had left it in the Shaarei Hessed synagogue they hurried to Rehavia. The caretaker, a Mr Kaminitsky, quickly found the hat. As soon as the grey trilby was in their hands the brothers noticed a name written in ink on the sweatband. Even though it was worn and smudged they could make out FAR-AN or FARKAN. They immediately took the hat to the Mahane Yehuda police station and handed it over to a British police inspector named John O'Neill. Public curiosity was now piqued by the story and new information reached them every day, some of it false and some of it potentially significant. In an important tip-off they were assured by an unknown source that Alexander had not been abducted as the result of any friction between Jewish underground groups. Later, a boy called at their home and left an anonymous letter typed in Hebrew stating that Alexander had been seized by a man in civilian clothes, carrying a pistol, and driven away in a car with the registration 993.[14]

Alarmed by this new information the family contacted a lawyer, Asher Levitsky. He was a well known and highly regarded Jerusalem advocate who was associated with the right-wing Zionists. From time to time he did pro bono work for the members of the Irgun Zvai Leumi who were arrested by the British. On 19 May Levitsky met with Detective Superintendent Hadingham of the Jerusalem CID. Hadingham reiterated what the police had said before; that Alexander was not in prison or in police custody, although it was possible that he was being held by the army. When Levitsky asked if the name FARKAN or FAR-AN meant anything to him, Hadingham said it didn't. The detective superintendent advised the family to check with the underground because 'in his opinion here was an abduction carried out by Jews'. The family discounted that hypothesis but followed Hadingham's suggestion to make further enquiries with the military. They contacted a British Army chaplain who on their behalf asked if anyone in the military police or army prisons had knowledge of Alexander Rubowitz or a youth matching his description. The results were entirely negative. It seemed that the military were not holding Alexander, either.[15]

A week after the first eyewitnesses had come forward news of the hat's existence leaked out. A major report in the *Palestine Post* on 22 May revealed that it had been found and handed to the police. But the Jerusalem CID reiterated to the Rubowitz family that the police had no knowledge of anyone by the name FAR-AN or FARKAN. CID officers also told the family that the registration number on the car as reported by eyewitnesses was either mistaken or the plates were false. (The number plate actually belonged to a doctor in Tel Aviv.) Strangely, the CID hinted that Alexander *had* been abducted by someone British, but went on to assure the family that he was not held in any British-run police or military installation.[16]

The next day the *Palestine Post* received an anonymous letter addressed to Miriam Rubowitz. The writer hinted that they had once been acquainted with the family but their current occupation was rather more pertinent than a forgotten friendship: the author was a handwriting expert.

> My dear Mrs Rubowitz,
>
> I have been following the Palestine Post re- the kidnapping of your dear son Alex, and the part clue given. I think that I might be able to assist you in the rest of the clue . . .
>
> I am an expert, of ink writing on cloth, absorbing paper, pipirus [sic] etc., and I can tell you, as anybody else might, that ink spreads blotches, etc. and that the name is not FARKAN or FARRKAN, but after the first 'R' there is a further 'R' which should read 'FARRAN'. The 'R' which might not be very clear, or might have spread and shows 'K'.
>
> The CID are right to have stated that the abductors were British, but they are not right in saying that they do not know who the person is, or do not know the person.
>
> I would frankly tell you, this man is a deputy superintendent of police, in the Criminal Investigation Department, and is often seen wearing civilian clothes.[17]

The anonymous correspondent was careful to explain that he or she did not belong to any political group and was acting impartially. But whatever the reason for getting in touch the information the letter contained represented a breakthrough for the family. Rumours now began to swirl around the Jewish community that Alexander Rubowitz was not the victim of internecine warfare between Jewish factions or prey to a criminal assault, but the target of an operation led by a British police officer. At the end of May the press reported for the first time that Rubowitz had been putting up Stern Gang posters at the time he was seized. It was not hard to put two and two together. All the evidence pointed to a deputy superintendent of police called Roy Alexander Farran.[18]

But Roy Farran was no ordinary policeman: he had previously served in the Special Air Service, an elite regiment that conducted daring operations behind German lines during the Second World War. Although he was only twenty-six years old he was one of the most highly decorated officers in the British Army. Farran's unit was one of two 'special squads' set up inside the Palestine Police Force to conduct covert operations against Jewish terrorists. These 'special squads' were the brainchild of the inspector general of the Palestine police, Colonel Nicol Gray, who was also a brilliant soldier. He had led 45 Royal Marine Commando in some of the toughest battles on D-Day and during the liberation of Europe. It was Gray who appointed another war hero, Lieutenant Colonel Bernard Fergusson, to recruit the officers who would spearhead the counter-terrorist offensive in Palestine, including Roy Farran. Fergusson had fought behind Japanese lines in Burma and was well versed in the dark arts of unconventional warfare. He had taught Farran at Sandhurst before the war and took pride in his former student's reputation as a daredevil warrior.

The story of how these brilliant, courageous young men came to be in Palestine is at the heart of Britain's war against Jewish terrorism. The scandal that erupted around them shook the British Mandate to its foundations and helped erode whatever legitimacy remained for British rule. Roy Farran's fate became entangled with the fate of the British Empire. The intermingling of diplomacy and counter-insurgency warfare would lead to a trail of bombs and bloodshed that stretched from the Middle East to Middle England, from David Yellin Street to Downing Street.

Jewish Rebels, Imperial Warriors and Colonial Policemen

In 1947 Palestine was a cauldron of discontent, rebellion and violence. Britain, which had ruled Palestine since General Allenby wrested the territory from the Ottoman Empire in 1917, faced the most serious challenge to its domination. The implications of this unrest spread far wider than just the Middle East. Although Palestine was a small place, roughly the size of Wales, it occupied a key position in the geostrategy of the British Empire.

British scholars, artists, explorers, missionaries and soldiers had long been fascinated by the Holy Land. But Britain only became strategically engaged in the Middle East when the Conservative government led by Prime Minister Benjamin Disraeli purchased a major share in the Suez Canal in 1875. During the high tide of British imperialism the canal assumed immense importance as the main artery carrying military and economic traffic to and from India and Britain's Far Eastern possessions. In November 1914 the Ottoman Empire, which bordered Egypt to the east, entered the Great War on the side of Germany and a few months later launched probes across the Sinai Peninsular towards the canal. British forces repulsed these incursions and eventually went over to the offensive. In 1917, after bitter fighting, the Allied forces commanded by General Allenby were on the way to Jerusalem. The city fell in December. At the same time as the military campaign was being fought, a diplomatic battle was being waged over the future of

Palestine that would inveigle Britain in the politics of this conflicted region for the next thirty years.[1]

In November 1917 the British Foreign Secretary, Arthur Balfour, issued a statement in the form of a letter to Lord Rothschild declaring that the government looked with favour on 'the establishment in Palestine of a national home for the Jewish people, and will use their best endeavours to facilitate the achievement of this object, it being clearly understood that nothing shall be done which may prejudice the civil and religious rights of existing non-Jewish communities in Palestine, or the rights and political status enjoyed by Jews in any other country.' The motives for the Balfour Declaration were mixed. Jews had lived in what they called Eretz Israel, the Land of Israel, since biblical times but the last vestige of an independent Jewish state was snuffed out by the Romans. Successive Jewish revolts resulted in the forced dispersion of the Jews and depopulation of the land. However, since the 1880s Jews had started emigrating to Palestine from countries, mainly in Eastern Europe, where they suffered discrimination and persecution. They bought land, set up farms and built towns. Various movements sprang up to facilitate this migration but it gained coherence, an ideology, and an organisation when Theodor Herzl founded the World Zionist Organisation (WZO) in 1897. The WZO was dedicated to obtaining a Jewish state in what the Jewish people regarded as their ancestral homeland. Zionist leaders, beginning with Herzl, appealed to one great power after another to help them achieve this goal. As soon as Turkey, which controlled Palestine, entered the war in late 1914 a few prominent British Jews and Zionist activists who happened to be in England lobbied the government to seize the opportunity to carve a pro-British Jewish state out of the Ottoman Empire. By early 1917 key British politicians, notably Prime Minister David Lloyd George, and various officials believed that a pledge to support Jewish national aspirations would win Jewish opinion in the neutral United States over to their side. They also hoped that a pro-Zionist policy would persuade Jews in war-weary Russia to encourage their leaders to soldier on. These beliefs, which reflect the desperation of the times, were based on a grotesquely exaggerated understanding of 'Jewish power'. The more rational holders of these stereotypical ideas were quickly disillusioned. However, there was an additional and more realistic impulse. British policymakers wanted a good excuse to hold onto Palestine once the war was won and to keep their imperial rivals, the French, out. By contrast, this ploy worked exceedingly well.[2]

In order to legitimise their occupation, in 1920 the British obtained from the victorious Allies at the San Remo Conference consent to remain in Palestine under a mandate on behalf of the new League of Nations. However, at no stage had anyone consulted the Palestinian Arabs: the Balfour Declaration was a supreme act of imperial hubris. Although Palestinian Arabs were slow to develop a local, let alone national identity, Muslim and Christian elites had been protesting against Jewish immigration and landbuying since the 1890s. In 1919 they formed the vast majority of the inhabitants, approximately 580,000 as against 65,000 Jews, and were developing distinct, national aspirations. They soon resented British rule for making it possible for Jews to immigrate en masse with a view to settling the entire country and turning it into a Jewish one. Local notables and members of the educated urban class formed associations and parties to articulate Arab opposition. Popular unrest, with a tinge of religious antagonism, led to riots directed against Jewish immigrants in 1920 and 1921; meanwhile Arab representatives lobbied the British locally and in London. It fell to Winston Churchill, as British colonial secretary, to put British rule on a stable basis and confirm its international legitimacy. In 1922 he issued a White Paper limiting the 'Jewish national home' to the area west of the River Jordan and linking immigration to what the local economy could absorb. The League of Nations then formally conferred the mandate on Britain, and it was accepted after much heated debate by Parliament. The mandate authorised the British to oversee the development of Palestine towards self-rule; the 'Jewish national home' was embedded in this mission. Its articles also included a provision to create a Jewish Agency to represent Jewish interests. The agency, which embraced Jews in the Diaspora as well as the Jewish community of Palestine (known as the Yishuv), evolved into a quasi-government of the Jewish population. In the early 1920s it developed a home guard-style militia, the Hagana, which was tolerated by the British authorities.[3]

Palestine was peaceful for most of the 1920s. The Jewish population expanded, somewhat fitfully, through immigration from Eastern Europe. However, the growing number and assertiveness of the Jews created unease amongst the Arab population. In 1929 Arabs in several cities rioted against the Jewish presence, causing a heavy loss of life. The British government despatched a Commission of Inquiry to investigate the disturbances. Its report blamed Jewish immigration and land purchases for the unrest. Consequently, the government introduced a White Paper proposing limits to Jewish immigration and curbs on land-buying. However, the White Paper was overturned after vigorous lobbying by the Zionist movement.[4]

After the Nazis came to power in Germany in 1933 Jewish emigration to Palestine climbed to unprecedented heights. Within half a decade the influx of Jews from Germany and Austria took the Jewish population up to 450,000 or one third of the total inhabitants. With the demographic balance shifting before their eyes, Palestinian Arabs fought to gain control of immigration but their efforts to achieve change by peaceful means were thwarted. Despairing of getting any satisfaction while the British remained in charge, in 1936 radicalised elements in the towns and the countryside launched an armed insurrection. It took the British Army, with some assistance from specially trained Jewish units, three years to suppress the uprising. This turbulence forced the government to seek a political solution to the clashing aspirations of Jews and Arabs and finally resolve the contradictory elements of the mandate. In 1936 a high-powered Royal Commission investigated the causes of the Arab rebellion and proposed ways to meet Britain's obligations to the Jews under the mandate while respecting the demand of the Arab population for self-determination. In 1937 the commission recommended partitioning the territory into two states, one Jewish and one Arab. However, the government rejected its proposals. In view of the darkening international situation and the threat of war it preferred to preserve the good will of the newly emerging independent Arab states who had come to champion the Palestinian cause. This ruled out the creation of a Jewish state in even a tiny part of Palestine.[5]

In early 1939 the British government convened a conference of Jews and Arabs in the hope of reaching agreement to a constitution for an independent Palestine that would allow both a measure of Jewish immigration and majority rule. The conference was a failure. The Palestinian Arabs wanted the British out and a complete halt to Jewish immigration; the Jews wanted the mandate to continue with a level of immigration the Arabs would not countenance. Finally, the government imposed a solution. It published a White Paper that limited Jewish immigration to 75,000 over a period of five years to be followed by independence on the basis of majority rule, effectively guaranteeing an Arab state with a Jewish minority. Ironically this success came just when the Palestinian national movement was militarily broken and Arab society, weakened by two decades of unequal economic competition with the Jewish sector, was left prostrate. Inevitably the Zionist movement refused to accept the White Paper, but the outbreak of the Second World War put the issue into suspended animation.[6]

Britain's retreat from the mandate provoked upheavals within the ranks of Zionism. During the 1920s and 1930s, the World Zionist Organisation saw the emergence of a multi-party system as movements with a rich variety of ideologies evolved into political parties. Dr Chaim Weizmann, who was credited with obtaining the Balfour Declaration, was the president of the WZO for most of the interwar years. He led no party of his own but presided over a shifting coalition of those who accepted his charismatic leadership and pro-British policy. The core of his support was the non-aligned General Zionist grouping. But the strongest single element in the WZO was the Labour Zionists whose dominant personality was David Ben-Gurion. In 1925 Vladimir Ze'ev Jabotinsky created a non-socialist and more aggressively nationalist movement that became the Revisionist Party. After a decade of conflict the Revisionists seceded and set up the New Zionist Organisation. These parties were also at odds over how best to negotiate with the British and how to deal with the Arabs. Their disputes were reflected in the social, economic and military organisation of the Yishuv. While Ben-Gurion advocated a policy of restraint in the face of armed Arab attacks on Jewish settlements in the 1930s, holding back the Hagana, Vladimir Ze'ev Jabotinsky favoured reprisals. In the early 1930s a section of the Hagana split off and formed a militant Jewish underground army, the Irgun Zvai Leumi (IZL), the National Military Organisation, or Irgun. The Irgun wanted a more active policy of reprisal against Arab terrorist attacks on the Jews and a tougher line against the British who were steadily reneging on their obligation to foster a Jewish national home in Palestine. An even more radical faction wanted the Irgun to become a fully independent liberation army. Their leader was Avraham Stern, a dynamic figure who blended messianic Jewish nationalism with admiration for the operational techniques of the Irish Republican Army. In August 1939 the Irgun staged its first military operations against the British but its leadership, including Stern, was quickly rounded up by the security forces.[7]

Stern and his chief lieutenants were languishing in prison when the Second World War started. To his disgust the heads of the Irgun pledged allegiance to Britain in the struggle with Nazi Germany. He believed that any enemy of the British Empire was an ally of the Zionists, even Mussolini and Hitler. In June 1940 Stern was released from prison and set about making contact with Fascist Italy. When that approach proved a dead end he tried the Germans. Meanwhile his band of underground fighters attacked British targets in Palestine; their favoured tactic was the assassination and their chief target was the Palestine CID. At a time when only the British Army stood between Palestine and the Germans, Stern's murderous tactics quickly alienated the Jewish population. The gang was successfully hunted down; Stern was killed by the police in February 1942. But two years later the survivors regrouped under the leadership of Nathan Friedman-Yellin (later Hebraised to Natan Yellin-Mor). Galvanised by the mass murder of Europe's Jews the Lohamei HaHerut b'Yisrael (LEHI) dedicated themselves to ejecting the British and creating a Jewish state. Unwilling as ever to await on outside events, LEHI embarked an a spree of assassinations. The climax came in November 1944 with the killing of Lord Moyne, Britain's top diplomat in the Middle East and a personal friend of Prime Minister Winston Churchill. The Jewish Agency was appalled and for a while the Hagana was ordered to help the British track down LEHI fighters, a period lasting into 1945 known as the 'saison' or hunting season.[8]

The assassination of Lord Moyne was a disaster for Zionist diplomacy. Winston Churchill was favourably inclined towards Zionism and after he became prime minister in May 1940 he began to inch British policy away from the White Paper and towards partition. By mid 1944 he had almost succeeded. But the murder of his friend by Jewish terrorists soured his mood; partition was shelved and he refused to consider the future of Palestine. In May 1945 he brusquely told Weizmann that the matter would have to wait for the post-war peace conference. By now the British and the Zionist movement were drifting towards a confrontation. The mass murder of the Jews in Europe had radicalised the Zionist movement. In 1942 an emergency conference convened in New York by the Zionist Organisation of America called for the creation of a 'Jewish commonwealth' in all of Palestine. This programme became the manifesto for the WZO. In early 1944, the Irgun denounced the refusal to allow Jewish refugees to enter Palestine and resumed its military operations against the British. Its fighters were now led by the Polish-born Menachem Begin, an implacable disciple of Vladimir Ze'ev Jabotinsky, who had escaped from Europe to Palestine.[9]

When the war in Europe ended in May 1945 the scale of the Nazi genocide against the Jews became clear. Around six million Jews had perished. The survivors of the great East European Jewish communities congregated in dismal refugee camps on German and Austrian territory. Numbering only a few tens of thousands they were a drop in the ocean of seven million Displaced Persons (DPs), but unlike most of those uprooted by the war they had no homes to go back to and, if they did, were not welcome. Most desired nothing more than to leave Europe and go to Palestine or America. The election of a Labour government in Britain in July 1945 led to a surge of optimism in the Jewish world that the gates of Palestine would be opened. The Labour Party had a record of pro-Zionism: its party conference in December 1944 had called unequivocally for scrapping the 1939 White Paper. Furthermore, the new prime minister, Clement Attlee, was under pressure from the US president,

Harry Truman, to admit 100,000 Jews to Palestine. Truman was responding to a report by an American official, Earl G. Harrison, who had investigated the condition of Jews in the DP camps in the US zone of occupation in Germany. Harrison's report concluded that the survivors overwhelmingly wanted to go to Palestine; 100,000 immigration permits would solve the Jewish DP problem. However, Attlee and his foreign secretary, Ernest Bevin, saw the problem in a different light. They believed that Europe should be made safe for Jews and the refugees enabled to return home. They were also warned by British representatives in Arab states and by the Palestine administration that a mass influx of Jews could spark anti-British unrest throughout the Arab world.[10]

In September 1945 a new Cabinet Committee on Palestine convened to decide the future of Palestine. Attlee was acutely aware that after six years of war Britain was bankrupt; so he was inclined to cut overseas commitments. Bevin was more impressed by the advice he received from Foreign Office officials and by what the chiefs of staff told him. They argued that Britain's military bases in Palestine were essential for its Middle Eastern and global strategy. Indeed, the army planned to send reinforcements to Palestine that would also serve as Britain's strategic reserve in the region. The Foreign Office and the military advised that nothing should be done to antagonise Arab opinion. So the colonial secretary, George Hall, agreed that pending a longer-term settlement the government should continue with the level of immigration (1,500 immigration permits per month) set under the White Paper. News of the government's decision provoked huge disappointment in Jewish circles. It also led to the first of many Anglo-American clashes over Palestine. Sweeping aside British sensitivities the Truman administration published Harrison's report, highlighting the demand for increased Jewish immigration to Palestine. Truman was not acting from humanitarian concern alone: he was also influenced by electoral considerations, aiming to win favour for the Democratic Party amongst Jewish voters in New York. Attlee and Bevin resented the mounting US pressure to increase immigration and blamed Zionist propaganda efforts in the USA for making a complicated international question into a plaything of American domestic politics.[11]

However, Bevin believed that the USA and Britain had to work together in world affairs. As well as his conviction that only America was strong enough to deter Soviet expansion, he knew that Britain was financially dependent on the US Treasury. So he was determined to involve Washington in the solution to the Palestine question. In response to the cry to admit 100,000 Jews to Palestine Bevin proposed the creation of an Anglo-American Commission of Enquiry to look into the situation of the Jewish DPs and recommend ways to alleviate their plight. Bevin gave the committee, comprising six American and six British members, four months in which to make its inquiries. He hoped, in a spirit of misplaced optimism, that its report would provide the basis for a joint long-term policy. On 13 November 1945 he announced the establishment of the Anglo-American Committee; the White Paper policy would continue in force for the time being.[12]

The Zionist movement responded to the continued restriction on immigration with a mixture of political pressure, especially in America, propaganda and acts of defiance. The Hagana began to organise large-scale illicit immigration from Europe. By chartering ships and loading them with refugees to run the British naval blockade the Hagana hoped to dramatise the iniquity of British rule. Within Palestine the mood swung towards favouring a demonstration of armed strength to change British minds. During September the Hagana overcame its ideological differences with the Irgun and LEHI. Despite their prior history of fratricidal conflict they formed a united Jewish Resistance Movement. On 31 October 1945, the resistance launched a wave of attacks to show that it could render Palestine unworkable as a British base. The Hagana cut railways in over 150 places and destroyed two police launches used to intercept illegal immigrants' ships. The Irgun destroyed rolling stock and locomotives at Lydda rail yards. LEHI struck the Haifa oil refinery. Six British police and soldiers were killed.[13]

The British government was determined to keep the lid on Palestine while it searched for a diplomatic solution, so at the same time as officials got to work on the formation of the Anglo-American Committee the security forces in Palestine were significantly beefed up. However, for over six months the government gave diplomatic manoeuvres priority over attempts at a military solution. From November 1945 to April 1946 the diplomatic track was dominated by the work of the Anglo-American Committee. It took evidence in Washington and London before splitting up so that its members could investigate how Jews were faring in Central and Eastern Europe. The committee reassembled to hear evidence in Cairo and then spent 6–28 March in Palestine. The team then flew to Lausanne to reflect and write up their conclusions. After much argument and compromise between US and British points of view the report was completed on Good Friday, 19 April 1946. It was unanimous. The committee recommended that 100,000 Jewish DPs should be allowed to enter Palestine immediately and called for scrapping the laws that prevented Jews buying land and building new settlements; but it also advocated UN trusteeship until the will existed amongst Jews and Arabs to live peacefully together in one state. It roundly condemned violence and the use of force by either side to achieve domination of the other.[14]

The Foreign Office and the chiefs of staff were dismayed by the report. They were convinced that the admission of 100,000 Jews to Palestine would provoke the Palestinian Arabs into revolt and alienate the Arab states on whom Britian depended for oil. By a fateful coincidence the importance of Palestine to the chiefs of staff was hugely increased by the concurrent renegotiation of the treaty between Britain and Egypt under which the British army and navy had the right to keep bases in Alexandria, the Nile Delta and along the Suez Canal. If Britain was forced to pull out then Palestine was the ideal place to which it could relocate its bases. But only if it were pacified. The mood in London and Jerusalem was further soured by several vicious terrorist attacks on the security forces. In response to the report the Cabinet decided that it would consider allowing the entry of 100,000 Jews if the Jewish resistance disarmed and if the US agreed to help with the cost and logistics of transferring so many people to Palestine. On 30 April the report of the Anglo-American Committee was published. The same day, and without consulting London, President Truman publicly endorsed the recommendations for the entry of 100,000 Jews into Palestine. Attlee was furious: he was hoping to use immigration as a lever to force the Jewish Agency to curb terrorism, but Truman was pulling the lever in the opposite direction. The next day Attlee told the House of Commons that there could be no mass immigration of Jews into Palestine until the 'illegal organisations' had been disarmed. Nevertheless, Bevin had little choice but to persist with the diplomatic track. He negotiated with the US administration to convene a group of experts to examine how the Anglo-American Committee's recommendations could be put into effect.[15]

Washington duly sent a team of experts to meet with British officials to examine the implications of the committee's report and consider how it might be implemented. The Americans were led by a diplomat, Henry Grady, the British by Sir Norman Brook, secretary to the Cabinet. After much wrangling a plan emerged to divide Palestine into autonomous Jewish and Arab provinces, under overall British rule. The immigration of 100,000 Jewish refugees would be permitted, with US support, once both sides had accepted the plan. When Herbert Morrison, the chairman of the Cabinet Palestine Committee, presented Parliament with the results of their discussions the proposals became known, rather misleadingly, as the Morrison-Grady plan. The Zionists hated it because it fell way short of full independence in all of Palestine. But Bevin, whose plan it really was, hoped that the Jews would buy it because British countermeasures against the Jewish resistance had momentarily weakened the Yishuv. He was wrong. The Zionists were able to retrieve their position thanks to their lobbying muscle in the United States. On 31 July 1946, while Herbert Morrison announced the provincial autonomy plan in Parliament, President Truman recalled Grady in anticipation of 'further discussions'. He did not say a word about implementing the plan, least of all with US assistance.[16]

Truman's reluctance to back the 'Morrison-Grady plan' crippled Bevin's Anglo-American diplomacy. The immediate question of the 100,000 was left hanging in the air with no viable long-term solution to the Palestine question in sight. Bevin followed up the unveiling of the plan by calling a conference at which he hoped the Jews and the Arabs would come together on the basis of provincial autonomy; but neither side was willing to play ball. The Zionist leadership would only agree to attend if the British consented to partition as a starting point for discussions. Bevin and Hall insisted that Zionist representatives could only participate if they accepted limited autonomy in parts of Palestine and the continuation of British rule. The result was a stalemate. The conference opened in London on 9 September, without Jewish participation. The Arab states (representing the Palestinian Arabs, too) insisted on immediate, full independence for Palestine. Bevin adjourned the proceedings on 2 October having failed to get agreement from the Arab delegates to any increased Jewish immigration, let alone limited self-government.[17]

Then, as a *coup de grâce* to British policy, President Truman issued a message to American Jews on the eve of the Yom Kippur holy day (4 October) reiterating his call for Jewish immigration to Palestine and appearing to endorse partition. Prime Minister Attlee was apoplectic. In his eyes the fate of the Middle East was being made to turn on Truman's bidding for short-term advantage in the American midterm elections. But the government had no options left. It decided to reconvene the London conference in a last bid to find an agreed settlement before trying to impose one. Bevin let it be known in Cabinet that in the absence of any mutually acceptable outcome Britain might take steps to hand the mandate to the United Nations, successor to the League of Nations. The diplomatic track had all but run its course.[18]

Bevin's diplomatic failure was made even more disastrous because the priorities of diplomacy had repeatedly cut across efforts by the police and the army in Palestine to curb the Jewish insurgency.

In November 1945 the Palestine Police Force (PPF) numbered about 9,000 full-time officers and other ranks distributed across three separate sections: British, Jewish and Arab. (There were also several thousand railway police and over 12,000 Jewish auxiliaries charged with the protection of rural settlements.) The force was divided into the regular police and the Police Mobile Force (PMF), the equivalent of a motorised infantry battalion equipped with armoured cars, trucks and heavy weapons. But these figures did not reflect the number of 'effectives'. For obvious reasons the authorities relied most heavily on the British section for countering the insurgency. Furthermore, both the regular police and the Police Mobile Force were roughly fifty per cent below their establishment, with respectively 1,672 and 919 effective personnel.[19]

The army was charged with giving support to the police in the event of civil unrest. At the end of the war the garrison comprised the 1st Infantry Division as well as RAF and Royal Navy units plus many service troops. In September 1945 the 6th Airborne Division arrived in Palestine as Britain's Middle East strategic reserve. By November the garrison included one infantry division, one airborne division and one independent infantry brigade, plus numerous logistical, air force and naval formations. On paper it mustered about 100,000 personnel, but only 25,000 were combat troops and of these only the rifle companies in the infantry and airborne divisions were appropriate for counter-insurgency tasks.[20]

The security forces confronted about 45,000 Jews in the Hagana, a part-time militia force that embraced almost every male Jew of military age spread through 550 towns and rural settlements. Most of the Hagana units were static and existed to protect the settlements where their members lived; only a few hundred were suitable for mobile deployment. The most effective Jewish force was the Palmach, which had evolved out of the Hagana. The Palmach totalled about 3,000 fighters, many of whom had received commando training from the British Army during the war. The Hagana, led by Moshe Sneh, and the Palmach, under Yitzhak Sadeh, had an elaborate command and control structure, as well as intelligence and logistic arms. They were ultimately responsible to the Jewish Agency. The IZL and LEHI operated under their own political commands for most of the time and were consequently known as 'dissidents'. The Irgun, under Menachem Begin, numbered some 1,500 in 1945 and was mostly concentrated in a few towns and cities: Tel Aviv, Jerusalem, Petah Tiqva, Lydda, Rishon l'Zion and Netanya. Its activist policy won it recruits from old settlers, new immigrants and from the Hagana so that it grew quickly to 5,000, but with a core of 500–600 fighters. LEHI had only 600 members. Of these Friedman-Yellin could probably rely on a mere 100–150 fighters as against the platoons of youthful volunteers who stuck up posters to make LEHI seem more ubiquitous than it really was. Its cells were buried deep inside the Jewish populations of Tel Aviv, Haifa and Jerusalem. From October 1945 to July 1946 a committee, known as 'Committee X', loosely co-ordinated the activities of all three organisations. The Hagana was the dominant partner but it never exercised much control over the militants and, anyway, agreed that they could pursue their own agendas to seize weapons and steal money to finance their operations.[21]

The Hagana and the Palmach preferred to strike targets that combined a symbolic with a tactical value, particularly installations connected with enforcement of the blockade, and attempted to minimise casualties. The Irgun was not so fastidious, classifying all the security forces and the Palestine administration as fair game. LEHI positively delighted in assassinating government, police and army personnel. In their attempts to seize weapons both the Irgun and LEHI targeted security-force installations, with inevitable casualties. Bank robberies and diamond heists were often accompanied by shoot-outs. Even while the resistance was nominally under a unified command there was plenty of scope for unrestrained violence. Palestine was about to start descending a spiral in which each brutal act triggered countermeasures that led to more cruelty.

The Hagana opened its offensive on 25 October with an attack on a coastguard station at Givat Olga that was used as a base for intercepting ships carrying illegal immigrants. Over a dozen policemen were wounded in the raid although the post continued to function. The united resistance unleashed its first wave of attacks on the night of 31 October, killing half a dozen British police and soldiers. On 27 December, the Irgun launched simultaneous assaults on the Palestine CID headquarters in Jerusalem and Jaffa, detonating bombs and spraying the buildings with automatic weapons fire when the survivors stumbled out. Ten policemen and soldiers were killed and a dozen wounded.[22]

Three weeks into the new year the Hagana returned to the coastguard station at Givat Olga and destroyed it in an action that left seventeen British soldiers wounded. A parallel raid on the radar station atop Mount Carmel went awry, though, and the Hagana suffered casualties of its own. A second attempt, a month later, succeeded in demolishing the facility, at a cost of eight wounded

RAF personnel. At the same time the Hagana was stepping up the rate at which it despatched ships from Europe to run the British blockade. Every time a ship beached and the Hagana took off its human cargo there was risk of a skirmish with police patrols. On 21 January 1946, the Palmach took the initiative and assaulted three camps of the Palestine Police Mobile Force in different parts of the country. In the fighting the Palmach lost four dead, while only one policeman was hurt. Next it was the turn of the Irgun. Its trademark was spectacular, simultaneous attacks. On the night of 25 February, Irgun raiding parties hit three British military airfields, destroying five planes and damaging seventeen more. Four IZL fighters were killed, but the RAF lost £750,000 worth of equipment. It was a powerful message that if the British wanted to use Palestine as a military base they would have to reach some kind of accommodation with the Jews or crush them.[23]

On 6 March the Irgun raided the armoury at the Sarafand army base, killing one guard and wounding a female civilian worker. The security forces subsequently captured nine Irgun fighters, several of whom were later sentenced to death. On 23 April the Irgun struck the police station in Ramat Gan in an attempt to seize more weapons, leaving four of their men wounded and three more policemen dead. Two days later LEHI mounted a murderous night-time assault on a paratroop detachment guarding a 6th Airborne Division vehicle park in Tel Aviv. The raiders grabbed fifteen rifles but five Red Berets were killed along with two other soldiers. Several were gunned down in cold blood while they lay unarmed on their camp beds.[24]

All three underground forces attacked the transport system. The Hagana sought to paralyse British military activity while the Irgun knew a soft target when it saw one. LEHI, with its anti-imperialist philosophy, wanted to make the occupation as economically costly as possible and was drawn time and again to attacking targets associated with the oil industry, including pipelines and the Haifa oil refinery. On 10 June the Irgun attacked four trains, wounding three members of the security forces. Six days later the Hagana destroyed or partially wrecked no less than eleven bridges, cutting road and rail links between Palestine and neighbouring countries.

This dramatic show of force cost the Hagana and the Palmach eight fighters; the police and army suffered five casualties. The following day, 17 June, LEHI lost no fewer than twenty-six of its men in a disastrous raid on the railway repair yard at Haifa. Twenty-four hours later the Irgun kidnapped six British army officers and proclaimed that they would execute them unless the death sentences passed on captured Jewish fighters were commuted.[25]

Although the Jewish underground suffered casualties, its ability to hit British governmental, military and police targets again and again exposed the limitations of the security forces. The British authorities seemed at a loss to counter the insurgency. The governance of Palestine was in the hands of the high commissioner who was also the commander-in-chief of all the security forces. On 21 November 1945, General Sir Alan Cunningham was installed as the seventh, and as it turned out the last, high commissioner. Sir Alan, aged fifty-eight, was a short, dapper man of great charm. He was the son of an anatomy professor but opted for a military career. In 1906 he was commissioned into the Royal Artillery and served with distinction on the Western Front during the First World War. Between the wars he held numerous postings, rising to the rank of a major general. In January 1940 he directed the scratch force assembled to eject the Italians from east Africa. His conduct of the campaign was quite brilliant: the Italian armies were defeated in four months. In mid 1941 General Claude Auchinleck, British commander-in-chief in the Middle East, appointed Cunningham to lead the 8th Army. He thereby became responsible for the autumn offensive intended to relieve Tobruk. At a crucial moment in the battle Cunningham lost his nerve, advising Auchinleck that it was time to go onto the defensive. Auchinleck was unimpressed and relieved him of his command. Cunningham returned to Britain to hold a number of administrative posts until the end of the war. He never escaped the shadow of failure and many who knew him suspected that he was determined to show he could fight to the end and win a battle. It so happened that Palestine would prove his final testing ground.[26]

Soon after his arrival Cunningham sent the first of his monthly reports to the Secretary of State for the Colonies, to whom he was ultimately responsible. He told George Hall that Jewish public opinion was largely supportive of the resistance. A few days later he reported that the security situation was 'grave though I do not despair of it being possible to solve the problem without an extensive military operation'. On the other hand, 'The question of when and how to disarm the country may well however make such an operation necessary.' It would greatly assist his job if the government could declare a clear policy for the future of the mandate and come up with a solution to the plight of the Jewish DPs. Here was Cunningham's dilemma. All those who met him agreed that he was perceptive and well meaning. An American member of the Anglo-American Committee, Bartley Crum, recalled that he was 'one of the few British officials I met in whom I found a sympathetic understanding of both the Arab and the Jewish positions'. Golda Myerson (later, as Golda Meir, to become Israel's prime minister), a Jewish Agency official, remembered him as 'an extremely kind and decent man'. He consistently strived for a political rapprochment but it was also his duty to maintain law and order. Unfortunately, without any viable concessions to offer the Jews (least of all enhanced immigration) he faced mounting unrest that propelled him towards ever more draconian measures.[27]

The first line of defence against the insurgency, and supposedly the chief means of rooting it out, was the Palestine Police Force. But the PPF was a flawed instrument.

The force was established in July 1920 and modelled on the Royal Irish Constabulary. When the RIC was disbanded after the partition of Ireland the new Palestinian force absorbed hundreds of Irish officers and constables. This gave it a curious Anglo-Irish flavour but not an infusion of real policing talent. During the 1920s and 1930s the PPF went through several phases of expansion and reform, each one driven by a major outbreak of communal violence between Arabs and Jews; but the persistence of political uncertainty combined with national, ethnic and religious antagonisms doomed the force to a state of perpetual tension. It was always torn between regular police work and maintaining security.[28]

Each burst of communal strife eroded the viability of the Arab and Jewish sections, obliging its commanders to import more reliable

British personnel. Yet the predominantly Anglo-Irish composition of the force increased its isolation from the population and reduced its ability to gather intelligence for criminal or political policing. During the Arab rebellion of 1936–9 the PPF became increasingly marginal to the restoration of order and fell under the operational control of the army. It developed a reputation for rough justice administered by poorly trained ex-servicemen who regarded violence as a quicker solution to most problems than routine palliatives or patient detective work.[29] A Criminal Investigation Department (CID) was established early on, but devoted more resources to intelligence gathering than crime fighting. By the mid 1930s the CID had separate political sections devoted to monitoring anti-British activity amongst the Arabs and the Jews. Even so, the political branches were small relative to the task they faced and poorly developed.[30]

Successive reports on the PPF argued that it had to develop its routine policing role, not least to build up the confidence and support of the local population. But there was an inexorable tendency towards militarisation. Although recruits, many of them ex-servicemen, spent some time studying legal ordinances, learning about the various communities, and mastering basic policing techniques, equal if not more attention was given to weapons training. During the Second World War the police remained under army control. At the initiative of the inspector general, Captain John Rymer-Jones, in 1943 the Police Mobile Force was established as a mailed fist to use against the terrorists. When Rymer-Jones left at the end of 1945, the debate over who could replace him brought to a pitch arguments about how best to use the police.[31]

The Colonial Office in London wanted to appoint someone with experience of colonial policing. Perhaps because they had a more realistic view of the security situation Rymer-Jones and Cunningham preferred to select candidates from the ranks of the armed forces.[32] The possibilities included Colonel John Hackett who had commanded a parachute regiment in the epic battle of Arnhem, and Colonel William Nicol Gray, the former commander of 45 Royal Marine Commando. However, Hackett's wife was Austrian and Cunningham thought the 'fact he married [an] Aryan Austrian has disadvantages vis-à-vis Jews'. Cunningham wanted someone steady who was also able to get along with the Jewish population. As he told London: 'I cannot take risks in this appointment'. Unfortunately, in plumping for Gray, that was exactly what he did.[33]

Nicol Gray (he preferred to dispense with the William) was a 37-year-old bachelor, six foot two inches tall, with a square jaw and a powerful physique. Born in Scotland, he was educated at Glenalmond boarding school for boys near Perth. Before the war he made a living as a farmer and land agent in Australia. In 1940 he entered the Royal Marines and became chief instructor at the Combined Training Centre at Darling, Argyllshire. Every commando unit that passed through the centre in 1943–4 remembered, and not a few disliked, him for his exacting standards and discomfiting candour. Gray relied on charismatic leadership and personal courage to compensate for the resentment he inspired.[34]

In January 1944 he joined 45 Royal Marine Commando as second in command. The unit went ashore in Normandy on D-Day, 6 June 1944, with orders to fight its way through to the British paratroops who had seized the key 'Pegasus' Bridge over the Orne River several miles inland. The commandos reached the bridge but while crossing their CO was hit by sniper fire and Gray took over. In the words of the citation for the DSO that he was subsequently awarded, he then led 45 RM Commando 'tirelessly for the next thirty-six hours until almost out of ammunition, when he received the order to withdraw. This he achieved successfully, and under difficult circumstances brought his unit back to our lines intact. Major Gray's tireless energy, devotion to duty and unfailing cheerfulness throughout all difficulties has been an example to all and it is largely through his fine leadership that his unit has inflicted heavy loss on the enemy.'[35]

In January 1945 Gray took his men into action in north-west Europe. But he now revealed a less certain grip on command. When ordered to take an island in the River Maas he launched the operation without adequate reconnaissance and support with the result that an entire troop was practically wiped out. Following that setback, though, he masterminded a textbook assault on the city of Wesel as part of the attack across the Rhine. He was wounded shortly afterwards and nearly lost an arm. Once he had recovered he led his men through a series of bitter encounters with diehard Waffen SS formations. When the Germans finally surrendered 45 RM Commando had reached the north German province of Schleswig-Holstein. Gray now displayed another side of his abilities by rapidly organising an efficient and humane occupation regime.[36]

Although he was a *Boy's Own* war hero, news of his appointment as inspector general of the Palestine police 'came as a shock to all ranks'. The popular choice within the force was Arthur Giles, the head of the CID. He was born in Cyprus into a family of soldiers and scholars, and was highly knowledgeable about Middle Eastern affairs. Having opted for a career in the Egyptian Colonial Police he rose to become assistant commandant of police in Port Said. His appointment in February 1938 to run the CID in Jerusalem was greeted with universal approval. In this office, where he was known as 'Giles Bey', he shifted attention to the growing threat of Jewish unrest and established the Jewish Affairs section. By contrast, senior officers viewed Gray as a complete outsider. According to one he 'was not a police officer, was not even a professional man-at-arms'. Consequently, he arrived in Palestine in March 1946 to take over a force that was seething with resentment at the way it had been treated, although this is exactly what Sir Alan Cunningham said he wanted to avoid. Edward Horne, the historian of the Palestine police who was then an officer in its ranks, understood why: 'The PP had never been led by someone who was not a policeman – or one of the clan – and everyone viewed his appointment with suspicion'.[37]

These suspicions were immediately confirmed when Gray ordered the disbandment of the Police Mobile Force, which many police officers believed was the key to defeating the terrorists. But Gray took over a force that was chronically under-strength. He tried to solve the manpower shortage by reassigning PMF personnel to regular police duties, relying on the enhanced garrison to supply the rapid reaction force. However, the troops lacked the intelligence and experience of the police. Nor could they be expected to mount small-scale, information-led seek-and-seize operations in urban settings. Gray seems to have resolved this dilemma by drawing on his wartime knowledge of British special forces, the SAS and the commandos. He planned to form undercover units that would operate in Jewish districts, gathering information locally and taking leads from district and national police headquarters. When they had identified the target his men, dressed as civilians, would set up an ambush and either arrest their prey or if there was armed resistance, kill them.[38]

In late October 1946, Gray travelled to London for a series of meetings with officials at the Colonial Office and the intelligence community. (By chance Attlee learned of his presence and asked to see him.) Ostensibly he was there to accelerate recruitment for the police and to explore a suggestion of the Joint Intelligence Committee to appoint a 'political warfare officer' with 'experience of Palestine conditions and especially psychology of [the] Jewish community'. He was also, less publicly, meeting with officers of MI5 and MI6. Gray was tapping into the network of ex-SOE agents and men who had fought in the SAS or other special forces during the war to find suitable officers to command an undercover anti-terrorist unit. Amongst the first he contacted was Lieutenant Colonel Bernard Fergusson, one of the heroes of Britain's war against the Japanese.[39]

Bernard Fergusson, aged thirty-five, came from an old Scottish family steeped in military service and imperial governance. His grandfather, Sir James Fergusson, a Grenadier Guards officer, had been Undersecretary of State for India and then served successively as governor of South Australia, governor of New Zealand, and governor of Bombay. His father, a major general, was Governor General of New Zealand from 1924 to 1928. Bernard Fergusson's family on his mother's side were no less prominent in Britain's imperial history. His air of insouciance, monocle, and fondness for poetry made him appear unworldly and unmilitary. In fact he possessed a strong sense of personal duty, immense physical stamina and steely resolution.[40]

Fergusson was educated at Eton and entered the Royal Military Academy at Sandhurst in January 1930. A year later he was commissioned into the Black Watch. In 1935 he was taken on as aide-de-camp to General Archibald Wavell, commanding officer of the 2nd Division. Wavell became his patron and through him

Fergusson met a succession of high ranking officers who would play leading roles in the war.[41] In 1937 his battalion was sent to Palestine, where Wavell was commander-in-chief of the forces suppressing the Arab rebellion. Fergusson was appointed the intelligence officer for the army's southern command and criss-crossed Palestine in an old Austin Seven motor car reconnoitring the terrain and sketching maps. It was there that he met Colonel Orde Wingate, the eccentric but brilliant young officer who initiated the Special Night Squads. These units were composed of Jewish volunteers with British officers. Wingate trained them in the pioneer techniques of counter-insurgency warfare and they achieved considerable success hunting down and destroying rebel bands. Fergusson would imitate the technique in Palestine a decade later, but under radically different circumstances.[42]

Fergusson held several commands during the first years of the Second World War and had another spell as aide to Wavell while he was commander-in-chief, Middle East Forces. But he ended up in Delhi on the Joint Planning Staff of GHQ India where he learned that Wingate, now a brigadier, was planning to mount a 'deep penetration' operation into Burma. Wingate's plan was to send columns deep into enemy territory and supply them by air while they disrupted Japanese lines of communication. Fergusson obtained a transfer and subsequently took part in the 'Chindit' expeditions in February-March 1943 and March-May 1944. During the first expedition the supply drops were only intermittently successful and the men suffered terribly from malnutrition and disease as well as the hostile terrain, not to mention frequent skirmishes with Japanese patrols. Of the 318 men Fergusson led into Burma, only 95 emerged alive. He was decorated with the DSO for his inspired leadership. The second expedition, launched in March 1944, was much stronger and the concept was changed to enable better supply, although the casualties were still horrendous.[43]

After the war Fergusson worked in Combined Operations Headquarters which he considered 'not very exciting' and stood unsuccessfully as a parliamentary candidate for the Conservative Party in the July 1945 general election. Ironically, in early 1946, he was offered the job of inspector general of the Palestine Police.

He declined to take it up because the War Office refused to second him for a fixed period and he feared that if he went to Palestine he would lose the chance to command the Black Watch, which was his dream.[44]

It is more than a little surprising, then, that he willingly accepted the posting to Palestine that Gray engineered just a few months later. According to his memoirs, *The Trumpet in the Hall*, in October 1946 the War Office contacted him to say that the Palestine Police Force had asked for a suitable candidate to take command of the Police Mobile Force with the rank of assistant inspector general. The War Office had *nominated* him. His first response was to refuse because this assignment was two ranks *below* the post that he had previously been offered. But he soon learned that the title and the role were not all they seemed. Nicol Gray approached Fergusson in person to explain that he would be in charge of 'anti-terrorist activities'. As Fergusson recalled in his memoirs, 'this as a job did sound extremely interesting'. He renewed his efforts to persuade the army to release him for a limited period and traded on his connection with General Browning, Military Secretary at the War Office. Browning cleared the way for Fergusson to go to Palestine for a couple of years and then return to command a regiment. However, when he reached Palestine he found that his anti-terrorist mission was on hold. Instead he was given the fag-end of a job reassigning the members of the PMF to the regular police and overseeing the training of new recruits coming to the force from Britain.[45]

In *The Trumpet in the Hall* Fergusson gave a muddled and not terribly convincing explanation for this 'misunderstanding'. He was led to believe that 'although my nominal job would be to run the PMF I would in fact have a specific responsibility for all anti-terrorist activities'. If the PMF job was purely 'nominal' it should not have detained him, whatever it involved. Even more confusingly, he blamed the elimination of the PMF on a controversial report about the Palestine Police Force written by Sir Charles Wickham. In fact, the decision to wind up the Police Mobile Force was made in Palestine in March 1946 and the official date for disbandment was 5 June 1946, months before Fergusson was recruited. And the Wickham Report was not delivered to the authorities until early December 1946. But the report *did* get in the way of his mission, if not as head of the PMF and nor for the spurious reasons he gave. The Wickham Report fed into a raging controversy over Britain's counter-insurgency tactics in Palestine and spelled a setback for Gray's plans for an anti-terrorist unit under Fergusson's leadership.[46]

Several months earlier, in the summer of 1946, the Colonial Office was doing its best to increase the number of men in the Palestine Police Force. At the same time, Sir Alan Cunningham was having doubts about how best to employ them. He wrote to the Colonial Office, 'Ever since I have been here I have been most concerned at the lack of information available regarding the terrorist organisations and individuals and the small success we seem to have in tracking them down.' Was this due to faulty police methods? Could investigation and intelligence-gathering techniques be improved? 'I am anxious to be assured that our police methods are the best that can be devised and I would welcome a visit from some expert'. He was thinking of 'a man of eminence in police work who had experience of terrorist activities in an unfriendly population'. The name that came to his mind was Sir Charles Wickham, recently retired after twenty-three years as inspector general of the Royal Ulster Constabulary. But Wickham was just completing a mission to reorganise the Greek police force and was not available until November 1946.[47]

When Sir Charles duly arrived in Palestine he was accompanied by Lieutenant Colonel William Moffat, head of the Special Crime Branch of the Royal Ulster Constabulary. They completed their investigation and drew up their report in less than a month. It was a scathing document. Wickham noted the Irgun and LEHI had 'seriously weakened the prestige of the government, done much damage to life and property, thrown thousands of the government forces onto the defensive and caused the withdrawal of the police from duty on the streets in their area of operations'. Against this, 'no repressive or offensive measures have met with any marked success' 'Terrorism', he asserted, 'is crime in its most highly organised form. It is a police responsibility to fight it by an intensification of their normal procedure, with limited army assistance.' The armed forces should only get heavily involved if the terrorists came out into the open. The trick was organising the police appropriately to conduct information-led operations against the terror groups. But the necessary information could only come from the public, so it was essential for the police to maintain the best community relations. Wickham could see how this might be difficult in Palestine, where many Jews sympathised with the terrorists and where fear of intimidation as well as language differences created barriers between police and public. However, this was 'no reason why it should be abandoned nor is it an argument in favour of any departure from recognised police procedure or punitive methods against the public generally which cannot fail still further to alienate the people'.[48]

Wickham commented acidly on the use of armoured cars and observed that there was 'no substitute for a foot patrol'. In what many serving policemen in Palestine considered a blatant disregard for actual conditions he pronounced: 'Motorised fighting police alienate the public. They resemble too closely the Gestapo and are inclined to forget the first lesson of policing – civility to the public'. Instead, he recommended reorganising the force, increasing its numbers, and providing better training in old-fashioned police work. Above all he urged the recruitment of more Jews into the force. 'There is no doubt that the introduction of more Jews could be dangerous, but without Jews the force must be handicapped and on balance the case for more Jews seems well founded if they can be obtained.' Moffatt added a report on the Palestine CID which was equally critical. He noted that the CID was undermanned, its officers were too inexperienced, and they lacked the necessary language skills. He concurred with Sir Charles that the panacea for these deficiencies lay in recruiting more locals and, in the short term, using secret-service funds to buy informants.[49]

The Wickham Report was a comprehensive indictment of the Palestine police. Not surprisingly, it was greeted with anger. One officer observed that it arrived at 'strange conclusions, all of them at variance with police experience in Palestine'. Cunningham himself must have been more than a little irritated because he had told Wickham expressly what he was after. 'As regards the scope of your inquiry', he wrote to him in early September, 'we

are particularly anxious to have your advice on anti-terrorist measures and on the organisation of the CID.' He did not want a
review of the whole organisation and distribution of the police.
Wickham had replied that 'I quite agree about the scope of the
inquiry'. Instead, Cunningham now found himself in possession
of a report that upset everyone and, worse, did not say what he
wanted it to say. The Colonial Office had little choice but to
accept its recommendations.[50]

This explains why the plan for anti-terrorist units that Fergusson
was intended to implement went into suspension for several months
and why he found himself in charge of not just one but two non-
existent forces. It would take months for Gray's plans for covert
anti-terrorist squads to get back on course. The bitter debate in
Palestine and in Whitehall about the best means to combat the
Jewish insurgency was only resolved by a dramatic change in British
government policy and the arrival of new military chiefs.[51]

The initial response to the Jewish insurgency was framed by Sir
Alan Cunningham who, as well as being the high commissioner,
was commander-in-chief of the forces in Palestine; by the General
Officer Commanding (GOC) the army General John D'Arcy; and
by the commander-in-chief of Middle East Land Forces, General
Sir Bernard Paget. As soon as the garrison was reinforced they insti-
gated the conventional measures intended to combat a guerrilla
force. They sent army units to cordon off Jewish rural settlements
and search for arms, set up checkpoints to curb the mobility of the
terrorists, tried to locate and seize the leaders of the underground
resistance, and attempted through police work and intelligence to
break up the terrorist groups. But the resistance operations compelled
the army to guard every army and naval installation as well as
patrolling railways and roads; its forces were soon stretched thin
and chopped into small packets of men tied to fixed positions where
they were sitting targets for any attacker.[52]

Cunningham and D'Arcy were soon convinced that the leaders
of the Jewish Agency and the Hagana were behind the attacks.
Consequently they wanted to discipline the agency and neutralise
the Hagana, but they were repeatedly held in check while the
government pursued the diplomatic track. As early as December

1945 they requested permission from the Colonial Office and the Cabinet to occupy the Jewish Agency headquarters and place Jewish Agency leaders under police supervision. Hall, Bevin and Attlee refused such drastic action as long as the Anglo-American Committee was at work. However, as a palliative measure, in January 1946 London permitted the high commissioner to extend the Defence Regulations for Palestine. The new regulations set up a system of military courts and delineated a very wide range of offences over which they had jurisdiction. Capital punishment was extended to cover a variety of acts merely connected with abetting terrorism, such as being found in possession of a weapon. The courts were empowered to order the expulsion, detention and confinement of offenders without trial or time limit. The presiding officers did not require legal expertise; there were no rules of procedure; and there was no appeal. Military commanders could order the seizure and destruction of buildings, control traffic and regulate trade as they saw fit. The press was subjected to strict censorship: protest was all but silenced. One Zionist historian concluded that 'unlimited power had been handed to the military'. Palestine was well on the way to becoming a police state; but the harsher the regime, the less Jews felt any inclination to co-operate with the authorities.[53]

Once the report of the Anglo-American Committee was completed, Whitehall relaxed the restrictions on army operations. By this time the chiefs of staff were champing at the bit. Constant attacks by Jewish terrorists were pushing the troops close to breaking point. At his last appearance before the Cabinet, on 20 June 1946, the outgoing Chief of the Imperial General Staff (CIGS), Field Marshal Viscount Alanbrooke, warned that 'if the existing state of affairs continued, troops in Palestine might get out of hand'. The Tel Aviv car-park massacre had led to revenge attacks on Jewish civilians and the morale of the troops was febrile. Alanbrooke reported that the chiefs of staff thought it was time to give the high commissioner and the army in Palestine a freer hand against the terrorists. But, again, Prime Minister Attlee counselled restraint. He argued that while it was essential to break up the Jewish 'illegal organisations' and isolate the 'extremists' who had seized the Jewish Agency, any attempt to disarm the Jews wholesale or shut down the agency would be a mistake. It would provoke a collision with the entire Jewish population and jeopardise co-operation with the Americans. Nevertheless, the Cabinet authorised the high commissioner 'to take such steps as he considered necessary to break up the illegal organisations in Palestine'. These measures included searching the Jewish Agency building and detaining agency officials.[54]

This was the authorisation that Cunningham needed. His resolve was stiffened by the arrival of General Sir Evelyn Barker as the new GOC and the installation of Field Marshal Viscount Montgomery of Alamein as the new CIGS. The arrival of Montgomery, in particular, shifted the balance between the diplomatic and the military tracks. Bernard Law Montgomery was 'the nation's most popular general'. He was credited with reversing the tide of the war in North Africa and leading the Allied armies to victory after victory through Sicily, Italy and the Normandy invasion. He had masterminded the climactic assault on the Third Reich and taken the German surrender at Lüneberg Heath in May 1945. Yet many eyebrows were raised by the announcement on 1 February 1946 that he would become the next Chief of the Imperial General Staff, Britain's top soldier. Montgomery had a well-earned reputation for tactlessness and had little political sense. Perhaps it was fairer to say that he had very firm views and could not grasp why anyone would disagree with him.[55]

Montgomery was a classic imperial warrior and Palestine occupied an important position in his strategic thinking. He was born in England in 1881, but raised in Tasmania where his father, a clergyman, was appointed a bishop. The young Montgomery was sent to England for his schooling, so from an early age he was aware of the vastness of the empire and the arteries that allowed it to function. He entered Sandhurst in 1907 and his first experience of soldiering was in India. In 1914 he commanded an infantry platoon in France but after just a few weeks in action he was severely wounded. When he recovered he held various staff jobs. Between the wars he served in Ireland, Egypt and India. In 1938 he commanded 3rd Division in southern Palestine where he directed a successful campaign against Arab rebels. He led the division in

France in 1939–40 and then held a number of key positions in the defence of Britain. In August 1942 he took over 8th Army in Egypt, a force that drew its strength from the Dominions and the empire. To Montgomery the British Empire was a marvellous thing in its own right and a precious asset to the motherland.[56]

But when he took office as CIGS on 26 June 1946 he inherited a terrible dilemma. The government was renegotiating the 1936 treaty with the Egyptians under which the British were able to maintain bases in Egypt. Given the nationalist mood in Egypt it was very likely that the treaty would be rescinded. This would entail the loss of the naval facilities at Alexandria as well as the army and air force installations in the Nile Delta and along the Suez Canal. It was becoming imperative to secure alternative bases from which to guard the sea routes to India and protect Britain's oil supplies from the Arabian Gulf. The chiefs of staff wanted Palestine. It was already the home to large army bases, had airfields that could accommodate bombers capable of reaching the Soviet Union, and in Haifa possessed a deep-water port that already functioned as a backup to Alexandria. Montgomery was also acutely aware that oil supplies for the armed forces and for the British economy were vulnerable to pressure from the independent Arab states. So he was convinced that Palestine had to remain under British control and that whatever solution was found to conflicting Jewish and Arab aspirations, it could not be one that alienated the Arab world. Britain had to reimpose its authority on Palestine and, one way or another, compel the Jews to accept the kind of settlement that would not upset the Arabs.[57]

He already had a firm view of what steps were needed. Before he took office he went on a month-long tour of British forces stationed around the world in order to familiarise himself with conditions at first hand. In Palestine he conferred with General Sir Bernard Paget, General Sir Evelyn Barker, Cunningham and Gray. According to his official diary Montgomery 'was quite definitely perturbed by what he heard and saw'. The Irgun and Stern Gang, 'with the approval and sometimes the co-operation of the Hagana and the Jewish Agency', were successfully mounting numerous attacks on British targets. The diary continued with extraordinary frankness that: 'he was firmly convinced that General Cunningham was not the man to be High Commissioner in these troubulous [*sic*] times. He appeared to be quite unable to make up his mind what to do and was pathetically anxious to avoid a show-down. This led to a state of affairs in which British rule existed only in name, the true rulers being the Jews whose unspoken slogan was "You dare not touch us."' Montgomery was 'astonished' to learn from Gray that the Palestine Police Force was fifty per cent below strength 'at a time when the situation was obviously about to boil over'. He was appalled to learn that the police included large numbers of Jews 'who unhesitatingly passed on information concerning future plans to their friends in the Jewish illegal organisations'. Montgomery did not hide his feelings about the Jewish opposition. 'All ranks must understand that they were in for a very unpleasant job: the first task was a political one, namely to re-establish British authority; this would mean that the army would have to strike a real blow against the Jews by arresting the heads of the illegal Jewish organisations and those members of the Jewish Agency known to be collaborating with the Hagana.' The Jews would use 'the weapons of kidnap, murder and sabotage: women would fight against us as well as men; no one would know who was friend and who was foe'.[58]

The day after he returned to England he issued an uncompromising directive to Paget. 'The high commissioner has been given a free hand to deal with the situation. This will lead to war with the Jews, with all that implies. On joining battle with the Jews you will give the General Officer Commanding Palestine [Barker] a clear directive to strike hard and with great speed and determination, with the object of completely and utterly defeating the Jews as soon as possible. You will ensure that every officer and man in any way connected with this struggle realises to the full the fanatical and cunning nature of his enemy, the unEnglish methods that this enemy will use'. All ranks had to realise 'now that the Jews have flung the gauntlet in our face, they must be utterly and completely defeated and their illegal organisations smashed forever'.[59]

Three days later, the security forces launched Operation Agatha.

Just before dawn on 29 June Royal Signals units disconnected telephone communications throughout Palestine while troops and police threw up roadblocks and cordons around the main cities. 10,000 troops and 7,000 police were mobilised. The Jewish Agency building in Jerusalem was occupied and searched for documents linking the Jewish leadership with terrorism. Members of the agency executive were arrested at their homes and offices, including Moshe Shertok the 'foreign minister' of the Yishuv and several Hagana chiefs (though not the commander, Moshe Sneh, who was tipped off in time). Whole units of the Palmach were interned at camps in Atlith and Latrun. By 2 July, 2,800 Jews had been rounded up in Haifa, Tel Aviv, Jerusalem and other towns. Units of British 1st Division and 6th Airborne also mounted cordon and search operations against Jewish settlements. At Kibbutz Yagur men of the 1st Division discovered a massive arms cache. The operation had been intended to catch people rather than to find weapons, but this haul seemed to more than vindicate the immense effort.[60]

Montgomery was delighted. When he attended his first Cabinet meeting on 1 July he used Operation Agatha to show what could be achieved by a combination of political resolution and the calculated use of force. Yet the success was illusory. The police and the army had missed the most dangerous elements of the Jewish resistance movement: the Irgun and LEHI. This was made cruelly apparent on 22 July 1946 when the Irgun blew up the wing of the King David Hotel in Jerusalem housing sections of the civil administration and the offices of the General Officer Commanding Middle East Forces in Palestine. Ninety-one people were killed in the blast, including sixteen British personnel. The operation was conducted with the knowledge and consent of the Hagana high command, though not the Jewish Agency, and it was deliberately designed to show the British that the resistance was unbowed.[61]

The Cabinet Defence Committee, now including Montgomery, met soon after news of the attack reached London. Montgomery demanded permission for the army to take on the Hagana, but the prime minister warned against premature action. To Montgomery's dismay the Cabinet opted for a surprisingly moderate line. Attlee and Bevin were desperate not to upset the chances of a political settlement and were influenced by evidence that elements in the Jewish population and the Zionist leadership were so disturbed by the crackdown and the bombing that they were more inclined to co-operate with the British. The prime minister was also shrewd enough to see that an attack on this scale coming so shortly after Operation Agatha showed that the army had been over-optimistic. So the Cabinet instructed that further security measures should be precisely targeted at illegal arms dumps and members of IZL and the Stern Gang.[62]

Cunningham (who was in London at the time of the atrocity) was astonished by this tepid reaction. He told the Secretary of State for the Colonies that they must 'do something drastic and do it quickly' or British authority would evaporate. Cunningham advocated a punitive suspension of Jewish immigration and a collective fine on the Jewish population. Barker in Jerusalem and General Sir Miles Dempsey, Paget's successor in Cairo pleaded for tougher action, not least 'to maintain the morale of the British community and soldiers in Palestine'. A week later, the government instructed the army to strike at LEHI and the Irgun in Tel Aviv and other towns known to be their havens. This operation, code-named Shark, involved over 20,000 troops, mainly from 6th Airborne. At dawn on 30 July they cordoned off Tel Aviv and then divided the city into segments, each controlled by a brigade. Each zone was subdivided into blocks which were sealed off while soldiers systematically searched for suspects and arms, building by building. 100,000 people were funnelled into makeshift cages and interrogated in stifling hot tents. Of these 10,000 were subjected to a full screening. The results were modestly successful. Over 370 terrorist suspects were detained, including Yitzhak Yzernitsky (later as Yitzhak Shamir to be prime minister of Israel), one of LEHI's top commanders. Several Irgun leaders were caught and five arms caches were uncovered, including a huge weapons dump concealed under the Great Synagogue.[63]

The two massive military operations and the outrage caused by the King David Hotel bombing rocked the Jewish Agency. At Weizmann's behest Moshe Sneh was sacked as commander of the Hagana and the alliance with the Irgun and LEHI was broken off. After July 1946 the Hagana never launched another assault on the security forces in Palestine and focused its energies on illegal immigration. The leaders of the Yishuv publicly condemned terrorism even if they still refused to co-operate with the security forces.[64]

Unfortunately, Barker compromised the wave of sympathy for the British by issuing a carelessly worded order against fraternisation. In a fit of anger he declared Jewish-owned cafes, restaurants and places of entertainment out of bounds with the intention of 'punishing the Jews in a way the race dislikes as much as any, by striking at their pockets and showing our contempt for them'. This was a gift to the Zionist propaganda apparatus, especially in the United States, which depicted the British forces as anti-Semitic.[65]

The Colonial Office was bombarded with demands to sack Barker, but Montgomery stoutly defended him. He told the colonial secretary: 'If he goes, I go.' Instead, Montgomery turned his ire on the high commissioner. He wanted Cunningham to enforce the death penalty imposed on several captured LEHI fighters by military courts. When Cunningham appeared to be dithering Montgomery wrote a private letter to the colonial secretary stating that 'It is my opinion that Cunningham is NOT the right man to govern Palestine at the present time'. As evidence of his unsuitability he cited the grounds for which Cunningham was dismissed from command of 8th Army in 1942. The letter became known in government circles and brought into the open a feud that would gravely weaken British leadership at a critical moment.[66]

Montgomery did not appreciate that Cunningham constantly had to align his actions with priorities in London. On 9 September Ernest Bevin opened the conference that was intended to bring the Jews and the Arabs together. In order to encourage Jewish participation, the British government instructed the high commissioner to release the Jewish leaders interned since June. This only confirmed Montgomery's withering opinion of the politicians in London and Jerusalem. Lacking any grasp of the political imperatives or the constraints under which Cunningham laboured, Montgomery steamed into Cabinet meetings demanding that the army be let loose and launching a stream of vituperation at the high commissioner. As his diary noted coyly, 'this caused somewhat of a stir'.[67]

During the autumn of 1946 a chasm opened up between the

army and the civilian policymakers. One historian has called it 'the most bitter civil-military feud in Britain's post-war counter-insurgency experience'. While the Cabinet was pinning its hopes on the London conference and wanted to keep all parties sweet, Dempsey, the C.-in-C. of Middle East Land Forces, complained that the release of the Zionist leaders was appeasement. The only way to persuade the Jewish leaders to combat terrorism was through relentless military pressure. 'We soldiers had the initiative in July and August', he wrote to Montgomery, 'and things were satisfactory. Then we stopped and handed over to civil government. We are getting mighty near now to the time when the soldier takes over again.' Dempsey feared that the morale of the security forces would plummet unless the Jewish population was seen to suffer the consequences of acquiescing in terrorism. As if to make his point on 19 November 1946 members of the Palestine Police Force went on a rampage in Tel Aviv and injured over thirty people as well as destroying property.[68]

The political and public mood in Britain was equally fevered due to the extension of Jewish terrorism to Europe and the threat that it would soon cross the English Channel. At 2:45 in the morning on Thursday 31 October 1946 a massive explosion wrecked the British Embassy in Rome. Four days later the Irgun 'Supreme Command' claimed responsibility for the bombing. The 'communiqué' stated in clipped military jargon that 'troops of Irgun Zvai Leumi attacked offices of British Embassy which is one of the executives strangling repatriation of Jews. All our soldiers returned to their bases with all their arms. The attack on the British Embassy in Rome is a symbol of the opening of the Jewish military front in the Diaspora. Britain has declared a war of extermination against our people in the world. Let every Briton who occupies our country know that the armed hand of the Eternal People will reply with war everywhere until our fatherland is freed and people redeemed.'[69]

This was the first indication that the Irgun had developed a capacity to strike at British targets in Europe. As far back as February 1945 MI5 officers in Palestine had warned the security services in Britain that the Irgun and LEHI were looking for ways to send agents to Europe. Sources, probably in the Jewish Agency intelligence service, informed British officers that LEHI intended to assassinate a military or political figure in the UK. This source was Teddy Kollek, the future long-serving mayor of Jerusalem. Operating under the code name Scorpion, Kollek helped the security forces to catch several Irgun and LEHI suspects in Palestine. However, he was acting in the interests of the Jewish Agency in its fight against the 'dissidents', rather than for the British. Once British policy alienated the Jewish Agency and it withdrew Kollek's co-operation his utility was exposed as an unhealthy form of dependence.[70]

At the beginning of 1946 Guy Liddell, MI5's director of counter-espionage during the war, passed on to Special Branch 'reliable' information that LEHI was 'training members for the purpose of sending them to the United Kingdom to assassinate members of Her Majesty's Government, Mr Bevin being especially mentioned'. This news contributed to the decision by the Colonial Office to impose more stringent checks on Jews coming to the UK from Palestine.[71] During the summer the threat level was raised still further when eighteen members of LEHI were sentenced to death in Palestine, prompting blood-curdling promises of retribution. J. C. Robertson, head of the Middle East section of MI5, warned Deputy Commander Leonard Burt, head of Special Branch, that 'Irgun Zvai Leumi and Stern Gang have decided to send five cells to London to operate in a manner similar to the IRA'. In more vivid language he told an official at the Foreign Office that their plan was 'to beat the dog in his kennel'.[72]

On 28 August 1946 the director general of MI5, Percy Sillitoe, personally briefed the prime minister, Clement Attlee, about the extent of the danger. A few days later, J.C. Robertson warned Security Service personnel that 'Reports that the Irgun Zvai Leumi or Stern Group may attempt the assassination of a prominent British figure outside the Middle East have been in fact growing in number since the beginning of the year and culminated a few days ago'. All visa applications made by Jews in the Middle East intending to visit Britain were to be vetted by the security services while Special Branch began to monitor more closely the activity of right-wing Zionist groups in Britain. Robertson explained that

'While there is nothing concrete to show that the Revisionists or their Youth Group are organising an underground terrorist movement, or planning acts of violence, there is always the possibility that some unpredictable act of violence may be committed by one of the more hot-headed members.' It was also possible that local militants would serve as a 'convenient point of contact' for any terrorist arriving in the UK seeking assistance or funds from a friendly source.[73]

The lynchpin of the Irgun's European operation was Eliyahu Tavin. He was born in Poland in 1919 and emigrated to Palestine at the age of nineteen. While studying history at the Hebrew University he became involved with the Irgun's student branch. Tavin was a brilliant young man and by 1944 was head of the Irgun's intelligence section and a member of its high command. During the 'hunting season' after the assassination of Lord Moyne in November 1944 he was kidnapped by the Hagana and held in secret for six months while he was repeatedly and brutally interrogated. Following his release he travelled to Italy as a stowaway on an oil tanker. Italy was a perfect base for Irgun activity. The country was awash with survivors of the ghettos and the concentration camps. Many were young and had been radicalised by their experiences. More than a few had acquired military training in the Jewish underground or various national resistance movements during the war. They were conveniently gathered together in Jewish Displaced Persons camps run by the United Nations Relief and Rehabilitation Administration (UNRRA) or were clustered in ports waiting to board ships intending to run the British blockade of Palestine.[74]

Tavin started organising survivors of the Revisionist Party who had arrived in the DP camps and recruiting radicalised young Jews to BETAR, its youth wing. He trained dozens as fighters and prepared them for illegal immigration to Palestine to join the underground. In October another leading member of the Irgun, the South African-born Samuel Katz, travelled to Europe with instructions from the Irgun high command (hidden in the heel of his shoe) to commence operations in Italy. Tavin was reinforced with further cadres of Palestinian Jews experienced in terrorist methods. Their job was to handle the operational and the technical aspects; there was no shortage of local recruits and volunteers for the more humdrum tasks.[75]

The Rome Embassy bombing was his first and most successful exploit. His agents had surveyed the building carefully over the preceding days. They had identified the vulnerable points and worked out when an explosion would wreak maximum havoc while causing minimum loss of life. In the early hours of the morning they placed two suitcases packed with explosives outside the main entrance. Balanced on top was a crude sign proclaiming 'Attenzione – Miny' (Beware – Mines), a curious blend of Italian and Polish, to deter any tampering by passers-by or security men. Placards with similar warnings were also placed at either end of the block where the embassy was located. The staff were asleep in quarters under the roof and the only other people in the building were the security officer and a few soldiers charged with guard duty. The suitcases were actually spotted by the embassy chauffeur who was returning late to the building, but he had no time to raise the alarm. The explosion, 'roughly equivalent to a 1,000 lb bomb', brought down the exterior wall as far as the roof, devastated the ornate entrance hall, and collapsed the grand staircase. The staff were tossed out of their beds by the force of the blast which shattered every window in the vicinity and badly damaged the building opposite. An unlucky Italian who was cycling past was blown off his bike and seriously injured. By good fortune he was the only casualty.[76]

Within hours of the attack both the Italian prime minister, Alcide De Gasperi, and the foreign minister, Pietro Nenni, sent messages of sympathy to Attlee and were quick to point the finger at Jewish terrorists. Embassy officials tended to concur. 'Suspicion falls on Jewish organisation', the security officer Carey Foster reported to London. The chargé d'affaires, Mr Ward, requested that investigators be flown in from Britain and that 'CID Jerusalem should be asked to provide since they have greatest experience of this type of investigation.' The Colonial Office was of a like mind, telling the Palestine authorities that the 'Outrage seems to have been the work of skilled terrorists and suspicion falls on Jewish organisation [sic]'.[77]

When the ambassador, Sir Noel Charles, arrived from London, where he had been on leave, he was shocked by the sight that greeted him and immediately agreed to demolition of the building as soon as the staff were relocated. In his first report to London he was careful not to rule out local extremists, such as neo-Fascists or even communists, but he too leaned towards the belief that the culprits were 'Polish Jews'. In a top-secret cable he informed London that 'the action is consistent with Jewish practice elsewhere and there are obvious motives e.g. the fact that the embassy is known to have been engaged in combating Jewish transit traffic here'.[78]

As the investigation got under way a joint committee was set up to co-ordinate the efforts of the Italian police, the British military police, British intelligence and their American counterparts. The Palestine government was anxious to assist. By chance Dick Catling, head of the Jewish Section of the Palestine CID, was about to leave for London with Nicol Gray to take part in talks about the future of the Palestine Police Force. Sir Alan Cunningham ordered him to break his journey in Rome for five days to offer advice and practical aid. He was accompanied by John O'Sullivan, an MI5 officer who was nominally an assistant superintendent, Palestine CID. O'Sullivan actually ran MI5's Jewish division and had achieved distinction for quickly identifying the men responsible for the King David Hotel bombing. The two arrived on 4 November disguised as officials from the Ministry of Works.[79]

The investigation led in two directions: to the Jewish DP camps near Rome and to the ports where Palestinian Jews had recently arrived from the Middle East. Sir Noel Charles told the Foreign Office that it was urgently necessary 'to bring under proper control the camp and administrative machinery for Jewish DPs in Italy'. The British vice consul at the port of Bari reported that camps in his area 'virtually represent an extreme Zionist enclave on Italian territory'. They 'are believed to be full of hidden arms'. However, the camps lay outside the jurisdiction of the Allied Commission for Italy and the Italian government was loath to interfere in their affairs because UNRRA had strong US support. There was little the British could do about them.[80]

Catling and O'Sullivan had more immediate success tracing

recently arrived Palestinian Jews. They identified two known Irgun operatives who had arrived in Genoa on 22 October from Haifa. The first was Moshe Krivoshein (Moshe Galili), an Irgun veteran who had organised illegal immigration on the eve of the war. He was apprehended boarding a flight from Rome to Athens on 12 November and taken into custody by the Italian police. He absconded the next day, though, and weeks passed before he was tracked down. When O'Sullivan went to search Krivoshein's hotel room he discovered it was being used by another Irgun suspect, Israel Epstein. O'Sullivan interrogated Epstein but did not appreciate just who he had found. In fact Epstein was a close friend of Menachem Begin and had known the leader of the Irgun since their days in BETAR in pre-war Poland. He had just been sent covertly to Italy to strengthen the Irgun's European operations but had no role in the embassy bombing. He, too, was taken into custody. Further leads pointed to Dr Israel Lifschitz, a South African born-Jew who was head of the local branch of BETAR. Its HQ in Rome was raided by the police and a warrant issued for the arrest of Lifschitz. Tavin himself was caught after a period on the run.[81]

However, once Catling and O'Sullivan left Italy the drive went out of the investigation. Lifschitz vanished, ultimately returning to South Africa. The Italian police did not have enough evidence to prosecute Tavin and released him after two months, allowing him to make his way to Paris where he re-established the Irgun's European headquarters in more hospitable surroundings. Krivoshein and Epstein were held in custody pending a decision by the British to extradite them to Palestine where the Jerusalem CID thought they might provide valuable information. But the lack of evidence for a prosecution in Italy applied equally well to the chances of obtaining a warrant for their extradition. Unaware of this logjam and increasingly fearful of repatriation, Epstein managed to contact Irgun activists who were still at liberty and concocted an escape plan. It went wrong. On 27 December 1946 he was shot by a guard while scaling the prison wall and mortally wounded. Krivoshein was released on condition that he report weekly to the Italian police and promptly disappeared. Nearly a year later the embassy in Rome commented bitterly to the Foreign Office: 'The Italians are not a persistent race and soon get bored with difficult subjects, particularly anything to do with the Jews, about whom their policy is to forget as far as possible'. While the Irgun cell in Italy was disrupted, none of the terrorist suspects was prosecuted.[82]

The disruption of the Irgun operation in Italy did nothing to calm nerves in London. While he was in Milan 'mixing with Palestinian Jews', Catling had obtained credible information that the Irgun was planning an action in Britain while LEHI might try to assassinate 'a British personality' in Paris where Foreign Secretary Bevin was about to attend a major diplomatic conference. A worrisome indication that Jewish terrorists had already entered Britain came on 6 November when a threatening phone call was made to Montgomery at the office of the CIGS. His military assistant (MA) took the call and recorded the message. 'Listen carefully my friend. If another drop of blood is shed in Palestine, retribution will follow to the War Office and to military officers. This will begin tomorrow. Tell Field Marshal Montgomery. You have been warned.' The MA reported that the caller 'spoke in a clipped accent. Typical screen villain.' But the melodrama played out over the phone coincided with fresh intelligence from MI5 'indicating a somewhat increased probability [that] Jewish terrorists may attempt outrage in UK'. 'It is all probably nonsense', commented Major General Templar, the director of military intelligence, 'but on the other hand one cannot take a chance.' It was a mark of how gravely the security services took the threat, and how short of intelligence they were, that they considered resuscitating their contact with Scorpion, code name for Teddy Kollek, in the Jewish Agency. This was a delicate manoeuvre because any such liaison would give the agency a window into British intelligence. But J. C. Robertson argued that 'we should not underestimate the benefits which may accrue from a contact of this kind'. The attack on the embassy in Rome was 'heralded by the Irgun as the first stage in their campaign outside Palestine, and the danger of outrages in this country is as real as our information on the subject is scanty'. After much internal debate involving Dick White, future head of MI5, and Maurice Oldfield, who was to become director general of MI6, it was agreed to go ahead but with a 'cut out'. Unfortunately, Scorpion moved to the USA soon after the decision was made and the opportunity was lost.[83]

The Rome bombing and the Irgun's pledge to mount a terror campaign in Britain triggered something akin to hysteria in Fleet Street. On 11 November under the banner headline 'Stern Gang here' the *Daily Mail* reported the threat to kill Montgomery and blow up the War Office 'unless British policy in Palestine is changed'. It was 'the first big Jewish terrorist threat to this country'. The usually restrained *Daily Telegraph* informed its readers that 'Almost unprecedented precautions for the safety of ministers and the protection of government buildings have been taken by Scotland Yard and chief constables throughout the country following consultation with the government. This follows threats of [sic] Jewish terrorists in Palestine to extend their activities to Britain.'[84]

By coincidence, the warning of Irgun operations in London came on the cusp of several state events in the capital. On the morning of Tuesday 12 November the king and queen were to conduct the State Opening of Parliament. In the evening members of the royal family and the government were due to attend the annual Festival of Remembrance at the Royal Albert Hall. Consequently London was flooded with Special Branch officers, plain-clothes police and military police. Armed guards were posted at key buildings and the homes of senior ministers. Immigration checks at ports and airports were intensified, while the coastguard patrolled landing spots that might be used by terrorists attempting to infiltrate from the Continent by boat.[85]

On the day of ceremonies itself thousands of troops from the Brigade of Guards were posted along the royal route. Armed police officers from Special Branch mingled with the crowds of onlookers and armed constables were stationed at the entrance to Downing Street. Special constables were drafted in from the suburbs and plain-clothes officers were told to watch out for 'members of Jewish terrorist organisations who may have slipped into Britain'. But nothing untoward occurred. The only 'terrorist' activity during the remainder of 1946 consisted of abusive and menacing letters sent to various politicians and personalities in the name of LEHI. The targets included the war minister, Frank Bellenger, the assistant commissioner of the Metropolitan Police, the head of Special Branch, Lord Vansittart, and, strangely, Hugh Trevor-Roper, the Oxford historian who had just published his book on the last days of Adolf Hitler.[86]

Despite the lack of hard evidence that any LEHI activists had reached the UK, the police fostered panic and prejudice by informing journalists that they were hunting at least one Palestinian Jew who was 'tall, dark of foreign appearance'. Special Branch made a great fuss about a news-sheet, *Jewish Struggle*, published by militant Zionists in London that was allegedly 'filled with terrorist propaganda'. The police considered referring *Jewish Struggle* to the Director of Public Prosecutions in case the content could be construed as 'seditious' but Arthur Creech Jones, the new colonial secretary, disagreed. He advised Sir Hartley Shawcross, the Attorney General, that he didn't think it was worth the trouble to prosecute. Creech Jones observed that Irgun support and influence in Britain was negligible, although he shrewdly noted that thanks to the Nazi atrocities many Jewish people had sufficient sympathy for the goals of the terrorists to react against any attempt to suppress their organ. If the case went to court the defence could claim 'fair comment' which would turn it into a trial of government policy, a potential embarrassment. 'Proceedings would also, I fear, lead to an increase in anti-Semitic feeling in this country.' Cooler heads prevailed and the contemplated action was dropped.[87]

An air of suspicion hovered over every Jew, especially those who 'looked' or 'sounded' foreign, but in practice the security services focused their energies on immigration controls. The first arrests of suspects came in Scotland. Acting on information from the Palestine CID, civil and military police in Glasgow detained a Polish Jew who disembarked from the SS *Marine Raven*, a troop ship that had arrived from Italy. The detained man had false papers identifying him as a soldier who had served in the Polish armed forces under British command in the Middle East and the Italian campaign. According to intelligence from Palestine, he was a member of LEHI. Next the police tracked down Rosalie Altabeb, a thirty-year-old Manchester-born woman who had lived in Palestine since 1930 where she had been involved with the Jewish underground. As a result of this dalliance she was registered by the Palestine police as a 'suspected person' and this alone warranted a much-publicised swoop on her Maida Vale lodgings. Altabeb told reporters that she had come to the UK to find work as a typist 'not to throw bombs' but her case added to the alarm.[88]

The security forces made a grand example of the Cunard liner *Ascania* when it docked in Liverpool on Thursday 14 Novermber. The ship had come from Port Said via Cyprus and Malta, carrying 534 passengers including members of the Palestine police and British government personnel on leave. Suspicion fell on twenty-nine Palestinian Jews, mostly students. No one was allowed to disembark until all the Jews on board had been strip-searched and their papers rigorously checked. The operation took several hours and was conducted under the glare of prearranged publicity. It represented 'the most stringent security measures' ever carried out on a ship berthing at Liverpool. Despite the huge inconvenience to the majority of passengers, not to mention the unpleasant experience of the Jewish arrivals, no one was arrested.[89]

The Jewish terrorist scare abated as quickly as it had flared up, but the consequences lingered. *The Times* correspondent in Jerusalem observed that it had been a triumph for the terrorists. 'When they read that the London newspapers are carrying flaring headlines about them, accompanied by photographs and colourful details – all this being reported back to Palestine largely with the object of suggesting that anti-Jewish hysteria has gripped England – the terrorists think themselves very fine fellows, and are spurred to further deeds. Each piece of irresponsibility is costing British and Arab lives here.' J. Bowyer Bell, one of the first historians to explore the terrorism of this period, observed that 'For the first time the Irgun's presence was felt in Britain.' The coverage was 'an unexpected gift' to Begin and his men.[90]

The extension of the threat, in fact or fantasy, greatly strengthened the case for breaking the 'illegal organisations' in Palestine that had spawned it, and as CIGS, Montgomery was as much responsible for homeland security as for Palestine or the rest of the empire. He now 'faced up' to the prime minister. He told the Cabinet Defence Committee on 20 November that seventy-six army personnel and twenty-three policemen had been killed over the previous month alone. The army had lost the initiative because it had been forced into a reactive role; the police were at half strength; terrorists got light sentences; and internees were released from custody. The army had to be set free to resume arms searches and mount manhunts. The new colonial secretary, Arthur Creech Jones, pointed out that the army's capacity had not changed since June; continuous arms searches were only suspended because they were unproductive. Attlee agreed with him. He recalled that in June the army had set out to break the illegal organisations. 'It appeared now that the actions had not achieved this object, in so far as terrorist activity was, in fact, increasing. He was not certain what was required by a request to allow the army to take the offensive against terrorism.' Montgomery retorted that the army had struck an effective blow against the Irgun and the Hagana, but had since been prevented from searching for weapons dumps and acting on intelligence to intercept terrorists.[91]

Montgomery's accusation occasioned the 'devil of a row'. Cunningham rejected the 'outrageous suggestion' that he had prevented the army from acting and demanded that Montgomery withdraw his statement. He observed that Operation Agatha had not been directed at the terrorists: the real aim had been to place pressure on the Jewish leadership and in this it had succeeded. A general crackdown 'would not have the slightest effect in reducing terror and might well increase it. I should say, with the example of Ireland and even the Arab rebellion before me, I am dead against reprisals as such'. The terrorists were not 'formed bodies' of the kind that the army could engage. Rather, it was the job of the police to go after them. 'I am having police methods examined by an expert at this time to see whether we can get some improvement in our hunting of these men and in catching them when on the job. I have always been clear that the best method of dealing with terrorists is to kill them.' It was apparent from Cunningham's brutally clear statement that the only difference between him and Montgomery was how you went about finding the terrorists. Unlike Montgomery he understood that they were buried so deep inside Palestine's urban population that cordon and search operations merely skimmed the surface.[92]

But Montgomery was convinced that Cunningham and Gray were failing where he, Dempsey and Barker could succeed. On 29 November 1946 he flew to Palestine to bring his commanders and Cunningham together to discuss the use of the army. They gathered on Friday evening in Government House, the elegant Lutyens building on the Hill of Evil Counsel overlooking Jerusalem. While they were in conference a gun battle broke out in the city below. Against this ominous background they agreed that the minimum of troops should be employed on guard duty. Instead the army should be engaged in 'mobile and offensive' actions intended to 'seize and keep the initiative'.[93]

While he was in Jerusalem Montgomery also met Sir Charles Wickham and listened attentively to his criticism of the Palestine Police Force, which was much to his taste. Back in London Montgomery used Wickham's comments to undermine Cunningham and Gray. 'It is no exaggeration to say that the police force in Palestine is quite ineffective. Every responsible soldier in Palestine agrees with this statement of fact and so does the Chief Secretary [of the Palestine government] and also Sir Charles Wickham.' He maintained 'that the first thing to do in Palestine is to organise the police into a proper civil police force doing its proper job. To do this the Inspector General must be an experienced policeman.' Nicol Gray was 'very gallant' but he was 'not the man for the job'. Nor was Cunningham the right man to run Palestine. 'Every thinking British person in the country realises that the thing is being handled in a gutless and spineless manner and that the whole business is just nonsense.' Montgomery had told the high commissioner that 'it is my opinion that his methods have failed to produce law and order in Palestine and that it is also my opinion that he will have no success until he organises his police in a proper way and uses the police and Army properly and adopts a more robust mentality in his methods to keep the King's peace'.[94]

Cunningham did not take this lying down. He warned the Colonial Office that the panaceas Montgomery recommended 'would be ineffective against the type of terrorism we are now experiencing. Moreover, the inevitable result would be the antagonising of the majority section of the population who are in agreement with us on the question of terrorism.'[95] The Colonial Office agreed. They too cited Wickham's report, but to quite different ends. 'He endorses the view of the High Commissioner that reprisals or punishment inflicted on the general public, unless direct connection between a section of the community and specific terrorist acts can be demonstrated, will not defeat terrorism but merely further alienate the populace on whose nascent co-operation present hopes of eliminating the scourge of violence are based.'[96]

So, just when the diplomatic track had reached an impasse it seemed as if the counter-insurgency track was paralysed by dissension at the very highest levels. On New Year's Day 1947 the Cabinet Defence Committee met to resolve the question of how the armed forces should be used in Palestine. It was freezing cold and the fuel shortage underlined Britain's desperate economic position, its dependence upon loans from America and oil from Arab countries. Unfortunately for Cunningham and Creech Jones events further conspired against them. In mid December the Zionist Congress in Basle dumped Weizmann and elected a hard-line leadership that signalled it was not interested in talks unless it got concessions on immigration or partition. On the eve of the Cabinet meetings in London, three British NCOs and a major were kidnapped by the Irgun and flogged in reprisal for the flogging of captured Jewish militants. More than any incident since the blowing up of the King David Hotel this outraged the military in Palestine and inflamed the public at home.[97]

During the meeting Creech Jones admitted that the army had been held back, but with some encouraging results. Moderates in the Jewish community were beginning to co-operate with the authorities. In these circumstances 'it would be most unfortunate if we were to adopt a more aggressive policy'. Bevin reiterated how important Palestine was: 'without the Middle East and its oil and other potential resources he saw no hope of our being able to achieve the standard of life at which we are aiming in Great Britain'. The time had come to make a decision and, if necessary, to impose a solution. Albert Alexander, the recently appointed minister of defence, concurred that 'retention of Palestine was a strategic necessity' and urged that 'all necessary discretion should be given to the army to prevent and punish terrorism'. Then it was Monty's turn. He argued that the recent outrages in Palestine illustrated beyond any doubt how far the government had lost control. 'The whole country was in the grip of lawlessness, and the Army, who conceived it to be their duty to support the civil power, were not allowed to do so to the extent that they could.' He wanted the country 'flooded with mobile columns of troops'. The police 'should be dressed in proper police uniform and used as police, and shooting should be left to the Army'. His bravura performance won the committee's backing. Attlee concluded that whatever long-term decisions were made it was essential to restore law and order: 'to continue the present policy placed the armed forces in an impossible position'. He instructed the War Office in consultation with the Colonial Office and the high commissioner to draw up a new directive to the GOC in Palestine that reflected the day's discussion.[98]

Thus, at the start of 1947 Montgomery and the military appeared to have got exactly what they wanted. But he still had to cajole Cunningham into giving the army carte blanche. On 3 January the high commissioner flew to London. He met Montgomery that evening at the Colonial Office in the presence of Creech Jones and senior officials. It was a stormy encounter. Monty came armed with a draft directive for Cunningham instructing that 'all possible steps will be taken at once to establish and maintain law and order in Palestine, using the police and military forces at your disposal as may be necessary'. Cunningham retorted that 'the army in Palestine had never been prevented from taking such action as they could against terrorism'. Montgomery reiterated that the army was condemned to a reactive, defensive role. 'He advocated thorough searches throughout the country, "turning the place upside down"; without waiting for evidence. It would be impossible to avoid upsetting the life of the population and in time they would tire of being upset and would co-operate in putting an end to terrorism.' If the Hagana were drawn into the open he welcomed the chance for a fight. He claimed that 'success had been achieved with similar methods in dealing with the Arab disorders before 1939'. Cunningham parried by noting that the rural settlements which Montgomery proposed to search were 'opposed to terrorism'. It was

not 1939, and Montgomery was not fighting the Arabs: 'The terrorists were based in Tel Aviv and the larger centres and general
searches of settlements would merely disturb innocent people.' What
Monty was proposing would lead to war throughout Palestine and
ruin any hopes of a political resolution. Creech Jones concurred
and added that 'War with the Hagana would be war against the
whole nation.' Montgomery was unmoved and simply stated that
he was ready to do what was necessary to suppress 'lawlessness'.
The two sides argued each other to a standstill.[99]

The following day in a private letter Montgomery thanked Creech
Jones for hearing him out. His real purpose, however, was to assert
his position as the government's sole authority on military matters
and to deride Cunningham. 'I consider that his efforts to maintain
order in Palestine are futile, are quite ineffective, have definitely
failed, and will continue to fail unless he resorts to more robust
methods'. Having said that, it was up to the colonial secretary to
decide between the divergent policies each had put forward. The
upshot was a new draft directive from the Defence Committee to
the high commissioner on 7 January. It stated that the government
had decided that 'further efforts will be made to stop lawlessness
and terrorism' and that 'all possible steps will be taken at once to
establish and maintain law and order in Palestine' using the military and police forces 'as may be necessary'. There was no question
of taking reprisals against innocent people but apart from this 'the
efforts of the police and troops should be designed to take the offensive against breakers of the law and to ensure that the initiative
lies with the forces of the Crown'.[100]

On 15 January the Cabinet approved the directive. When it
came to this last hurdle Montgomery was aided by another wave
of incidents in Palestine. On 7 January the Irgun launched a flame-
thrower attack against the headquarters of the Tel Aviv Military
District and five days later the Stern Gang blew up the Haifa police
headquarters with a truck bomb killing four and wounding sixty-
three – including fifteen British personnel. Consequently in Cabinet
'there was general agreement with the view that more vigorous
action should be taken against the terrorists; that this would be
welcomed by the law-abiding elements of the population; and that

leniency towards the terrorists would not strengthen the influence of the Jewish Agency'. Montgomery immediately fired off a message to Dempsey telling him to pass on the word to Cunningham and Barker that it was time to crack down on terrorism. His urgency was all the greater because he had heard mooted in Cabinet for the first time the possibility that Britain would pull out of Palestine if the Jews and the Arabs could not agree to live together under British rule. The Cabinet's consent to a 'troop surge' might be the military's last chance to save its precious bases and preserve this lynchpin of empire.[101]

Roy Farran and the Special Squads

Montgomery's policy coup in Whitehall has been described as 'nothing less than a "blank cheque" from the Cabinet' for the security forces in Palestine. Within a few weeks the atmosphere in Palestine was transformed. On 23 January 1947, General Barker issued a stark, new operational policy to his commanders: 'The object is to kill or arrest terrorists and to obtain possession of their arms.' Barker ordered them to draw up plans for police and army units, each supporting the other, to scour areas known to harbour terrorists, stop and search suspects, and mount mobile patrols at points where terrorists were suspected of moving around. On 2 February, following a spate of kidnappings by the Irgun and LEHI, Cunningham ordered the evacuation of 2,000 British civilians. He was determined to restrict their scope for seizing hostages and holding them against the lives of terrorists facing the death sentence. Over the next days the British also began to withdraw all essential civilian and military personnel into heavily fortified cantonments. The decks were being cleared for an all out struggle.[1]

In addition to giving the army another chance to prove its mettle, Montgomery's policy enabled Nicol Gray to revive his plan for anti-terrorist squads within the police force. At first sight this appears as something of a paradox given that Montgomery endorsed Wickham's strictures against militarisation of the police. However, it was precisely because Montgomery had trounced the Colonial Office, and temporarily established his ascendancy over security matters in Palestine, that Cunningham was more keen than ever to see the police take the initiative. Furthermore, Gray's plan fitted perfectly with his conviction that it was necessary to strike with precision against the underground groups rather than mount large-scale, dragnet operations of the kind favoured by the army. If the 'special squads' succeeded Cunningham would have the dual satisfaction of defeating the terrorists *and* proving Montgomery wrong.[2]

In early February 1947 Fergusson travelled to London on a purchasing mission for the police. This was cover for his real purpose: 'I was authorised to recruit in great secrecy up to four officers with the sort of qualifications set out in my specifications: who had planned and executed behind-the-lines operations successfully during the war.' The 'specifications' were contained in a short memorandum blandly entitled 'Secondment of Army Officers to Palestine Police' that he wrote in London on 12 February 1947 to explain his mission to baffled civil servants. Deceptively managerial and bureaucratic in tone, it came to be interpreted as a warrant for extrajudicial executions by members of the police.[3]

Fergusson explained that 'I was directed by the inspector general [Gray] to study the problem of terrorism in urban areas of Palestine and make proposals for steps to counter it in addition to current police methods.' He proposed adding several new posts to the establishment of the PPF for the purpose of countering terrorism: three Deputy Superintendents of Police (Operations & Training), one each to serve in the main urban areas of Palestine: Jerusalem, Lydda and Haifa. These appointments were necessary because 'there have been frequent occasions recently when comparatively large-scale terrorist operations have taken place necessitating special measures for which normal resources and organisation are inadequate. The proposal is that these Deputy Superintendents of Police (Operations & Training), who will be unencumbered by routine police duties, shall assume this responsibility in each area.' The DSPs would work under the direction of the local superintendent but they would be answerable to Fergusson in the same way that CID officers answered to the assistant inspector general in charge of the CID. 'Their command will consist of a flying squad of ten constables, drawn from the district to which the officers are allotted, since intimate local knowledge will be essential to success.' Fergusson made a clear break with normal policing. 'It is imperative that these officers should have experience and knowledge of terrorist methods. They do not require police experience, nor is it economic to tie up experienced police officers in these duties when they are urgently needed to discharge their own.' The memorandum continued: 'There is in the army a small number of officers who have both technical and psychological knowledge of terrorism, having themselves been engaged in similar operations on what might be termed the terrorist side in countries occupied by the enemy in the late war.'[4]

Fergusson worked fast. He went first to the War Office and consulted General Ward, director of military operations, and General Browning, about potential candidates with the right background. Browning was known as a proponent of special forces and was well connected with like-minded officers. Within a few days Fergusson had conducted a number of interviews. Once he made his selection Browning consulted with Montgomery who was said to be 'keen'. Montgomery gave his approval; his only condition was that the Colonial Office make a formal application to the War Office for the secondment of the officers.[5]

The resulting exchanges between the Colonial Office and the War Office suggest that officials in London were not previously informed of the plan and confused, perhaps intentionally, about what it entailed. The Colonial Office found Cunningham's messages on the subject 'unintelligible to us until Brigadier Fergusson who is seconded from the army as Assistant Inspector General, Palestine Police, kindly furnished the note' (his memorandum of 12 February). Sir Eric Speed, the permanent undersecretary at the War Office, referred to the secondment of officers to the Palestine Police Force 'for the purposes of training that force in anti-terrorist methods'. Cunningham simply asked Creech Jones to give his consent to the secondment of serving army officers 'for special duty'. Eventually the permanent undersecretary at the Colonial Office, Sir Thomas Lloyd, knew enough to inform his opposite number at the War Office that the officers were 'to assume responsibility for operations against terrorists'.[6]

Much later Fergusson claimed sole credit for the initiative. 'It seemed to me, baffled as I was, that we needed people with experience of terrorism or something closely allied to it: people who would foresee the sort of plan that might occur to the imagination of terrorists: people, in short, who had been something like terrorists themselves: not to terrorise or to repay in kind, but to anticipate and to give would-be raiders a bloody nose as they came in to a raid. I sold this idea to my superiors'. However, Gray had mooted the idea of anti-terrorist squads months earlier and had almost certainly discussed it with Cunningham. The high commissioner visited the Home Office, 'to discuss certain police matters' while he was in London during late December 1946 and early January 1947. He also met Browning in Palestine a few weeks later. Given that Cunningham, Gray and Fergusson conferred regularly and shared views on how to fight the insurgency it is most likely that they developed the project together. It was probably when it all went wrong that Fergusson gamely shouldered the blame. What is beyond doubt is that officials at the very highest levels in London and Jerusalem were informed of the scheme in some form or other. It may have come as something of a surprise to the Colonial Office, but Fergusson carried with him the authority of the high commissioner to fulfil a brief set by the inspector general of the Palestine Police Force. It was seen and approved by Arthur Creech Jones, the colonial secretary, by General Browning at the War Office and by Montgomery, the Chief of the Imperial General Staff himself.[7]

By chance, while he was in London, Fergusson bumped into John Rymer-Jones in the United Services Club. After Fergusson told the former inspector general that he was going back to Palestine 'to the police, to run counter-terrorism', Rymer-Jones asked rather indignantly 'Why police? You are no policeman.' When Fergusson replied that 'Monty is very keen on the idea' Rymer-Jones told him bluntly that 'I think you are both crazy.' When asked if he would be using the 'remarkable CID intelligence', Fergusson said 'No.' At this point Rymer-Jones lost his temper and predicted disaster. He was the only person in London who seems to have appreciated the true dimensions of the scheme and its inherent perils.[8]

Fergusson liked to say how much he admired the professional police, men like Rymer-Jones, but the preparation of his 'special squads' had nothing to do with regular police work. Edward Horne, the historian of the Palestine police, later blamed Fergusson for mishandling Gray's original concept. 'Gray pressed the idea to its acceptance but then it seemed someone else introduced some muddled thinking, so that the new "recruits" who were rushed out from England were given command of the squads instead of training up selected police officers to do the work for which they would have been suited'. As a result 'some curious features developed'. This is unlikely. The surviving documents show that Gray and Fergusson were in frequent contact while Fergusson was in London and Gray saw the proposals that he put before the War Office and the Colonial Office. In any case, both men were veterans of commando operations and shared a faith in the efficacy of unconventional warfare.[9]

Everything about the officers who were chosen to lead the squads indicates their one and only function. The squads were to be led by men trained in commando tactics, fieldcraft, ambushes, weapons use, unarmed combat. The officers were selected precisely because they had *no* police background and the intention was not to 'waste' police time on their operations. This all points to their function as hit squads intended at best to snatch suspects or provoke gunfights. Fergusson later told the historian Nicholas Bethell: 'We planned to be unorthodox, but not illegal. The idea was to provoke contact, to look for confrontation, but not to fire the first shot. It's wrong to say that we were assassination squads.' They may not have been 'assassination' squads, but they were trained and equipped to shoot-to-kill once they engaged their target. A task for which no one was better prepared than Roy Farran.[10]

Roy Alexander St Thomas Farran was a war hero. At the age of twenty-six he was one of the most highly decorated officers in the British Army. He had served with British special forces behind enemy lines during the Second World War and was considered a leading exponent of guerrilla warfare. That is why he was picked for the Palestine mission: the poacher turned gamekeeper. But Farran was not just a skilled tactician for whom Palestine was merely another assignment. He was a child of empire and like many of the imperial warriors who ended up fighting the Jews in Palestine the conflict touched on cherished, personal beliefs.

Although he liked to give the impression that he was born in India Roy Farran was actually born in Kingswinford, near Dudley in England, on 2 January 1921. His father, Stephen Farran, was a warrant officer in the Royal Air Force. Shortly after the birth of his son he was posted to India and took his wife Mary (known to the family as Minnie) and Roy with him. Roy's earliest experiences were of the military cantonments in India where service personnel lived, a boyhood landscape that Kipling would have recognised instantly. Roy once told a Canadian journalist that it was 'at the foot of the Khyber Pass, that he got his first taste of adventure'. In middle age he described himself as 'a relic of Kiplingesque times'. His father had roots in Ireland and like many other service families with such a background the Farrans were devout Roman Catholics. As a child Roy developed a deep, almost primitive faith that sustained him throughout his life.[11]

He was educated at the Bishop Cotton School in Simla, the oldest public school in India. Bishop Cotton had a long record of turning out imperial administrators and soldiers, symbolised by the school's ornate and impressive war memorial chapel. Amidst the white, pillared Victorian buildings set in lush grounds at the foothills of the Himalayas, Roy absorbed the values of the British Empire. His Kiplingesque childhood informed the way he understood history and politics, and shaped his notion of manhood: he was raised to be an imperial warrior.[12]

India also taught Roy about the tensions within the empire. When he was just six years old he and his father were caught up in a nationalist riot. They were on a car journey when their vehicle was surrounded by a rampaging mob that had already killed two Europeans. With moments to go before the car was overturned Stephen Farran pulled out his service revolver and forced the terrified driver to plough through the crowd until they reached safety. Roy never forgot the incident. His father had given him a lesson in courage and cool-headedness while the mob had provided a first-hand demonstration of anti-imperialism. Despite his devotion to the empire, by the time he was an adult Roy was capable of empathising with those who bridled under foreign rule. He never quite reconciled his authoritarian role with his own nonconformism and the broad streak of rebelliousness that he traced to his Irish ancestry. His ability to see both sides and, ultimately, remain detached from either, gave his character a somewhat mercenary quality.[13]

In 1939 Stephen Farran was transferred back to Britain. By now Roy had three brothers: Raymond, Rex and Keith. While his younger siblings resumed their schooling in England, Roy decided to follow his father into the services. In May he entered the Royal Military Academy at Sandhurst. The time he spent there was another formative experience. In addition to military training he was taught leadership skills and soldierly values. Although he was never at ease with matters of discipline (least of all his own) or the routine duties of a subaltern, the martial arts and the masculine ethos of the officer class came naturally to him. At Sandhurst he also acquired contacts who would assist him throughout his army service. One of his teachers was Bernard Fergusson. He was not to know that this gifted young officer of the Black Watch would later have a profound, and not wholly welcome, influence on his life.[14]

At Sandhurst Roy set his heart on joining the cavalry. He loved horses and was a fine equestrian. However, the cavalry regiments of the British Army were being converted into armoured formations so he joined the officer training wing of the Royal Armoured Corps. He passed out of Sandhurst on 27 April 1940 with a commission in the 3rd Carabiniers (Prince of Wales's Dragoon Guards). After further training he was posted to the 3rd King's Own Hussars, known as 'The Galloping 3rd'. This was one of the oldest cavalry units in the British Army with battle honours won under Marlborough and Wellington. The regiment had also fought its share of nineteenth century colonial wars. It was mechanised in 1935 as a light armoured unit, but still retained the panache of the cavalry. According to the regimental history it boasted a 'curious diversity of talents'. Farran's colourful, rumbustious personality blended in perfectly.[15]

By this time Roy had matured into a handsome, sturdy young man. He was only of medium height, five foot eight inches, but he was well built and strikingly good-looking with lustrous light brown hair and twinkling blue eyes. Everyone who met him agreed that he was immensely charming. Although he could be shy and disliked large social functions, he was naturally gregarious and was never short of female company no matter how unlikely the place and the time. He fizzed with energy and sheer joy in life, what Bernard Fergusson called his 'smiling, frivolous, Hibernian' temperament. Another officer recalled Roy's 'irrepressible character'. He was constantly using his charm to smooth his way into and out of trouble, with his superiors and with the ladies. But Roy was also prone to black moods, especially when he had been drinking, and bursts of anger that were as intense as they were short-lived. The darker side of his character was accentuated by his wartime experiences. Physical courage and recklessness about his own safety were matched by mercilessness towards his enemies. He had a capacity for deep compassion and, equally, for murderous detachment. While outwardly appearing single-minded he could be inwardly wracked by doubt. The fear of God hovered over everything he did; he prayed publicly and privately with genuine fervour. And he believed in sin. He was periodically assailed by such powerful feelings of guilt that he launched himself into hare-brained acts of atonement and attempts at self-immolation.[16]

In September 1940 Roy shipped out of Liverpool with the King's Own Hussars as part of an armoured brigade destined for Egypt. While most of his unit was transferred into the Western Desert to acclimatise men and machines, he spent several weeks at the base near Cairo. This gave him plenty of opportunity to indulge his predilection for women, drinking, hunting and horses. He became a habitué of the cabarets in Cairo and got to know many of the artistes. The fun ended in early October when he was ordered to join his unit, now part of 7th Armoured Division, in the vicinity of Mersah Matruh some hundred miles from the border between Egypt and the Italian colony of Libya. Here a small British Army confronted a much larger Italian force that had launched a timid invasion a few months earlier. In the British 8th Army (as it became) Farran found himself rubbing shoulders with officers and men of the 4th Indian Division as well as Australians and New Zealanders. He fitted comfortably into a quintessentially imperial force fighting an imperial war.[17]

For the nineteen-year-old Lieutenant Roy Farran the shooting war began in October 1940 when he led a squadron of light tanks in the offensive that routed the Italian Army. The Hussars pursued the fleeing Italians through Cyrenaica until the retreating horde was trapped by the main British force at Beda Fomm. On 5–7 February 1941 the Italians launched wave after wave of tank and infantry attacks in an attempt to break through the British line. Farran's light tanks patrolled the desert flank and watched the Italian disaster unfold. Afterwards Roy and his men had the grisly task of recovering abandoned or wrecked Italian tanks, and burying dead crew. The Galloping 3rd remained at the front for several more weeks although it was so depleted by battle damage and mechanical fatigue that it had to be re-equipped with salvaged Italian vehicles. In March 1941 the newly arrived Afrika Korps counter-attacked, outmanoeuvring and ovewhelming the attenuated British forces. Farran fought in several desperate rearguard actions until his much inferior tanks were all destroyed. Then he joined the flight that continued until the survivors reached Tobruk. From there he was evacuated to the Nile Delta where his regiment was reforming and rearming.[18]

Meanwhile, the Germans had overrun Greece and threatened the island of Crete. Roy commanded one of two squadrons of Mark IV light tanks sent to Crete in April 1941 as reinforcements. They sailed from Alexandria to Suda Bay without trouble, but the German air force attacked the convoy as it attempted to dock, hitting the ship carrying Farran and his tanks. Only twelve were salvageable. Once ashore Farran's column moved to the area around Galatas where he was positioned to support New Zealand troops. The Germans began their invasion with an airborne assault on 20 May and Farran's tanks were thrown into a succession of counter-attacks against the German paratroops. In these confused skirmishes, fought through olive groves and shattered villages, little quarter was given by either side. Innocent civilians suffered as much as the combatants. Farran was enraged when he saw an old woman cut down by crossfire between his tank and an unseen German enemy. A little later a Greek peasant pointed out a German paratrooper lying in the road. Farran fired warning shots with his pistol and tried to make the prone German surrender. Whether he refused or was unable to move Farran lost patience. He later recalled that he told the gunner to turn the tank's gun on the prone soldier. Farran now embarked on a killing spree. A little further on they came across two other Germans who were also mown down. Five more paratroopers came out of the olive grove with their hands up but he was not in the mood, as he put it, to be deceived by any German tricks and he was still too enraged by the fate of the old Greek woman to care. He ordered the gunner to fire and saw three drop dead, while the rest limped to safety in the trees. In his memoirs he reflected that he would not make a practice of shooting prisoners, but in Crete it was different and he had no time to think in the heat of the moment. In fact, this would not be the last time that Farran killed prisoners.[19]

As the tide of battle turned in favour of the Germans, Roy's surviving Mark IVs were in constant demand to cover the withdrawal of battered Commonwealth units. On 25 May his last pair of tanks supported a desperate attempt by New Zealand infantry to recapture Galatas. The first was struck by anti-tank fire as soon as it entered the town. Farran went to the rescue but his Mark IV was also hit and he was badly wounded in the leg. Eventually a party of New Zealand troops managed to drag him to safety. Roy was evacuated to a dressing station but three days later the hospital was overrun by the Germans. Roy, lying helpless on a stretcher, became a prisoner of war.[20]

Along with other wounded he was flown to Greece and sent to a hospital in a prisoner of war camp at Kokinia, near Athens, where British and German doctors treated him. Although weeks passed before his leg healed he did not waste a second before he started working on ways to escape. By late July he could get around with the aid of crutches and asked to be transferred into the main POW camp. When it turned out that the hospital actually offered better prospects for an escape attempt he feigned a relapse. Back in the sickbay he manufactured civilian clothing from items begged or bartered from other patients and scraped together some Greek currency. Then, on a hot day in mid August, while he was sunbathing, he noticed that one of the guards on the perimeter had dozed off. He seized the chance to make his way through the wire and scampered to a row of nearby houses where the inhabitants gave him food and shelter. Their hospitality was so fervent and his charm so irresistible that he had to fend off several amorous advances from the young women of the neighbourhood. After a few hours of euphoria it was time to move on and he was guided to the hideout where a small group of fugitives, some of whom had previously escaped from the Kokinia camp, had assembled. They included a pipe major from the Black Watch, two Australians and two Jews serving with the Palestine Pioneer Corps. The Palestinians had broken out of a prison camp at Corinth under the leadership of a Polish-born Jew called George Filer who had also helped several New Zealanders escape from Kokinia.[21]

The Allied escapees spent a month in hiding, well taken care of by the Greek underground. The household Farran stayed with included a beautiful young girl named Elpice and, inevitably, a romance developed between them. Sadly, this liaison had to end. In mid September a contact put the fugitives in touch with a band of Greeks who planned to sail to Egypt to join the British Army. The Greeks offered to take them if the Allied group could raise the money to buy a boat large enough to carry everyone. Farran grabbed this opportunity and organised a fund-raising drive. George Filer was crucial to its success because he had taught himself enough Greek to go out and solicit money from friendly sources. Within two or three days they had amassed enough cash to buy a thirty-foot fishing boat, a caique, and made their way to Piraeus to begin the voyage to freedom. The group comprised Farran, Lieutenant Sinclair, Staff Sergeant Wight and a mixed bag of British, New Zealand and Australian other ranks, plus Filer and ten Greeks. The caique had just enough food, water and fuel to cross the Mediterranean.

At first all went well. However, once they passed Crete they were hit by a storm and used up precious diesel just riding the waves. Calm returned, but on the fifth day they ran out of food. Next the fuel went. They tried to paddle, but the exertion only made them weaker. The Greeks, who had previously stolen much of the food, were now in a mutinous state. Farran and Sinclair had to alternate spells guarding the remaining water supply. On the evening of the eighth day they were spotted by Allied planes and expected to be picked up at any moment. But no help arrived. They only survived the next twenty-four hours because the resourceful staff sergeant managed to distil drinkable water from seawater by means of a primitive distillery assembled out of bits of the motor. On the night of the ninth day at sea they were rescued by a Royal Navy destroyer. Astonishingly, they were just forty miles from Alexandria. Farran was awarded the Military Cross for his valour in Crete and a bar in recognition of his leadership in this extraordinary escape.[22]

After debriefing and a spell in hospital for treatment of his leg, in January 1942 Roy was appointed intelligence officer of 7th Armoured Division. He had barely held this post when General 'Jock' Campbell VC, the divisional commander, took him on as his aide-de-camp. The appointment was both prestigious and promising, but it ended in tragedy. While Roy was driving the general's staff car on the return leg of a long journey they had made to inspect positions around Tobruk, he hit a patch of unmade road and lost control. The car overturned and Campbell was killed, although Roy escaped with minor injuries. He was subsequently exonerated of any wrongdoing by a court of inquiry and General Frank Messervy, Campbell's successor, mercifully reappointed him as divisional intelligence officer.[23]

The shock and the sense of guilt at having deprived the army of a rising star soon wore off, at least superficially. Within the month he was back at the front line combining his intelligence duties with hunting gazelles. On 26 May 1942, while Farran was on leave, the battle of Gazala erupted. By the time he reached the front the 7th Armoured Division was so scattered over the battlefield that the normal collection and distribution of intelligence was impossible. Farran was given command of a hastily assembled headquarters protection unit named 'Frigforce'. Given the futile character of British tactics this moniker was a good example of army humour. He ended up commanding a series of rearguard actions until there was hardly an undamaged tank or armoured car left in his command. With 8th Army defeated he and his men joined the retreat. In early July he reached the El Alamein position and was assigned a sector of 7th Armoured's front at Qaret al Himeimat. After just a few days there he was caught in a German bombing raid and seriously injured.[24]

Roy was taken on an agonising three-day journey by field ambulance to Cairo where his damaged arm was patched up. True to form as soon as he could get out and about he was to be found by the swimming pool at the Gezireh Sporting Club. His convalescence continued pleasantly until mid July when he was evacuated by train to Suez and placed on a hospital ship to England. The convoy broke the journey for a short time in Mombasa and then for six weeks in South Africa where he had a glorious time flirting with nurses, shooting ducks and hunting. This idyll ended when he was shipped back to England. What greeted him there was grim and disappointing. He found it difficult to get on with civilians. His relations were no better with officers based on the home front. Looking back he could see how the years of battle had put him out of step with them. He astonished a medical board by pleading to be graded fit for active service and, having succeeded with them, he implored senior officers of his acquaintance to get him posted back to 8th Army. Eventually, in February 1943, he was placed with a replacement unit bound for North Africa. He arrived in Algiers only to spend weeks in an Armoured Corps transit camp. His efforts to get an attachment to 8th Army were all frustrated. Just when he despaired of seeing action again he ran into Sandy Scratchley, an old friend from the desert campaign, who was now in the Special Air Service. Farran was fascinated by what Scratchley told him about the SAS.[25]

The Special Air Service had emerged from the experience of long-range operations behind Rommel's lines. Lieutenant David Stirling, attached to a commando unit in North Africa, came up with the idea of dropping commandos by parachute to attack vulnerable targets, such as supply dumps and airfields, deep in the enemy's rear and bringing them back on jeeps sent across the desert to meet them. In October 1941 Stirling sold his idea to General Auchinleck, commander-in-chief in the Middle East. The early raids were hardly promising, but during the first half of 1942 the SAS converted its approach method to jeeps rather than parachutes and scored a number of successes. Dozens of Axis planes were destroyed on the ground, rail links were blown and valuable supplies destroyed. In February 1943, Stirling was captured and the original SAS unit was disbanded. But development of the SAS passed to his brother, Lieutenant Colonel William 'Bill' Stirling, who was building up a second regiment at Philippeville in Algeria.[26]

Farran was immediately drawn to the SAS and used all his contacts to get an interview with Stirling. Whereas senior officers bridled at Roy's unconventional dress, his rather louche demeanour and impatience with administration, Stirling recognised his energy, fighting prowess, and capacity for quick, independent thinking. In return, Farran was enamoured of Stirling's can-do approach, the informality of the SAS and its driving sense of purpose. He later reminisced about the interview that they were transported to a world in which there were no obstacles, in which they felt as though they were finally doing something concrete to win the war. It was a perfect match. Farran found his métier with the SAS and Bill Stirling became a lifelong friend.[27]

It was in the SAS that Farran learned the skills of unconventional warfare. He took a parachute course, studied sabotage techniques, mastered infiltration methods and built up his strength on endurance marches. He was also taught close combat skills and shooting by Colonel Grant-Taylor, a curious figure who played an important role in training special forces during the war. Grant-Taylor had served in the Chicago Police Force in the 1930s and had adopted the technique of local gangsters who habitually sprayed fire with a tommy gun held at hip level. This proficiency led to his nickname 'Tac Tac'. Grant-Taylor was also known to his students as 'Killer' in homage to an article he published in December 1943 in *Reader's Digest* entitled 'Killing is my Business'. Farran would prove an adept student. Whereas he had previously been constrained by military bureaucracy he now relished his freedom of action. He soaked up everything necessary to function as the new kind of warrior.[28]

Major Victor Dover provides a wonderful sketch of Roy at the threshold of his career in special forces. Dover was the adjutant of the 1st Parachute Brigade when Roy reported to him at Mascara near Algiers where he was supposed to take a parachuting course. A 'devilishly good-looking, blond young cavalry officer' strolled into the major's tent and announced that he was present for a training session. Dover sized him up in one glance: 'He was an 8th Army type wearing a neck scarf and suede "desert boots".' His 'casual attitude' immediately irritated the major, but he noticed that the young captain already wore the Military Cross and bar. 'This was obviously no ordinary man with whom to play the role of the heavy adjutant.' Dover advised him that the course would start soon and take one week, only for Roy to reply that he absolutely had to jump the same day in order to prepare for an imminent mission. He did, and suffered a serious back injury as a result of his impetuosity. But Dover was forgiving. 'I got to like him and respect his very special courage. He was a buccaneer, and always gave me the impression that he had been born three centuries too late.'[29]

Roy began his operational career in special forces as second in command of a squadron of 2nd SAS Regiment under Sandy Scratchley. Their first mission in July 1943 was to capture a fortified position around a lighthouse at Cape Passero on the south-east coast of Sicily as a preliminary to the Allied invasion. Like many early SAS operations it was slightly farcical: the batteries of machine guns that supposedly threatened the invasion beaches turned out to be one emplacement manned by three terrified Italian conscripts. Following the invasion Farran was given some leave in North Africa, to be followed by a trip to Cairo to seek recruits for the SAS. In September 1943 the Allies launched the invasion of Italy and Roy was placed in command of a squadron of jeeps equipped with powerful twin Vickers machine guns. His mission was to land at Taranto and reconnoitre ahead of the main invasion force, wreaking havoc behind German lines wherever possible. Once ashore his jeeps roared into the countryside and for a week operated up to eighty miles beyond the nearest Allied forces, shooting up German transport columns and spreading confusion. Roy revelled in this style of warfare. Although he made contact intermittently with the Canadian and British vanguards, he preferred to live off the land so that he could continue waging his own independent war.[30]

His squadron was next attached to 4th Armoured Brigade at Bari from whence they were again launched northwards in a reconnaissance role. Farran infiltrated the German positions and embarked on a series of ambushes, firefights, and hair-raising escapades. However, as the German defences solidified across the peninsular the opportunities for this kind of freewheeling operation diminished. The special forces now shifted from reconnaissance and overland raiding to amphibious operations that could take advantage of the Germans' open flank along the Adriatic coast. On 26 September 40 Royal Marine Commando and 1st SAS Regiment were landed at Termoli, a coastal town several miles ahead of the British advance guard. When the Germans launched a ferocious counter-attack Farran and 2nd SAS Regiment were pressed into service to hold the line, taking heavy casualties in the process.[31]

His last operation in Italy that year was a classic SAS sabotage mission. The objective was to cut the railway that fed supplies down the Adriatic coast to the German front line. The insertion point was far to the north, between Pescara and Ancona, and the team was expected to operate in enemy territory for a week. Farran and a squad of sixteen men were transported northwards by motor torpedo boat and transferred to rubber dinghies for the last stretch. Despite filthy weather and exhausting terrain the mission was successful: a key stretch of the railway was blown and the Germans were forced to divert precious resources from the front. The pick-up went perfectly and the team made a clean getaway. When they returned to base the men got a 'thank you' gift of newspapers and cigarettes from General Montgomery; Farran earned a second bar to his Military Cross.[32]

At the end of 1943, after three months of near-continuous fighting, the SAS were taken out of the line to prepare for the invasion of north-west Europe. Roy now found himself part of a Special Service Brigade earmarked for critical and highly risky operations during the invasion. To his immense frustration, though, a bout of malaria and a knee injury meant that he missed the D-Day assault. In mid August he was flown to Rennes, in France, to command a jeep column on a long-range operation behind enemy lines. It was to go down in military history as one of the most daring and successful of its kind. Beginning on 19 August, sixty SAS men riding in twenty jeeps under Farran's leadership slipped past German outposts and drove deep into enemy-occupied territory. They used forests for cover and were resupplied by air. Moving fast, and appearing as if from nowhere, the jeep columns spread panic amongst the retreating Germans. By the time Farran's men linked up with the Americans advancing from the south they had killed or wounded some 500 Germans, destroyed twenty-three staff cars, six motor-cycles, thirty-six lorries and troop carriers, a petrol tanker and a dump containing an estimated 100,000 gallons of precious fuel. All this was achieved at a cost of seven killed and two wounded, with three men captured or missing. For this tremendous accomplishment Roy was decorated with the Distinguished Service Order. The French later paid tribute to his role in the liberation of France by giving him the Croix de Guerre.[33]

The 2nd SAS Regiment was then withdrawn and transported to its base in Southampton for rest. Roy managed to snatch an uproarious week in Paris but he was in no mood to stay on base. He wanted to take part in the liberation of Greece. Disregarding his routine duties as a base commander, he obtained an attachment as an official SAS observer to the HQ of the British forces operating in the Adriatic theatre. This enabled him to get to Athens, where he celebrated with old friends. He also joined a commando assault on Salonika and spent a week idling on the island of Skythos with Xan Fielding, another legendary special forces officer. But this was not simply skylarking: all the while he was reporting back to his commanding officer, Colonel Brian Franks, on the counter-insurgency operation against communist guerrillas in Greece.[34]

In December 1944 Roy was summoned back to England and, much to his surprise, placed in command of 3rd Squadron of the 2nd SAS Regiment in northern Italy. The headquarters of Allied 15th Army Group had agreed to proposals for special forces to be dropped behind German lines to work with the Italian partisans disrupting German supply routes prior to the planned spring offensive in 1945. Farran was picked for this mission because of his achievements in France. However, from his point of view there was one snag: he was ordered to plan and oversee the operations but not to take part in them himself. At first he settled down to his task and dutifully masterminded two missions. The first of these, Operation Cold Comfort, went seriously awry. He ordered a twelve-man team under Captain Ross Littlejohn to parachute close to the Brenner Pass with the aim of blocking it. The scheme was wildly overambitious and weather conditions were atrocious. Unable to make progress the team requested extraction, but before they could be evacuated the Germans captured Littlejohn and Corporal Dave Crowley. Both were tortured and executed. Even though the second mission, under Captain Robert Walker-Brown, was a success Farran was assailed by guilt over the failure of Cold Comfort.[35]

He conceived Operation Tombola at least partly to redeem himself and the SAS. The plan was to insert teams of SAS men into the mountains to the rear of the German front line, inland from La Spezia. This area sat astride a number of vital arteries feeding the German divisions which blocked the American advance up the Mediterranean coast. Just as important, it boasted a number of well-organised Italian partisan units of various political colours that just needed encouragement and guidance to inflict major damage on the Wehrmacht. However, 3rd Squadron was more a paper than a real force. Farran had to recruit officers and men from local depots and put them through a crash course in parachuting, weapons training and physical fitness. Because he could not find an experienced senior officer to command the men in the field he made a conscious decision to disobey orders and go with them.[36]

Farran's breach of orders says a great deal about his strengths and weaknesses as a soldier. His resolution to accompany the troops was not simply a response to the lack of good senior officers. As he confessed in his autobiography he dreamed of himself as a G. A. Henty figure leading an army of partisans. He relished the freedom that went with operating behind enemy lines, far from the military bureaucracy, where he developed a profound contempt for the staff. 'We were special troops and almost a law unto ourselves: we lived in the present and cared little for the years ahead.' He was also driven by remorse for the fate of Littlejohn and Crowley: 'I never really forgave myself for committing them to such a wild plan so close to the end of the war.' Guilt and the desire for redemption thus mingled with romantic fantasies and sheer bravado. It was a potent blend and not one conducive to cool judgment. Yet, having committed himself to an act of disobedience, Roy had to succeed and was consequently under still more pressure to take risks. But wasn't this the whole point of the SAS, with its motto 'Who Dares Wins'? He felt that the nonconformity and daring of the SAS gave him licence. He later wrote that orthodoxy had never been the strongpoint of special forces. As long as the mission went well his liberties would be forgiven. On the other hand, if he failed he would not be the only one to pay the price. He understood this only too well. The trouble with 'private armies', he observed in his auto-biography, was that they had so many malicious critics that they could not afford to have a failure. But fear of failure can be corro-sive of sound military judgment and luck the only thing that stands between triumph or disaster.[37]

On 4 March 1945, US Dakota transport planes dropped fifty SAS men and their gear onto Mount Cusna, in the Apennines south of Reggio in the province of Emilia Romagna. Farran posi-tioned himself by the door of his Dakota and as the plane passed over the drop zone he 'fell out'. As he floated down he reflected that 'having flagrantly disobeyed orders, I was in acute danger of ending my regular army career with a court martial'. Success was essential. With the help of the Allied liaison officers Farran forged an agreement between the local partisan brigades. He also estab-lished an 'Allied battalion' that included one company of Italians and one made up entirely of Russian deserters from the German Army. Having sorted out his partisan legions he requested the US Army Air Force to drop a Russian-speaking liaison officer, more interpreters, heavy weapons, a 75 mm howitzer, and a piper 'complete with kilts and bagpipes'. The piper was intended 'to stir the romantic Italian mind and to gratify my own vanity'. His vanity was further gratified by an attractive girl partisan called Norice who became his girlfriend. For the duration of Tombola they lived together, Norice providing the home comforts that Farran's batman, Morbin, was incapable of supplying.[38]

For two weeks he trained the new battalion and set up defen-sive positions. When his base was secure he felt ready to launch a raid against the headquarters of the German LI (51st) Corps at Albinea, in the Po Valley. 15th Army Group HQ agreed to the raid, only to change their minds a few days later. Unbeknownst to Farran, the army group command wanted the attack delayed to coincide with the main Allied offensive. Otherwise it might put the entire German force on the alert. However, Farran was irked by the reversal. He radioed Walker-Brown, who was his liaison at special forces headquarters in Florence, who in turn consulted General Mark Clark, the commander of 15th Army Group. Clark was emphatic that the raid should be postponed, but when Walker-Brown replied to Farran he gave Roy enough leeway to do what he thought was right under conditions in the field. Assuming that the postponement was just another case of prevarication, and afraid that his febrile partisan force might lose heart, Farran ordered the attack to go in on 25 March. This confusion over orders would later cause serious ructions.[39]

The assault on Albinea involved a hard and perilous march across the mountains and a night attack on a heavily defended position. Farran carried out the manoeuvre so skilfully and deployed his forces so well that he gained complete surprise. It was a short, vicious battle for 'the main object was to kill the German officers and to set fire to their HQ'. With merciless efficiency several officers were gunned down or blown up before they could even react. (Unfortunately, the corps commander was away that night.) After twenty minutes the raiders withdrew and commenced a twenty-two-hour non-stop return march. Due to his old leg wound Farran struggled to keep up and had to ride part of the way on a pony. When they finally made it back to 'Tombola Valley' he collapsed onto a bed and slept for fourteen hours.[40]

Following a brief recovery period Farran asked to be supplied with a number of jeeps. Once they had arrived by parachute he embarked on a series of spectacular raids, but this time he co-ordinated his actions with the US 5th Army attack towards La Spezia. His mobile raiders operated with devastating effect on German supply columns and reinforcements moving up to the front. On 19-20 April, the German line began to crumble and a general retreat began. Tempting though it was to enjoy the laurels of victory Farran and his men slipped quietly back to base.[41]

He now had to face the consequences of his unorthodox behaviour. Colonel Riepe, who ran special forces headquarters, complained that he 'had considerable trouble with a turbulent member [of the SAS] who apart from disobeying orders forbidding him to drop . . . also disobeyed a clear order' not to attack the enemy HQ. Farran claimed that he had been away from his wireless set when the instructions were transmitted, but an SOE liaison officer with the partisans confirmed that Roy had received the 'stop' signal. It looked as if he would face a court martial. Fortunately, the Americans had a change of heart once the extent of the damage inflicted on the Germans by Farran's irregulars became clear. As he recalled, 'The British faction that wanted to try me . . . was narrowly defeated, largely through the support I received from Colonel Riepe, the US officer at 15th Army Group in charge of special operations. He even went so far as to recommend me for a US Legion of Merit – an ace in the hole because I could hardly be court-martialled for something for which I had been decorated.' He would not always be so lucky.[42]

With the war in Italy winding up, Farran returned to England. He arrived just in time to take part in the VE Day celebrations on 8-9 May. The night of rejoicing passed in a whirl of dancing, drinking and kissing. Farran got very drunk and eventually fell asleep under a tree in Hyde Park. But the following day he felt utterly depressed. In his memoirs he remembered feeling as though the clock had stopped ticking. His life had been geared to winning the war, but that objective had now been achieved. He felt out of step with the happiness of the civilians. All around him people embraced peace but he could only see an end to comradeship, excitement and a sense of purpose. In his memoir he lamented that he would never be at the centre of things again; there would not be any more adventure. He dreaded the dull monotony of barrack life, being subservient to staff officers who had done well behind a desk. His depression over the end of the war was temporarily staved off when the SAS Regiment was sent to Norway to oversee the disarming of the German occupation force. Farran spent a month in Bergen, during which he and his fellow officers drank their way through 300 bottles of champagne that were discovered in a cache left by the Germans. When this assignment ended he was buoyed up by the prospect of joining an SAS raiding force being prepared for operations against the Japanese in China. But the atomic bombs on Hiroshima and Nagasaki put paid to that. To Roy it was as if someone had blown out the candle. He would either have to make a supreme effort to settle down to being a peacetime soldier or drink himself to death.[43]

Farran arranged to rejoin his old regiment, the 3rd King's Own Hussars, which was in Syria taking part in an operation to eject the French from their former colony. As he was now a major he become second in command of the unit, but this entailed mainly desk work. The regimental commander, Lieutenant Colonel Philip Labouchere, used to tell his officers that to keep the men happy 'The points of entry and exit are the key.' A successful unit had to have a good cook and clean latrines. But this was not what got Roy Farran out of bed in the morning. In October 1945 when the regiment was sent to join the British garrison in Palestine, Labouchere removed Roy as deputy commander. Instead of having to worry about hygiene and the canteen he was placed in charge of an armoured car squadron.[44]

Now came his first encounter with what he termed the Jewish trouble. Initially he approached the conflict with an open mind. In his memoir he asserted that he and the other British troops sent to Palestine were not anti-Semitic. In his eyes British soldiers were essentially good-natured men who cared little about politics. Indeed, Farran had not displayed any previous antipathy towards Jews. He got to know several during the war and developed a high regard for them. Yet, if Farran was without prejudice nor was he terribly sensitive to the religious identity of others. One of his jeep drivers was a Polish Jew called Kalkstein. When Kalkstein was killed in France in August 1944 Roy arranged for him to be buried in a churchyard, though he later wondered rather archly whether the ceremony would quite have accorded with the Jewish faith.[45]

Once he was in Palestine, Farran developed more intense but contradictory impressions of the Jewish people. In early July 1946 when he was interviewed by a Jewish journalist 'he asked with interest and goodwill and apparently admiration, about the Hebrew settlements'. This exchange took place while he was an expert witness at the trial of a British paratrooper who had used a Sten gun to hold up an Arab street-seller. According to the *Palestine Post* 'In conversation with reporters during the trial he showed a considerable knowledge of Jewish and Zionist matters. On several occasions he is reported to have said "We must find a just solution to this problem. I am sure that a just solution for the Jews will be found."'[46]

He expressed similar sentiments in his memoir where his interest in young women jostled with political observations. He admired the shapeliness and endeavours of the youthful women workers on the kibbutzim who had brought modern husbandry to barren land and made it fertile. He could not stop himself giving them credit for the miraculous transformation of desert soil. To him the kibbutz always conjured up the image of attractive girls toiling in the hot sun in their blue work-shorts. He was impressed by Tel Aviv, a modern town that had sprung up like a Hollywood film lot. It was clean and prosperous unlike other Middle Eastern cities. But upon closer examination, and after greater experience, the Jewish metropolis lost its charm for Roy. He was repelled by what he saw as the cheap artificiality and the phony prosperity that seemed to ape American consumerism. He noticed the prostitutes in Hayarkon Street and suspected that the young Jewish men with earnest expressions actually had bombs in their pockets. In distinctly unpleasant terms he envisaged fat, cigar-smoking Jews presiding over the city's affairs. In the course of one blood-soaked year he was embittered by the nature of the war the underground waged on the British security forces.[47]

The Galloping 3rd was stationed at the British base at Sarafand in central Palestine where it was attached to 6th Airborne Division as a reconnaissance unit. Initially its duties were guarding military installations and government buildings, patrolling the streets and enforcing curfews. Later it was used for cordon and search operations. In common with his fellow officers Farran bridled at the restraints imposed on the army. The fact that captured terrorists usually escaped the death penalty only heightened his frustration. He did have one opportunity to fire back,

though. At midday on 6 March 1946 an Irgun unit dressed in paratrooper smocks and wearing red berets drove a truck into the base
and parked it outside the KOH ammunition store. They held up
the sentries, broke in and started loading the truck with munitions.
By chance the Jews were spotted and a firefight started. Roy was
having lunch in the officers' mess when the alarm was raised. He
dashed to his quarters to get his pistol and charged off to the main
gate. When he was under a hundred feet away he noticed something odd about the red berets at the guard post. They were clearly
not the regular sentries. He fired at them, only to attract a return
volley of bullets from several Sten guns. It was an unequal contest
and he was lucky not to get hit. Next the truck came hurtling past,
picked up the Irgun covering party at the gate and roared off. Farran
emptied his pistol into the tailgate and then sprinted to his armoured
car to lead the chase. The pursuit had some success: two wounded
Jews were apprehended, the truck was found and most of the munitions recovered. But the incident was a turning point for him. He
was indignant when he found out that a young woman who worked
in the camp canteen had been seriously wounded in the crossfire.
And he was shocked that the raiders cold-bloodedly shot a Jewish
policeman who they had been holding prisoner by the gate.[48]

His disillusionment was increased by the Tel Aviv car park killings
and the attack on the King David Hotel. In his memoirs he berated
the Jews for not fighting fair and killing soldiers at random. He was
disgusted that although Jewish leaders ritually condemned acts of
terror, Jews never came forward to assist the police. In his eyes,
though, the rot began in London where pusillanimous government
policy encouraged disorder. There was simply no excuse for the lack
of determination to maintain the rule of law. It was with a sense
of relief that he left Palestine in August 1946 to take up a teaching
post at Sandhurst.[49]

From here onwards Roy Farran's career might have followed the
conventional path: a period as an instructor, then a staff position,
followed by command of a battalion and finally a regiment. Instead,
in March 1947 his life took a fateful turn. He later recalled that
he was summoned by the military secretary and told that he was
to return to Palestine where he would put his knowledge of under-

ground warfare at the disposal of the Palestine Police. He regretted leaving a little but mainly felt that, at last, he was getting a chance to overcome the frustration he had experienced when he was previously stationed in Palestine. He believed that with the complete backing he was promised he might well be able to smash the terrorists who murdered innocent people for political ends. He understood that he was to set up special anti-terrorist squads with full power to operate as they pleased. The mission was actively to hunt down the dissidents.[50]

The summons from the War Office did not come out of the blue. Since the end of the war Farran had stayed in touch with Brigadier Mike Calvert, the last commander of the SAS, and Colonel Brian Franks who were leading a campaign to preserve the SAS for peacetime counter-insurgency duties. They had experienced some success in getting a small team of former SAS personnel attached to the British Military Mission in Greece to act in a training role. Palestine offered potential for another display of SAS prowess. Bernard Fergusson, who approached Roy, was part of the loose network of officers who saw a place for special forces in the defence of the empire against nationalist insurgents and communist subversion. He had in mind the kind of mission for which Roy seemed to be perfectly suited. Unfortunately, it was also perfectly suited for all of his weaknesses to go unchecked.[51]

By a strange symmetry, at exactly the same time that Bernard Fergusson was arranging for Roy Farran to go to Palestine to fight terrorism there, Nathan Friedman-Yellin was sending some of his best fighters in the opposite direction to carry the terrorist war to Britain. During 1946, LEHI had established a base in France. The head of operations in Europe was Ya'acov Eliav, a brave and highly intelligent young man whose entire adult life, like Roy Farran's, had been spent in armed struggle. Born Ya'acov Levstein in Russia in 1917, he arrived in Palestine with his parents when he was eight years old. He joined the Irgun Zvai Leumi in 1935 and was one of the select group sent to Poland for training with the Polish Army on the eve of the Second World War. Eliav specialised in bomb making, for which he possessed a devilish genius. One of his inventions was the 'explosive coat'. He took an ordinary coat but with the help of a skilled tailor replaced the fabric in the shoulder pads with plastic explosives, concealing the wiring needed to arm it in the lining. The beauty of this device was that it could be 'worn' to the target and left there in the most innocuous of guises. Eliav was involved in a number of murderous attacks on British members of the Palestine CID until he was caught and sentenced to two years in jail. In 1940 he followed Avraham Stern into LEHI. He carried out several missions for Stern under the *nom de guerre* Yashka, but in 1942 he was again captured by the British and imprisoned. After two years he escaped. While still on the run Eliav tried to unite the underground but the time was not yet ripe for that. In mid 1945 he left Palestine for Egypt and made his way from there to France where he started recruiting for LEHI. He also co-ordinated the activity of experienced fighters who were smuggled into Europe from Palestine, via Italy or southern France, and then sent to establish cells in other countries.[52]

When he reached Paris Eliav made contact with David Knout, a Jewish writer and poet who had been a leading figure in the French-Jewish resistance during the war. Knout (his name was also spelled Knut) had been an enthusiastic follower of Vladimir Ze'ev Jabotinsky and became a LEHI supporter, but his daughter was the cell's secret weapon. Betty Knut, also known as Elizabeth or Gilberte Lazarus, was a pretty nineteen-year-old. Her mother, Arianna Scriabin, was the daughter of the composer Alexander Scriabin. She had fled the Soviet Union and settled in the White Russian émigré community in France. David Knout was her second husband. In 1940–1 he had called for Jews to resist the German occupation and helped establish L'Armée Juive, an entirely Jewish partisan force, in the southern, unoccupied zone of France. At the tender age of fourteen, Betty worked as a courier for the underground organisation. After the liberation she joined a French military newspaper reporting from the front, but was forced to quit when she was injured by a landmine. Around 1945 she was approached by envoys of the Jewish Resistance Movement keen, perhaps, to capitalise on her experience of clandestine warfare. Probably influenced by her father's ideology she eventually threw in her lot with LEHI.[53]

Eliav and Betty Knut gradually built up the LEHI cell, drawing in sympathisers and pumping out propaganda via their news-sheet *L'Independence*. They established safe houses, weapons dumps and trained new members. The French government tolerated this activity out of hostility to Britain, which had helped throw the French out of Syria in 1945. It was the same rationale that made southern France the point of departure for many of the Hagana's illegal immigration ships. But for LEHI France was temptingly close to Britain and they were soon planning an attack on the British mainland. The first recorded attempt was made by Jacques Martinsky, a veteran of the French resistance who had lost a leg in the war. As a French citizen his request for a visa would not be subjected to the rigorous screening to which applicants from the Middle East were subjected. Bizarrely his prosthetic limb was another asset: Eliav devised a way to smuggle explosives into the UK inside the artificial leg. The plan was for Martinsky to assemble the bomb once he was in the country and send it by post to the Colonial Office. However, Martinsky was known to MI5. When he attempted to enter Britain through London Airport on 6 March 1947, he was denied leave to land because he could not show good cause for his visit.[54]

But another member of LEHI got through. Just before 7 p.m. on 7 March 1947, an explosion blew out the doors and windows of the British Colonial Club, a recreational facility for British service personnel and students from the West Indies and Africa housed on the second floor of a building sandwiched between St Martin's Place and St Martin's Lane, just off Trafalgar Square in central London. Ambulances, fire engines and police cars converged on the site, battling through snow and skidding on thick ice. Several injured black servicemen were evacuated by ambulance to Charing Cross Hospital while others were given first aid on the spot. Although the blast was initially attributed to a 'gas pipe', police cordoned off the block and searched the building. Shortly afterwards LEHI issued a communiqué in France and Palestine claiming responsibility for the explosion: 'On Friday 7 March at 6:56 p.m. our fighters launched an attack on the centre of British power in London. Notwithstanding the defensive measures and numberless precautions our fighters were successful in penetrating "Trafalgar Square" where they attacked and destroyed the "British Colonial Club" – one of the centres of imperialist intrigue. The enemy sustained damage. All our fighters returned to their bases safe and sound. The secret Jewish movement will continue and will strengthen the attacks against the enemy on his own soil and everywhere they will be vulnerable – until the occupier will be driven from our country.'[55]

The bomb was planted by Robert Misrahi, the son of Turkish Jews who had moved to Paris in the 1930s. Misrahi was a student at the Sorbonne where he was a protégé of Jean-Paul Sartre. Some time in 1946 or early 1947 he befriended a delegation visiting from British universities and was, in turn, invited to Britain. This was the chance Eliav was waiting for. He equipped Misrahi with a 'coat bomb' that he was able to carry with him across the Channel and all the way to London. Eliav later reflected, 'The execution was perfect. I learned an important lesson. No security measures can stop sophisticated imaginative planning.'[56]

Eliav next launched Betty Knut. Taking advantage of her French citizenship she too was able to evade security checks at the border and entered Britain around 14–15 April 1947. She rented a hotel room in central London and studied her target: the Colonial Office. On the morning of 16 April she began assembling the explosive device provided by Eliav, but the pocket-watch detonator fouled up and she had to postpone the mission for twenty-four hours and buy a new one. The following afternoon she dressed in a smart outfit, topped off with an expensive coat, checked out of the hotel, and put her baggage in a locker at Victoria Station. Her plan was to make her getaway for France as soon as the deed was done. From Victoria she made the short journey to Whitehall with the bomb wrapped in copies of the *Evening Standard* and the *Daily Telegraph* concealed under the coat draped over her arm. She headed for Dover House, an annexe of the Colonial Office located at the southern end of Horse Guards Parade. Security was tight following the recent execution of the Irgun fighter Dov Grunner in Palestine. Nevertheless she went directly up to the guards at one of the entrances and asked to use the ladies' cloakroom. When the guard asked for her identity card she feigned desperation and suggested it was ungallant of him to delay her while she was in discomfort.

Although the reason was phoney her agitation was genuine: she had set the detonator on the bomb and knew that she had only a few minutes to get into the building and plant the device. The guard relented and let her through. Knut then hastened down to the basement where the cloakrooms were located and left the bomb on a toilet seat. With an expression of authentic relief she made her exit and went on her way. Some time after she had left the building a cleaning woman called Lizzie Hart checked the toilets. She noticed the package and took a look at it. As she peeled away the wrapping she accidentally disconnected the wiring on the bomb. Luckily for her there was no booby trap attached to the detonator. In fact, the hands of the watch had jammed against the face preventing it from going off. Hart warned the security men and army engineers were summoned to dismantle the device. Whitehall had had a lucky escape.[57]

Commander Leonard Burt, head of Special Branch, later wrote that if the bomb had not been faulty it 'would have blown the sort of hole in the Colonial Office that was blown in the King David Hotel'. This juxtaposition underlines the gravity of the counter-insurgency struggle the British security forces were waging in Palestine and just how much rested on its outcome. Although Farran probably did not know it, the future of British rule in Palestine and the safety of the imperial capital were connected. The front line against Jewish terrorism in England ran through Tel Aviv and Jerusalem.[58]

On 17 March 1947, Farran flew into Lydda Airport. He was decked out in the resplendent blue uniform of a Palestine police officer, the first and last time he ever wore it. With him was Alistair McGregor, the only other officer whose secondment Fergusson had been able to secure so far. McGregor had also been taught by Fergusson at Sandhurst. After leaving the Royal Military Academy he joined the Royal Scots but during the war he carried out covert missions for the SOE in Italy and Yugoslavia and fought in France in the SAS. Like Roy, he had previously served in Palestine but they did not meet until the formation of the special squads. McGregor later told a historian that Farran filled him in about the details of their mission while they were in the gents' toilet at the

Berkeley Hotel, in London, before they left for Palestine. Fergusson met them at the airfield and drove them up to Jerusalem where they were briefed at police headquarters in the Russian Compound, the picturesque nineteenth-century pilgrims' rest that had become the heavily fortified home to the courts and police.[59]

Afterwards Fergusson took his new DSPs for dinner at the King David Hotel. Neither there nor at police HQ was there much talk of training policemen. On the contrary, Farran confirms in his memoirs that he and McGregor were primed for offensive action. He recalled that they were told they would each have the power to operate as they pleased within their own specific areas. As well as advising on anti-terrorist measures they were tasked with hunting down the dissidents, directly and actively. Although Fergusson's memorandum had spelled out the chain of command quite carefully, Farran understood things differently. He recollected that to all intents and purposes he had carte blanche, a prospect that filled him with excitement. He was getting a free hand to fight terror while other forces had their hands tied.[60]

For the next two weeks McGregor and Farran roamed around the Palestine Police Force looking for suitable men. There was apparently no shortage of volunteers. Two weeks later they gave Fergusson lists of who they wanted. He reviewed the names and thought they had 'chosen well'. The candidates were mostly ex-servicemen including a couple of former commandos, an ex-cavalry sergeant, and an Irish-American fighter pilot. Farran was able to pick no less than five men who had served with him before. The NCOs included sergeants Murphy, Faulkner and Clarke; the other ranks were constables Harry Carson, William Pilkington, Burke, Jones and Cade, who was the unit's truck driver. Another man, who Farran called Said, may have been an Arab. Fergusson quickly obtained the release of these men and they were sent for training.[61]

The main base for the special squads was at Jenin where a depot had been established for the Palestine Police Mobile Force in 1943. Since the disbandment of the PMF it was used to train recruits pouring in from England. As well as these facilities Jenin had the added advantage that it was an Arab city and therefore free from prying Jewish eyes. The two weeks of training seem to have consisted

mainly of learning and practising ways to kill people. Farran star-
tled the regular instructors by teaching his boys, as he called them,
'to pepper a playing card with bullet holes from forty feet'. He passed
on what he had learned about the use of the tommy gun from
Colonel 'Tac Tac' Grant-Taylor. With Fergusson's assistance they set
up a training ground in the hills outside the city. The area could be
approached by only one track and for added security Fergusson had
it closed off for two hours every morning. He recalled that 'we
converted it into the equivalent of a clay-pigeon shoot, where we
were able to erect devices corresponding to the sort of ambush they
might easily encounter'. There was every kind of terrain in which
the squads might operate, except for a built-up area. Fergusson was
frustrated that he could not simulate the conditions for urban warfare
but he was reluctant to commandeer a stretch of shops and houses.
That would have attracted too much attention. As a result the
squads were unable to train in the environment of which they were
supposed to be the masters and in which their enemy was most at
home. Nor was there any training in intelligence gathering, investigation or interrogation. For what they had to do Fergusson and
Farran seemed happy that the men were in top physical condition,
and had been taught to shoot according to 'Tac Tac's' methods.[62]

When this eccentric training was completed the squads were
issued with the kind of clothing that young Jews tended to wear.
Farran was convinced that in this get-up they looked like typical
kibbutzniks and he felt reassured when they were hissed at by the
locals as they passed through Arab villages. Each squad was supplied
with two battered civilian cars and an outwardly innocuous truck.
But the cars concealed souped-up engines and the trucks were
adapted to carry squad members along with their weapons and
ammunition. The squads were each assigned a safe house in the
city where they would be operating. It was stocked with enough
supplies, including petrol, to make the unit independent for at least
one week. They were also equipped with a radio to enable them
to stay in contact with Fergusson at headquarters in Jerusalem.[63]

At the beginning of April 1947 Farran's squad left Jenin for the
safe house from which it would cover the Jaffa-Tel Aviv-Jerusalem
area. It says something about his state of mind and his mission that

he later compared his truck to a 'Q' ship sailing deep into enemy waters. The 'Q' ships were British merchant ships that were adapted during the First World War to destroy German U-boats. To all outward appearances they were unarmed merchant vessels, but much of their superstructure was false and concealed heavy guns. The aim was to pose as a vulnerable cargo ship tempting a German submarine to surface and use its deck weapons rather than valuable torpedoes. Once the German sub was near enough the superstructure of wood and canvas was pulled aside to reveal a deck bristling with armaments. 'Q' ships were U-boat killers.[64]

However, it was soon apparent that the design and deployment of the special squads was riddled with flaws. Because they had no police experience or independent intelligence-gathering capacity the squads had to draw their information from the Jewish Affairs branches of the Palestine CID. But the police force was infiltrated by the Jewish underground so each time the squads made contact with a CID officer there was a risk of exposure. Farran mocked the police for clinging to their forts and surrendering the ground to the terrorists, but he soon discovered that it was impossible to travel through the Jewish districts of Palestine without being observed. 'The biggest snag', Fergusson admitted, 'was that none had more than a smattering of Hebrew and a few even that.' How were the squads expected to observe and interpret what their targets were doing if they could not understand what they were saying? How could they plan to intercept terrorist actions if they could not eaves-drop on their preparations? Looking back, Dick Catling, the highly respected deputy head of the Palestine CID, thought that Farran's operation 'hadn't got a hope'.[65]

For the next four weeks Farran's squad spent its time on stake outs and trailing suspects, but rarely arresting anyone. Other than what he and Fergusson later recorded in their carefully edited memoirs, there is very little information about what the squads actually did or what they achieved. The operations we know about hardly match up to their vaulting ambition to break the illegal Jewish organisations. Nor do they give substance to the mystique that has come to surround Farran's exploits in Palestine.[66]

The first successful mission stemmed from information, probably supplied by the CID, that an Irgun man was going to make a rendezvous outside a cinema in Jerusalem. He was part of an Irgun group that had previously beaten up a Jewish youth and stolen his ID card, presumably for some nefarious purpose. The meeting, which the authorities had learned about, was arranged so that the card could be returned to its rightful owner. Farran proposed to seize the Irgun men at the rendezvous, but for what ought to have been a routine police task he devised a highly elaborate plan. He intended to hijack a van to use in tandem with his own, stuff the two vehicles with his men, and position them so that they could snatch the terrorists when the opportunity came. To do this he 'borrowed' a section of the Argyll and Sutherland Highlanders commanded by a not unwilling young lieutenant, Colin Mitchell, who later achieved fame commanding the Highlanders in the Crater District of Aden in 1967. Mitchell already knew of Farran and hero-worshipped him, so he needed little persuasion to set up a bogus roadblock on the approaches to Jerusalem. The 'Jocks' duly stopped a dry-cleaner's van and detained the driver on false pretences. Farran's squad, wearing uniforms, then piled into the back and drove to the cinema in convoy with their own lorry. Once in position the drivers, disguised as Jews, loitered around until four tough-looking youths arrived for the rendezvous. They were joined by another young man and a girl, and finally, the boy whose 'hot' ID card was the cause of all this skulduggery. When the group started to transact its business Farran blew his police whistle, the squad members leaped out of the two trucks and rounded up four of the gang. Two escaped. The Jews who were captured were carrying enough evidence to prove that they were members of an illegal organisation and were handed over to the police. Farran reflected that the manoeuvre did not lead to the capture of anybody very significant, but it worked smoothly and his team congratulated themselves for being jolly clever.[67]

This may have been so, but the operation required extensive preparations and resources that were out of all proportion to the value of the target. Farran also showed a blatant disregard for the law. On his say-so a van was hijacked and its driver held for no good reason, acts that could easily have led to a formal complaint.

The operation resulted in the detention of four teenage members of the Irgun, something which a squad of plain-clothes police could have accomplished with fewer resources and no danger of a legal backlash. The other operations we know about were equally unimpressive in conception, execution and outcome. One night his squad staked out the home of a Jewish woman code-named 'Bella' who was the girlfriend of an imprisoned Irgun paymaster. Farran had reason to believe that Irgun men still visited her. In an attempt to catch them two men armed with tommy guns were inserted into the grounds at the rear of the house, presumably to gun down anyone who was flushed out in their direction. The constable referred to by Farran as 'Said' was dressed up as a Yemenite Jew and instructed to hang around at the front of the house. If he saw anything suspicious he was to signal by throwing a stone over the wall surrounding the building. If he needed backup from Farran, who was some distance away with the car, he had to set fire to a piece of paper and toss it into the air. Farran was worried that his men might be outgunned because it was a bad area, but, as he later wrote, nothing happened except for spending many nervy hours in the darkness keeping watch, disengaging, and departing with the anxiety of suddenly coming under fire. It is striking that Farran had not arranged any back up and lacked the means to summon support. Communications within the team were also primitive, to say the least. A cat scrambling over the wall and dislodging a fragment of cement could have triggered a storm of bullets, while a breeze strong enough to extinguish a knot of flaming paper tossed in the air could have left 'Said' facing Irgun gunmen by himself.[68]

Some time later Farran took his team into the coastal town of Netanya, an Irgun stronghold, to a Jewish fundraising dance being held in a cinema. His unit had been tipped off that an Irgun suspect code-named Oscar would be there. For this mission Farran posed as the rookie driver of Police Sergeant Murphy. Constables Burke and Jones were stationed in the car park outside. Farran and Murphy went into the cinema to watch for Oscar. Farran played his part so well that as the evening wore on he got more and more drunk. He started flirting with an attractive, blonde Jewish girl and was dancing with her when he finally spotted Oscar. Just at this moment his pistol slipped from the waistband of his trousers and was about to clatter onto the floor when he managed to disengage from the girl. Although Roy avoided embarrassment or a self-inflicted wound, Oscar saw him retrieve his weapon. It turned out that their Irgun quarry was none other than the waiter who had been plying them with beers all evening. The only 'success' came when Burke and Jones nabbed two men who had climbed onto the roof of the cinema with the intention of throwing leaflets through a skylight. Unfortunately the leaflets were spreading the Hagana anti-terrorism line and both suspects had to be released. Farran once complained that police methods in Palestine were so amateurish that they made even a non-policeman like him wince. But there is little in this episode to arouse admiration for his technique.[69]

Farran complained that on several other occasions he was ordered to release suspects because they were members of the Hagana rather than Irgun or LEHI gunmen. He railed against this distinction, but it was crucial. The special squads were intended to disrupt terrorists operating against British targets but by this stage of the insurgency only the 'dissident' groups were launching these attacks. Since July 1946 the Hagana had restricted its activities to illegal immigration.[70]

Yet this did not stop Farran leading his men on exciting if futile missions against the Jewish Agency militia. One weekend he had the idea of tracking down some Hagana men engaged in illegal training. The unit borrowed two jeeps from the army and his men put on army uniforms. Thus disguised they drove up and down the beach south of Netanya for several hours until they stopped to go for a swim. While they were frolicking in the surf the constable posted on guard duty told them he had seen a group of 'schonks' up to something on the cliff top. Farran and the others put on their trousers, grabbed their guns, and started up the cliffs. They managed to surprise and surround a group of ten juveniles who were training under the eye of a Hagana instructor (who happened to be a Jewish policeman). The squad took them by jeep to the nearest police station but instead of extending congratulations to him the duty officer told Roy their captives were Hagana men and reminded him that the Hagana was doing its best to help the security forces. Farran protested that they were engaged in an illegal activity, but a quick call to police HQ in Jerusalem confirmed what the local officer had said. To Roy's disgust the Jews were released.[71]

Whatever he may have thought about the value of seizing a Hagana squad, it would not have had the slightest impact on the terrorist campaign. Indeed, in May-June 1947 the Hagana mounted a small 'season' against the 'dissidents' and saved the British from at least one potentially catastrophic attack on the army HQ in Tel Aviv. Farran's irritation when his 'successes' were dismissed may indicate a drastic misunderstanding of his mission, which is hard to believe, or a refusal to obey orders he didn't like, which was more in character. His dubious methods are further indicated by another mission, this time to a suspect settlement. He recollected later that they were not getting any leads from the CID so he decided to send a uniformed patrol through the settlement late at night to see if they came across anyone suspicious-looking. While Farran, Clarke and Cade stayed with the truck, a sergeant and three men went in. They stopped a man and demanded to see his identification papers, which only provoked a showdown with a crowd of Jewish women who poured out of the residential quarters. Fortunately, Farran was able to extricate his team who suffered nothing more than cuts, bruises and wounded pride. The next day, however, a complaint was made that they had assaulted a member of the settlement.[72]

The details of this operation are revealing. Again, Farran seems to have been operating without any backup and no means to summon it. Had the settlement been home to an Irgun or LEHI team his men could have been cut off and wiped out. It is more likely, though, that it was a kibbutz garrisoned by a disciplined Hagana unit. In such cases it was common practice to let women deal with army intruders rather than provoke an exchange of gunfire. Once more, Farran was working without any intelligence, sending his men on a fishing expedition in the wrong place.

For every success there seems to have been a more or less embarrassing failure. Acting on good intelligence his men were able to pick up a suspect in Petah Tiqvah, but a raid on a fruit-packing factory near Ramat Hakovesh was a farce. Six armed Jews were reported skulking in the vicinity of the plant, an isolated location surrounded by fruit groves, but the raid led to nothing more than a complaint from the local Arab village chief that the constables had broken into the premises and stolen some water sprinklers. While they were returning with a suspect caught in Petah Tiqvah a remote-control bomb was detonated under their truck. This could have been a lucky hit by terrorists who were waiting for targets of opportunity, but since Farran's squad used an adapted civilian vehicle it is more likely that a trap had been laid specifically for them. Another time their car was fired on in broad daylight. Farran writes dismissively of this incident but it has grave implications. The car was not identified as a police unit and Jewish snipers would hardly open up on any old car in the middle of the day. This attack suggests that Farran's cover was a complete failure, that his squad was under observation.[73]

Farran was aware of these flaws and considered giving up. Indeed, he reflected bitterly in his memoirs that after battling against the current for a month he should have resigned. Yet at one level the special squads did succeed. Farran and his men created a mystique that briefly lifted the morale of British troops and may have worried the terrorists. Colin Mitchell recalled that 'The terrorists did not make all the running. For three months at the beginning of 1947 they were to experience counter-terrorism at its most efficient'. According to Mitchell, 'Roy Farran's actions terrified the terrorists. But eventually they began to identify what was happening, identified Roy and were determined to put an end to his activities. To do this by force would have been difficult, if not impossible, because the Farran team were as tough and experienced as any Jewish terrorists. They therefore snatched eagerly at what seemed like a scrap of evidence.' They accused Farran of abducting and murdering Alexander Rubowitz.[74]

According to Farran's recollections frequent articles began to appear in the *Palestine Post* about the abduction of a youth. The reports mentioned a hat found at the site of the incident. He could prove that at the time he was disguised as an Arab, having dinner with Arabs in Givat Shaul, a Jerusalem suburb, but that didn't seem to matter. Despite what he considered the absence of evidence, the finger of suspicion pointed at him. In an equally injured tone Fergusson remembered that 'a young Jewish dissident disappeared from the streets of Jerusalem and Farran was at first suspected, and eventually accused, of having murdered him. Heaven knows that plenty of British had been murdered . . . but British policemen and British soldiers were not supposed to go around murdering people, whatever the provocation.'[75]

Both were lying. On the evening of 6 May Farran and four members of his team were on patrol in Rehavia, a smart area of west Jerusalem, looking for suspects. As usual they had no particular leads and were not acting on intelligence from the police; they were simply cruising the streets 'watching for illegal pamphleteers'. It was then they spotted Rubowitz, a figure of such lowly importance in LEHI that they could not have known he was involved with the underground had they not noticed he was carrying wall posters. But, once he was in their hands, they thought that with a little encouragement he could lead them to bigger fish. Roy decided they should take the boy to a secluded spot for 'further questioning' and headed out of Jerusalem. At 9:20 p.m. British soldiers manning a checkpoint on the Jericho Road, to the east of the city, logged the passage of a police saloon with number plate M419N. The driver's name was recorded as 'FARRAND'.[76]

Having passed through the checkpoint they drove on until the car neared Wadi Kelt, a steep-sided valley that cuts through the Judean Hills all the way from Jerusalem to Jericho. At some point they turned off the metalled road and drove across broken ground until they reached an olive grove. Rubowitz was then dragged out and tied to a tree. For over an hour he was 'interrogated' about his contacts in the underground. Despite the terrifying situation he was in, Alexander said nothing. Finally, in what was either a misjudged application of violence or a deliberately brutal termination of the 'questioning', Roy Farran picked up a rock and smashed it against the boy's head. After one or more blows Alexander Rubowitz died.[77]

With Farran's track record of killing prisoners and his pitiless attitude towards enemies what happened is hardly surprising. But even if the murder was not premeditated, the attempt to get rid of the body was calculated. The policemen released the body from the tree and for reasons that remain obscure stripped it of clothing and stabbed the corpse again and again with knives or bayonets. Perhaps they wanted to make it look as though Rubowitz had been savagely attacked by bandits or militant Palestinian Arabs, for such killings were commonplace. Or perhaps they hoped the scent of blood would attract the jackals that roam the desert at night. Whatever the reasoning, having completed this bloody work they burned the clothing and scattered the debris. Then they returned to the police car and drove back up to Jerusalem. At one minute to midnight the car was logged again at the same army checkpoint, travelling in the opposite direction. We know for certain what had happened in the intervening period because the next morning Roy Farran went to Bernard Fergusson and told him everything.[78]

3

Cover-Up and Scandal

The day after the murder of Alexander Rubowitz, Ray Farran met with Bernard Fergusson at the police officers' mess in the Katamon district of Jerusalem and confessed what he had done. Farran also gave Fergusson a wad of papers his men had found on the slain boy. The pages appeared to contain lists of names and Farran hoped they were valuable intelligence. We do not know if they discussed the implications of what had occurred or whether Fergusson recommended any particular course of action to Farran. We do know that although he was nominally a senior policeman Fergusson did not immediately order an investigation. He did not order that Farran should be charged with murder, held in custody or even suspended pending further inquiries, which would have been normal police practice in the case of a person who said they had killed someone in cold blood.[1]

Fergusson did report the conversation to Dick Catling, the acting deputy head of the CID and one of his few friends in the Palestine police. Catling ran the Jewish Affairs section of the CID and would have recognised the seriousness of what Farran had done. Despite this he did not trigger an official response, either. In fact, nothing happened for three days until *Ha'aretz* newspaper reported the abduction. This was the first signal to Fergusson that the disappearance of Rubowitz was not going to go unnoticed. So, on the evening of 10 May, Fergusson went to see Nicol Gray. He chose to visit him at his home rather than at his office, and late in the evening, which suggests that he wanted a very private meeting.

Gray subsequently recalled that Fergusson 'told me that Major Roy Farran, Deputy Superintendent of Police, who had been on duty with some British police watching for illegal pamphleteers had (a) killed a Jew (b) obtained Stern Gang documents including forty-five names'. Gray's response was surprising, to say the least. The head of the Palestine Police Force remembered that 'I merely expressed displeasure and informed Colonel Fergusson that I would consider the matter and discuss it with the assistant acting inspector general, CID.' The following morning Gray decided not to take any action for the time being. He reasoned that it was more important to check on the forty-five names listed in the papers taken from Rubowitz. Further inquiries could lead to arrests and 'might well have caused the break up of the Stern Gang in Jerusalem'. Gray considered that 'had Major Farran been arrested or even suspended from duty following his oral report to Colonel Fergusson the follow up of the documents would have been seriously prejudiced'. Consequently, on 11 May, he told Catling to give priority to examination of the documents and postpone investigation of the killing.[2]

It should be recalled that during all this time the Rubowitz family were being told by police officers that there was no trace of their son and that no one in the Palestine Police Force knew anything about his disappearance. Undeterred by this misinformation, they published photographs and descriptions of Alexander in the Hebrew press which led to the trickle of information that pointed to a kidnapping by armed men who spoke English. Catling reported these developments to Gray on 13 May, but again the inspector general stymied any investigation. Instead, as Gray subsequently explained, 'I instructed the Acting Assistant Inspector General CID that normal police action was to be taken in respect of any evidence from this or other sources.' It is not clear what Gray meant by 'normal police action' because when a murder is reported, and a person admits responsibility for it, normally the police detain and question the suspect. Gray did nothing of the sort. His rationale was that 'two British police constables had been murdered in Jerusalem on the evening of 12 May and the arrest of a British police officer following this incident would have had in my opinion a disastrous effect on the morale of the force. I therefore decided that it was in the best interests to refrain from taking any action in regard to Colonel Fergusson's report particularly as at this stage the Stern Gang were not aware that Rubowitz had fallen into the hands of the police and it was reasonable to suppose that they would assume, in view of the spate of mysterious abductions at that time, that this particular disappearance was the work of an opposing faction.' They might leave their guard down while Gray's men pursued the names on the list. 'In these circumstances', he concluded, 'I felt I was justified in delaying formal criminal proceedings.'[3]

Gray's efforts to block an investigation were unavailing. Evidence continued to appear and, more worryingly, it entered the public domain. First, the two boys who had seen the abduction in Ussishkin Street made statements to the police. Then the hat came to light. Farran now understood that he was in real danger. On 14 May he went to see Fergusson again and told him that he had loaned his hat to one of the men in his squad who 'had lost it whilst making the arrest'. Fortunately for Farran, either by design or by accident, the CID laboratory to which the hat was sent for forensic examination played its part in the obfuscation of the evidence. Superintendent Kenneth Hadingham, who later reviewed the entire investigation, found that 'The laboratory examiner was unable with certainty to discover the full name owing to a missing middle letter but said that it was FAR-AN or possibly FARSAN. A later examination by the Government Chemist at the Central Government Laboratory failed to throw any further light on the name.' The laboratory technicians may have had an excuse for their ignorance but Gray, Fergusson and Catling must have known who it belonged to. After the *Palestine Post* published the leaked information about the hat and gave FARKAN as the name on the sweatband their procrastination threatened to transform an internal affair into a public scandal.[4]

Gray nevertheless waited another week before he finally set in motion an investigation. On the eve of an official trip to London he called in Deputy Inspector General Arthur Giles and 'instructed him to go into it in detail and to take such action as he considered correct'. Even though the police had still not traced all forty-five names on the seized documents he must have felt that he could not delay the inevitable for any longer, least of all while he was out of the country. Anyway the list was useless. When inquiries were eventually completed they revealed that forty-four out of the forty-five names were merely contributors to Stern Gang funds. The one person who was an 'active terrorist' had already been arrested. Having run out of plausible reasons for stonewalling, Gray abandoned Farran to his fate. Almost as soon as Gray's plane for England had left the ground 'Giles Bey' went into action. This was the moment he had been waiting for ever since he had been denied the top job in the Palestine police the previous year. It was the perfect opportunity to administer a drubbing to the military men who had been parachuted into the command of his beloved police force: Gray, the inspector general and former Royal Marine Commando; Fergusson the monocled toff who ran special squads packed with ex-commandos; and Farran, the SAS hero.[5]

On 30 May, Giles personally informed Sir Henry Gurney, chief secretary of the Palestine government, of the truth concerning the disappearance of Alexander Rubowitz and the evidence pointing to Farran's culpability. Gurney had taken over as the chief civil servant of the Palestine government in August 1946 having enjoyed a distinguished career in colonial administration as a district commissioner in Kenya, assistant colonial secretary of Jamaica, chief secretary of the government of Kenya and colonial secretary of Gold Coast. So he must have realised the gravity of what he heard. He reflected for a full day before he instructed Giles to 'proceed with the case as an ordinary criminal offence with the object of bringing Farran and any other accused to trial'. Now that he had the green light from the Palestine government Giles showed that he meant business. He placed Superintendent Kenneth Hadingham, one of his best detectives, in charge of the case. Hadingham had risen through the ranks of the Palestine Police Force and could be relied upon to show no quarter to interlopers like Farran and Fergusson. Giles instructed him to begin by taking a statement from Colonel Fergusson.[6]

Hadingham formally interviewed Fergusson on the morning of

Monday 2 June 1947. He was accompanied by two other officers from the Jerusalem CID, a sign of how seriously the matter was now being taken. What they heard was, indeed, sensational. Fergusson told them everything he had heard from Farran the day after the murder. Little time elapsed before their report was on Giles' desk. That same afternoon Giles presented it to the acting Attorney General, Leslie Gibson, and Vivian Fox-Strangeways, the permanent undersecretary in the Palestine government responsible for police and judicial affairs. The details of the operation on 6 May and Farran's reported confession offered sufficient prima facie evidence to charge him with murder. However, they decided to seek instructions from Gurney and Cunningham before arresting him. The reasons can be easily surmised. They not only possessed evidence of a murder, but of a cover-up that implicated an assistant inspector general and the inspector general himself. If the case against Farran was proven, then Fergusson and Gray were potentially culpable of obstructing the course of justice. There was a tangible threat that the police force and the government would be engulfed in scandal.[7]

Farran was now ordered to Jerusalem and confined to Fergusson's house pending the outcome of the investigation. Another officer of the special squads was staying there and Fergusson thought he could keep an eye on Roy. But on Monday evening Farran received a tip-off from a friend that he was likely to be arrested the next day. He was stunned. As he recalled in his memoirs, he had not appreciated the possibility that there might be a trial. Everything he had done had been reported to the government which had permitted him to continue his operations until early June. To the best of his knowledge his mission had not been changed: he believed he had carte blanche, as before. As he brooded in Fergusson's house a horrible conspiracy began to take shape in his mind. He knew that a UN committee was shortly to arrive in Palestine to determine the future of the country. The Jews would be sure to use the allegation that he had murdered Rubowitz as evidence that the British were unfit to rule. So it would be convenient for the government if he could be tried in the shortest possible time. That would be a fine demonstration of British impartiality. In his memoirs, where he naturally depicted himself as the innocent party, he asserted that this was the only credible explanation because no one could be brought to trial on what he characterized as such slender evidence. Yet he rather gave the game away by adding that the authorities would face embarrassment if they allowed the special squads to come under scrutiny in a courtroom. He felt certain they would require a prior undertaking that he would not bring up certain evidence in his defence. However, Farran's belief that he could use the terms of his mission as leverage only makes sense if he was sent to Palestine to do something other than train policemen to combat terrorism. In other words, if he was charged with murder he was prepared to expose his illicit mission. He thus convinced himself that he could bargain his way out of trouble if he just had time to explain to the authorities the dangers of making what he considered to be a stupid move.

He decided he had to find refuge in a neighbouring country from where he could argue his case via British diplomatic channels. Even if the Palestine government remained bent on charging him it would take days to complete the extradition process. By then the UN committee might have moved on and Jerusalem might relent in its determination to put him on trial. He would play for time and make a run for Syria. Money would not be a problem because as a precaution he had already obtained £100, surely another hint that he was not quite as innocent as he pretended to be. His decision was confirmed the next day when he was summoned to police headquarters for an early morning interrogation. On his return he told the other officer in the house that he was desperate to go back to Jenin to collect some fresh clothes. Despite the gravity of the situation neither Fergusson nor Farran's unofficial 'keeper' seemed overly cautious. At around 9 a.m. Roy stole a CID car parked outside the house and sped northwards. Before he left he changed the car number plates in case Hadingham alerted police and army checkpoints to his flight. Driving as fast as possible along the poor roads he reached Jenin at noon. Instead of going into the depot he paid an Arab street urchin to carry a message to his squad to meet him outside at a nearby cafe.[9]

One by one sergeants Murphy, Faulkner and Clarke, and

constables Carson, Pilkington, Burke, Jones and Cade emerged. When they were all gathered around him Roy spelled out their predicament: he was a wanted man and they would probably be arrested too. He was going to Syria and they were all welcome to accompany him, but he advised those who opted to stay to prepare their own escape plan. He remembered in his memoirs that some of the team looked at him as though he were mad. Others couldn't believe that the Government could be, from their point of view, so fickle. He saw in their anguished looks the struggle between loyalty to their leader and fear for their own prospects. In the end only Bill Faulkner and Harry Carson decided to go with him. They topped up the petrol tank of the car with fuel from the 'Q' truck and after brief farewells tore off along the road leading down into the Jordan Valley. Only two of the fugitives had passports and none had travel papers, but Farran managed to bluff his way into Transjordan. Emboldened by this success they crossed the country heading northeast until in three hours they reached the border with Syria. So far they had only had to deal with frontier posts and checkpoints manned by the Transjordan Frontier Police and the British-officered Arab Legion who were deferential towards a car containing a British officer. Once they reached Syria, however, the going would be tougher. At the first frontier post Faulkner, who had no passport, had to hide in the boot of the car while Farran tackled the Sûreté officer who checked travel documents. Using all his charm and knowledge of French, Farran convinced the officer that they wanted to make a brief detour to Damascus for the purposes of a romantic assignation. This worked but to be sure Farran again changed the number plates of the car as soon as they had put some distance between themselves and the border. They also released Faulkner from the boot. After further scrapes and near misses they reached Damascus just as night was falling. They concealed the car in a garage and took rooms in a crummy hotel near the bazaar, telling the proprietor that they were oil drillers from Beirut.[10]

Back in Jerusalem Fergusson had to deal with the consequences of Farran's disappearance. On the same morning he had flown up to Haifa in his private plane to tell Alistair McGregor that the special squads were being stood down. When he returned home he found Farran gone and a message requiring him to see Giles. It was not a pleasant meeting. Giles no longer had to maintain a facade of civility towards Fergusson and addressed him in a curt, aggressive tone. He told him that he had issued orders for Farran's arrest and demanded to know where he was. All Fergusson could do was repeat the rather lame story that Farran said he was going to Jenin to get fresh clothes. He suggested that they wait until he returned. However, later in the day Giles received a signal from a frontier post reporting that Farran had crossed into Transjordan with two other men. When this information reached Fergusson it did not take him long to figure out that Farran was making for Syria. He could sense that a full-blown international crisis was now brewing. Fergusson believed that he might be able to prevent the worst happening if he could only get to Farran before the police did, but he was convinced that Giles would never give him the chance. So he decided to go over the head of the acting inspector general and appeal directly to Sir Henry Gurney. By the time he reached Government House it was dinner time and Sir Henry invited him to stay for a meal and then to watch a film. It was not until late that he was able to speak with the chief secretary in private. He told him that Farran had probably gone to Damascus and pleaded for forty-eight hours to persuade him to return before formal charges were issued. Gurney was sympathetic and quickly agreed.[11]

The next morning Fergusson went to police headquarters to tell Giles that the chief secretary had given him and another special squad officer a day to bring Farran back before putting the legal apparatus in motion. Giles had to give way, but he was unremittingly hostile and reiterated that the squads would have to be broken up. Fergusson pleaded with Giles not to victimise the men. He asked him to let them return to their previous duties, if possible serving alongside other ex-squad members. However, when Fergusson landed in Jenin to tell Farran's men that their undercover operation was over he found they were being held under guard in a single, small room in the training depot. He was furious with Giles for breaking his word and felt humiliated that the squad was being detained in a facility that was supposed to be under his own jurisdiction. But there was nothing he could do. The men had no idea about the politics and personalities behind their downfall; they just felt betrayed and did not hide their feelings. Fergusson took off for Syria with their curses ringing in his ears. Some time later they were interrogated by detectives. Hadingham reported that 'the majority stated they knew nothing of the incident, while some refused to make a statement'. Whatever they felt about Fergusson their loyalty to Farran was undiminished.[12]

Farran had meanwhile started his day in Damascus in a cafe opposite the British Legation, fortifying himself with coffee and cigarettes for the next phase of his plan. When he felt charged up he crossed the road and entered the building. To begin with his requests to see the first secretary, Charles Dundas, were met with indifference. When he insisted that he was there on a matter of national importance he was allowed to explain himself to a junior official. This man was struck by what he heard and took Farran to see Peter Scrivener, the minister. Scrivener listened with what appeared to be an air of sympathy as Farran unfolded his tale. He agreed to send a message to the government in Palestine setting out Farran's terms for returning and threatening that he 'would apply to the Syrians for political asylum if the terms were rejected'. In fact, Scrivener was bewildered about what was going on. Since he had no idea what Farran had been doing in Palestine the story seemed 'incoherent'. He was only sure that Farran would not return to Palestine unless 'he were guaranteed freedom from arrest and immunity from trial. It was virtually an ultimatum.' Farran told Scrivener he would return in person to collect the answer, but he had no intention of sticking around Damascus. He did not anticipate a quick surrender by Jerusalem and reckoned that the British authorities would either ask the Syrians to arrest him prior to extradition, or try to avoid a messy, public procedure by sending 'some plausible official' to persuade him to return. He decided it would be safer to drive north to Aleppo which was close to the Turkish border. From Turkey he could easily reach Greece where he had friends who would help him. Greece also had the advantage of lacking an extradition treaty with Palestine. Farran rounded up Faulkner and Carson and they hit the road again.[13]

A few hours after they had left, Fergusson strode into the British

Legation seeking information on Roy's whereabouts. He apparently did not know that Giles and the Palestine government had no intention of sticking by the agreement to get Farran back by voluntary methods. Hard on Fergusson's heels Scrivener received a signal from Jerusalem instructing him to request the Syrian authorities to arrest the fugitives on a charge of 'absconding with police property'. This was just a holding charge and was possibly intended to deflect public curiosity. But the net was closing in. Police officers working under Hadingham began to take statements from all the witnesses who had come forward, while teams of mounted police scoured the desert where Farran had told Fergusson they had left the boy's body. The members of Farran's squad were also brought to Jerusalem for an identity parade. It was held a few days later but none of the five eyewitnesses could pick out anyone connected with the abduction.[14]

Farran remained one step ahead. He and the two others had holed up for the night in a town about halfway to Aleppo where they conferred with an Australian (a wartime deserter from the British Army), who Carson and Faulkner heard might be able to get them into Turkey. They resumed their journey early on Thursday and reached Aleppo at 11 a.m. While the sergeant and the constable looked into selling the car to raise money for the next stage of their escape, Farran went to the British consulate to find out the response of the Palestine government. He was allowed to telephone Damascus where Dundas, the first secretary, played for time, telling him that the official response would reach him by telegram in the evening. Farran knew what that meant. Either an arrest warrant or an envoy of the British authorities was on its way to Aleppo. Nevertheless, he opted to stay overnight and then attempt to cross the border by a smuggler's route the next day. In order to avoid detection by the Syrian police, the Sûreté, he and his companions steered clear of respectable hotels that required registration and evidence of identity. Instead they hooked up with three Armenian prostitutes and prepared to spend the night in a brothel. They wiled away the evening in a cabaret with the Armenian girls for company and got increasingly drunk.

Fergusson, meanwhile, had not given up the chase. He hoped to track down Farran in Aleppo but bad weather made it impossible to fly so he and his companion had to travel there by taxi. They reached the city in the evening and checked into Baron's Hotel, familiar to Fergusson from a stint in Syria in 1941. He then went to see the British consul who was no less bemused by the parade of British officers passing through his office than Scrivener had been. However, at Fergusson's request the consul asked local Syrian officials to block the exits from the city to prevent the fugitives from making a break for the border. Since Farran had told the consul that any messages for him should be left at Baron's Hotel Fergusson went back there in case there was any word. While he was having a cigarette on the veranda Fergusson heard Farran shouting in the street. There is some confusion between their accounts as to what happened next, possibly because Farran was extremely drunk at the time. According to his hazy recollections, after three hours of boozing and dancing in the cabaret he had tired of his companions and gone outside for some air. When he wandered into the vicinity of Baron's he spotted Fergusson and shouted at him to meet at the bar across the road. Fergusson rushed down and followed Farran into 'a dubious hotel full of dubious people'.

Once his eyes had adjusted to the gloom Fergusson espied Farran seated at a table, 'looking as black as thunder'. Fergusson joined him and at first they conducted their negotiations over the noise of the cabaret music and general hubbub. Farran recalled in his memoirs that because he was so bitter towards the Palestine police he was very bellicose at first. But Fergusson was persuasive, despite the din from the band. Farran could see tears welling up in his eyes and could not help remembering their long friendship. Then Fergusson appealed to Roy's patriotism, saying that Britain's prestige in the Middle East was in jeopardy. After a while they adjourned to the 'dingy room' where Farran was staying and continued talking and drinking. Fergusson was filled with compassion for Farran who faced a murder charge and, if convicted, the noose. He felt terribly guilty because his ex-student and friend 'was now in a mess where he would not have been but for me'. Farran did not make things any easier. As he got more and more drunk he warned Fergusson that 'he would not get out of the room alive'. As if this were not bad enough, Carson and Faulkner now erupted onto the scene. They had rousted out Fergusson's companion and forced him at gunpoint to accompany them to the brothel where they threatened to execute the other officer. Farran calmed them down but the inebriated men kept returning at intervals during the night to ask their commander 'Shall we do him now, sir?' Fergusson was never sure if either of them would see the morning, but by daybreak Farran had sobered up and saw the sense of what Fergusson was telling him. He agreed to return to Jerusalem to face the music, as long as it was recognised that he was going voluntarily. The clinching argument was that he risked damaging the empire by remaining a fugitive. Fergusson was doubly relieved: he had survived the night and he had succeeded in persuading Farran to go back.[15]

On the morning of 6 June Farran arrived at Aleppo Airport where Fergusson's plane had now caught up with him. Faulkner and Carson agreed to drive back with the other officer and return the stolen car. Unfortunately for Fergusson, halfway across Syria a sandstorm blew up, forcing them to land at Damascus. By now the Syrians were fully acquainted with the Farran affair. Having been sympathetic to British requests for co-operation, the Syrian government had learned that Roy was a feared adversary of the Jews and had come to regard him as a hero. Instead of offering assistance to Fergusson, immigration officials detained him and his pilot on the grounds that they did not have the correct travel papers. Fergusson watched helplessly as a group of Syrian officers escorted Farran away as if he were a VIP. To them he was. The Syrians subsequently offered Roy a commission in their army with the rank of colonel if he would train their soldiers in the techniques of unconventional warfare. He was tempted to accept when he learned from Syrian police officers that the Palestine government had issued a warrant for his arrest. To him this was yet another breach of trust: he had consented to return with Fergusson only on a voluntary basis. So he told the Syrians that he would be glad to stay for a day or two to think it over.[16]

Roy was to remain in Damascus for ten days. While he enjoyed royal treatment as a guest of the Syrian government the carefully contrived secrecy that had shrouded the affair was blown apart.

Thanks to Arthur Giles and his single-minded, not to say gleefully vindictive, pursuit of the culprits the case erupted into the world's press. The abduction of Alexander Rubowitz turned into an international incident sucking in Cunningham, the Colonial Office, and the prime minister.

On Friday 6 June Giles flew to Damascus to achieve by more forceful methods what Fergusson had failed to accomplish by persuasion. Meanwhile, on his orders, Hadingham went to the chief magistrate's court in Jerusalem to obtain a warrant for Farran's arrest on a charge of premeditated murder. Three days later the police submitted the extradition papers to the Palestine government for transmission to the Syrian authorities. The sharp-eyed Jerusalem press corps, Jewish, British and foreign, observed this activity and it did not take genius to piece together what was going on. The British censors could still scotch the story in Palestine, but the international press were under no such constraints. On 7 June Reuters reported that the Syrians were holding a British officer who was wanted by the Palestine police. The officer was named as Roy Farran.[17]

Extradition proceedings necessarily drew the Foreign Office into the imbroglio and it is through the involvement of officials on the Middle Eastern desk that it is possible to follow the increasingly bizarre and embarrassing developments in Damascus. Following the instructions from Jerusalem the day after Farran legged it to Syria, the legation staff sought the assistance of the Syrian authorities to apprehend the fugitive. However, when they learned from Fergusson that Farran was prepared to return of his own accord they rapidly backtracked. Unfortunately, by this time it was not so easy to secure Syrian co-operation. Scrivener, the head of the legation, warned the Foreign Office that 'reversing of administrative machine has been tricky having regard to the fact that the officer did a good deal of talking' and also 'to Syrian sympathy with *any* opposition to Jewish activity'. Scrivener went to see the Syrian president to smooth things over in person and returned to the legation optimistic that a solution was in sight when 'officers suddenly withdrew their agreement to return and demanded political asylum'.[18]

Farran had taken a few days to think over the Syrian offer of asylum and decided to accept. A desperate attempt by Fergusson to change Roy's mind failed dismally because Farran had lost trust in his former patron. He insisted that they meet in the presence of Syrian officials and played up to his hosts by accusing Fergusson of being 'pro-Jewish'. It was, Fergusson remembered miserably, 'an uncomfortable interview'. Scrivener reported to London that Farran had 'made a written statement to the Syrian police (which is being kept secret) admitting that he might be put on trial for murder of a Jewish terrorist and definitely asking for political asylum in Syria'. There was, then, every likelihood that the Syrians would protect him. After another appeal by Fergusson proved futile, Jerusalem seemed left with no alternative to extradition. This would entail further unwelcome publicity and might have an adverse outcome as there was a good chance a Syrian court would refuse on the grounds that Farran merited political asylum.[19]

But Cunningham and Gurney had one, last card to play. If Fergusson had forfeited Roy's allegiance, perhaps regimental loyalty might still prevail. They had already informed the new General Officer Commanding in Palestine, Lieutenant General Gordon MacMillan, that Farran was absent without leave. Now they arranged for Lieutenant Colonel Philip Labouchere, Farran's commanding officer from the Galloping 3rd, to travel to Damascus in the hope of talking him round.[20]

Labouchere arrived on Friday 13 June accompanied by his adjutant Major D'Arcy Muirhead, and Arthur Giles. They found that Farran's determination to stay had weakened since he had learned a bit more about what the Syrians wanted from him. He later recalled that if he had stayed in Syria, where he was very happy and felt much at home, he would almost certainly have been sucked into the Palestine imbroglio. And although he was prepared to fight what he called aggressive Zionism, he was not willing to train Arab forces in terrorist methods that might be used against British troops. Regardless of this, he thought that the Syrians would have been willing to let him stay, but thanks to Labouchere there was no need to test their hospitality. Roy was willing to listen to his own colonel who he considered was purely a soldier, with no political axe to grind. He was impressed by the argument that refusing to go back would cause great embarrassment to Britain. Roy was ultimately convinced that it was his duty as a regular soldier who had taken an oath of allegiance to the King to return and face his accusers. If he remained a fugitive it would amount to a tacit admission of guilt. Labouchere said he could not prevent a trial going ahead, but assured Farran that he was not without friends. There were people in Palestine and England who would raise the money to pay for legal counsel to represent him properly. Roy backed down. On Sunday 15 June in the presence of the Syrian chief of police he signed a statement that he was willing to return to Palestine voluntarily. On 17 June he was driven to the border with Palestine, accompanied by Labouchere and D'Arcy Muirhead. They crossed over at 9 a.m. and proceeded down the road to Rosh Pina at which point Farran passed into the jurisdiction of the British Army.[21]

This break came just in time for Cunningham. Four days earlier he had belatedly informed London about the extraordinary goings-on. His account was full of omissions and puzzling silences. 'I think you should know', he told the colonial secretary, 'that on 6 May a Jewish youth named Rubowitz, suspected of Stern Group activities, was arrested by British police in Jerusalem. He was taken by Major Farran, a Deputy Superintendent of Police seconded from the Army, to a lonely spot between Jericho and Jerusalem, where, in the course of interrogation, he was killed. It appears the body was stripped and left, and police have since found no trace of it.' Cunningham reported that the next day Farran had informed his superior officer, Colonel Fergusson, but the Palestine government, in the person of Sir Henry Gurney, had not been alerted to the matter until 30 May – three weeks later. Gurney had immediately issued instructions that 'statements should be taken from all concerned' and after Fergusson had been interviewed 'it was clear that a charge of murder lay against Farran'. Before he could be arrested, though, Farran had fled. Cunningham concluded, 'There could scarcely be a worse time to disclose this murder (as it appears to be); but I am afraid it must come to light very shortly.'[22]

Indeed, with the fate of Palestine hanging in the balance the timing could not have been worse. During the first weeks of 1947 successive Cabinet meetings weighed the options of partition, favoured by the Colonial Office, as against some kind of unitary state under British rule, favoured by the Foreign Office and the military, or handing Palestine to the UN. The Cabinet decided to wait for the outcome of the London Conference, which resumed on 27 January, and discussions with both Zionist and Arab representatives. These consultations were fruitless. The Zionists would now countenance partition but would never accept a united Palestine under an Arab majority; the Arabs would not accept anything but that; both rejected the idea of limited autonomy under overall British rule. When Bevin threatened that he would pass the issue to the UN the Jewish envoys thought he was bluffing, while the Arabs believed that their case would prevail before the General Assembly. Consequently, on 13 February Bevin wound up the London Conference. The next day he announced that he would ask the UN to take the Palestine question into consideration. Although he was ambiguous about whether Britain might remain in Palestine if the UN wished, and speculated that the prospect of an uncertain outcome might scare both sides into an agreement, he was clear that the British public and the troops were at the end of their tether. A week later, Attlee announced that Britain would quit India in August, which transformed the strategic rationale for holding onto the Middle East in general and Palestine in particular. Britain was also facing financial meltdown because it had reached the limits of a massive loan from the USA; the country simply could not afford extensive overseas commitments.[23]

For Montgomery, as for all the service chiefs, the February decision in Cabinet was a catastrophe. The government's readiness to contemplate withdrawal from Palestine, the decision to wind up British rule in India, and the termination of military aid to Greece seemed the end of everything that he had fought for and believed in. 'The month of February was a black month', his diary recorded. 'We were going to give up any attempt to hold the situation in Palestine and place our case without any British recommendation to the Security Council of the United Nations Organisation.' He foresaw the loss of Greece to communist rule, leading to the collapse of Turkey, and Russian intervention in Palestine. 'These were devastating decisions.' However, the chiefs of staff continued to argue that the bases in Palestine were essential and clung to the belief that if Palestine was pacified the UN would acquiesce in Britain remaining in charge. Until the UN reached a final decision, there was all to play for. Montgomery resolved to fight on, tooth and nail.[24]

Since there was no hope of convincing the Cabinet that Palestine was a strategic asset as long as the population was in open revolt, it was imperative that the army restore and maintain order. The year had opened with a wave of cordon and search operations but the garrison no longer had the manpower to sustain them for any length of time, while the February announcement gave heart to the underground. On 1 March the Irgun blew up the club for British officers in Goldsmith House, Jerusalem, killing thirteen and wounding sixteen. In reprisal the army imposed martial law on Tel Aviv and parts of Jerusalem. This had a crippling effect on the local economy but could not be kept up for more than a fortnight. When the Cabinet met on 20 March, Creech Jones defended the use of martial law for this short period arguing that it had led to sixty arrests and shocked the Jewish community into seeing sense. But his colleagues were unconvinced. 'It was the general view of the Cabinet that the results achieved by this imposition of martial law were disappointing. Some arrests had been made, but terrorism had not been brought to an end. Serious outrages continued, both during the period of martial law and afterwards.' The suspension of martial law actually made the government and the armed forces look weak.[25]

Montgomery, who was on leave at the time, was unable to defend the army. To his frustration the Cabinet asked for a plan to maintain law and order for the next six months while the UN deliberated, although as far as he was concerned the only way to do that was to smash the terrorists. He complained that the colonial secretary 'showed that he was unable to distinguish between the maintenance of law and order and the elimination of terrorism, and that altogether he was pretty hazy of [sic] the points at issue'. In a chilling indication of how far he was prepared to go to keep bases in Palestine (and, incidentally, how far he was removed from the realities there) Montgomery added that 'to eliminate terrorism would entail the most ruthless measures (such as razing to the ground villages to get at hidden weapons)'. But Palestine was not irrevocably lost. On 2 April Britain formally applied to the UN for a special session of the General Assembly to appoint a committee that would prepare a report on the future of Palestine. The UN agreed and on 15 May 1947 the UN Special Committee on Palestine (UNSCOP) came into being. Its brief was to take evidence from all the parties interested in the future of Palestine and recommend a system of governance acceptable to Jews and Arabs. By refusing to make any recommendation to the UN about what solution Britain preferred or saying how it would respond to the committee's report, Bevin left a glimmer of hope for those who wanted to hold on. Montgomery knew that the only hope for this lay in delivering a decisive blow against the terrorists. Having pinned such substantial hopes on Fergusson's scheme it is no surprise that Farran's misadventure, at this particular juncture, came as a cruel disappointment.[26]

The implications of failure were no less grave for homeland security. At the beginning of June 1947 Eliav and LEHI struck again. Eliav's fertile mind had developed a highly effective letter bomb. After experimenting with plastic explosive stuck onto cardboard and a variety of detonators he worked out how to make a device small and slim enough to fit into an innocuous-looking envelope. Getting the addresses of potential targets in England proved almost more difficult than manufacturing the bombs. The team spent 'tedious' hours combing through address books and directories. To avoid compromising France and causing a backlash in their relatively safe haven, once the targets were located the bombs were transported to northern Italy and posted from Turin. This part of the operation was handled by two other LEHI members, Zimka Rendel and Herzl Amikam, who had been based in Paris since 1945.[27]

On 5 June 1947, eight letter bombs containing gelignite were found in the mail of Ernest Bevin, Stafford Cripps MP, the Chancellor of the Exchequer, Anthony Eden MP, the shadow Foreign Secretary, and other political figures. The first one to be discovered was intended for Arthur Greenwood MP, a former leader of the Labour Party, but it was accidentally mailed to the owner of a laundry in Gypsy Hill, South London, with the misfortune to have the same name. It was he who raised the alarm. The chancellor's secretary had a narrow escape after she started to open the letter and noticed it getting hot. With great presence of mind, the messenger who delivered it grabbed the envelope and dropped it into a pail of water kept in readiness for such an eventuality. Eden was also lucky because he had slipped his letter into his briefcase and carried it around for a whole day. All the postal bombs were addressed with the same typewriter and sent from Turin. Given the clear indication that a campaign was now underway, Special Branch set up shop in the central London Post Office and brought in X-ray equipment to examine all mail sent to members of the government and the royal family.[28]

Eventually, a total of eleven letter bombs were intercepted. Any doubt about the motives behind this campaign was dispelled when LEHI issued a 'communiqué' in Tel Aviv claiming several successful detonations and crediting the effort to its 'European branch'. A warning letter was also sent to the British Consul General in Turin. On 7 June a third wave of bombs arrived, this time bigger and potentially more destructive. They were directed to Hector MacNeil MP, a Foreign Office minister, John Hynd MP, Chancellor of the Duchy of Lancaster, William Paling MP, Postmaster General, Lord Citrine, a trades union leader who served on government committees, Winston Churchill and Admiral of the Fleet Lord Fraser, who commanded the Royal Navy in the Eastern Mediterranean in 1946–7. When one of these bombs was tested by Home Office explosives experts it blew a hole in a steel plate. Realising the scale of the assault the police now brought in Hugh Watts, the Home Office inspector of explosives, to assist the investigation and appealed to the Palestine Police Force for help.[29]

Just then LEHI's European campaign ran into trouble. Eliav was plotting to blow up the British Embassy in Belgium but because the LEHI cell in Belgium was weak and the operation was so complex he decided he had to go there himself and take charge. He set off with Knut and another woman, Judith Rosenberger. Knut had sticks of gelignite concealed in her clothing; all three were lugging cases with false bottoms containing dozens of letter bombs. Eliav and Knut were travelling under the names Jacob Elias and Gilberte Lazarus. However, either by chance or because they had a tip-off, the Belgian frontier police detained them at the Quevy border crossing. After customs inspectors discovered letter bombs concealed in Knut's suitcase they were both arrested. Knut was also found to be wearing a girdle packed with explosives. Rosenberger managed to evade detection, but Knut and Eliav were taken to Mons police station and held in custody.[30]

The Belgian police immediately suspected that Knut was the woman who planted the bomb in the Colonial Office and notified the British. On 9 June several British CID and Special Branch officers travelled to Belgium to interrogate the suspects. Detective Inspector George Wilkinson of Special Branch was able to identify Elias/ Eliav as a known member of the Jewish underground and connected him via fingerprinting to the unexploded bomb in London. Eliav's capture was a huge blow to LEHI and a big opportunity for the British security services. As soon as Wilkinson and his colleagues returned to London they conferred with officers who had just arrived back from a five-day consultation with the Special Intelligence Bureau in Palestine. Eventually the investigation into the LEHI cell drew on the resources of the CID, Special Branch and the security services in Britain, Europe and Palestine. A report into the abortive attack on the Colonial Office was sent to the Director of Public Prosecutions by Commander Hugh Young, head of CID, but progress ended there. It proved impossible to extradite Knut and Eliav because the Belgian Ministry of Justice considered their crimes 'political'.[31]

The Chambre du Conseil at Mons ordered the pair to be detained for one month while investigations continued. A week later the French government successfully applied for the extradition of the couple to France on the grounds that they had obtained the explosives by criminal means on French territory. They were duly deported and tried in Paris later that month. However, thanks to her exploits in the resistance Knut was treated as something of a heroine by the French public. In any case, French opinion was generally sympathetic towards the Zionist cause. Prominent members of the French Jewish community even helped provide them with legal aid. Eliav was sentenced to eight months for smuggling explosives into Belgium but was released after just two. Knut was sentenced to one year in a juvenile prison for the illegal importation of explosives. She too was granted an early release.[32]

The near miss in Whitehall and the arrests on the Continent gave rise to another panic in the British press. This time it alighted on news that a substantial quantity of gelignite and 500 detonators had been stolen from two quarries near Exeter in Devon. The foreman, Mr Jack Jones, who raised the alarm, said he had noticed 'mysterious Jewish-looking foreigners' in the vicinity. According to the *Daily Express* front-page story, police were hunting a black Morris 8 car carrying the stolen explosives. Radio alerts warned all cars to be on the lookout for 'two men, foreign-looking and of Jewish appearance'. They were 'suspected associates of Jewish terrorist associations' and spoke 'broken English'. Even the *Manchester Guardian*, which normally steered clear of such stereotypes, repeated the claim that police were after two young men 'said "to be of Jewish appearance"'. Scotland Yard fanned the hysteria by announcing that its Record Office had checked the list of known safe blowers to eliminate the possibility that a criminal gang had stolen the dynamite. This revealed that 'not one is of Jewish origin or appearance', which was enough to satisfy the police that the theft must have been the work of Jewish terrorists. The Jewish community may have been relieved to know that none of its number were safe blowers, but the notion that a 'Jewish-looking' person might automatically be suspected of terrorist affiliations caused deep unease.[33]

On 16 June 1947, in the middle of this latest scare over Jewish terrorism and the crisis over Farran's delinquency, the UN Special Committee on Palestine arrived to take evidence. This coincidence could not have been more painful. The Farran affair cast a lurid light over the methods by which the British were holding onto Palestine. And just when the security forces should have been moving to extinguish a threat that reached as far as Britain, they were on the back foot due to accusations that they were out of control. Needless to say, the propaganda organs of the Jewish underground as well as the general Jewish press were unsparing. Around the time that Farran fled Palestine LEHI issued a wall poster summarising the information about the abduction of Alexander Rubowitz and mentioning that the name FARKAN was written in the hat found at the scene. 'More than three weeks have passed since the abduction. Close investigation of the events leads us now to assume the fate of the lad: **Alexander Rubowitz has died at the hands of his abductors – the British (and the gentiles [sic] of the world).** If the enemy powers do not reveal, in the next few days, where Alexander Rubowitz can be found, this assumption will become a fact. **In which case the British criminals will pay the price**.' On 11 June, the Irgun radio station Voice of Fighting Zion referred to the kidnapping in a two-pronged critique of the British and the Jewish Agency, who it accused of collaboration: 'they *know* what happened to young Rubovicz [sic] who was kidnapped by British Secret Police and whose traces have been lost'.[34]

Concern about Rubowitz spread beyond the nationalist and right-wing militants in the Jewish community. *Davar*, a left-wing paper, wanted to know why the British were able to free their own people when they were kidnapped but could find no trace of Rubowitz. In the same vein the *Palestine Post* asserted, 'There can be no reason why the authorities should have failed in this case to act with the same alacrity and zeal which they displayed two days ago in recovering the men [two British police officers] abducted in Ramat Gan.' *HaMashkif*, a paper aligned with the right-wing Zionists, and *Davar* both reported rumours that unnamed British officers were involved in the abduction of Rubowitz and that members of the British Union of Fascists who had infiltrated the Palestine police were responsible for this and a spate of other mysterious disappearances. On 13 June, the Jewish press published the first reports that British officers were being detained in Syria. Two days later, *Ha'aretz* finally named Farran as the officer whose extradition was being sought. The circumstances could not have been more inconvenient for the British. For weeks the Palestine police and the army had denied any knowledge of the abduction. When it was suggested that British police were involved they denied that too. After a name very similar to Farran's was revealed in the hat found at the crime scene they eschewed any knowledge of such a person. Now, with the UN Special Committee about to arrive, it was beyond any doubt that Farran, a senior police officer, who must have been known to the police and the government, was involved in the affair.[35]

The implications certainly did not escape the British prime minister. On 14 June Attlee had asked Creech Jones, Secretary of State for the Colonies, to find out why the high commissioner had not reported the business earlier. His request triggered introspection and despondency in the Colonial Office. William Mathieson, one of the officials handling Palestine, explained that in view of the growing press interest in Britain, and even more so in America, it was urgent to get the details. So far no statements had been issued by the government, but with the US press on the trail of a 'sensational story' that included allegations of British fascists infiltrating the Palestine police it would not be possible to stonewall for much longer. Another official responded glumly that the Farran case provided material for anti-British propaganda 'which will be deeply embarrassing for its background of truth'. The Rubowitz affair was becoming an international scandal and the British Embassy in Washington had to prepare for the moment 'if and when the story breaks'.[36]

That moment was not long in coming. The same day the *New York Times* carried a long account of what was known to date. This was bad, but the *NYT* special correspondent pointed out that what was not yet known was potentially even worse. 'Extreme embarrassment on the part of the Palestine government was apparent tonight as a result of the sinister-sounding mystery surrounding the arrest in Syria of three British officers of the Palestine police.' Whenever the subject of the arrests was raised 'government officials displayed extraordinary caution and had an air of men expecting some acutely unsavoury scandal to break just on the eve of the opening of the United Nations inquiry on Palestine'. For two days they had fended off journalists with assurances that everything would soon be made clear, but all that appeared were 'two cryptic announcements'. The second declared that an extradition order had been issued against Major Farran but the charge was not stated and no reason was given why the other 'officers' no longer figured. The press corps was able to pick up fragments of the story from 'official circles', presumably regular policemen who were only too glad to dish the dirt on the seconded army officers. They learned that Giles had travelled to Damascus and that Farran was expected back soon. In a wry aside the *NYT* correspondent added, 'All this must seem like doubletalk to readers in the United States but, in the absence of an official statement, correspondents here cannot honestly and fairly offer any further explanation. The full story will soon be told and the general expectation is that it will be a sensation.' For the moment the rumour mill was in overdrive. Stories were circulating that a cell of the British Union of Fascists (BUF) existed in the police force; that 'the British police in Palestine have their own "underground", a counter-terrorist unit operating independently of the central police command; and that one or more of the officers held in Damascus are wanted for questioning in connection with the disappearance of Alexander Rubovitch [sic]'.[37]

With the Farran affair all over the press on the very day that UNSCOP arrived in Palestine, Attlee addressed a personal minute to Creech Jones couched in the sort of restrained language that indicated the opposite of how he really felt: 'I do not understand why this important incident was not reported at the time. Unless you already know of an explanation, one should be sought from the High Commissioner.' All that Cunningham had provided to Creech Jones until then was the rather lame summary of the case which begged far more questions than it answered. Stung into renewed efforts to get at the truth, Creech Jones fired off a terse cable to Jerusalem. 'PM has enquired why this important incident was not reported at the time. I would be grateful for material for reply earliest.' The next day, his private secretary forwarded to the prime minister's office copies of the telegrams from Jerusalem and from Damascus 'about a very unfortunate occurrence as he thinks that the PM should know about it'.[38]

The explanations from Jerusalem left Creech Jones unsure of how to respond to the growing clamour. 'Great interest is being shown in this case by the British press,' he telegraphed Cunningham, 'and I should welcome your views on the line to be taken in reply to enquiries by them.' He was also concerned about the suggestions that the officers were associated with the British Union of Fascists. 'So far no comment has been made here in response to the press enquiries but the flow back from the American press may at any moment produce [a] situation in which some statement may be required.'³⁹ Cunningham duly updated the Colonial Office although, again, his reply could not fail to raise eyebrows. 'It was not until 30 May that [the] matter came to the notice of government. Further investigation was ordered the next day as what had happened and what steps could be taken were far from clear. The Inspector General was in England at the time. The incident was reported to you as soon as the Inspector General returned and the results of police investigations were reasonably clear. FARRAN has now been returned to this country and has terminated his contract with the police on secondment at his own request. He has been taken over by the Army for Court Martial.'⁴⁰

Creech Jones was hardly reassured. While not saying whether he thought it was a case of incompetence or malfeasance, with great acuity he pinpointed all the flaws in the way the affair had been handled. 'I cannot regard it as satisfactory nor am I sure that there should have been such a long delay on the part of the police in reporting to you an incident of this character which had been under investigation for some three weeks. It was also important that no report was made to London until 13 June. Nor is it clear why FARRAN was not placed under arrest earlier pending further investigation. I do not wish to add to your difficulties in connection with a case that is already sufficiently embarrassing but I feel the above point requires further elucidation. The good name of the British administration in Palestine is bound to be attacked over this incident and already warnings about the incident are entering in [sic] Press. I shall therefore be hampered in explaining and defending their action unless I am in possession of most detailed information available. I shall be glad if you will also keep me fully informed regarding progress of court martial proceedings.'⁴¹

Cunningham was alert to the implications of Creech Jones's message. He made a blatant effort to distance himself from the conduct of Fergusson and Gray, who stood to be accused of a cover-up and obstructing the course of justice. 'I am of course fully aware of the unsatisfactory aspects of this unhappy case and have called for a report in writing from the police as to the reasons for the delay in reporting. In regard to the action of this government I trust you do not imply that there was any intention of withholding information from you. If so nothing could be further from the truth.' He blamed the time lag on Gray's absence. 'I decided that he should be heard before reporting but unfortunately he was delayed and did not arrive back until the evening of 10th. After he had been seen you were informed.' Cunningham's defence against charges of complicity in the cover-up was thus to aver that he had been kept in the dark. This was a viable legal defence but it was politically toxic because it suggested he lacked a grip on the security forces. It implied that the police were carrying on certain operations without his knowledge.[42]

The prime minister's reaction was no less remarkable. Rather than expressing concern about alleged illegal actions perpetrated by the British security forces in Palestine, with or without the knowledge of the government, he seemed more preoccupied with news management. After digesting Cunningham's latest telegram Attlee told Creech Jones: 'This, to my mind, shows that it is already urgent that an official statement on the case should be issued as soon as possible either by the High Commissioner or by yourself in the form of a statement in the House. In a case of this kind, HMG is always at a disadvantage if the first official statement is made to correct garbled versions of the story which have appeared first in the press. Once this happens it is almost impossible for the government to abandon the defence and to put the official statement across convincingly. It is now inevitable that some publicity will be given to the Farran case, and it is surely better that HMG should not delay any further putting out some statement, however cautious that may have to be.'[43]

These reflections would have brought a blush to the cheek of a modern 'spin doctor'. But they missed the point. It was left to officials in the Colonial Office to spot the hostages to fortune in Cunningham's explanations. William Mathieson observed in a minute, 'The answer is unsatisfactory and fails completely to explain the serious delay on the part of the police. It is incomprehensible that the Acting Inspector General, a few hours after the Inspector General had left for the UK, should then report to the Chief Secretary a serious matter over which the police had been concerned for three weeks. Particularly since the Chief Secretary would feel obliged to seek an explanation from the responsible head of the force who was not then in Palestine'. He could see how the latest information for the prime minister was so patchy it 'would be likely to evoke a sharp request for more help'. Creech Jones himself added that 'it seems to be still in need of explanation why an incident so obviously important and explosive was not reported to you the very day it came to the notice of the secretariat, i.e. 30 May instead of waiting until June 13th'.[44]

However, the recriminations between London and Jerusalem and between Government House and police headquarters were overtaken by even more dramatic events. At one o'clock on 17 June Farran had arrived at the Allenby Barracks, a collection of military buildings in south Jerusalem, escorted by Labouchere and D'Arcy Muirhead. A district superintendent accompanied them although Farran was technically under army jurisdiction and had not yet been arrested. Labouchere handed Farran over to two detective superintendents, T. B. Wood and K. W. Horner, who had previously been detailed to meet him and provide his police guard. At 3 p.m., Kenneth Hadingham arrived. He placed Farran under arrest and charged him with premeditated murder contrary to Section 214 of the Palestine Criminal Code Ordinance 1936. In a gesture of defiance that boded ill, Farran refused to make any statement or even to sign the charge sheet. He was then taken to a three-room flat in the married officers' quarters where Lieutenant Colonel Niven, the Assistant Adjutant General, HQ Palestine, arranged the military guard. One soldier was even detailed to sleep in Farran's flat and all his meals were to be carried up to the second-storey apartment by military mess staff. However, Niven was not taking these precautions to keep Farran under close supervision. He believed that his task was to prevent an assassination attempt by Jewish terrorists. The troops on guard were there to stop anyone unauthorised from getting in, not to prevent Farran from getting out.[45]

The army was not unduly worried about Roy attempting anything so silly. He had given his word and he was an officer and a gentleman, after all. Labouchere later swore that he was sure Farran 'intended to face the charges and felt that he could refute the evidence against him'. The next day Farran formally submitted his resignation from the Palestine Police Force, which was accepted, and officially reverted to the army. Labouchere and D'Arcy Muirhead notified him that he would now be tried under the Army Act. The next step in the court martial proceedings would be to collect the evidence in the form of official police and army investigation reports and sworn statements. This was known in military legal parlance as the 'summary of evidence' and it would form the basis for the prosecution and the defence. At some point during the day Farran set about writing down all he could recall of the events surrounding the abduction of Alexander Rubowitz. A guard later reported that when he had finished he sat back and said, 'Well, that's that.' This statement, in the form of a diary, written in pencil in an exercise book with the addition of some press cuttings, would later assume huge legal significance.[46]

Farran was also visited by Assistant Inspector General Henry Shaw who was organising an identity parade for later in the day. Like Giles and Hadingham, 'Ben' Shaw had risen from constable to senior officer in the ranks of the Palestine police and it is unlikely that he brought much comfort to the incarcerated officer. In the early evening Farran was taken under guard to the Old City Central Police Barracks where the identity parade was to be held. Ten men from his squad, including sergeants Murphy, Faulkner and Clarke, constables Carson, Pilkington, Burke, Jones and Cade were also there. It was the last time they would see each other together. However, it was hardly a reunion. Farran was kept on his own and the men were forbidden from speaking to one another. Shaw and an assistant superintendent, Reginald Sims, were in charge of the proceedings. They waited until 8:30 p.m. when the light was similar to the conditions prevailing when Rubowitz was seized. Then the first of three line-ups was led into the courtyard. Over the next ninety minutes as the gloom deepened the eyewitnesses, a woman and four young men, scrutinised the suspects. Two failed to identify anyone. Mrs Sherlin and the two teenagers who had seen the incident claimed to recognise Farran, but were mistaken.[47]

The government of Palestine subsequently issued a press statement summarising the state of play. 'Investigations into this matter are proceeding but no trace of Alexander Rubowitz has been found. Major Farran, an officer of the regular army whose extradition was requested from Syria last week, returned to Palestine on Tuesday. He was charged on the same day in connection with the disappearance of Rubowitz. An identity parade was held in the Old City Police Barracks on Wednesday night. Major Farran was not identified by any witness.' The statement added that 'The General Officer Commanding has elected that on the charges preferred against him Major Farran shall be dealt with under the provisions of the Army Act, to which he is subject, and further investigations into the charge preferred against him are being pursued by the military authorities.' Finally, the government denied that there were any 'grounds for suggesting that he is connected with the British Union of Fascists'. The press were advised that the case was *sub judice* and journalists were asked to show restraint.[48]

Not surprisingly the Hebrew press was anything but restrained and the British could hardly censor factual reports of an offical process. But the stories that appeared on the morning of 19 June wrongly stated that three witnesses had *positively* identified Farran. Even the normally accurate and authoritative *Palestine Post* stated that two witnesses had failed to identify anyone, leaving open the possibility that three others might have identified him. This was bad news for Farran. 'I was appalled by the relentlessness with which the police were pursuing my case (a new feature in Palestine) and by the unwarranted accusations of some of the Jewish papers'. His mood darkened. At two o'clock in the afternoon he was visited by Lieutenant Colonel Niven who later reported that Farran 'was perturbed by information that he had recently obtained to the effect that the police case against him had been considerably strengthened by additional evidence'.

This should have been the moment to check the security arrangements but the opposite happened. Because Farran had passed from police custody into the jurisdiction of the army the police officers assigned to watch him, Horner and Wood, were inclined to relax. Niven, on the other hand, still thought his men were only there to keep out intruders. At eight o'clock in the evening, when the fierce heat of the day had subsided, Farran listened to the BBC news and then asked to take exercise. Horner escorted him downstairs but instead of exercising Farran suggested they go to the officers' mess. Horner agreed and they had a beer at the bar in mess 'D'. While Farran was enjoying his drink, Lieutenant Colonel Adderley of the Royal Artillery entered. He started chatting to Farran and the three men had another round. When Adderley suggested that Farran join him for dinner Horner expressed no objection, although he declined an invitation to join them himself. Instead, while Farran followed Adderley down a corridor towards the dining room, Horner stayed at the bar. He lazily assumed that Adderley knew Farran and was aware he should keep an eye on him. However, when Adderley reached the end of the corridor from the bar and turned one way into the dining room, Farran went the other way into the latrine. Adderley took his seat and when his fellow officer did not appear guessed that he had changed his mind. Horner, who had lost sight of Farran, supposed that he was now in the dining room with the colonel. At 9 p.m. District Superintendent Wood turned up and asked Horner where Farran was. When he heard what Horner had to say he immediately went into the dining room to check that Farran was there. He was not and Adderley had no idea where he was. Within minutes Wood telephoned Fergusson to raise the alarm. Fergusson informed the Jerusalem district superintendent of police, but it was too late. Farran had escaped – again.[49]

Farran was always recondite about how he managed to evade his guards and what happened next. It was one thing to clamber through the latrine window into the street outside. He then had to pass through the heavily fortified security zone around the barracks and cross several checkpoints. He was not in uniform and had no official identification papers. According to the description that was flashed to police and military posts, as well as to British embassies and consulates in neighbouring countries, he was dressed in grey flannel trousers, desert boots, a white open-necked shirt with a fawn and red muffler, and a brown and white sports jacket. Yet according to the official report on his escape he received no outside assistance and thus equipped was able magically to pass through Jerusalem and disappear into the desert. According to Fergusson he took refuge with a Bedouin sheikh with whom he had struck up a friendship and went native, 'lost to all eyes, swathed in the appropriate dress'. For the next ten days he travelled with the Bedouin, crossing Transjordan and getting as far as the frontier with Saudi Arabia.[50]

Fergusson was hardly surprised by this turn of events. He expected Farran to make an escape bid because 'putting him under close arrest was a clear breach of an undertaking I had given, and was morally binding'. He thought that once he was charged with murder Farran would feel under no compulsion to keep his word, so it was only a matter of time before 'he slipped his cable'. But that was not how it was seen from Government House or Whitehall. Farran's breakout caused consternation in London, fuelled suspicions in Jerusalem and fanned outrage in the wider Jewish world.[51]

Cunningham informed the Colonial Office on 20 June and called for an urgent report into the circumstances of the escape. Fergusson was suspended from all duties, other than supervising training depots, and the contracts of the other army officers on secondment to the Palestine police were terminated. Creech Jones responded to the news with a pained message: 'This is a most unfortunate occurrence as the case has already received considerable notice and speculation'. He wanted to know 'at once' under what conditions Farran had been held, the circumstances of his escape, and the steps being taken to recapture him. To answer these pertinent questions a court of inquiry comprising a superintendent and two deputy superintendents was rapidly convened. The whirlwind investigation culminated in a final session at eleven-thirty at night on Monday 23 June. The report concluded that 'there is no suggestion of DSP Mr K. W. Horner having in any way connived at Major Farran's escape, except by his negligence'. His conduct was 'inexcusable' and a clear case of 'neglect of duty'. In mitigation, the court found that both police officers were unclear about their tasks and their orders were confused. There was nothing to suggest that Farran was assisted by 'accomplices of any description'. Instead, 'the evidence suggests that he seized a sudden opportunity to escape while in a perturbed state of mind'. Horner was charged with neglect and subsequently dismissed from the police. Wood was censured for conduct that was 'far from satisfactory' and his contract was terminated.[52]

By chance, Montgomery flew into Palestine for a conference with senior officers soon after Farran's escape. The meeting was held at the Sarafand base under a massive security blanket which vividly illustrated to Montgomery how bad things had become. Though it was not the reason for his visit, the Farran case could not be avoided. In a stunning, but characteristic, volte face he disavowed the special squads. He told the meeting that 'he expected that the high commissioner would soon ask for the withdrawal of all army officers on loan to the Palestine Police. These officers, although admirable men, did not understand the proper functions of a police force and the experiment of secondment had consequently proved a failure.' In a gesture that was presumably intended to indicate generosity but which actually reeked of hypocrisy he said 'he had always been against this secondment and he was willing to accept these officers back again as soon as asked to do so'.[53]

Farran's spectacular vanishing act was front-page news in London. The story of his suspected involvement in the abduction of Alexander Rubowitz, his flight to Syria, the charges against him and rumours about the special squads were regurgitated in every newspaper, with varying degrees of accuracy and sobriety. The *Daily Mail* front-page headline screamed 'Farran Freed By Own Men', which was doubly embarrassing to the government. No less worrying, it described his unit as one of several 'special "operational columns" enlisted to combat terrorism by "unorthodox" commando methods'. The *Star* won the prize for the most lurid account headlined '"Pimpernel" Major Escapes'. It informed its readers that Farran was 'reported to have been a member of a special secret anti-terror squad. During the war he was known as the Scarlet Pimpernel of the Special Air Service.' Unofficial briefings by the Colonial Office disclaiming the involvement of 'regular police officers' and denying knowledge of an '"anti-terror" column' only fuelled the suspicion that an irregular, undercover operation had gone wildly wrong.[54]

Over the following days the rumours about Farran magnified but more facts began to emerge as well. These revelations, while UNSCOP was taking evidence in Jerusalem, added to British discomfort. Julian Melzer, special correspondent to the *New York Times*, reported that 'The escape of the 26-year-old tough, hard-bitten

former commando leader of wartime European resistance movements was his second jolt to the British authorities.' Their attempt
to hush up his getaway to Syria had been spoiled and now he had
broken out of a barracks 'in the heart of the British security canton-
ment'. Melzer credited Farran with carrying out 'anti-terrorist
missions' that both the police and the army were now at pains to
disavow. Officers eager to distance their respective services from
the special-squad pariahs spoke openly or off the record to the
British press. Gene Currivan, also writing for the NYT, had picked
up on rumours that Fergusson and Gray were both 'contemplating
resignation'. He related this to longstanding unease in the PPF over
the special squads. 'Their police squad, working virtually independently of the regular department and using more or less unorthodox
methods, has not been popular with the regular force. There has
been friction in the upper brakets [sic] and the latest development
has not helped their situation.'[55]

Speaking against the background of rumours about a 'purge' of
three dozen officers allegedly involved in the anti-terror initiative,
Lieutenant Colonel C. W. Norman, chief of the general staff intelligence at British military headquarters, 'categorically denied' a news
agency report that thirty-six British Army officers were 'operating
their own war against the terrorists'. With a nice touch of irony
for a beleaguered intelligence officer in Palestine he told the
Manchester Guardian's correspondent, 'If any army officers were
waging a war in this country we would know about it'. When he
was asked if there could be special units in the police he replied
dismissively, 'The police run their own show'. Two days later the
Palestine police delivered their riposte. According to the Daily
Express special correspondent in Palestine, 'These methods have
been strongly criticised by British and Jews alike in Palestine.
Orthodox police have objected to the employment of Army officers and men more used to battle than tact.'[56]

In a belated attempt to stem the rumours and innuendo in the
press, Cunningham authorised another press statement. 'Suggestions
have been made that Major Farran was a member of a special unit
employing unorthodox methods against terrorists. No authority has
ever been given for the use by any member of the police force of

other than ordinary police methods in dealing with apprehended persons and there is no suggestion of this ever having occurred in any other case.'[57] However, the Palestine government had irretrievably lost the initiative in the press and propaganda war. It was now accepted that special anti-terror units had been established in Palestine within the police force. Thanks to briefing and counter-briefing from antagonistic factions within the security services a clear outline of the special squads' structure and operations was emerging. The only item of contention was whether they had been authorised to exceed normal measures or had run out of control.

According to the *Daily Express*, on 26 June, 'the phantom police force formed unofficially in Palestine to counter the terrorists is tonight almost broken. Its fate is bound up with Major Roy Farran.' Peter Duffield, the paper's special correspondent in Jerusalem, provided an accurate summary of how the squads operated: 'Wearing plain clothes, sometimes in disguise, and with private cars or trucks at their call, they have carried out lightning arrests and taken the suspects to the heavily fortified British zones for interrogation.' The next day the *Daily Graphic* reported that a 'major purge in the highest ranks of the Palestine police is about to take place'. The purge was described as 'the sequel to the discovery that specially recruited plain clothes "infiltration squads" have been using unorthodox methods against terrorists'. In a sign that the Colonial Office was also running for cover an unofficial Whitehall source told the paper that 'Investigations may lead to high police officials in Palestine being dismissed. A serious view is taken. This sort of thing should not have happened, and must not happen again.' The article attributed the formation of the special squads to Nicol Gray and stated that his associates said he was 'preparing his resignation in the face of an inquiry into the unit's methods'. A 'British Army brigadier, a former veteran of Burma who fought with Wingate's Chindits' who admitted heading an 'anti-terror operational column', was quoted saying that 'Since the Farran business I have been sacked.'[58]

A singularly perceptive article appeared in the *News of the World* the following weekend under the byline of Claire Hollingsworth, one of the few women correspondents covering Palestine. 'It is clear', she wrote, 'that the Palestine government are doing their best to throw a veil of mystery over the activities of that valiant soldier Major Farran'. With impeccable accuracy she went on: 'There has undoubtedly been a tendency to introduce into the Palestine police a number of ex-commando officers, men of the most distinguished war records, who have formed what might be termed "anti-terrorist squads" – and used against the terrorists much the same methods that they used during the war against the Germans.' Then she asked the key question: 'Is the Secretariat [the Palestine government] aware of all this? If so, it is highly reprehensible for such methods sully the name of a British administration. If they were not aware of what has been going on, then I suggest they should have been. I was; I heard all about those squads in cafes in Jerusalem and Tel Aviv.' Hollingsworth had clearly also heard about Sir Charles Wickham and was privy to the argument over tactics that had bedevilled the Palestine Police Force. 'No one could have a higher opinion than I of many individual members of the Palestine Police. They are fighting a losing battle, not so much against a highly trained and superbly organised body of fanatical terrorists to whom life literally means nothing, but also against a *system* that gives them practically no chance at all of success.' The generals thought they could win using masses of troops and tanks, but a 'distinguished former police officer who visited Palestine in 1946' knew better. She agreed with Wickham that the only way to defeat the terrorists was by treating them as criminals. 'I believe that, at long last, the Palestine police are now adopting this advice. Had they done so sooner there would have been no need for illegal anti-terrorist squads.'[59]

The Jewish press were already in a sceptical frame of mind after reports that the identification parade had actually been futile. The Rubowitz family were 'amazed' because several witnesses told them 'they were quite sure they'd identified the man'. An editorial in *Ha'aretz* newspaper asked 'If the witnesses didn't identify him . . . why did he have to flee?' And why had the two men who returned with Farran from Syria not been questioned? When the government appointed the court of inquiry into Farran's escape, *Ha'aretz* published an editorial that pinpointed one question after another, giving the Jewish public a set of benchmarks by which to judge the administration. It could not have made happy reading in Government House: 'Major Roy Alexander Farran proved that he really has excellent commando skills. He was outstanding in the army. He excelled, apparently, in the police special units against terror, too. But – he was too good. The special court of inquiry which has been appointed now to look into his two escapes will need to clear up a lot of very important details. It will need to clarify how much time went by from 6 May (when the lad Alexander Rubowitz was abducted in Jerusalem) until the first rumour was heard that Major Farran and his two comrades were connected. It will need to check whether any of the officer's superiors knew anything of the matter before the accused parties fled to Syria. It will be necessary to find out what in fact happened to the major's two comrades who travelled abroad with him, returned, and of whom since then nothing has been heard. Are they under arrest? Or have they returned to work? Although no one can identify them, the accomplices to the main accused party sat, apparently, in the car, while the boy was captured and pushed into the car by the man who lost his hat with something very like the name Farran written inside it. And, finally: how could such a thing happen, that a man under arrest with such grave accusations against him could be allowed to move around the officers' mess in the camp in such a manner and to disappear without anyone being aware of it?' The newspaper wildly overestimated the inquiry's terms of reference but its comments were prescient nonetheless. The Farran case put the entire administration on trial: the police and the army for the conduct of the war against terror, the government and the judicial apparatus for their handling of the charges, and, ultimately, the legitimacy of British rule in Palestine.[60]

Government denials in London and Jerusalem about the existence of special squads rang hollow, not least because the Jewish press could now piece together a narrative showing that police and government officials had systematically lied to them. It was clear that the police had denied knowledge of Farran for days after he was first named in connection with the abduction of Rubowitz, even though he was well known at police headquarters. It was also established that when the government charged Farran with going absent without leave in Syria and stealing government property they already had grounds for indicting him for murder. So it was unsurprising that repeated denials that he had received assistance for his second escape met with derision. Inevitably, Jewish suspicions multiplied and grew more fevered. The newspaper *HaZofeh* wrote that 'In Jerusalem we remember the number of "mysterious" night-time attacks on Jewish passers-by and the posters which appeared at that time on the notice-boards in the city, signed by the BMO (Brit Milah Organisation – Organisation of the Covenant) threatening to blow up the Jewish Agency and the *Palestine Post* buildings if the terrorist attacks against the British continued.' The BMO was, allegedly, the Palestine branch of the BUF. Even the normally sober *Ha'aretz* began to indulge in speculation that members of the British Union of Fascists had been involved with Farran.[61]

Concern in the Jewish community crossed the normal political and factional lines. Despite confirmation that Rubowitz was associated with LEHI his cause was taken up by the newspaper of the Marxist Zionist youth movement Achduth HaAvodah. Accusing him of 'murder in cold blood' the paper demanded to know why Farran wasn't arrested as soon as his name was found inside the hat. Who helped him to escape? What lay behind his rapid transfer from the police force to the army? The government accused the Jewish community of not helping it to detect criminals who they were seeking, so who would be punished for not revealing where Farran had gone? Reverting to its doctrinaire analysis of the world, *Achduth HaAvodah* suspected that Farran was a fascist or represented the germ of fascism. In hiring him the government 'made a covenant with Satan'. Farran's conduct was 'a blemish on the environment which raised and educated him. Bevin must answer: Where is Farran? How is this Farran possible? How is such an environment possible?' Even Natan Alterman, the bard of the Labour Party, felt impelled to write a poem, 'Where is the Boy?' for his weekly column in *Davar*, the newspaper of the Jewish trades unions. That left-wing Jewish youth and hardbitten trades unionists could embrace one of a nationalist terror group was a stark indication of how the Rubowitz affair had united the Jewish population and how it contributed to the evaporation of British legal and moral authority in Palestine.[62]

Of course much of the Jewish press comment was hyperbole, based on a distortion of the facts or sheer invention. But the Hebrew-language newspapers were able to draw on articles appearing in the British and American press that claimed to reveal the existence of a secret anti-terror unit with shoot-to-kill orders. The conviction that this was the case gained such momentum within the Jewish community that the Jewish Agency, too, was moved to act. Whereas the British government had been courting the Jewish leadership to join the fight against the 'dissidents', it now found itself receiving official representations on their behalf by the very people it had hoped to turn against them. On 23 June a courier arrived at Government House with a letter for Sir Henry Gurney from Goldie Myerson, a member of the Jewish Agency executive. Myerson, who was later to achieve fame as Golda Meir, Israel's prime minister from 1969 to 1974, was acting head of the agency's political department while Moshe Shertok was interned. In this capacity she was the official channel of communication between the agency and the Palestine government. Her letter informed Gurney that information had reached the agency concerning the disappearance of Alexander Rubowitz and 'the subsequent behaviour of the alleged abductor, Major Farran and certain superior officers'. This report had been received from a usually reliable source. 'Your Excellency will appreciate that this cause has given rise to deep anxiety in the Yishuv, not only because the details, as far as they are known, are shocking in themselves, but because of the apparent existence of a most distressing state of affairs within the Palestine Police Force.'[63]

The Jewish Agency submission opened with the assertion that 'Alexander Rubowitz was kidnapped by Major Roy Alexander Farran, with the help of two or three other members of the police force'. They were members of a 'so-called "strong-arm squad"' charged with the fight against terrorists. According to the agency's informant, 'The boy was taken down the deserted Jericho Road, "grilled" and tortured for about an hour. Finally Rubowitz succumbed

135

to the torture and died on the spot. The policemen tried to get rid of the body, and finally handed it to some Bedouin in the neighbourhood and asked them to dispose of it.' The report alleged that Farran did not inform Fergusson until a week later and that Fergusson 'advised Farran to "skip" away'. Farran then left Palestine with his 'accomplices' but no inquiries were made by the police and Fergusson did nothing for another five days when he told the inspector general. 'Colonel Gray also is said to have waited for a few days and then to have mentioned it to Mr A. F. Giles, Deputy Inspector General, who had become very concerned about the disappearance of the four men.' The statement claimed that Farran was identified by eyewitnesses after he returned from Syria and alleged that his escape had been 'assisted, if not actually engineered, by members of his own particular police unit'.[64]

Gurney assured the Jewish Agency that the matter was 'under active consideration by the Government' and promised an early reply. However, instead of responding to the points made by Myerson he subsequently asked her to give the police force any information that was in the agency's possession. This added insult to injury because it implied that the Jews had intelligence that the British lacked and suggested they should entrust it to an institution which had shown itself to be blatantly untrustworthy. Gurney concluded that 'In the meantime no comment is offered on the accuracy or otherwise of the statement enclosed in your letter, since the case is under active investigation.' Shortly afterwards, the head of the Jewish Community Council of Jerusalem called on the Jerusalem district commissioner to express the anxiety of his constituency. This sort of protest could be safely brushed aside, but it was a different matter when the Hagana issued a wall poster announcing that it was looking for Farran and intended to bring him to justice. Fergusson's idea for a surgical operation to strike at the underground that left the Hagana untouched had only served to drive the official Jewish militia closer to the 'dissidents'.[65]

Farran's escape also triggered awkward questions in London. On 26 June the high commissioner transmitted to London reports of no less than four separate investigations intended to answer at least some of them. First was Hadingham's inquiry into the alleged abduction and murder of Rubowitz and his review of the subsequent investigation. Next, Gray gave his account of why the incident on 6 May was not reported for nearly a month. He also submitted an initial report on Farran's escape. Finally, Cunningham sent London the proceedings and recommendations of the court of inquiry. Creech Jones needed all of this material in order to placate Attlee. He also had to deal with questions in Parliament from Tom Driberg, the maverick Labour MP who took a close and friendly interest in all manner of Jewish issues. Driberg had asked the colonial secretary for a full statement on the Farran case, the events preceding and following his arrest, including the disappearance of Alexander Rubowitz.[66]

The information that Sir Henry Gurney provided to the colonial secretary for his reply to Driberg was a masterpiece of evasion: 'It is believed that Rubowitz was found on the evening of 6 May distributing Stern Group literature. He was not brought to any police station or military installation and no trace of him has since been found. In the course of the investigations into the matter initiated by the Government Major Farran took refuge in Syria. A request for his extradition was made to the Syrian government. He returned to Palestine on 17 June, was taken into custody and was charged in connection with the disappearance of Rubowitz. On the night of the 19th he escaped from custody. Intensive efforts are being made to discover his whereabouts and all surrounding territories have been notified. A Court of Inquiry set up to investigate the circumstances of the escape has found no evidence to suggest that he was assisted in his escape by accomplices of any description. Of the two police officers responsible for his custody one is being dismissed for negligence and the engagement of the other terminated.' The statement also repeated the formula that no authority had been given for any police units to use 'unorthodox methods' in dealing with captured persons 'and there is no suggestion of this having occurred in any other case'.[67]

When Creech Jones gave his reply to Driberg he did not reveal the latest and most damning information that had reached him from Jerusalem. For, on the previous day, Cunningham told the colonial secretary that a 'written statement found in Farran's quarters at Allenby Barracks, Jerusalem, after his escape on 19 June, unsigned, but believed to be in Farran's handwriting, stated that he had killed Rubowitz'. On the strength of this discovery renewed efforts were made to find the body. Fifteen policemen in mounted patrols led by three experienced sergeants scoured the area between Jerusalem and Jericho. After several days spent in unproductive searching and questioning local Bedouin, the patrols gave up. On 24 June, Hadingham summoned the Rubowitz brothers and in a curious ritual read them a letter 'that had been given to him to inform the family of the boy's death'. It stated that the police could find no trace of the missing boy 'but they had information which led them to believe that he was no longer alive'. When the brothers asked for more details, Hadingham refused to say anything. When they proposed hiring Arabs to continue the search in the Wadi Kelt area, he said it was too dangerous.[68]

If the Palestine government and the police intended to put the family out of its misery, they failed. All they had done was fuel the mystery surrounding Alexander's disappearance. If the police had not found a body how could they be sure he was dead? If they knew he had been killed, why didn't they say so? Why couldn't they identify the alleged culprit? In the absence of these details the family kept alive the hope that Alexander was only missing. In a pitiful interview with a journalist from *HaBoker* newspaper they said they were sure he was still alive, somewhere. In order to protect Farran and their own reputations, the police force and the administration subjected the Rubowitz family to continuing mental torture.[69]

LEHI drew its own conclusions. The day after the announcement it began a campaign of kidnappings and shootings in revenge for the murder of Alexander Rubowitz. The underground group made it clear via their contacts in the international press that they would not let up until Farran surrendered. On Saturday 28 June alone, Jewish snipers killed four soldiers relaxing on the Tel Aviv beach while LEHI gunmen sprayed automatic weapons fire into the Astoria Restaurant in Haifa, killing one officer and seriously wounding two more. In its weekly intelligence appraisal for London, the Palestine government reported that 'The week has been marked by a number of assassinations and attempted assassinations of British soldiers. It is believed that these were the work of the Stern Group and that they are a reprisal for the death of Rubowitz, the victim of the Farran case.' One of the officers killed at the Astoria Restaurant was a friend of Roy Farran.[70]

Somehow, even though he was deep in the desert, Roy heard about the wave of killings. In his reminiscences he wrote that notwithstanding his successful escape he faltered at the prospect of becoming a permanent renegade and felt responsible when he got reports that the Stern gang had begun to take reprisals because of him. So he decided to give himself up. At 11:20 in the morning on Sunday 29 June, Farran materialised at the main gate of the Allenby Barracks and surrendered to the sentry. When he was brought to the duty officer, Captain MacDavid, he simply announced 'I am Major Farran and I have come to give myself up to the army.'[71]

4

Court Martial

Farran's magical reappearance in the middle of Jerusalem was a sensation, but it created as many problems as it solved for the government in Palestine and London. He was briefly held at the Allenby Barracks, where he was given a military uniform to replace his civilian clothes, and then transported under heavy guard to the fortified headquarters of the Oxford and Buckinghamshire Light Infantry in the Notre Dame building in west Jerusalem. Extraordinary precautions were taken to keep him safe while he was there. No one was allowed in the vicinity without an armed escort and soldiers with machine guns stood on watch constantly. Newspaper reporters who got wind of his return were roughly turned away.[1]

The authorities were just as surprised as everyone else. In the afternoon senior army officers, including the GOC, Lieutenant General MacMillan, gathered for an emergency meeting to consider how they should handle him. It lasted three hours. They eventually decided to charge the errant major with going absent without leave and hold him pending the summary of evidence. This was in line with standard practice under military law to detain a suspect on a holding charge while investigations were made and only then to take written statements, examine witnesses and question the accused. The summary of evidence would serve as the basis for a decision to go to trial by court martial or dismiss the charge. Farran was then unobtrusively taken from Jerusalem to the military prison on the base at Sarafand and placed in a cell.[2]

Meanwhile the Palestine government imposed a news blackout and made no statements. Inevitably, the Jewish press was left bursting with questions. Speculation ran amok. It was rumoured that Farran had never left Palestine, but had been concealed by the British at a military base in the south of the country. Or that he had taken refuge in a Jesuit monastery until the wave of LEHI killings flushed him out. *HaBoker* asked if his mysterious return would shed any light on his equally baffling departure: 'The mystery that enveloped the disappearance of Farran also accompanies his turning himself in. The curt official announcement that Farran had given himself up to the authorities, doesn't clarify a thing about his very complicated disappearance.' *Ha'aretz*, as usual, asked the most awkward questions. 'The fact that Major Farran is once again under military arrest has been well received by all circles in the Yishuv and one assumes that, to a certain extent, the British in the country are also pleased that a stain has been removed from the efficiency of their military processes here. We hope that now the sad affair of the kidnapping and death of young Rubowitz will be cleared up. This is, of course, the most important question in the whole matter. But with the reappearance of Farran some more questions arise and the public is entitled to get clear answers to them. We want to know for what reasons and with what help Farran managed to escape from his first arrest. Then we want to know all his movements and the places he was in, between his escape and his return, and we also want to know the motives for which Farran agreed to be rearrested, and for exactly what reasons he was charged. The cryptic language of the official announcement makes us demand these further explanations.'[3]

Conjecture also swept through the security forces. John Watson, a national serviceman in the Royal Air Force who was working at the British forces radio station in Haifa, reported the gossip in his letters home. He told his family, 'There's a lot of scandal here about a certain Major Farran. He was in the commandos (behind the lines in Germany) during the war, and was appointed as counter-espionage "anti-terroristic commando extraordinary" recently by the government. Unfortunately he arrested (secretly) a Jewish youth pasting up pamphlets for the IZL, and "liquidated" him. So in time

Farran was handed over by the Syrian government to the Palestinian one, as he'd gone there to get away from the law, under fishy circumstances he escaped his escorts at an officers' club in Jerusalem; today he has given himself up again, as the IZL says that the latest shooting of three officers in the Astoria Cafe here, was a retaliation to Farran's unlawful "liquidation" of Jews.' Watson's letter shows just how much information about the special squads had leaked into public circulation. Even if it was garbled, the essence was correct and it was highly compromising to the Palestine government.[4]

The international press amplified what was known and benefited from non-attributable briefings by police officers who seized the moment to finish off Fergusson. 'Police sources' informed the *Chicago Daily Tribune* that 'strong-arm squads' within the force were being broken up following Farran's arrest. The case had 'brought to light an unorthodox group of war-seasoned army officers lent to the police to use their commando experience against the Stern Gang and Irgun Zvai Leumi'. The *Associated Press* was clearly being used by certain officers in the Palestine Police Force (whose identity can only be guessed at) to blacken Farran and the special squads. Only this can account for the highly accurate details in its bulletins. According to *AP*, the squads, numbering about thirty-six men in all, had been set up after 'consultations between London and Jerusalem' four months ago. Twelve-man units in plain clothes using civilian cars were sent 'to prowl the Jewish quarters outside the security zones' of Jerusalem, Haifa and Tel Aviv. Sometimes they had seized youngsters putting up posters for the underground and taken them to police HQ for questioning: Rubowitz was one of them. 'One brigadier already has reported privately that he has been fired for heading such flying squadrons. At least two high ranking police officers were reported as resigning in a shake-up.'[5]

The Palestine government was under enormous pressure to respond to these allegations. They understood only too well that after the previous farcical goings-on their every move would be closely watched. Cunningham told London that 'The comment on this case which has been permitted by the censorship to appear in the local press has continued to be relatively restrained, but the excised matter testifies to the increasing disposition of the Jews to make political capital out of this unfortunate affair and to exploit it in order to embarrass the administration.' Any decision would have ramifications in London, too, where the Parliamentary Question tabled by Tom Driberg several days earlier still awaited an answer. The Colonial Office urgently wanted to know what evidence there was for presuming the death of Rubowitz, beyond Farran's statement, and details of the charge on which he was being held.[6]

Unfortunately, Farran's transfer from civil to army jurisdiction meant that any answers to questions about the evidence and about his status tended to seem less than straightforward. Instead of detaining Farran on a holding charge and going through the process of taking evidence, it would have been much simpler for Creech Jones and officials in London if Farran had been arrested and charged with murder immediately. Cunningham replied that 'Reasons for presuming death of Rubowitz are: (a) oral statement by Farran to Fergusson that he, Farran, had killed Rubowitz (b) written statement found in Farran's quarters at Allenby Barracks, Jerusalem, after his escape on 19 June, unsigned, but presumed to be in Farran's handwriting, stated that he had killed Rubowitz (c) fact that, in spite of prolonged search and enquiries, no trace of Rubowitz can be found.' These were the grounds on which he had *previously* been charged with murder. But he was *currently* being held on a military holding charge of being AWOL 'pending the taking of summary sworn evidence, when it is probable that he will be charged with murder'.[7]

Moreover, when Major Styles, Undersecretary of State at the War Office, reviewed this argument he alerted the officials working under Creech Jones to something of which they were not aware. According to Styles 'under the strict rules of evidence governing trial by court martial, Farran will not be charged with murder unless the sworn summary evidence gives solid evidence for such a charge'. In army eyes that evidence did not yet exist. Despite the statement in his own hand he had not made a sworn confession. No one had identified Farran in connection with the abduction of Rubowitz. The hat that bore his name, or something like it, had been borrowed by another squad member. In any case, the government laboratory had not established that the hat definitely belonged to him. Dick Catling even assured William Mathieson at the Colonial Office that there was a hat shop in Jerusalem called Farrans. (About which another, less credulous, civil servant had added the marginalia, 'Yes, but the name was written in the hat in ink.') Within a few days Mathieson was writing that 'On the information here, prima facie, there is no evidence on which Major Farran could be convicted on a charge of murder.' Apart from his own statement there 'is likely to be no evidence connecting him with the disappearance of Rubowitz'.[8]

Under military law there was a long way to go before the charge of murder could be made to stand up and the taking of evidence had not even begun. Hence the reply made by Creech Jones to Driberg on 2 July did not actually mention murder. Creech Jones merely stated that Farran was 'in military custody on a holding charge of being absent without leave pending the taking of a summary of sworn evidence on which a decision will be taken whether further charges are preferred against him'. This statement caused amazement in the Jewish press. How was is possible that the Palestine Police Force had sought Farran's extradition from Syria on a charge of 'wilful murder' yet in Jerusalem he was only charged with going AWOL?[9]

As Cunningham had predicted the Jewish press and politicians in Palestine and England maintained their pressure on the administration. Reuven Nochimowski, a well-known Tel Aviv lawyer and nationlist firebrand, led the charge by demanding that Farran be tried in public, in a civil court. He wrote an open letter to the chief magistrate of the Jerusalem district court challenging him to explain why the court had abrogated its jurisdiction. The call was, naturally, taken up by a brace of Jewish newspapers. It was echoed in London by Marcus Lipton MP, a Jewish Labour MP elected in 1945 who was rapidly making a name for himself. At Parliamentary Questions for the Colonial Office on 9 July, he asked the Secretary of State on what charge Farran was arrested. Creech Jones referred him to the written answer he had given to Driberg a week earlier. In his supplementary question Lipton then asked Creech Jones if he could request the authorities in Palestine 'to make up their minds as quickly as possible about the charge on which this officer is to be tried, and that the trial, when it does take place should be held in public'.[10]

Farran himself was now under guard deep inside the base at Sarafand. The elaborate security arrangements, dubbed Operation Buffer (Farran was Buffer) were as much a precaution against a revenge attack as a sign of determination to prevent him absconding again. He was confined to his cell for the entire day excepting visits to the latrine, the shower, and a daily exercise period. An officer was with him constantly and the guards had orders to open fire if he attempted to escape. One of the officers assigned to watch him was Colin Mitchell, the same young officer from the Argyll and Sutherland Highlanders who had co-operated in one of Farran's operations in Jerusalem. He later recounted how 'I would be locked into Roy's cell with him for twenty-four hours at a time, sometimes being allowed out to play badminton with him under guard.' They naturally spent a good deal of time talking and Mitchell recalled that these conversations with the 'hard, cold-eyed young man' taught him a lot about warfare. Never one to be idle, when he was not distracted by Mitchell or reading novels, Farran spent his time writing up his war experiences in the form of a memoir. It contained several chapters detailing his misadventures in Palestine. These passages are distinguished from the rest of the book by the tone of anger, regret and guilt. He asked himself how he had got into such a mess? And he quite explicitly wondered how he got involved in murder? He wrote that he could never have dreamed while he was evading enemy forces during the war that one day he would end up, in his eyes, being hounded by the authorities of his own country.[11]

As he ruminated on his fate Farran's political outlook hardened. He denied vehemently that he was a fascist or anti-Semitic, although one can take with a pinch of salt the resentment he expressed against his accusers for allegedly forgetting the long years he was, in his words, fighting a crusade on behalf of persecuted Jews. Farran had probably never given Jews much thought prior to arriving in Palestine. Since then he had developed firm views about Zionism, at least. He now believed that the new Jewish state was being constructed on neo-fascist lines and felt sympathy with the Arabs. He claimed he had never allowed these feelings to influence his behaviour, though, and there is a ring of truth to his mercenary declaration that he was employed by the British government to fight terrorists and would have acted no differently if the outrages had been committed by Arabs or Germans or Chicago gangsters.[12]

Roy now wondered why he had bothered. But, if he felt betrayed by his country, as Philip Labouchere had promised his friends did not let him down. As soon as he was committed to a court martial the officers of his regiment started a subscription to pay for his defence. D'Arcy Muirhead held the fund. Letters appealing for contributions were sent to fellow officers in Britain, too. One of these reached Major General Robert Laycock, chief of Combined Operations, who had pioneered special forces during the war and headed commando operations in 1942–3. Laycock was in close touch with Farran's former commanding officers in the SAS, Bill Stirling and Brian Franks. As well as sending Roy messages to keep up his morale, they formed a powerful and wealthy support group. Franks had worked at the Dorchester before the war and became general manager of the Hyde Park Hotel after the SAS was disbanded. Together with Stirling he helped raise money for Farran's legal counsel and may have directed Roy's family to Laurence Collins and Fearnley-Whittingstall, the firm of London solicitors who would prove formidable advocates. The case became a cause célèbre. Members of the Long Range Desert Group, which had operated alongside the SAS in North Africa, started a fund for Roy. And although he had alienated many senior police officers in Palestine, even veterans of the force in Britain rallied to his aid. They were organised by Raymond Cafferata, a highly distinguished assistant superintendent who ran the PPF London depot.[13]

The question of legal representation soon came to a head because of a decision made at the regular security conference held at Government House in Jerusalem on 11 July, attended by Cunningham, Gurney, MacMillan and Gray. MacMillan informed them that the summary of evidence would be taken in a week's time with the intention of holding the court martial on 11 August. Farran thus had to obtain counsel and have them ready, in Jerusalem, within days. However, the army had not yet decided where the trial

אלכסנדר רובוביץ

בן 16 וחצי שנים מרח" דוד ילין
22 ירושלים. יצא מביתו ביום
שלישי, 6.5 ש.ז. בשעה 6
אחה"צ ומאז נעלמו עקבותיו.
תיאורו: רזה, גבוה, חובש ברט
בחיל, תולצה חקי, מכנס' וחוך
ארוכים. נעל'ם שחורות. **חורב-ב
משקפים.** כל היודע על מקום
המצאו יודיע לתחנת משטרה קרובה
או למשפחתו לפי הכתובת דלעיל.

Portrait of Alexander Rubowitz and missing
person description from Hebrew press. The
photograph and the description triggered a
flood of information to the family.

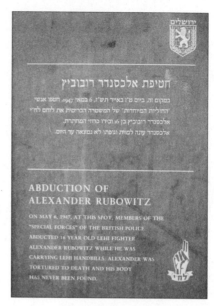

Plaque commemorating
the abduction.

Ussishkin Street, Jerusalem, where Rubowitz was abducted. A blue plaque on the wall
on the right side of the road (visible above the barrier) marks the exact spot.

Roy Farran in the SAS, leaning against a jeep, at Stavanger airport, Norway, May 1945. The officer standing next to him is Col. Paddy Mayne, legendary commander of the SAS.

Bernard Fergusson, photographed while leading a Chindit column in the Burmese jungle in 1943.

Nicol Gray as Inspector General of Palestine Police Force, 1946.

THE BRITISH EMBASSY IN ROME

The hole blasted in the wall of the British Embassy in Rome by explosives left in suit cases.

IRISH TRIBUTE TO C. P. SCOTT

GARDENING

Fruit Trees in

As did other newspapers in Britain, the USA, and around the world, the *Manchester Guardian* gave prominent coverage to the damage inflicted on the British Embassy in Rome by an Irgun bomb, 31 October 1946 (picture attribution unknown).

COMBATTANTS POUR LA LIBÉRTÉ D'ISRAEL

COMMUNIQUÉ

Le vendredi, 7 mars, à 18 h. 56 P. M. nos combattants ont déclenché une attaque contre le centre de la puissance britannique à Londres.

Malgré toutes les mesures de défense et les précautions innombrables nos combattants ont réussi à pénétrer dans " Trafalgar Square ", où ils ont attaqué et détruit le " British Colonial Club " — un des centres de l'intrigue impérialiste.

L'ennemi a subi des dégats.

Tous nos combattants ont regagné leurs bases sains et saufs.

Le mouvement clandestin juif continuera et renforcera ses attaques contre l'ennemi sur son propre sol et partout où il sera vulnérable — jusqu'à ce que l'occupant soit chassé de notre pays.

"Combattants pour la Liberté d'Israël"
GROUPE STERN

LEHI Communiqué, issued in Paris, March 1947, claiming responsibility for the explosion in British Colonial Club, London. A similar communiqué was distributed in Tel Aviv.

MINISTRY WILL STOP 'BAD' EXPORTERS   **STRACHEY TALKS FOOD WITH AUSTRALIANS**   **2,000 FACING SACK FROM AIRLINE**   **FARRAN CASE OFFICER REFUSES EVIDENCE**

'SELL ABROAD OR SHUT' FIRMS TOLD

No materials if they miss the target

Express Industrial Reporter TREVOR EVANS

IF British firms fail to sell enough goods overseas they will be shut down. This warning was given yesterday by Mr. John Wilmot, Minister of Supply.

All engineering firms making consumer goods are to be watched. Every three months they must make a return of the goods they have made and the amount sold overseas.

Any firm that fails to reach its target will have its supplies of steel and other raw materials stopped. These supplies will be transferred to more successful firms.

Any firms which are not considered necessary to the home or export trade will not be licensed. They must either close down or switch to essential goods.

Those that are left will be divided into two groups —

1. Makers of capital goods, that is, heavy electrical plant and machine-production plant. They will be given first priority for labour and materials.

2. Most of the others, including makers of cars, motor cycles, bicycles, radio sets, refrigerators, cookers and fires. They will have individual quotas for exports.

This quota will be generally about three-quarters of total production.

On own record

Up to now, raw materials have been issued to industries as a whole, each individual firm getting its share, irrespective of whether their products were sold.

For the future, our makers were given an export target for the whole industry, but individual firms who failed to achieve their target were not penalised for their failures.

Now each firm must show on its own record, and those without the necessary previous experience of exports will get their supplies cut and their negotiations filtered into policy.

All this will mean "a very hard squeeze" in the supply of goods for the home market, said Mr. Wilmot.

Whatever goods go across the counters they have to give the consumer fewer.

Ranked all over and beyond stuffs will be offered to you after Butter-and-Overseas Avenues and Bacon and American Airways.

'Limit claims'

WAGES: Mr. Attlee told the Trades Union Congress general council that the Government is now holding peel to a hard wage freezing policy.

Wages, he explained, will naturally affect industries but he looked there will be no more to wages cutting.

HOMES: Mr. Charles Key, Works Minister, warned that building industry leaders shall act unbuildingand owing to shortage of materials started new homes many million workers into a housing black market.

COAL: The Cabinet has sharpened its approach to the miners' plan to allow each absented hours to be resolved.

Some districts are giving to devote Saturday morning shifts other more week may only fall 20p a day for the years. But we have to Cabinet, nearer on Mr. Revival, mark Saturday many years opened in a miners' work, followed by Wilson labourincreased absenteeism.

SMALL POOLS SAY: WE CARRY ON

Express Staff Reporter

PROMOTERS of the smaller football pools said last night that they will try to keep their independence despite a cut in the under paper ration. They are outside the "Big Eight," who formed the wartime Unity Pool.

If they find they cannot carry on individually, they will combine forming a Second Unity Pool of their own.

Mr. Sydney Zeiger, director of Zetter Pool, London, said—

"A number of small pool men have arrived close applied to join the Big Eight. But we have not been accepted. We do not expect to be invited to join any new big pools first.

Mr. A. W. Belcher, Perth, secretary Secretary to the Board of Trade, said an hour's section easy with promoters yesterday and told them they had a shortage of paper for the future.

He did not open a new Unity Pool but it was clear this is that the present development.

A second meeting will be held in 10 days.

2,000 die in camp raid

NEW DELHI, Wednesday.—Two thousand Sikhs and Hindus were slaughtered by Moslem raiders who attacked their refugee camp near Lyallpur in Punjab, it was disclosed tonight.

In the second raid on the Jullundur area in three days, the 118 non-Moslems killed by the raiders were killed by the armed guard.—B.U.P.

Mrs. Paton says no to £900 a year

Mrs. Amy Paton, 49-year-old, ex-nature of Chapelmount masseuse of Sheffield, stepson at Manchester Corporation salaried officer because "cooking for mine a more important." The organisers pools for 10,000 makers 15, 25 customs.

Non-starters

Captain C. A. Kershaw, general secretary of the English Industries Association, said last night: "Hundreds of non-starters betting by one firm for export order because they locked the plastic mines for the new starter trade."

► BACK PAGE, COL. ONE

Australia asks—

HELP US TO GROW FOOD FOR YOU

By GUY EDEN

A THREE-POINT plan to import more food from Australia will be discussed by Mr. Strachey and Mr. J. A. Beasley, High Commissioner, in London today.

1. Britain will be asked to provide capital for the development of Australia's food industry.

2. Broadley is believed to be in favour of this investment, swinging to millions of pounds, because of the extra food returns.

3. Britain will be asked to give a long-term guarantee of markets.

Dr. Beasley is there to recommend his owner to the Cabinet, which will make the final decision.

Australia will then examine of her cattle and grassland industry in Beach and Western of markets and in Queensland.

It will be able to send more pounds of produce—representing, owing to the—in a short time and extra dairy produce for us.

Agralia is prepared to produce beef production in a new high next year for shipping payments for Britain. A proposal to use much of the Commonwealth future military and essential services stockpile for the war. This will save time and money.

Primary sales between Whitehall experts and Australia for food deliveries are continuing. The extra food may be produced direct stations for Commonwealth supplies.

First subsidy off-potatoes

THE potato subsidy is the first to go under the Government's squeeze plan. And Thursday housewives are paying the "old" prices but they must pay down the full next year.

Prices of the tonnage subsidy disappears normally starts in October if each year, with the beef, passed on to the consumer.

Last year the retail price was set by most months. This week it will be 45d., and will increase to 1gd. in Jan.

But subsidy, paid in prices has been kept on Sunday news.

Bread subsidy to go up?

BREADS world food prices have risen the Food Minister may not be able to avoid an increase of 2s. 6d.—the 1946-48 figure now.

Income from prices were nearer than the Canadian farmers bid. a dollar-and-a-half wheat—in excess of 2s. 6d. 1946-48 figure.

This subsidy officials have been forced to make more than ½d. a loaf that have in the next the rise in the bread price.

Alexander Price, Canadian Importer, interrupted a Cabinet session in Ottawa yesterday to announce the new wheat prices.

More dollars, says Rank

Savings income from films in the U.K. and on American markets is steadily up., a reason why J. Arthur Rank, in a statement issued with Odeon-Corm, said yesterday.

In two main streams of distribution, "a review statement broadcast regularly in Eastern fare." On 30 British film fare in over 12,500 theatres for the last six years in their U.S. Hollywood.

"It is stopping us export," said, "but maybe we are doing it."

No, no

OXFORD, Wednesday.—the women's colleges at Oxford have pruned.

They voted tonight by 150 to 68 against more students to be at Somerville. The question was raised by Italy and Poland have voted they GMO business the bright for students, but were then quite against now admission of Germany, Japan and Bulgaria as well.

CROWDS TURNED AWAY FROM BIG FIRST NIGHT

The Ayes have it at the Hustings

By WILLIAM BARKLEY

NORTHAMPTON, Wednesday.—Great crowds had to be turned away from the first Daily Express Hustings held here tonight. What a pity!

Seats were true to the first comers, except for a small number of tickets issued equally in advance to the party machine. Even Tories, fighting back against their earliest, got their free seats at the party recreation ground.

The issue was, "Does the country need a choice of Government?" No doubt of this meeting's views.

After being sixty Tory Page Beech Files M.P., had replied the Conservative gentlemanita, and pondered, but emotional Socialist H. T. Page, M.P., for Northampton, had cracked the Tory hands before and was thrashed by 1,000 for the Government.

The Mayor, Councillor A. Strickland, as a wealthy plain chair, read the poll amid emotional cheering and shouting. His 525 NO votes floating on sounded probably to his opponents' 558 and his adversaries as they essayed to assure no-plurality.

'I'M IN FAVOUR'

The Ayes produced seven clear decisions as Socialist Page's declare. He said, "Our country has a Coalition Diana on a system of quote-concharge, as the Dominions could not secure a first secured to plan.

But he added a putting politic plan he hoped this Empire Clusters first would include the socialist Europe.

"Please charge yourself on the debris, looked that this Government had reduced one occasional risk of miserable hanging our eggs were now decent in one basket."

He and Pages are both the Socialists on the same years. They are 26 and 41 in age. "Cry old men," said Page. "But are they not members less on that system."

'NOW I BELIEVE'

Of the Government he said "It would be easier to stand a day time putting on the soft borders positive and performance. When I was in the Army soldiers were there to be hit. Now when you are there to be ruled. A plan after plan has been revealed. Proud rationing—none, and in-all meat already with itself have been, over-manning a set of issues." 'He doesn't think this will far, 'but he does meat rationing from there and issue he said anything.'

(Laughter.)

"His worst enemy wants on excuse line of cheering where he is going. 'he should go the Government wrong lines, not now shutting off, but he didn't—and flashed. 'I believe," said Beech.

"The Government are to the grip of old the time they themselves were programmed for 20 years.

"First he summed up in clear Arthur Greenwood's statement that, 'No. 2, no fewer mentioned—

"I ASK YOU

He was in favour of the American Loan as the time. But all it meant was that we had had £1,350,000 American debt wortern far as the working. To borrow money, young fellows to pay and will meet nothing. It is stupidly immoral. Unless —

"To derive money, youngsters, to hold out, your feats and all the tones you are in. If you shorten moneylenders's run only the loan. It is stupidly immoral. Unless you think that you can do away with the American loan at any means.

"Mr. Attlee said last week that we did not want youth necessarily to choose the rocky trail in most pleasurable or good-like.

"I ask you what does my mother want for her son. Nearly man and the power half her plan, for he wants and put the past page for her. So was she the. The fellows we willing to take living at the beck of labour, hesitating trends of wheat and labour's pay for being its master. There they now hear, they not say they no. And fight the plan?"

(Laughter.) seven long trade leaders seem late of taking away the bit —

► BACK PAGE, COL. ONE

POLICE HOLD UP FAMILY

Stopped at airport on way to London

Express Staff Reporter

POLICE stopped a man, his wife and three children, from boarding a London Airport last night.

The family had reserved seats, and were going through the Customs when four airport officers arrived.

They spoke to the man, then drove the family to Harlington Police Station, near the airport. The wife was in tears.

The police said: "We are only interested in the man, who has been detained at the request of the Glasgow police." He was escorted to Glasgow.

The wife and three children—a boy of six, a girl of three, and a nine-months-old girl—were given food and shelter for the night in the police station recreation room.

Two sisters flying to Lourdes for health reasons left Northold 24 hours late last night after being asked to strip to their shifts and search them.

They travelled from Bradford on Tuesday hoping to get an overnight plane. Customs officers ordered a search for currency.

A woman officer told the sisters, twins Monica Illingii was found. But the plane had gone.

Sisters asked to strip

PROSECUTION GIVES PLEDGE, BUT—

Colonel says 'I won't tell'

WHAT FARRAN TOLD HIM

From PETER DUFFIELD: Jerusalem, Wednesday

COLONEL BERNARD E. FERGUSSON, ex-Chindit leader, now Assistant Inspector-General of Palestine Police, today refused to testify before the court-martial where Captain Roy Farran was accused of murdering 16-year-old Jew Alexander Rubowitz.

Fergusson, tall, monocled Scot, was asked by the prosecution: "Used you to meet Farran almost daily in the officers' mess at Katamon (a district of Jerusalem)?"

"We met daily," replied Fergusson.

"Do you remember a conversation in early May in the officers' mess? What did Farran say?"

Fergusson, still an assistant to this court, I am not prepared to give any details of that conversation because, in particular circumstances, if details became known, it might tend to incriminate myself."

The court, taken aback, rose for three hours of Jewish wedding troubled by a Hebrew interpreter; now sat still.

COLONEL FERGUSSON, in Chindit days.

The seven stare

For a moment the Seven of his officers and the bewigged R.C. Judge Advocate-General stared back on Fergusson, immaculate in his scarlet uniform.

Then the prosecutor said: "The court martial authorities have decided that this officer will not be prosecuted in any of his statements he may be permitted to make but he may be prosecuted in other respects."

After legal discussion, the Judge Advocate, Mr. Holland Stevenson, K.C., asked Fergusson: "I imagine you have taken legal advice?"

"Yes, sir."

"And, having done so, you refuse to answer?" "Yes, sir."

Then Mr. Arthur Stevenson said: "This is a case where a witness is asked a question the answer to which might incriminate him. He is entitled to refuse to answer."

He withdraws

"That is quite enough," said the Judge Advocate. "This is a position where this witness on grounds of common sense, because people on oath saying that the question incriminates themselves. Colonel Fergusson is not bound to answer his law. You may go."

Colonel Fergusson then withdrew. He saw the captain of 15 witnesses whom the prosecution could have called but refused to appear was the eighth.

He told the court, when the legal point concerned Rubowitz on July 22-1050, and another s Perger for 2000.

He owed no knowledge.

For a year—on the name of Berry-Brien—he owned two ploys and had lines at Croydon. One was an actress, GAHDJ, which he sold to July, tinge people knew in which they had lies on time.

LEFT MONEY

The second was an Austin GARAGE, which he had previously owned at Kew-in, Walland, the Scilly Isles and one little London in Stoneham, Sussex, with a garaging away—though Brien held for several of commercial firms.

For a clerk Brien had a flying partner in a former Dutch Girls' Vetkhagen Van Leeuwen held Vetkhagen Van Leeuwen. A stunting spinster in Johannesburg in January had been hiding with a garage with a well-known, Breens Amorous Irony at Johannesburg in January.

Yesterday, at four page near The Hague, Miss Van Zalen said: "Brien was a commercial wen" on in Cape Town.

Then the Window arrived at Dover last night from Calais on her way to her private business. He goes to Lloyd Dudley's home at Chingford, Essex, Lady Dudley is one of the Duchess's friends.

BRUCE PLANTED CASH IN AFRICA

Went to meet a woman

By RALPH CHAMPION

DOUGLAS BRUCE, the six-ft., four-times convicted Croydon crook who was released and buried in a private drum near the Transvaal diamond fields, went to South Africa to meet a woman. So Scotland Yard reasoned last night.

But was she the blonde 26-year-old with the Veronica Lake hair style whom the South African police went to interview, one of several slaps of the flamboyant, much-operating playboy-gambler?

That was on no certain Scotland Yard.

Inspector, land Yard thought, as Bruce pinned fresh police saying on Bruce's last residuals in this country.

Now it is known that Bruce, several of an investigation into his career, plansed money all over the world. So if the murder is to a private store.

School first team goes on strike

A school Rugby team went on strike yesterday and refused to play on Saturday because their gloomy mother had owned Monday.

Mr. Dennis Flagon, the master of Morley Road, Southchurch, put on the has after Monday's game, and when twenty to one cases, he said: "Other team are risking too bad."

The headmaster, Mr. E. L. Dormer, has given the boys a half-holiday Monday to change their minds.

'Atom cures baldness'

Some forms of baldness can be cured by atomic rays? according to Dr. Patrick J. Ferrey, a skin specialist of the London Hospital, in a report published today.

He pointed the brain of a new bald method, and so exposing varnish consuming structure X, a roshine-contented. The rays stimulated the growth of new hair in the cases.

The patient had been the skin to radio to which the skin was inactive.

Screaming woman at Consulate

A screaming woman was taken from the Polish Consulate in London yesterday, when she had been driven away in a car. Today a 25-year-old woman will appear at West London court charged with using insulting words.

Bound woman found murdered

In Regent's Park

Express Staff Reporter

AN unknown woman aged about 30 was found murdered in Regent's Park shortly after midnight. She was bound and gagged and battered.

She was lying within 100 yards of the Outer Circle road, near Albany-street, 100 yards within a quarter of a mile of the spot where Mrs. Olive Nixon, 57-year-old widow, was found dead.

4.30 a.m. LATEST

RUSSIANS SEIZE TWO AMERICANS

BERLIN, Wednesday.—Lieutenant John P. McCall, of U.S. Army headquarters, Berlin, and Mr. A. Vandit, state prosecutor, U.S. military courts, were seized by Russians in Soviet zone of Berlin, held several hours, then released without commission or papers. German News Service reports tonight. Each officiall absently.—Reuter.

CENtral 8000

nearly a year ago. Her murderer was never found.

The woman was lying on the grass in a slight hollow.

Detective Inspector Spooner, Jamison, with a squad of detectives from Albany-street station, searched the grass by torchlight for the weapon.

The woman was expensively dressed, and had recently manicured nails, several detectives were broken. There was a every sign, one of the police said, that she fought for life before the murderer did his deadly work.

The grass in the hollow was trampled, and showed many foot prints.

The discovery was made by a man who was taking a short cut home across the park.

Police were unable to move the grass in a hollow. A technical team made an underground examination, which he or carried out.

Canon shot in Arctic

WINNIPEG, Wednesday.—Canon J. R. Turner, 61-year-old Church of England missionary from Pemehwayo, Suffolk, is reported outright to have shot himself accidentally through the lip on board Moose Island, 100 miles away in the Arctic. He is seriously ill.

His wife Joan, is along with the survivors of the 1,000 hundreds of miles—early Johnson. Their rescue was carried through in a mercy plane. So the Army had broken down. Police think the murder was done in the air.

THE MARCH OF LIGHT

The Romans only had terra-cotta lamps to light their houses...

today there's

Osram

the wonderful lamp

ADVT. OF THE GENERAL ELECTRIC CO. LTD. ● A B&G PRODUCT

AIRWAYS TO SACK 2,000

Through travel cut

Express Staff Reporter

BETWEEN 2,000 and 2,500 men and women are to be sacked by the State-owned British European Airways Corporation, it was announced last night.

This is a third of the 7,000-strong staff employed to run the 100-plane line. The corporation says—

"The pleasure season ends and the foreign pleasure travel ban will similarly regret B.E.A.'s wings and activities.

Ranked air crews and ground staff will be offered in low other state-owned lines Overseas Airways and British American Airways.

50 builders migrate

Mr. William Ritchie, 48-year-old Sheffield builder, is closing his business and taking 50 of his workers to Australia to build houses for the New South Wales Government.

The men and their wives will sail in the ship as the first emigrating building team.

Said Mr. Ritchie: "It is hopeless in this country trying to get materials. All my men are handicapped. I could take a thousand there accommodation."

Letters opened—cash hunt

Officials put aside every 12th letter for abroad at Liverpool post office yesterday, and many were opened in a search for currency being sent out of the country. Little was found.

POCKET CARTOON
—By OSBERT LANCASTER

"So Sir Stafford Cripps and Diana Anne Laughlin are perfectly happy, are they, Vicar?"

SPECIAL TRIP

"I had no idea that Bruce was suspected of diamond smuggling or any other racket. I only knew him slightly and thought he was a decent fellow," said—

"I met him while I was staying instructions to Johannesburg, and planned out just for then flight. Bruce felt finished for the last leg of the journey."

Johannesburg police report that Bruce's young girl secretaries is to go to a garage fire a ward-down, 20-stored diamond fields was done in the air.

Duke of Windsor: private visit

The Duke of Windsor arrived at Dover last night from Calais on his way to his private business. He goes to Lord Dudley's home at Birmingham, Essex, Lady Dudley is one of the Duchess's friends.

IBA VAN ZANTEN
—No idea ...

Football pool in church

A play about football in church—with the congregation invited to join in on the penalties—is to be staged at St. Luke's Church, Blackrock, Dublin, on Sunday.

Rita seeks decree

HOLLYWOOD, Wednesday.—From film star Rita Hayworth today filed a divorce suit against Orson Welles in which because they locked the plastic mines for the new-starter trade.—Express News Service.

Mrs. Paton says no to £900 a year

Roy Farran being decorated with the US Legion
of Merit by Gen. Clayton Bissell in London,
October 1947.

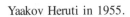

Yaakov Heruti in 1955.

Daily Express, front page report of the explosion at Farran's home in Codsall which killed his brother, Rex. The story made the front page of many British newspapers.

Roy Farran, flanked by his surviving brothers, follows his parents at the funeral of his brother Rex in Codsall on 7 May 1948.

Street in the Jerusalem suburb of East Talpiot named after Alexander Rubowitz.

It was a sign of the times that Alexander Rubowitz was finally commemorated in Israel.

would be held. This matter was to generate a great deal of argument, the first of several controversies that delayed it.[14]

Brigadier Shapcott, the deputy Judge Advocate General for the Middle East, wanted the trial moved to a criminal court in London because a murder case in which the body of the alleged victim was missing raised complicated questions of law that might tax the ability of the army's judicial branch. There was also concern that a court martial might be suspected of going easy on a 'brother officer'. If Farran was found not guilty the verdict would be 'savagely attacked by the Jews in Palestine and in the American press'. Finally, under the rules of a court martial if he were found guilty there would be no chance of appeal except to the king. The War Office therefore thought it might be preferable if Farran were transferred to London, passed into the jurisdiction of the civil authorities, and put on trial at the Old Bailey (the Central Criminal Court). The matter was so sensitive that the Attorney General, Sir Hartley Shawcross, was brought into a meeting with officials from the Colonial Office and the War Office. Shawcross told them that if they wanted to move the trial to London they should consult the Director of Public Prosecutions (DPP), but as it was a political question the decision ultimately rested with the Secretaries of State at the Colonial Office and the War Office. 'If ministers decide that it was politically expedient to have Major Farran tried at the Central Criminal Court then he, the Attorney General, would raise no objection to this procedure.'[15]

The DPP agreed, but asked the Colonial Office to arrange for a senior police officer from Scotland Yard to go to Palestine to review the case before a final decision was taken. This raised all sorts of tricky issues. John Gutch, on the Middle East desk, noted that Scotland Yard would want 'to investigate certain points on which the Palestine Police have not been altogether forthcoming, e.g., none of the police party who had seized Rubowitz and accompanied Farran to interrogate him had so far been identified'. In which case, it might be better to opt for a civil trial, but in Palestine. This was the direction in which Creech Jones leaned. He wanted to blunt the charges of 'deliberate delay' that were already being made by the Jewish press and 'avoid giving that press the grounds for the complaint that the altogether unusual step of removal to this country was being taken for some ulterior purpose'. However, it turned out that it would require special legislation to move Farran from military to civil jurisdiction in Palestine whereas it was possible to remove him for trial in England and hand him over to the civil power under the Offenders of the Person Act 1861.[16]

When MacMillan and Cunningham were consulted they were both firmly against moving the trial to London. MacMillan, the senior soldier in Palestine, considered that a court martial would be 'fully capable of dealing with the issues involved' if it could be 'assisted by a first-class Judge Advocate provided by the War Office'. Cunningham, like Creech Jones, saw the political pitfalls of further delay, which was how the Jewish public in Palestine and the USA were bound to regard a change of venue. His argument for holding the trial in Palestine was unexpectedly strengthened when violence there spilled onto the streets of British cities.[17]

On 12 July, the Irgun kidnapped two British sergeants from Field Security who were off duty in Netanya and held them hostage against the lives of three captured Irgun fighters who were in Acre prison under sentence of death. Despite the imposition of martial law on the Netanya area and an intensive manhunt by the 1st Infantry Division, the army and the police were unable to discover where the captured sergeants were being concealed. But in line with the 'get tough' policy, this time the civil administration and the army did not back down: on 29 July the Irgun captives were executed. The next day the two British NCOs were hanged from a tree in an orange grove near Netanya. When the dead men were found on 31 July a mine seriously injured a sapper trying to cut them down. News of this atrocity spread like wildfire through the security forces. British troops and police in Tel Aviv went on the rampage, killing five Jews and injuring fifteen. Back in Britain, grisly photographs and reports were splashed across the newspapers on the eve of the August bank holiday weekend. Over the following four days synagogues and Jewish-owned properties were attacked and damaged by mobs in Liverpool, Manchester and Glasgow. Anti-Jewish incidents also occurred in Hull, Brighton, Leicester, Plymouth, Birmingham, Bristol, Cardiff, Swansea, Newcastle and across London. The anti-Jewish riots had been brewing before the atrocity in Palestine and were partly a reaction to continued food shortages and the perceived association of Jews with the black market. Yet the connection with Palestine was tangible and in the wake of the riots, some Jewish traders put notices in their shop windows denouncing Jewish terrorism. The riots reinforced Cunningham's opinion that there was little to gain and much to lose by shifting the venue of the trial. He wrote archly to the Colonial Office that 'the impartiality of [an] English jury in the present state of British public opinion against terrorism is as likely to be challenged as the impartiality in local courts'.[18]

A few days later, Frank Bellenger MP, the Secretary of State for War, informed civil servants at the Colonial Office that the War Office had dropped its objections to a trial in Palestine. He instructed the commander-in-chief of Middle East Land Forces that Farran should be tried by court martial in Palestine. In view of the legal and political sensitivities of the case, the War Office agreed to provide a 'first-class man from here as Judge Advocate for the trial'. As a signal of their intent, Lord Russell of Liverpool, a colonel in the Judge Advocate General's department, was assigned to oversee arrangements for the trial. Russell was immensely experienced. He had either tried or managed a number of very difficult cases during the war and was responsible for prosecuting Nazi war criminals and Wehrmacht officers in Germany in 1946 and 1947. This background made him sympathetic towards the Jewish cause, but he had also been deputy Judge Advocate General to the C.-in-C. Middle East Land Forces in 1946, in which capacity he had been responsible for the trial of Jewish terrorists. He was a safe pair of hands and he could be trusted to take a balanced view.[19]

Steady nerves and impartiality were at a premium because only a few weeks after the agitation over the hangings another sensational story of Jewish terrorism erupted onto the front pages. Acting on a tip-off, police in France arrested an American rabbi who planned to drop leaflets and bombs on London.

Rabbi Baruch Korff, the man behind this hare-brained scheme, was born in Russia in 1914. He was the scion to a long line of distinguished rabbis, but war and revolution were bringing the traditional life of Russian Jews to an end while he was still a child. His mother was killed in one of the pogroms that swept across Russia during the civil war and in 1926 his family emigrated to the USA. Korff studied rabbinics in America and Poland, where he was ordained in 1936. But he sprang from the obscure ranks of the US rabbinate when he tried to rouse interest in the fate of the Jews in German-occupied Europe during the Second World War. It was then that he drifted into the orbit of right-wing Zionist militants and set up the Political Action Committee for Palestine (PAC) along with an ex-New York state congressman, Joseph Clark Baldwin. Together they raised prodigious amounts of money to campaign for the entry of Jewish DPs into Palestine and published large adverts in the New York newspapers lacerating British policy. In June 1946 Korff attracted more attention with a bizarre plan to surmount the British naval blockade of Palestine by parachuting Jews into the country. An American reporter who interviewed the rabbi in his office in a New York hotel could not help noticing a stack of parachutes in one corner of the room. 'They are not souvenirs', Korff told him. Baldwin later elaborated on this scheme by asking the PAC's friends in Congress to request the president to lend a fleet of DC-4 Dakota airplanes to the Zionist movement. These would be used for an 'Exodus by Air', transporting DPs from Europe to isolated airstrips in Palestine.[20]

In August 1947, Korff travelled to Europe ostensibly to campaign for the admission of Jews to Palestine. He installed himself in the luxurious Hotel Crillon in Paris and negotiated personally with the French Foreign Ministry. Behind the scenes he made contact with the LEHI cell that was previously responsible for the bombs in London and the explosive-letter campaign. For some time these activists had actually been receiving funds from Korff's American front organisations. In no time at all his interest in aviation morphed into a plan to hire a private aircraft and pulverise London with propaganda and bombs. Having obtained a plane he secured the services of a pilot, Reginald Gilbert, an American citizen who was originally from England. Next, Korff printed thousands of leaflets addressed to 'the people of England' in the name of the Freedom Fighters of Israel, LEHI. The text declared that 'Your government has dipped His Majesty's crown in Jewish blood and polished it with Arab oil'. Linking his mission to recent history and current events in Palestine it continued, 'Oswiecim [Auschwitz], Dachau and Treblinka made way for the "Exodus" to the Hitler-Bevin alliance – the murder of survivors whom Hitler's wrath could not reach.' It then threatened in quasi-biblical terms: 'We will carry the war to the very heart of the empire. We will strike with all the bitterness and fury of our servitude and bondage.' Korff ended with the message 'People of England! Press your government to quit Eretz-Israel now!' He planned to drop the leaflets over the Houses of Parliament on 2 September, but various problems forced him to delay for a week. By that time the French police were on the case. When Korff arrived at Toussus-le-Noble airfield, near Versailles, armed French policemen disguised as mechanics surrounded him, his glamorous red-headed 'secretary' Judith Rosenberger, and Gilbert. The police seized suit-cases containing 10,000 leaflets, but no bombs.[21]

It turned out that Gilbert had betrayed the plan to the French police as soon as he found out that Korff intended to inflict real damage on London. Over the following hours police searched Korff's hotel room and raided numerous addresses in the Paris area. Seventeen people were finally arrested, including Jacques Martinsky, the LEHI agent who made the first attempt to get into the UK; Robert Misrahi, who successfully planted the bomb in the British Colonial Club; and Herzl Amikam, who had posted the letter bombs from Turin. The French police were directed to several of their targets by British intelligence who had been watching Martinsky since his abortive mission. The raids and searches never revealed anything more lethal than sketches for improvised bombs made from fire extinguishers packed with explosives and fitted with fins, but they crippled LEHI's European operation.[22]

When Rabbi Korff was taken to Paris police headquarters for questioning he denounced Gilbert as a traitor and flamboyantly declared to the crowd of reporters that he was on hunger strike. But, like Knut, he enjoyed remarkably lenient treatment and was released without trial. This may have been because his crazy scheme unfolded against the saga of the Hagana ship *Exodus*. Public opinion in France, as elsewhere, was outraged when the Royal Navy and the British

Army used force to prevent Jews on the blockade-running *Exodus* from entering what was supposed to be the Jewish National Home and, still worse, returned them to Europe where most had suffered appallingly at the hands of the Nazis. The Palestinian militants were ably defended by Maitre André Blumel, the well-connected head of the French Zionist Association who was himself deeply involved in illegal immigration to Palestine. Guy de Rothschild covered the costs. Korff was able to return to the United States where he resumed his quixotic career of Jewish public service, ending up as a confidant of the disgraced President Nixon.[23]

At around the same time, but with much less publicity, MI5 scotched another Jewish terrorist effort involving aviation. This time the assault was mounted by the Irgun. After the intelligence services had disrupted the Irgun's Italian operation the organisation's European commander, Eli Tavin, relocated to Paris and started rebuilding its capacity to strike at British targets. His eyes were inexorably drawn to the British mainland, so tantalisingly close. Tavin was assisted by Samuel Merlin who had arrived from the USA where he used to run the American League for a Free Palestine and also the Hebrew Committee of National Liberation along with Hillel Kook (also known as Peter Bergson). Merlin and Kook/Bergson were followers of Vladimir Ze'ev Jabotinsky who had been sent to the United States from Palestine in 1940 to make propaganda for the Revisionist movement. They subsequently became involved in efforts to rescue Jews from Nazi-occupied Europe and made a considerable impact with their bold public-relations stunts. At the end of the war they reverted back into advocates for Revisionism and started raising money for the Irgun's activities across the Atlantic and in Palestine. Merlin had rooms in the Hotel Lutetia, once the luxurious accommodation of the German occupation authority, but now home to the European headquarters of the Irgun. Tavin was also joined by Samuel Katz, who had been promoted to the Irgun high command, and Eliyahu Lankin, who had escaped to France from a British prison camp in Eritrea.[24]

Lankin's arrival was especially significant. He was born in Russia in 1914, but raised in Harbin, China, where his family settled in the wake of the Bolshevik Revolution. He entered BETAR as a student and enrolled in the Irgun after he emigrated to Palestine in 1933. Lankin was one of the select few who were sent to Poland for military training on the eve of the war. This made him a valuable asset for the 'dissidents' and by 1944 he was commander of the Irgun in Jerusalem. It also made him a prime target for the Hagana and the British. A year later he was arrested by the British on a tip-off from the Jewish Agency and shipped to a detention camp in the Horn of Africa. His escape was an epic of ingenuity and fortitude. When he reached Paris he was appointed commander of all Irgun forces in the Diaspora. This grand-sounding title concealed the real weakness of the underground in Europe: it suffered from a shortage of funds and a lack of trained officers experienced in clandestine warfare. There were plenty of willing volunteers, but they tended to be naive and careless. Their poor security sense even made them a liability. With his keen organisational skills and wealth of experience Lankin set about rectifying these deficiencies.[25]

The greatest obstacle to a strike against Britain, though, was the fierce scrutiny of Palestinians attempting to enter the country. For months the group pondered how to get someone through the heightened security checks. The solution was provided by a young South African-born Jew called Boris Senior who had served in the RAF during the war. Senior underwent conversion to militant Zionism when he was demobbed and learned about the mass murder of Europe's Jews. He dropped his studies at London University and made his way into the ranks of the Irgun via Samuel Katz who was an old friend of his family. Katz introduced Senior to an Irgun agent in London, probably Yoel 'Leo' Bela, who in turn passed him on to the Irgun centre in Paris where he was introduced to Eliyahu Lankin and Eli Tavin. They taught Senior to make explosive devices and instructed him in the techniques of covert operations. However, as Senior recalled, the British members of the Irgun 'could act only in a supporting role, for none had any experience in handling delayed-action bombs'. Senior volunteered to solve the problem of getting an experienced operative into England by flying one over in a private plane. Emulating SOE missions to France during the war, but in reverse, he proposed to pick up the Irgun agent at an airfield outside Paris and land on farmland near Canterbury where he would be collected by someone from the UK cell.[26]

For this part of the mission Senior approached Ezer Weizman, another ex-RAF pilot who was studying in London. Weizman was the nephew of Chaim Weizmann, the Zionist leader. He was born in Tel Aviv in 1924 and grew up in Haifa where he entered the Hagana as a teenager. It was while he was on a Hagana leadership course in 1941 that he saw a dogfight between the RAF and Italian aircraft over the port and decided to become a pilot. He enrolled in the RAF the following year and ended the war in India. Not having any interest in a peacetime career in the British air force he demobbed and in July 1946 he travelled to London to study. Frustrated by the sense that great events were happening elsewhere, and irritated by his uncle's pro-British outlook, he drifted into militant Zionist circles. He met Senior at the Palestine Club for Jewish and Palestinian servicemen in London and discovered they shared a passion for flying. Senior also 'began to talk me into aiding the IZL in its operations. I did not need much persuading: I'd been looking for some national occupation.' Weizman went with Senior to Paris, where they met Tavin and Lankin. The Irgun veterans completed the recruitment process and gave the two ex-RAF pilots 'underground crash courses in all kinds of sabotage tricks'.[27]

Weizman, like Senior, seemed like a gift to the Paris cell. Although he hailed from Palestine and had a distinguished uncle in the Zionist movement, he had no political ties and was therefore 'clean'. Unfortunately for the plan Yoel Bela was not. He had long ago been identified by MI5 as the Irgun's key man in London and he was constantly watched by Special Branch. So was Senior, whose flat Weizman was sharing for the duration of the escapade. Unaware that he was under suspicion, in the summer of 1947 Senior purchased an Auster aircraft using £1,000 of his own money and made a few recreational flights to establish a cover for the mission. Meanwhile, the Irgun team in Paris selected a Palestinian Jew, Yoel Eilberg, to go to Britain and spearhead the attack. He had served in a Welsh regiment during the war and had passable English as well as the necessary bomb-making skills. The target was General Evelyn Barker who had left Palestine in February 1947 and moved to Chobham, near Aldershot in Surrey.[28]

On the appointed date Senior interrupted the journey he had agreed with flight control in France and picked up Eilberg near Paris. He flew across the Channel and landed in farmland in Kent en route to his official destination, Croydon Airport. Weizman picked up Eilberg and drove him to Senior's Bayswater flat. They were joined there by Paul Homesky, a pilot who had flown with the Free French during the war before signing on with the Irgun. But none of them had any idea where Barker lived. Eilberg was alarmed to find that this half-baked Irgun unit did not have any arms or explosives, either. During July they wasted days driving around the country in Homesky's large sedan in a highly amateurish and ultimately futile attempt to locate their prey. Eventually police visited Senior's flat, which was awash with Irgun literature, and briefly interviewed Senior and Eilberg. Soon afterwards Senior was informed that his pilot's licence had been revoked; he beat a quick retreat to Johannesburg. Weizman was told he was no longer welcome in Britain. (Amazingly, in 1951–2 he was permitted to study at the RAF staff college which helped him on the way to command of the Israeli air force which, in turn, provided the platform for a long political career that ended with the presidency of the state of Israel in 1993–2000, a position whose first holder was his uncle in 1949.) Eilberg was left at large a bit longer. In desperation he contacted Bela, but he had previously been observed by Special Branch meeting Homesky in Paddington Station to conduct a transaction that involved several grenades. This time the police moved in on the Irgun cell. Eilberg was detained for several months and then deported as an illegal alien. Bela was arrested, too, but released without charge and kept under observation. Although the Irgun went on to hit various British targets in Germany and Austria, this was its last attempt to penetrate the mainland defences.[29]

While Jewish terrorism raged almost unchecked in Palestine and threatened again to reach England's shores, the summary of evidence in Farran's case got underway in Jerusalem at the Allenby Barracks. At nine in the morning on 17 July, five Jewish witnesses appeared at the entrance to the security zone in which the barracks was located and were escorted past the barbed-wire entanglements to where an army staff car was waiting to drive them the rest of the way. They were then ushered into the room where a lieutenant colonel conducted the examination. Farran was present wearing a perfectly pressed major's uniform. He was represented by Mr John Bickford-Smith, a solicitor who had been despatched to Palestine by the firm of Laurence Collins and Fearnley-Whittingstall two days earlier. According to one report, Farran showed little interest in the proceedings and ostentatiously read the Bible for part of the time. Bickford-Smith, however, allowed little to get past him. Most significantly he challenged the evidentiary status of the notes Roy had made while he was in the Allenby Barracks on 19 June, which the prosecution had produced as 'Exhibit B'. In a letter to Lieutenant General MacMillan, Bickford-Smith asserted that the notes were intended by Roy to be used for his defence and, hence, were covered by privilege and could not be used as evidence. The process was completed on 23 July and he returned to London to work on the defence. Farran returned to his hot cell in Sarafand, badminton with Colin Mitchell, and his memoirs.[30]

As the legal process dragged on, always behind closed doors, anger and suspicion welled up in the Jewish community. Yitzhak Ben-Zvi, the president of the Vaad Leumi, the national council and main representative body of the Jewish population in Palestine, expressed these feelings in a letter to Sir Henry Gurney: 'We deem it our duty to bring to your notice the unfortunate impression made on Jewish public opinion in Palestine by the method in which, it was reported, the legal proceedings are now conducted against Major Roy Alexander Farran.' Ben-Zvi complained that no member of the Rubowitz family or even a legal representative was allowed to be present and no information had been vouchsafed to them. They had no idea of the charge or any other details. 'The whole matter is shrouded in impenetrable secrecy', he wrote. 'The unfortunate events which have led up to the present proceedings have created a widespread belief that attempts are being made to hide the whole truth in connection with the kidnapping and murder of Rubowitz from the public, and to shield those responsible for such a crime as may have been committed. The fact that the case is being handled by the military authorities in secrecy greatly adds to that belief.' The letter observed that in England Farran would have been tried in a civil court and although the commander of British troops in Palestine was within his rights to try him by court martial, in a matter of such concern, and not one of army discipline, a civil trial would seem more 'consonant with the requirements of the situation'. Ben-Zvi ended by eschewing any desire to impugn British military justice; but he admonished that an open trial would be the most effective and fair way to proceed.[31]

Ben-Zvi's letter had absolutely no effect on the British authorities. However, the failure of the Jewish Agency and the Vaad Leumi to elicit any significant response from the Palestine government encouraged the Rubowitz family and more militant elements in the Jewish community to explore other avenues. In late July, Alexander's brothers Ya'acov and Nehamiah appointed Reuven Nochimowski as their attorney. He wasted little time before applying to the Jerusalem magistrate E. Y. Levy for a public inquiry into the boy's disappearance. Nochimowski's zeal was not matched by his attention to detail, however, and the application was dismissed on the grounds that he had not filled out the legal forms correctly. The Crown counsel, Mr Hooton, turned the knife in the wound by saying that if he had any new evidence he should give it to the police.[32]

Nochimowski quickly came up with a new stratagem. On 4 August, he submitted to the high court in Jerusalem a writ of habeas corpus in the name of Nehamiah Rubowitz for an order nisi calling on Colonel Gray, Brigadier Fergusson, Mr Kenneth Hadingham and Major Farran to show cause why they should not produce the body of Alexander Rubowitz. As supporting evidence the text of the application made reference to an affidavit by the Jerusalem district superintendent of police accusing Farran of kidnapping Alexander Rubowitz (presumably generated in the course of the extradition proceedings in June). It also stated that because Gray and Fergusson were his superior officers 'it is probable that he acted under their orders, and it is certain that they were immediately informed by Mr Farran about the incident'. Despite the heat and the holidays, the high court convened on 7 August for Acting Chief Justice B. V. Shaw and Acting Justice S. N. Weldon to hear the application.

In his plea, Nochimowski appealed 'to the legal mind and the human conscience'. He told the court that the family had been treated very badly. They believed that Alexander was still alive, but they had not been allowed to see any results of the police investigation and their lawyer had been barred from the summary of evidence taken by the army. He reviewed all the evidence in the case, alleging that Farran had been positively identified in the line-up on 18 June, and argued that Farran should now be subjected to civil proceedings. Despite his eloquence, the court rejected the application. The justices deemed it was surmise that the three officers – Gray, Fergusson and Hadingham – had issued orders concerning Rubowitz or ever had him in their custody. Most significantly, it was not necessary to issue an order nisi if an alternative remedy was available and Farran had been charged. Finally, and this was of course the true rationale of Nochimowski's ploy, it was not the function of the high court to investigate the case. Nochimowski's persistence was probably intended to embarrass the official Jewish leadership as much as the British. At the same time as he applied for habeas corpus he wrote to the Vaad Leumi that he was 'amazed' the Jewish Agency had not taken more forthright action and criticised them for meekly accepting the jurisdiction of the army when Farran had been a serving police officer.[33]

At the end of August he returned to the courts with yet another application for an inquiry. This time he used the Criminal Procedure (Trial Upon Information) Ordinance to apply to the Jerusalem examining magistrate, George Stultz, for a public inquiry into the abduction on the grounds that although the accused appeared to have vanished, no one had been charged or tried, and evidence was being concealed. The hearing took place on 30 August in a tiny courtroom in the well-guarded Russian Compound. It was packed to overflowing by members of the Rubowitz family, their legal advisers, representatives of the Palestine government, the police, the army and court officials. The government was represented by Crown counsel, Mr Maurice Heenan, and the army by Lieutenant Colonel R. H. Cowell-Parker, of the Judge Advocate General's department. Since it was the nearest thing to an open legal process that had yet taken place in connection with the Farran affair the press was there in force. During the first hearing, which lasted for three hours in the stifling heat, Nochimowski argued that because Farran was a police officer at the time of the alleged offence he should not be tried by the army but, instead, given into the custody of the civil authorities so that the case could be heard in public. Further, although it could be inferred from the evidence that someone had been murdered, no one had been charged or taken into custody and no complaint had been lodged in the civil courts by the police. He demanded an inquiry so that the evidence could be presented. The next day Crown counsel, Maurice Heenan, conceded that the court might consider the application if no one was detained, but he was authorised to state that Farran was 'in military custody on a holding charge of murder' and that due process was taking its course. Stultz, who had no competence to determine if Farran was in the army or the police, consequently rejected the application for an inquiry.[34]

Although Nochimowski had been thwarted he had at least elicited the important new information that Farran was being held on a murder charge. He may also have derived encouragement from the examining magistrate's closing remarks. In front of the press and government representatives Stultz expressed 'astonishment' that the police had not replied to requests from the Rubowitz family for information on the progress of the investigation and expressed the hope that the authorities would 'bring this regrettable and most worrying matter to finality'. Prominent members of the Jewish community now added their voices to protests against the continuing procrastination. The government spokesman was forced to issue one statement after another in a vain attempt to reassure the Jewish population that justice would be done and seen to be done. What the Jews did not know and what the government could not say was that postponement of the trial reflected a strenuous tussle between Farran's lawyers, the Colonial Office, the high commissioner, the police and the army over the way the trial would be conducted.[35]

In the few weeks after Bickford-Smith had returned to London and reported to Robert Fearnley-Whittingstall on the summary of evidence, Farran's legal team had been hard at work. Robert's brother, William Fearnley-Whittingstall KC, was instructed as counsel and brought with him important knowledge of military law. Aged forty-four, he had been educated at Malvern public school, studied law and was called to the bar in 1925. He built up a successful practice until 1939, when he was commissioned into the Royal Artillery. For two years he commanded a light anti-aircraft regiment, ending the war with the rank of lieutenant colonel. Initially, though, the main concern of the solicitors was to get hold of the documents that would set Farran's activity in context and, possibly, even negate the prosecution.[36]

Robert Fearnley-Whittingstall wrote to the Secretary of State for the Colonies explaining that Roy Farran was his client and asking for a copy of the memorandum that Fergusson had written proposing to establish 'anti-terrorist squads from among the Palestine Police as a result of which Major Farran was selected to train and lead such squads'. His intention may be divined from the explanation that 'It is important that the defence shall be in a position at Major Farran's trial to show precisely the nature and extent of the duties entrusted to him.' Fergusson's memorandum would at the very least enable them to argue that Farran was obeying orders. But the request also served notice that they knew the squads had a purpose that the British authorities, in London and Jerusalem, might not want exposed to public scrutiny. Without waiting for a response one way or the other they asked for an appointment in order to inspect the memorandum and 'other relevant documents'. This pushy style was to characterise their conduct of the case throughout. They suspected that the government had something to hide and with a mixture of innuendo and outright threat they used the fear of exposure for the maximum leverage.[37]

Farran's solicitors had definitely touched a raw nerve. The immediate response within the Colonial Office was to refuse the request and to claim privilege. In so doing the Colonial Office was invoking the right of government, recognised in law, to withhold a document or refuse to answer questions on the grounds that to do so would be injurious to good governance and the national interest. The legal adviser to the Colonial Office was unequivocal when he was asked whether the Secretary of State should follow this course:

'I am inclined to think he should do so. It seems to me a report of a highly confidential character.' Harold Beeley of the Foreign Office Eastern Department and Bevin's adviser on Palestine, minuted ominously: 'The letter creates difficulties. We, none of us, know the real facts of the Farran case, but the feeling I have gained from such reports as have been sent and from conversations in Palestine is that, while Major Farran was clearly going outside any instructions officially given to him, there may nevertheless be something to be said for the contention that his superiors knew something of the dubious methods adopted, the abuse of which caused the unfortunate death of Rubowitz. Thus I think everyone concerned on the British side hopes that Major Farran's sentence will not be severe. On the other hand, nothing could be more disastrous than our taking action which will give any grounds for the suspicion that the Palestine Government or HMG were trying to steer the case in Major Farran's favour. Thus, I think that we must stick to the formal letter of the law and refuse co-operation with his solicitors.' On 15 August, after further badgering, the Colonial Office informed the solicitors that the documents they asked to see 'are as you will be aware privileged from production in a court of law and the Secretary of State regrets that in these circumstances he feels unable to disclose them'.[38]

However, as Farran's diligent solicitors widened their demand for access to potentially explosive documents the claim to immunity proved increasingly contentious and eventually came to divide the government. The firm next wrote to Lieutenant General MacMillan, GOC in Palestine, asking him to provide a copy of the Fergusson memorandum. This drew the War Office into the debate. Officials of the Colonial Office were reassured to learn that under regulations governing the admission of evidence in a court martial it was normal procedure for the Secretary of State to claim privilege, although in the case of a capital offence it might be necessary for an official to appear in person with an affidavit giving the reasons for withholding the document in question. Brigadier Shapcott also advised that 'Fergusson must similarly claim privilege in any court proceedings if he is questioned about the contents or nature of the documents'. The Colonial Office duly alerted Jerusalem to the strategy

Whitehall had agreed upon to keep the inflammatory papers out of the public eye.[39]

At this point, Roy's powerful friends in London attempted to help via backstairs channels. His solicitors had contacted Brian Franks requesting a testimonial as to Roy's character and also asking for help in obtaining Fergusson's memorandum. Franks asked Laycock to help, too. As he explained, 'Bernard Fergusson in March last wrote a document setting out the whole scheme at the Colonial Office – this was approved by Creech Jones and copy sent to MB. The solicitors are most anxious to get a sight of this & have written to the colonial secretary asking for it but no reply has been received – and it seems likely that they will not reply – it follows that the document is fairly hot. Can you suggest a means of seeing it?' Laycock readily agreed and told Robert Fearnley-Whittingstall, who had made a formal appeal for a testimonial on Roy's behalf, that 'I understand from Lieutenant Colonel B. F. Franks, who is also inter-ested in this case, that you are anxious to have a look at a certain document issued to Major Farran by a Brigadier Fergusson. I am doing my best to obtain permission for this.' Because Laycock wanted more details, Fearnley-Whittingstall recalled the genesis of the memorandum, describing it as a proposal to 'combat the terror-ists by "extra-police" methods'. He noted that it was written at the request of the Colonial Office and accepted by the War Office, although the chances of either giving permission to see it were slim. Laycock resolved to do his best and contacted 'Boy' Browning on what he called the 'old-boy basis'. 'I am fully aware,' he wrote to him, 'that the whole question of Farran's trial is complicated by important political aspects and that, therefore, the greatest care must be exercised in preventing undersirable "dirty linen" being washed in public. On the other hand it seems very unfortunate if evidence is withheld which might help in the defence of an officer as gallant as Farran who, in the past, has served his country so admirably and whose life is now at stake.' Nevertheless, Laycock was rebuffed. Browning replied two weeks later that it was for the court to decide on matters of privilege and until that time it would be wrong for him to allow Farran's solicitors to see the document.[40]

However, unease began to develop about the use being made of privilege. Legal advisers questioned whether the documents at issue would really qualify for being withheld in the national interest, especially in a capital case. To help resolve these doubts, William Mathieson, in the Colonial Office, sought advice from Lord Russell. He subsequently reported that 'I examined the document with Lord Russell and formed the opinion that there was nothing in it which should make it necessary to claim privilege. I felt that there was evident advantage in producing this document if we could, as otherwise it would be assumed both by the court and by the public that we had something serious to hide, and it might also be alleged that by withholding this evidence we had seriously prejudiced Major Farran's chances of acquittal.' Privilege should not be claimed 'unless there were *exceptionally strong grounds* for doing so'. Opinion in the Colonial Office now swung the other way. Cunningham was informed that, for the purposes of the trial, Fergusson's memorandum was no longer considered secret. 'Privilege could only be claimed if disclosure of the contents of the documents would clearly be contrary to national defence. Exposure to public criticism or administrative inconvenience are not in themselves reasons for withholding; this is particularly so in a capital case.' The Colonial Office left it up to him to decide whether to draw the line at the communications exchanged between Jerusalem and Damascus.[41]

A request from Laurence Collins and Fearnley-Whittingstall for access to these exchanges inveigled the Foreign Office in the privilege debate, too. The legation in Damascus had good reasons to join the united front and assert privilege. Peter Scrivener told London that while it was 'obviously wrong' to give the court some documents while withholding others, 'To give all might embarrass the Government of Palestine and would involve the head of the Syrian state.' Furthermore, 'It should be remembered that Farran made a false statement to the Syrian Police, the contents of which we do not know'. Surprisingly, though, the Foreign Office took a less rigid view of privilege. London told Damascus that it was up to them. If possible, sensitive documents should be produced in camera with the prior agreement of the Syrian government. Otherwise, the presentation of these papers was 'unobjectionable' from a British point of view. It appears that Foreign Secretary Bevin had, himself, intervened. To Bevin, as to some others, it was unacceptable for government to seek to protect itself from embarrassment when a man's life was at stake. The message was driven home so hard that Scrivener, the head of the legation in Damascus, wanted it made quite clear 'should the matter arise, that it is the government of Palestine and not the Legation or HMG which decided initially to claim privilege in this case where a man is on trial for his life'.[42]

As a consequence of these deliberations a date was not set for the court martial until mid September 1947. The delay was frustrating to the Jewish community in Palestine, but it was crucial to Farran's defence. What had started out as a device by the Colonial Office to prevent a potentially embarrassing document entering the public domain ended up providing the Fearnley-Whittingstalls with a potent weapon. The government had wanted to use privilege in the sense in which official documents can be withheld in the national interest. However, Brigadier Shapcott had pointed out that privilege could also be invoked in the case of certain evidence in the possession of a witness. If government could claim immunity because the disclosure of documents might be damaging to the national interest, a witness in a court martial could decline to testify if the content of their testimony was likely to be self-incriminating. Robert and William Fearnley-Whittingstall saw the potential of this device to undermine the prosecution case and used it to devastating effect. Curiously, though, it only worked if the key witness *was* guilty of something. This was certainly true of Fergusson. Precisely because Fergusson was a party to the cover-up, because he knew the *truth*, it was possible for Farran's representatives to co-opt him into their defence strategy.[43]

Fergusson could never admit this, of course, and in his memoir came up with a convoluted explanation of what it was he had to hide. He recalled that he was permitted to travel to Cairo to consult a British lawyer and ex-army chum John Besley, who was legal adviser to the British Embassy. Fergusson recounted to him that 'Although I had not been involved in whatever Roy Farran might have done, I had sailed pretty close to the wind in order to cover up for him; my chief concern at that stage of the game being to keep the squads in being.' This was not only a lie, it was a bad lie. In reality, Fergusson had to protect himself from accusations that he concealed a murder. In protecting himself he also insulated the police and the Palestine government from charges that they were running hit squads. Even if he was telling the truth and he was a party to a 'cover up' for the sake of the mission, this was still no reason for obstructing the course of justice. But John Besley apparently accepted his explanation and Fergusson was quite correct when he reflected that 'it stood me in good stead'.[44]

On 24 September 1947, the government of Palestine finally announced that Farran's trial by general court martial would be held on Wednesday 1 October at the military court in the Talbieh district in south-west Jerusalem. In anticipation of the huge international interest in the case, arrangements were made to accommodate twenty-four foreign journalists and seventeen local reporters. This announcement overshadowed Nochimowski's last bid for a public hearing in a civil court. He again applied to the supreme court for a decree nisi calling upon the Jerusalem magistrate to show why the application for a hearing should not be granted. The court rejected the request, but granted Nochimowski a moral victory by expressing the opinion 'that it was in the public interest that the authorities should expedite proceedings in this matter'. As a last, rather absurd ploy he also wrote to the public coroner asking for an inquest. The Jerusalem coroner threw out the petition on the not unreasonable grounds that it was impossible to have an inquest without a body, and he was not aware of one having been found.[45]

The trial of Roy Farran took place under conditions of extraordinarily tight security. The court was located in one of the elegant buildings that adorned the leafy suburb of Talbieh, home to the wealthy members of Jerusalem's Arab community. But there was nothing pretty about it that day. The doors and windows of the building were sandbagged and it was surrounded by coils of barbed wire. Soldiers and policemen were posted all around and even on the roof. No one could enter the area without special passes issued by the army and everyone, including the press, was thoroughly searched, once at the checkpoint on the street and again before entering the courtroom. Thirty journalists and a small crowd of photographers were there when Yedidya Rubowitz, his sons Ya'acov and Nehamiah, and his daughter-in-law, appeared at 9:00 a.m., an hour before the proceedings were scheduled to begin. Along with their attorney, Asher Levitsky, they were amongst the few Jews who were permitted to attend. At half-past nine, an armoured car escorted by a truckload of battle-equipped troops drove through the checkpoint and halted outside a heavily screened entrance. Farran quickly exited the armoured vehicle and entered the building escorted by an officer of the Argyll and Sutherland Highlanders.[46]

The courtroom was small (to make more space the dock had been shifted into a corner and tipped on its side) and soon filled to capacity with an impressive array of uniforms and costumes. Several policemen from Farran's squad attended along with a number of army officers. Major Chichester, aide-de-camp to the high commissioner, was there to observe the proceedings for the government of Palestine. Fergusson found himself alongside a Bedouin sheikh who had assisted Farran when he was on the run in June. Fergusson recognised most of the members of the court: they were his fellow officers. The prosecutor, though, was not a member of the armed forces. To avoid any impression of going easy on Farran the Judge Advocate General's department had brought in Maxwell Turner, a well-respected London barrister. Adjacent to him were William Fearnley-Whittingstall KC, the defence counsel, and John Bickford-Smith, his solicitor. The Judge Advocate General, who was there primarily to rule on points of military law, was Aubrey Melford Stevenson KC. This was the 'first-class man' the War Office had promised to provide and he was, indeed, a distinguished choice. Stevenson went on to enjoy a high-profile career as a barrister that included defending Ruth Ellis, the last woman to be hanged in England. As a High Court judge he presided over the sensational trial of the Kray twins in 1969.[47]

At 10 a.m. the court took its seats. It comprised Lieutenant Colonel Eustace John Nelson of the Grenadier Guards; Lieutenant Colonel A. W. A. Malcolm, Welsh Guards; Major Slade, Suffolk Regiment; Major A. R. A. Cocksedge, Royal Inniskilling Fusiliers;

Major George Brooke, 17/21 Lancers. The president of the court, Brigadier Richard Maxwell, commander of the Palestine southern district, entered a few minutes later. The Judge Advocate General swore him in followed by the other members of the court as well as the court officials, two sergeant interpreters and the stenographer. Then Roy Farran was marched in wearing a peculiar combination of attire including a 'salmon-red forage cap' and a bush jacket adorned with his parachute wings and two rows of decorations. He was asked to stand and the charge was read to him: 'Committing a civil offence, that is to say murder, in that he on the night of 6–7 May 1947, near the Jerusalem-Jericho road, murdered Alexander Rubowitz'. He was asked how he pleaded and replied 'Not guilty.'[48]

Farran went through the next few hours in something of a trance. He was suffering from a bad cold, and Melford Stevenson offered to adjourn at any time if he was in need of a break. But a cough and a temperature did not explain his almost hallucinatory state of mind. In his memoirs he recalled feeling a great weight on him which prevented him registering any emotional response. He mused vaguely that he had given his body to his country to use as it saw fit and if Britain wanted to treat him as a criminal, so be it. If he was set free, then it would be like the end to a comic dream through which he was sleepwalking.[49]

Maxwell Turner opened the trial by describing the events of 6 May as far as they were known from eyewitness statements: how Alexander Rubowitz had left home and had not been seen since that day, despite searches for his body; how he was seen two hours later being pursued by a man in civilian clothes; how he had been grabbed and forced into a waiting automobile; and how a hat bearing a name resembling Farran's had been recovered from the scene of the incident and later handed to the police. He also referred to a conversation between Major Farran and Brigadier Fergusson on the morning following the incident, without giving any details. Moving on to the events of 3 June, he described how Farran had told Sergeant Faulkner 'that he had been let down' and subsequently went with him and Constable Carson to Syria. He returned from there two weeks later and was placed under arrest on 19 June.

The court then heard how Farran had escaped custody, but left behind a notebook and cuttings. Turner did not elaborate on the precise significance of this evidence because 'there was an objection raised to its contents'. Instead, he wound up his opening statement and proceeded to summon the witnesses for the prosecution.[50]

The first to be called was Ya'acov Rubowitz. Speaking through an interpreter he testified to last seeing his younger brother when he left their home at 6 p.m. on 6 May. He recounted how several days later he had come into possession of a light grey felt hat which he handed in to the Mahane Yehuda police station. Maxwell Turner produced the hat and asked Ya'acov to identify it, which he did. The trilby attracted great interest and was 'passed from hand to hand and examined attentively by the court and counsel'. However, under cross-examination by Fearnley-Whittingstall, Ya'acov admitted that in his original statement he had said he could not read all the letters inscribed on the sweatband. Turner next called Inspector John O'Neill who had been on duty at the police station on 13 May and taken the hat from Ya'acov Rubowitz. He testified that 'The hat was not in the same condition as it is now. There were five letters plainly written on the band – F-A-R and A-N – where there is now a smear mark.' Asked if he knew how it had been altered he replied that he had no idea. O'Neill was stood down and the interpreter again took his station for the next witnesses. In succession the three juveniles – Jacob Jacobson, aged thirteen, Moshe Khesin, aged thirteen, and Meir Cohen, aged fifteen – told of seeing a youth being chased along Aharon Street, caught and pushed into a car. But Jacobson admitted that he had not been able to identify anyone in the identity parades and Khesin declared that he had seen the car *twice*, the second time with a different number plate. Turner then called Deputy Superintendent Reginald Sims who was responsible for the identity parades. He confirmed that Farran had not been identified by any of the eyewitnesses at any of the three identification parades with the men of his squad.[51]

There was no doubt that the next witness, Bernard Fergusson, was familiar with Farran. When asked if he recognised the accused, Fergusson 'looked at him, and got a grin back'. Turner then asked the monocled colonel if he used to meet Farran almost every morning in the police officers' mess in Katamon, a suburb of Jerusalem where many service personnel were quartered. Fergusson said yes. Turner then asked if he remembered 'a conversation in early May in the officers' mess? What did Farran say?' Fergusson later wrote that this was his 'cue for refusing to reply'. He told the court that he was 'not prepared, with all respect to the court, to make known details of that conversation because certain of them might in certain circumstances tend to incriminate himself'. This response caused murmurs in the courtroom and the press realised that something was afoot. Turner suspended his examination and turned to address Melford Stevenson. As he did so he reached for a law book adorned with markers that was perched atop a pile on the table and accidentally knocked them onto the floor. While he picked them up and tried to find his authority, Melford Stevenson pre-empted him. Their exchange hinged primarily on the question of whether Fergusson was liable to incriminate himself by answering the question and secondarily on the jurisdictions under which this was at risk of occurring. Turner argued that if his evidence placed him in jeopardy from a private prosecution the Attorney General of Palestine might stay proceedings against him. However, that protection did not extend to England where Fergusson could be prosecuted as 'an accessory after the fact'. Melford Stevenson asked Fergusson to confirm that he had received legal advice on this point, which he did. The Judge Advocate then advised the court that 'English law provided that if a witness were asked a question he might refuse to answer if the answer might expose him to prosecution, and it was his duty to tell the court that they ought to accept the witness's claim.' Thus prevented from getting an answer to the one question that mattered Turner had nothing more to ask. There was clearly no need for Fearnley-Whittingstall to add anything. Fergusson had performed on 'cue' and to perfection.[52]

However, Turner seemed unfazed by this development and moved on briskly to examine a number of policemen who had searched for the body of Alexander Rubowitz. He then called Sergeant William Faulkner who had served under Farran in the special squad. Faulkner testified that Farran told him he was going to Syria because he had been 'let down' and explained how he and Carson felt it was their 'duty' to go with their commander. When Turner had completed his questions, Fearnley-Whittingstall chose to cross-examine Faulkner. He asked him if it was correct that around this time there were certain allegations against Major Farran. Faulkner confirmed that after the publicity about the hat 'rumours were being circulated against Captain Farran and that he was not being given a chance as far as gossip was concerned'.[53]

The case then proceeded chronologically to the events following Farran's return to Palestine and his brief incarceration in the Allenby Barracks. Turner now proposed to introduce as evidence Exhibit B, the notebook in which Farran had written while he was in detention between 17 and 19 June. However, Fearnley-Whittingstall objected 'on the grounds that it contained newspaper cuttings and notes made by Farran in preparation for his defence'. The implications of this were critical for the prosecution. Under the rules governing a court martial, as for a civil trial, the notebook would be covered by legal-professional privilege (more familiar from American TV dramas as client-attorney privilege) if it had been intended by Farran for use by his lawyer. In order to establish the status of the notebook, Turner called the two police officers, Wood and Horner, who had guarded Farran. Wood had returned to England after he had been dismissed from the Palestine Police Force and had been brought at taxpayers' expense all the way from a farm near Droitwich in Worcestershire. Despite this, he was not sure that the notebook produced in court was the one that Farran had written in while in custody. But he did remember 'a superior police officer' telling Farran to make notes about the case and not to rely on memory. Horner recognised the exercise book and recalled how Farran had finished pasting in the cuttings and then exclaimed 'That's that.'[54]

At around two in the afternoon, having apparently continued without a pause since convening, Brigadier Maxwell adjourned the court until 10 a.m. the next day. Perceptive observers filed out into the Talbieh streets knowing that it had not been a good start for the prosecution. Fitzhugh Turner, the correspondent for the European edition of the *New York Herald Tribune*, cabled his paper that 'tonight, with the trial possibly half over, it had not been proved that Captain Farran was involved or indeed that a crime had been committed'. Farran himself realised that the worst was over. Thanks to his lawyers, and with the help of military law, the two pieces of evidence that could have led him to the gallows had been struck out. It was in more than a spirit of jest that he replied to a supportive telegram from his father offering help: 'Don't worry. No help needed.'[55]

When the court reconvened on Thursday morning Turner immediately addressed the admissibility of the notebook. He summoned Lieutenant Colonel Philip Labouchere who recounted how he had accompanied Farran back from Syria on 17 June and been with him when he was placed under guard in the Allenby Barracks. He recalled telling Farran that he would get a court martial and in the presence of Superintendent Kenneth Hadingham 'told Farran that he was to regard him [Labouchere] as his legal adviser'. What Maxwell thereby elicited was actually of more help to the defence than to the prosecution because he had confirmed that Farran understood the established military practice whereby the colonel of a regiment is regarded as the legal counsel of all his subordinates. If Fearnley-Whittingstall could show that the notebook was inspired by Labouchere or intended for his eyes, then it was indeed covered by legal-professional privilege. When Fearnley-Whittingstall cross-examined the colonel he asked what had transpired between him and Farran in that room on 17 June. Labouchere explained that he had given the major a letter of resignation from the Palestine Police Force, which Farran had signed. He added that 'I told him to write down all matters to do with the case he could think of.'

Turner then re-examined Labouchere, but made a hash of it. He asked the colonel if he had any legal qualifications to which Labouchere replied: 'A commanding officer is always a legal adviser to his officers and men'. This was absolutely correct and exposed Turner as woefully uninformed to act in a court martial. Turner next asked the colonel if he was aware that Farran had left the document in his quarters and gone to Syria. By means of this question Turner presumably intended to make the point that Farran had treated the notebook most strangely if he had wanted it used in his trial. He had not asked for it to be given to his colonel and nor had it been obviously left for him. But Labouchere only replied that he knew Farran had left the document and did not know where he had gone. In fact, he added, no one then knew where Farran had disappeared to. Turner unaccountably left it at that. Instead, the prosecution, defence and the Judge Advocate became embroiled in a discussion of legal-professional privilege that went on until past midday when Maxwell adjourned the court for half an hour to enable its members to examine the document in question. Melford Stevenson instructed the court to look at the notebook and to decide whether the defendant had 'written purely to unburden his mind', as the prosecution submitted, or if it appeared to be intended for use in a legal process. When the court reconvened nearly an hour later the president announced that it did consider the notes had been written for a legal purpose, that the exercise book was accordingly covered by legal-professional privilege, and was not admissible as evidence. This decision crippled the prosecution case. Turner went through the motions by finishing his examination of Wood and Horner. He then called the officer on duty when Farran surrendered and asked him to recall what occurred. The reply was as short as it was useless. The prosecution concluded on this lame note.[56]

Fearnley-Whittingstall then stood. He wasted no time calling defence witnesses. Instead he submitted that the accused had no case to answer. There was not a 'shred of evidence against Farran'. The evidence was 'too flimsy to prove that the young man forcibly taken into custody on 6 May was Alexander Rubowitz'. None of Farran's squad had been identified as the man who chased the boy. None of the eyewitnesses had identified Farran, either. 'Whoever it was who took that young man – or a young man – into custody, it was not one of Farran's squad. It was not Major Farran.' As for the hat, it could not be traced to the major and 'there were other Farrans in Jerusalem'. Having dismissed the evidence as insubstantial Fearnley-Whittingstall turned to a crucial point of law, citing a decision made in 1758. 'For generations now no man has ever been convicted of murder or manslaughter unless there was evidence of the death of the person he was charged with killing. There is no evidence of the death of Alexander Rubowitz.' To be sure there was evidence that he had disappeared, but arduous investigations had failed to locate a body. As a parting shot he said that although it had not been entered in the trial, there was evidence that when he disappeared Rubowitz was allegedly putting up posters for the Stern Gang.

After Fearnley-Whittingstall had completed his oration, Maxwell Turner rose. His concluding statement was short and half-hearted. He told the court that 'He had first to prove that there had been a killing, and then that it amounted to murder by the accused. There was no evidence of the dead body of Alexander Rubowitz, and it was necessary to fall back on strong circumstantial evidence.' Consequently, his case had rested on the written statement by Farran and on the testimony of Colonel Fergusson, but neither was admitted by the court. 'I am bound to say', he continued, 'there is no strong circumstantial evidence, and it would not be proper for you to convict. In these circumstances there is no case for Major Farran to answer.' Unaccountably Turner did not call Superintendent Hadingham as a witness although this officer had conducted the investigation into the alleged abduction of Rubowitz and had taken Fergusson's statement. Nor, apparently, did he attempt to use Hadingham's report which had reconstructed the events on the night of 6 May. The reasons for this astounding omission can only be guessed at. The court adjourned for lunch and when it reconvened in the afternoon to hear the ruling the atmosphere had changed appreciably. The Bedouin next to Fergusson whispered to him, 'It must be all right: they don't look like people who are going to punish somebody.'[57]

It only remained for Melford Stevenson to perform his role as Judge Advocate and advise the court of the relevant military law. He said that even if it was assumed that it was Rubowitz who was abducted on 6 May 'there was no evidence, direct or circumstantial, showing that Rubowitz was dead; there were discrepancies in the evidence on the lettering which had been on the hat; and where no body or part of a body had been found the law was clear that the accused could not be convicted unless there was evidence of killing. In the absence of such evidence no onus lay on the accused to establish innocence and, even if there had been a confession, this confession could not be acted on without other evidence.' The court retired at ten minutes to three in the afternoon. Fifteen minutes later the six officers of the court reassembled. Brigadier Maxwell stood to deliver their verdict and had just begun when he noticed that Farran was not there. Maxwell paused while the defendant was hurriedly brought into the room. He then announced 'The court has considered that no prima facie case has been established against you and you are acquitted.'

At this there was a spontaneous burst of applause from army officers and policemen in the audience. One of them shouted 'Good show.' Yedidiya, Ya'acov and Nehamiah Rubowitz sat in stunned silence. Farran, his face flushed, shook hands with Lieutenant Colonel Labouchere and walked briskly out of the courtroom. Fergusson did not even have time to speak to him. But a pretty young woman who had been sitting with the officers of the Galloping 3rd rushed over and squeezed Farran's arm before he was hustled out of the building. Then he vanished again, this time legally and a free man.[58]

5

The Hero's Return and the Terrorists' Revenge

As soon as Roy Farran stepped out of the courtroom he was literally grabbed by two officers, rushed through the building and bundled
into an armoured car that was waiting at an exit with its engine
running. Once he was on board it roared off through Jerusalem
with jeeps to the front and rear, each mounting a heavy machine
gun and manned by battle-ready troops of the Highland Light
Infantry. From Talbieh he was driven to the British Army camp at
Gaza where he spent the night. Soldiers guarded him while he slept.
At dawn the next morning he was flown in a light plane to the
British military base at Fayid in the Suez Canal Zone. From there
he went to Port Said and embarked on the troopship *Orduna* bound
for Liverpool with 1,900 soldiers and 100 civilians on board.[1]

The departure of the other principals was equally unceremonious.
John Bickford-Smith and William Fearnley-Whittingstall were
packed and ready to go. M. W. Jacobs, the sharp-eyed reporter for
the *Palestine Post*, noted that when the court had reconvened on
Thursday morning 'three or four bundles of law books brought by
Mr Fearnley-Whittingstall from England, were already lying tied
up on one of the tables, labelled "Not required on journey." It was
plain from the close of business on the previous day, and possibly
even earlier, that he harboured few doubts about the outcome'.
Bickford-Smith and Fearnley-Whittingstall were driven at speed to
Lydda Airport in an army staff car with a heavily armed escort.
The distinguished counsel was hurried out so quickly that he didn't
have time to make a much-needed visit to the toilet. Midway to

the airport while the convoy was still deep in the Jerusalem hills he insisted on stopping so that he could relieve himself. The officer commanding the escort had been ordered not to stop under any circumstances and agreed only under protest. Fearnley-Whittingstall met the call of nature by the roadside, surrounded by nervous squaddies with rifles and Sten guns at the ready.[2]

Bernard Fergusson was summoned to police headquarters and 'invited' to resign, which he did without hesitation. He remembered being told 'to be out of the country for the sake of my skin within thirty-six hours'. The advice was hardly necessary and he made his preparations to leave with extreme caution. When he flew out of Jerusalem's Qalandiya Airport at dusk the next day he felt lucky to be alive. But he was convinced that his career was in ruins. 'I was turning my back on a disastrous episode', he wrote in his memoirs, 'one on which I had embarked with high hopes of being effective. Far from doing any good, I had inadvertently done positive harm.' He flew directly to Aqsa camp near Gaza where he stayed overnight. A relay of NCOs voluntarily guarded his quarters throughout his stay, a gesture of solidarity and respect that greatly moved him.[3]

These hasty and furtive departures were completely understandable. Jews in Palestine regarded the verdict as a blatant whitewash. The militants seethed with hatred and plotted revenge. There was little patience for the view expressed by Fergusson that 'the prosecution case was compiled with the utmost thoroughness, and that the police authorities, smarting from the scandal, had leaned over backwards to make it stick'. Even a few in the armed forces had their doubts about the quality of 'British justice'. John Watson wrote to his mother that 'Anti-Semitism and fascism in Hyde Park or even in the East End – like communism – is understandable, but in the army, and in high places is ominous. Farran, who tortured and murdered a Jewish youth has been let off scot-free, because the body couldn't be found, though even pro-British Army people here make no secret of their suspicions that the army search parties found the body, and had it liquidated, though of course they add "Jolly good show, what!"'[4]

In his weekly intelligence summary for 4 October 1947, the high commissioner reported that 'the reaction of the Jewish press and public is bitter'. With strained sobriety the *Palestine Post* told its readers that 'The case is closed, the law has had its way. The correctness of the judgment in law is not to be disputed.' But then the questions began. Of what did Fergusson fear to be incriminated? 'A court of law should draw its own conclusions when a witness declines to give evidence.' Jewish suspects were imprisoned 'on even fewer shreds of evidence than those which were so surprisingly missing in the Rubowitz case'. Finally, abandoning any pretence of equanimity it concluded: 'A good show indeed, and the applause was well deserved.'[5]

Over the next few days the criticism grew still fiercer as journalists picked holes in the investigation and the judicial proceedings. Jacob Ruthenberg in the *Palestine Post* neatly summed them up. Why hadn't the police inquired into the ownership of the car used for the abduction on 6 May? Why did the court not hear any information about Farran's activities on that day? Why was no legal action taken against any other persons involved in the abduction? Why wasn't a lawyer representing the Rubowitz family present at any of the identity parades? Why was no effort made to see if the hat belonged to Farran, or even if it fitted him? How could the charge allege that Rubowitz was murdered near the Jerusalem-Jericho road if there was apparently no evidence that he had been abducted or killed? If the evidence was really so slight why did the authorities feel it warranted prosecution at all? Ruthenberg ended with sentiments that echoed those of the Jewish community: 'it is, unfortunately, the general feeling that it was not Captain Farran who was "let down" by his superiors, but that the people of this country were badly let down by the police'.[6]

The international press was no less sceptical. Fitzhugh Turner, for the *New York Herald Tribune*, was puzzled that Fergusson had been allowed to get away without making any declaration. 'The court accepted his silence although it was pointed out [that] Palestine civil and military authorities had promised him immunity.' He concluded that 'What happened to the Rubowitz boy — a question of considerable interest to the Jewish residents of Palestine — remained after the trial as great a mystery as ever.' Perceptive commentators in Britain also registered disquiet. According to the left-wing *New Statesman* (the assistant editor was Dick Crossman, a member of the Anglo-American Committee and one of Bevin's chief antagonists), 'It is widely believed that flying squads have been given a free hand to counter-attack the Irgun by the use of its own methods so rough that in certain circumstances the victim died and the body had to be disposed of.' The weekly recalled Sir Charles Wickham's warning 'against this sort of commando campaign which merely intensifies the hatred and increases the risks to decent policemen in uniform'. It called for a parliamentary inquiry into what had gone wrong. But this was an unusual reaction. Most British newspapers celebrated the result without reservation. The *Daily Express* and *Daily Mirror* reporters tracked down 'Minnie' Farran and extracted some cloyingly sentimental expressions of relief from her. The verdict was 'the news for which we have all been hoping and praying', she said. But she had known it would be all right when, the night before the judgment, she heard on the radio Roy's favourite melody, 'The Road to the Isles'. This was the Farran family 'signature tune' and she knew then that he would return safely as he had done during the war. In the best tradition of jingo-journalism the *Daily Mail* proclaimed gleefully, 'Fighting Farran Is Coming Home'.[7]

This triumphalist chorus had the Jewish underground spitting fury. LEHI had suspended its operations while the future of Palestine was being debated at the UN, but within hours of Farran's acquittal it issued a statement that the ceasefire excluded 'provocative acts by the British'. Friedman-Yellin, the operational commander of LEHI, was already planning to exact revenge for the death of Alexander Rubowitz and he would not rest until then. Nor had the Rubowitz family given up hope of redress by legal means. Within days of the verdict Ya'acov Rubowitz filed an application for the arrest of Roy Farran on a charge of murder. For good reason the War Office refused to disclose his whereabouts.[8]

Roy was oblivious to the immediate fallout from the verdict. He spent the voyage home on the *Orduna* reading, sunbathing and strolling on deck. It was like a rest cure. Although he was supposed to be travelling anonymously, knowledge of his presence on board soon spread beyond the two officers with whom he shared a cabin and he was treated like a celebrity. The unprecedented security arrangements that heralded his arrival in Liverpool on the evening of 13 October certainly befitted a star or a statesman. Before the ship berthed the landing stage was cleared and cordoned off with barriers. Troops, military police and the local constabulary were posted around the docks. Police cars were stationed at the entrances and special passes were required to get into the security zone. Even the Mersey was illuminated with floodlights while police launches kept an eye on the shipping lanes. As part of the security arrangements Roy disembarked half an hour before anybody else, escorted by two officers. As he descended the gangway hundreds of troops crowded along the side of the ship raised a cheer that was echoed by the dockers down below. In Roy's words, he was received like a popular hero.[9]

The warmth of this reception was not only a reflection of Farran's heroic reputation or even his recent acquittal. It was also a vivid expression of public opinion in Liverpool. Since the anti-Jewish riots on 1–4 August, Liverpool had seethed with hostility towards the Jews. The disturbances there had been more serious and prolonged than anywhere else. On the night of Saturday 2 August a Jewish-owned furniture-making factory was set alight by arsonists and extensively damaged. On the Sunday a clothing store in Myrtle Street belonging to a Jewish family was smashed up by a mob 'several hundred strong'. Other shops were damaged, too. Twenty arrests were made over the weekend. Crowds gathered in the streets again on bank holiday Monday. They threw bricks through shop windows and looted the already battered clothing store. The damaged cabinet works was set on fire again. Police were forced to disperse mobs throughout the day and made two arrests for suspected arson. In an effort to calm the atmosphere the lord mayor made a statement to the local press condemning the riots as 'unfair' and 'unEnglish' because they hit at innocent Jews who had nothing to do with the events in Palestine. Whereas in other cities the ill-feeling over the murder of the two sergeants subsided, Liverpool continued to simmer. For weeks afterwards workers in the local abattoir refused to co-operate with Jewish butchers in the slaughter of animals according to the Jewish dietary regulations, forcing Jews to import kosher meat from Manchester. Jews were verbally abused in the streets and stones were thrown at their cars. The Liverpool dockers who cheered Farran were a lingering articulation of the antipathy generated by Jewish terrorism.[10]

Once he was on dry land the 'bronzed' and 'smiling' Farran was taken to the Movement Control Office where his papers were quickly processed. He then appeared at a press conference that had been arranged by the War Office. The flashbulbs and the barrage of questions came as a bit of a shock and he announced at the outset that he would not answer any questions of a 'political or controversial nature'. In reply to enquiries about his future he merely said that he had no idea what lay in store for him. He had to report to the War Office for a formal interview and it was conceivable that he might be posted back to his regiment in Palestine. In the meantime, his father had told him to 'go away somewhere quiet'. He regaled the journalists with the story of his high-security exit from Palestine, but when asked about the menacing statement issued by LEHI he retorted 'I am not afraid of threats.' The army and the police were not so blasé. He was driven away at speed in a police car with a military escort to an undisclosed destination. Having shaken off the press he travelled to Dunblane in Scotland to stay with Bill Stirling, his former commanding officer in the SAS and one of his staunchest allies while he was under arrest. With Stirling's help and the connivance of the army Farran expertly dropped out of sight. But he left a trail of controversy behind him.[11]

While the press conference in Liverpool had added to Farran's celebrity in Britain it did not meet universal approval. A Labour MP, George Thomas, asked the Secretary of State for War, Emanuel Shinwell, to explain just why Farran was given this privilege and 'whether he now proposes to grant similar facilities to other members of the army returning from that country'. Shinwell replied that the interview was arranged 'in response to the numerous enquiries received from the press'. 'In view of the very exceptional circumstances in which Major Farran returned to this country' he did not anticipate that such an eventuality would arise again. However, for the next year Farran's name was never far from the front pages. His situation remained 'exceptional'.[12]

Even while he was on board the *Orduna* the Rubowitz family were in hot pursuit. Reuven Nochimowski, their legal adviser, had dug up an obscure statute that enabled the authorities in one part of the British Empire to take legal action against a person resident in another part: the Fugitive Offenders Act 1881. On 17 October, Ya'acov Rubowitz applied under this Act to the Jerusalem magistrate's court for the issue of an arrest warrant against Farran on a charge of kidnapping for the purpose of murder. This move took the authorities quite by surprise but the judge, Dr Stultz, had to reserve judgment over the Sabbath which gave them a chance to organise a response. When court business resumed the Attorney General, Leslie Gibson, issued a stay – that is, he blocked the application – on the grounds that Nochimowski had not provided any new evidence or new eyewitnesses.[13]

Nochimowski did not give up. He enlisted the assistance of the Jewish Agency to locate a suitable English law firm to represent the Rubowitz family in London. The agency expressed willing and while they argued about who would bear the cost Nochimowski went ahead with another application. Against his better judgment and with no expectation of success, on 22 October Stultz issued an arrest warrant against Farran under Section 236 of the Criminal Code Ordinance (Abduction for Murder). The government of Palestine responded by arguing before the magistrate that the local judicial authorities would have to be satisfied that there was a prima facie case before they could take any action. But the Colonial Office, the Home Office and the War Office took no chances and put civil servants to work trying to understand this arcane legal procedure.[14] The flurry of activity ended when the Attorney General of Palestine again quashed the application. In a letter to the Rubowitz family Leslie Gibson explained, for the second time, that there had been no positive identification of Farran while the hat was circumstantial evidence and by itself did not provide sufficient grounds to justify criminal proceedings.[15]

Farran was not unaware of these legal battles. He stayed in touch with Robert Fearnley-Whittingstall and when the first effort was made to issue an arrest warrant, broke his silence by speaking to a journalist from the *Daily Herald*. With a mixture of black humour and weariness he said 'I am certainly no fugitive', but added that 'I had no idea it was so complicated.' A few days later he admitted to another journalist that 'It is quite a shock. Surely they cannot go all over it again. I was acquitted on the major charge, and I do not see how they can start proceedings on a lesser charge.'[16]

On 30 October, Farran appeared in public for the first time since his return. The occasion was a ceremony at the home of the American Ambassador at Princess Gate in Kensington, London, at which he was presented with the US Legion of Merit. The medal had been awarded to him in April 1945 by President Truman in recognition of the raid he led on the German Army corps headquarters near La Spezia. Roy's mother and father attended the presentation, proudly seated on gilt chairs under a glittering chandelier. At the appointed moment Farran marched into the room 'parade-ground style' and came to attention in front of Major General Clayton Bissell with such vigour that the floor shook. Bissell read the citation, which Truman had signed personally, and warmly shook hands with the hero. Farran then did a smart about-turn and marched out – only to realise that he had forgotten to collect the medal. Afterwards he held a press conference at which he revealed that his memoirs had been accepted for publication. He explained to the crowd of journalists: 'I suppose I am an expert in the underground way of warfare; and it sets out my adventures. It also describes how I got into a fix in Palestine, how I got to Syria, and back again to Palestine.' Asked about his future he said that there was no question of his resigning from the army. 'In fact, the army is anxious that I should do no such thing.' If he eventually decided to end his military career he said he would go to East Africa 'and manage a bush-clearing firm. That offer is open to me.'[17]

The ceremony was overshadowed, though, by threatening letters that had been received at his parents' home over the preceding days. They emanated from the E1 postal district in London which was contiguous with the predominantly Jewish-populated East End. The message in Hebrew spelled out 'Revenge'. Farran made light of the threats. 'I find the whole matter rather amusing', he told the

Daily Herald. However, in the light of the previous Jewish terrorist attacks, Scotland Yard took them very seriously indeed. The letters were sent to the police laboratory at Hendon for forensic examination. Farran and his parents were discreetly protected by Special Branch during the whole of their stay in London.[18]

The wariness of the security services was more than justified. In October 1947 Nathan Friedman-Yellin set in motion an ambitious operation to take revenge on three of LEHI's most hated adversaries. It had threatened several times to assassinate Bevin and Sir Evelyn Barker. Now Farran was added to the list. To carry out the mission Friedman-Yellin selected Ya'acov Heruti, a young Palestinian Jew who had already distinguished himself in the ranks of LEHI. Heruti was born in Tel Aviv in 1927 of Polish parentage. He was educated at the elite Herzliya Gymnasium and on graduation enrolled in the Jewish settlement police, an auxiliary arm of the Palestine Police Force. While still a teenager he became enthralled by the nationalist poetry of Uri Zvi Greenberg and the writings of Avraham Stern, LEHI's founding ideologist and organiser. Soon after joining the police Heruti secretly entered the ranks of LEHI and gravitated to the technical department where he specialised in bomb making. Although he was only twenty years old by the time he arrived in London he was already a hardened terrorist with ample experience.[19]

As cover for his mission Heruti posed as a law student and enrolled in London University. He then set about recruiting local helpers. As MI5 had predicted the cell members came from right-wing Zionist groups like BETAR and the Hebrew Legion. During 1946–7 these groups had grown in size and militancy thanks to the British determination to prevent the survivors of Nazi mass murder reaching Palestine. Heruti was able to marshal a dozen volunteers to gather information about the targets and perform routine tasks as couriers. The operation was mainly funded by wealthy local sympathisers, one 'Park Lane Jew' in particular. This was where British Jewish circles intersected with the Palestinian terrorists and where they were most vulnerable to penetration by the security services. The Hebrew Legion was formed in late 1945 as a breakaway from the non-political Association of Jewish Ex-Servicemen. Its inspiration came from Major Samuel Weiser, an ex-regular army officer aged forty-two, and Lieutenant David de Lange, twenty-nine years old, a member of the Royal Navy Volunteer Reserve. De Lange had seen active service with the RNVR from 1942 to 1946, when he was demobilised and went to work for a shoe-making company. Like Weiser he was a right-wing Zionist. Together they aligned their new creation with the Hebrew Committee for National Liberation in America. This was one of several front-organisations set up by Hillel Kook, operating under the *nom de guerre* Peter Bergson, that were used to channel funds to the Irgun. The committee also specialised in vituperative anti-British propaganda, much of it written by the playwright Ben Hecht. The legion emulated this propaganda work, bringing out a news-sheet, *The Legionnaire*, that hovered on the edge of sedition. Weiser also organised speakers at Hyde Park Corner, where he was a regular (and courageous) performer. More seriously from the standpoint of the security services, the legion attracted young British Jews returning from military service and there was a danger that it radicalised them so that they moved from violent language towards violent action. Given its connections in the USA and Palestine, MI5 also believed it was likely to serve as a 'point of contact' for any terrorists sent by the Irgun or LEHI to Britain. For all these reasons it was held securely in the sights of MI5 and the domestic counter-espionage agencies.[20]

J. C. Robertson, MI5's expert on Zionism, was absolutely right when he identified right-wing Zionist groups such as BETAR and the Hebrew Legion as potential 'points of contact' for Jewish terrorists arriving from abroad. Doris Katz, a member of LEHI, considered Weiser and de Lange amongst the few like-minded activists she could count on when she arrived in London in the summer of 1947. Heruti, too, was able to draw on this reservoir of support. Local militants provided the cell with a safe house in a North London suburb where they stored their small arsenal of revolvers and explosives. He obtained the dynamite by the simple expedient of writing to LEHI sympathisers in the United States who sent it to him by post. It still took several months for him to build up the operation and while he was accumulating the necessary resources he concentrated single-mindedly on getting intelligence about Bevin. The Foreign Secretary remained target number one because the Jewish underground still regarded him as the greatest threat to Jewish statehood.[21]

Between Farran's detention and his trial, the UN Special Committee on Palestine had conducted its research and published its report. It unanimously recommended ending the British Mandate and a majority proposed partition, with Jerusalem as a UN trust, after a two-year transitional period supervised by Britain. Attlee was content with partition, which was unfolding in India, while Cunningham was positively eager to wind up the mandate. The chiefs of staff clung to the hope of retaining bases and influence in post-mandatory Palestine: however, they knew they lacked the means to enforce a settlement that both Jews and Arabs rejected. Bevin regarded partition as unfair to the Arabs and was determined not to expend British resources enforcing a solution that he regarded as unjust, and certainly not one that antagonised the Arab states. He advocated announcing British withdrawal, unconditionally, so as to escape any odium for whatever settlement prevailed. Consequently, on 26 September 1947 the colonial secretary informed the UN that Britain would withdraw without imposing a UN-dictated solution on Palestine. The Zionist leadership believed this was a bluff, and Bevin may have harboured a distant hope that the prospect of a rapid pull-out would scare both Jews and Arabs into accepting British rule after all. But the army had begun thinning its forces and informed the government that they could be out by the start of August 1948. On 11 November 1947, the Cabinet agreed to this date as the termination of the British presence. Meanwhile, in New York, UN committees and subcommittees deliberated the future of Palestine amidst intense diplomatic activity. British representatives declined to get involved. Eventually only partition was left in play. On 28 November the UN General Assembly approved by a two-thirds majority the division of Palestine into a Jewish state and an Arab state, with Jerusalem under international control. For the next six months, while communal warfare between Jews and Arabs flared across Palestine, the British armed forces remained studiedly neutral; their orders were to engage only if attacked. Perversely, the Irgun and LEHI refused to believe that Bevin meant what he said, that the British would really leave, and continued to strike British targets.[22]

The events in Palestine still cast their shadow over Farran. In December 1947 Roy resigned his commission from the army and became free to do and say what he pleased. Soon afterwards he published an article in the *Daily Express* setting forth his views on the fighting that was raging between Jews and Arabs, with British troops caught in the middle. Drawing on his own observations he explained the 'disillusioned hopelessness which has led the Arabs to war'. They had lived in Palestine since ancient times and helped Britain in the war against the Turks only to find that British troops stayed in their land to help foster a Jewish national home. So it was that 'the poisonous flower has been planted by us'. Arabs were the most hospitable people 'so long as the guest does not abuse the rules of hospitality by turning out the landlord', which was exactly what the Jews were trying to do. True, they performed wonders cultivating the land, but as more Jews arrived, fleeing from persecution, their demands became increasingly strident. They had resorted to violence and now had aspirations to control all the territory from Egypt to Iraq. 'Small wonder', he wrote, 'that all the nations of the Middle East regard aggressive Zionism as a menace to their security.' The bearers of Judaism had become a 'bellicose nationalistic race'. But he prophesied that they would be defeated and, at the same time, that anti-Semitism in England would escalate. The Jews had no one to blame for this except their extremist leaders.[23]

It was hardly surprising that after venting such sentiments a rumour gathered momentum that Farran was going to fight for the Arabs. The *Palestine Post* and the *People* newspaper in London reported that he was amongst dozens of British ex-servicemen who were offering their skills to the Arab Office in London. A spokesman for the office denied that they had been in contact with Farran, but the canard fuelled the impression in official circles that he was a loose cannon. There was real anxiety inside the Foreign Office that his memoirs would reveal details of his mission in Palestine that could damage the government. According to Jon Kimche, a well-connected journalist on the Palestine beat, two weeks after the first instalment of Roy's memoirs appeared in the *Sunday Express* the Foreign Office 'privately approached' the paper and suggested that 'it might be advisable to cease publishing them'. Apparently the Foreign Office was worried by 'Farran's extraordinary and almost embarrassing frankness in these articles'.[24]

Indeed, anyone familiar with the facts of the Rubowitz affair would have been able to infer a good deal more about the special squads and Farran's own activity than the government preferred. But Roy allowed the confessional style of the opening and closing chapters on Palestine to go only so far. His account of his own behaviour remained ambiguous, the fate of Rubowitz an anomaly. In any case, few British readers were going to weep over the unexplained fate of a Stern Gang member. On the other hand, they thrilled to Farran's wartime exploits, brilliantly rendered in vivid, unaffected prose. Farran adopted a self-deprecating, mock-heroic style that was hugely endearing, while his racy descriptions of the young women who crossed his path gave the book a distinct sex appeal. It was a fantastic success, ran through several editions, and sold 300,000 copies. Thanks to *Winged Dagger* Farran was able to repay his legal debts and look forward to a comfortable life.

However, there was a shadow hanging over him. Since the end of the court martial, Robert Fearnley-Whittingstall had been trying to get his hands on the notes Farran had compiled while in detention in June. His chief object was to have the incriminating notebook and any copies of it destroyed. The Judge Advocate General complied with his request within a few days and got rid of all the copies in England. At the end of October, Fearnley-Whittingstall obtained from the army in Palestine a sworn affidavit that thirteen copies of the notes had been destroyed on 2 October at the military court in Jerusalem and two more copies on 15 October at police headquarters. One was still held by the chief secretary of the Palestine government and one by the Palestine Police Force. However, Fearnley-Whittingstall was disturbed that any were left and demanded that Sir Henry Gurney eliminate them. Gurney was unwilling to comply. He disputed whether the decision of the court martial that the notebook was privileged 'imposes an obligation to destroy documents made in the course of a criminal investigation'. This reply infuriated Fearnley-Whittingstall who vehemently contested the suggestion that the notes were composed in relation to a 'criminal investigation', presumably because his client had been acquitted of any criminal acts. He bluntly warned Sir Henry that unless he had a positive response within ten days he would write to the Secretary of State for the Colonies 'with a view to the matter being ventilated in Parliament'.[25]

Vivian Fox-Strangeways, now the Solicitor General for the Palestine government, tried to explain to the Colonial Office why they thought the demand for destruction of the document was 'somewhat unusual'. 'It formed part of a CID case file, is therefore the property of the Palestine police, and should be held with the file to which it relates for as long as that is preserved.' Furthermore, there were 'other people concerned in the case'. There was no danger of it falling into the wrong hands as it was kept 'in what we regard as absolutely safe custody'. In the New Year, Gurney elaborated: 'So far as the police are concerned the disappearance of Rubowitz and his presumed murder is an unsolved crime, in which others besides Farran are believed to be involved. The case has not yet been closed and in the ordinary way until it was concluded the police would not destroy any evidence in their possession throwing light on the matter.' Gurney referred to Nochimowski's attempts to revive the case as an example of what might happen in future, although he doubted that another effort to arrest Farran would ever be made. 'If, however, further evidence were to be produced similar proceedings might have to continue. In that event the statement made by Farran would be relevant and I am advised that another court, particularly a civil court, might not accept the plea of privilege if raised before it.' Although it was unlikely that the document could be admissible in evidence in the trial of anyone but Farran, 'nevertheless, a detailed and apparently correct account of important incidents on the night in question is of great assistance to the police in assessing the value of evidence put forward in connection with the crime'.[26]

This was an extraordinary statement. Eight months after the abduction of Alexander Rubowitz, the government of Palestine seemed to show an interest in who, apart from Farran, might have been involved in his disappearance. At the court martial William Fearnley-Whittingstall had successfully persuaded the court that there had been no abduction, no death, no murder, no crime and no criminal; but despite the part they played in reaching this verdict, the most senior officials in the Palestine government now referred to the death of the boy and described it as a 'crime'. This objection to destroying the evidence implies that there was a grotesque miscarriage of justice on 1–2 October 1947. Cunningham, Gurney and Gray were now behaving as if there had been a kidnapping and a murder, and that the criminals were still at large. If they had always believed this, how could they have connived in Farran's acquittal? How could they envisage the possibility of another trial for kidnapping and murder unless they rejected the findings of the court martial? But this was precisely what Robert Fearnley-Whittingstall and Roy Farran were afraid of. Because they knew the truth, they could not allow the incriminating documents to survive. The issue was, like the trial itself, a matter of life or death.

Officials at the Colonial Office who did not grasp this were naturally exasperated. William Mathieson minuted 'I am at a loss to understand why at this stage the Palestine government should concern itself with a wrangle of such small consequence.' They were especially irritated when Fearnley-Whittingstall arranged for a Conservative MP, Brigadier Anthony Head, to ask a Parliamentary Question about the document. On 21 January 1948, Head, a future Secretary of State for War, asked Creech Jones, 'Whether he is aware that the Palestine Government has refused to deliver up possession of certain copies of a document exhibited at the summary of evidence taken against Captain Roy Alexander Farran on a charge of murder on which he was acquitted, and which the court which tried him ruled was a privileged document; and what action he proposes to take about it.' Creech Jones replied that he was aware of the matter and was in communication with Jerusalem about it. Head persisted with his supplementary question and asked the Secretary of State to 'see that they destroy this document immediately'. To which the minister wearily responded that he would try to speed up progress although it was 'a matter of considerable legal complexity'.[27]

The Colonial Office wilted under this pressure. Creech Jones told Cunningham that since it was unlikely the notebook could be used in a subsequent trial this justification for retaining it was indeed shaky. Cunningham finally caved in. The Rubowitz case was 'to all intents and purposes, closed and there would be the obvious disadvantage in having public opinion again stirred up as it would be if Farran's solicitors brought an action to recover the copy'. The Palestine government agreed to inform Laurence Collins and Fearnley-Whittingstall 'without admitting the justice of their claims' that it would be destroyed on 1 April 1948. Even so, Cunningham and Gurney refused to supply an affidavit of destruction; that was more than their dignity could bear.[28]

This still did not satisfy the terrier-like Robert Fearnley-Whittingstall. The threat of a further delay elicited an astounding letter to the colonial secretary. After he had recited the arguments for destroying the notebook Fearnley-Whittingstall continued: 'You may, however, consider that there is a more far-reaching aspect of this matter, in the fact that if, by some mischance the failure to destroy any outstanding copy of this document were to result in its falling into the hands of a militant Jewish organisation, it will clearly be suggested, not only that our client was in fact guilty of the charge of which he was acquitted, but that the conduct of his trial upon that charge was a deliberate and successful attempt to pervert the course of natural justice.' In other words, Fearnley-Whittingstall believed that the most compelling reason for compliance was that Farran was a murderer and that if the proof of his culpability emerged it would expose the entire Palestine administration to accusations of criminal conduct. This sort of behaviour was more typical of gangsters, but Fearnley-Whittingstall had got the measure of the men he was dealing with and they got what they deserved from him.[29]

Remarkably, at the same time as Robert Fearnley-Whittingstall was blackmailing the Colonial Office into ordering the destruction of evidence relevant to an ongoing murder investigation in order to protect his client, his firm were applying to the Foreign Office for assistance in launching a libel case against Sumner Welles, former Undersecretary of State in the US government, who had repeated the allegations about Farran's role in the murder of Rubowitz in the *New York Times* in August the previous year. In a letter to Bevin they drew attention to the article which contained 'not only the gravest allegations against Captain Farran, but a singularly outspoken attack against the policy of HMG towards Palestine'. Farran's legal representatives explained with uncharacteristic solicitude that 'he recognises clearly that it might embarrass His Majesty's Government if he failed to refer the matter to you before initiating proceedings'. In fact, their real objective was to get a meeting with government officials to enlist their aid in the case. Foreign Office legal advisers took the matter seriously and tried to set up a three-way meeting including Lord Russell and Colonial Office personnel. But when one of them approached the Colonial Office they received a stinging reply. William Mathieson reported to his colleagues that 'I said that we did not wish to be involved in this. I also warned him about the character of the solicitors for Captain Farran.'[30]

In the end their unscrupulous methods worked. On 24 April 1948, the high commissioner for Palestine sent a message to the Colonial Office enclosing a 'Certificate of Destruction' signed by the acting assistant inspector general of the Palestine CID. This was the last in a series of tetchy letters and telegrams between the high commissioner, the Colonial Office and Fearnley-Whittingstall confirming the destruction of every last copy of Farran's confession. It was one of the final acts of the mandate. Beginning in mid November 1947, Lieutenant General Sir Gordon MacMillan had conducted the masterly withdrawal of 70,000 personnel in the army, RAF, navy and Palestine Police Force, as well as 210,000 tons of stores. Some units relocated to Egypt, where Britain retained the right to station troops thanks to a decision of the UN, others to Tripolitania and the UK. At the start of 1948 MacMillan regrouped the diminished garrison and began to pull units out, sector by sector. 6th Airborne, veterans of the campaign, commenced its departure at the start of March. In April the 1st Infantry Division set up a fortified enclave around Haifa to prepare for the withdrawal of all remaining military and civilian personnel. On 13 May, the high commissioner, the General Officer Commanding the armed forces in Palestine, and the Palestine Police Force evacuated Jerusalem.

The following day David Ben-Gurion declared the independence of the state of Israel. Twenty-four hours later Sir Alan Cunningham boarded a Royal Navy vessel and sailed out of Haifa. It was perhaps fitting that a document recording the exploits of the special squads, which had contributed so much to the erosion of British legitimacy, should have figured so prominently in the death throes of the mandate.[31]

By contrast, fortune smiled on Roy Farran. The publication of *Winged Dagger* was a runaway success and Roy was feted at a Foyles literary lunch held in the Dorchester Hotel. On 10 February he was decorated with the Distinguished Service Order and received the second bar to his Military Cross at a ceremony held in Buckingham Palace. The medals were presented by King George VI who had apparently followed Roy's adventures and travails over the past year. Afterwards Roy informed reporters that 'The king told me he was very glad the whole business was over. I told the king that I had resigned from the army and was now engaged in industry.' In March the *London Gazette* announced that he was promoted to the honorary rank of major, a mark of the esteem in which he was held by his regiment and the army.[32]

Farran did not neglect his prospects as a newly minted civilian. To gain experience in a non-military field he took up an engagement with Keir and Cawdor Ltd, a Glasgow-based construction company. Keir and Cawdor was responsible for a hydroelectric project on Loch Sloy where he worked as a quarry manager for six months. But his real interest in the company lay with their extensive undertakings in East Africa: this was where he saw his career leading. While he was in Scotland he spent much of his spare time hunting and fishing with his former SAS commanding officer Bill Stirling at his home near Dunblane in the Perthshire countryside.[33]

He did not know that he was being stalked. Early in 1948 Friedman-Yellin called off Heruti's operation against Bevin because LEHI headquarters thought it was unnecessary in view of Britain's imminent withdrawal from Palestine. But the plan to kill Barker and Farran advanced inexorably. At first Heruti's team had no idea where to find Farran. All they knew was the name and address of his solicitor, which became public knowledge during the trial.

Heruti placed them under observation in the hope of catching Farran making a visit, but to no avail. The press coverage of Roy's activities finally gave them the break they needed. Details about Roy's home had appeared in newspapers as long ago as August 1947. One of Heruti's team later stated that he followed Farran to his home, but events suggest this was untrue. The LEHI group certainly found out where he lived, but there was no accurate reconnaissance of the address. Only this could explain the tragedy that followed.[34]

On the morning of 3 May 1948, Mary Farran, Roy's mother, left the family house on Histons Hill, Codsall, near Wolverhampton, to go to work. Stephen Farran had already left for the factory where he was employed. As Mary walked down the road she passed Eileen Hayes, the part-time postwoman, who cheerfully told her: 'Nothing much for you – only a parcel.' Mary knew that her younger sons, Rex, aged twenty-five, and Keith, aged eighteen, were at home with their grandmother so that someone would be in to collect it. A few minutes later while she was standing at the bus stop she heard 'a distant explosion'. Back in the house Keith Farran heard and felt the detonation. He rushed downstairs and saw smoke billowing from the dining room. The windows had been blown out and scraps of paper and other debris were scattered all around. He went in and found Rex lying in a corner, his stomach ripped open.[35]

Rex was a draughtsman in the Bolton-Paul aircraft factory. Unlike his eldest brother Roy, he was a quiet and thoughtful young man who was often to be found dreamily puffing on his pipe. His family nickname was Pud. What had happened to him was easy enough to guess. The postwoman had delivered a package addressed to R. Farran. Since the publication of *Winged Dagger* many fans had sent Roy copies of the book for his signature so there was nothing unusual in the arrival of a parcel with the dimensions of a hardback. The family were used to forwarding Roy's correspondence to his solicitors in London. However, this parcel contained a volume of Shakespeare and as Rex tore away the wrapping he did not know that it was intended for his brother and had been hollowed out to conceal explosives and a detonator. At 8:10 the bomb went off. The blast was so strong it stopped the clock on the sideboard. By some miracle Tiger, the family cat who was also in the room, escaped injury. Rex was not so lucky. Keith called a doctor and an ambulance but his brother died of his wounds in hospital two hours later. According to Keith his last words were 'Am I brave enough for a Farran?'[36]

Within hours of the blast the police arrived in force. The strong investigative team included Inspector Burgess, CID, and Detective Sergeant George Baker, Special Branch. In an unusual move Scotland Yard recalled Superintendent Tom Barratt from his annual leave to lead the investigation under the overall direction of Commander Leonard Burt, head of Special Branch. The Home Office explosives expert, Dr Hugh Watts, was brought in to examine the bomb fragments. Initially the police had little to go on other than a postcode, E1, signifying that the package had been mailed from the East End of London. This fuelled suspicion that Jewish terrorists were responsible. On the basis of information about known LEHI 'agents' officers immediately began making inquiries there. They also reopened channels to colleagues on the Continent who had cooperated in the hunt for Jewish terrorists the previous year.[37]

Roy was sure he knew who was responsible. He told a reporter for the *Daily Telegraph*, 'The bomb was no doubt the work of the Stern Gang. I have been careful about opening parcels since I arrived home. Everyone at Codsall has been warned, too.' As soon as he had received the awful news he drove to Renfrew Airport and flew to Wolverhampton in a privately chartered plane. From there he was driven to Codsall, arriving in the evening. By now the house was surrounded by police and the entire neighbourhood was on high alert. Instead of alighting outside, Roy gave instructions to be dropped off on the other side of fields that backed onto the grounds of his home. He crossed hedges and fences and slipped in, unseen, by a rear entrance. For as long as he was at the house the guard was stepped up and everything arriving by post was intercepted and checked.[38]

The inquest for Rex was opened and adjourned *sine die*. He was buried on Friday afternoon in Codsall Parish Church. It was a beautiful sunny day and there was a large turnout of friends and well-wishers, though the police kept spectators at a distance. A local constable was posted at the entrance to the church and quizzed anyone unfamiliar. Each of the hundred wreaths was scrutinised before it was allowed through. Officers scoured the lanes between the house and the cemetery two hours before the funeral cortège was due to pass. It was led by a police car and motorcycle patrolman. Superintendent Barratt joined the procession and when he reached the church sat with other detectives who were scattered amongst the congregation.[39]

In what was probably an unconscious echo of Roy's trial, the event that sparked the tragic chain of events that led to Codsall cemetery, the wreath from Roy, Raymond and Keith read, 'Good show, Pud, from Brothers.' The family was united in grief, but Roy carried a heavier burden than the rest of them. After the ceremony was over he knelt alone at the grave as if he had a personal message for the brother he lost as a result of something dark and secret that he had done, a year ago and far away. Two days later he departed unannounced and unobserved to a secret destination. Keith told the press, 'I honestly have not the slightest idea where he has gone. But he is always like that. He is terribly upset about the whole affair and he has not talked about it much.'[40]

The murder of Rex Farran made front-page news in Britain for several days and rekindled fears about an onslaught by Jewish terrorists. In a statement to Parliament the following day the Home Secretary, James Chuter Ede MP, said 'I am sure the House will be as shocked as I am by this wicked outrage'. He offered the sympathy of the whole House to the Farran family. But in response to a question from his Conservative opposite number he could shed no light on the investigation other than to say it was continuing. In fact, on the basis of Watts' forensic report Scotland Yard had already concluded that the bomb maker was one of the suspects who had been arrested and later released by police on the Continent, that is to say Eliav. Special Branch had been in contact with the Sûreté in Paris, although Eliav was long gone. At this stage no one seems to have suspected that another LEHI agent had penetrated the mainland and was using techniques that had presumably been shared throughout the cell while it was still intact. Meanwhile, the head of the CID had called together senior officers at Scotland Yard to co-ordinate what was said to be 'the greatest hunt for Jewish terrorists ever held in Britain'.[41]

Any doubt about the badge of the culprits was removed when the LEHI radio station in Palestine claimed responsibility for the bomb. They admitted that they killed Rex Farran by mistake but showed not an ounce of contrition: indeed, the statement said they would get Roy 'next time'. The point was crudely underlined when two postcards arrived at the house in Codsall. One bore the words 'It is your turn to mourn' and the other a simple drawing of two staring eyes to remind Roy that he was being watched. The implication that the culprits were still at large in Britain was unsettling. British Jews especially feared the consequences of yet another bout of Jewish terrorism. The incident occurred against the backdrop of turmoil in Palestine as the British completed the last stage of their withdrawal. Jewish forces engaged with Arab irregulars in bloody struggles for territory that often sucked in British troops, resulting in yet more army casualties. The small Jewish community in Wolverhampton spoke for almost all Jews in the country when it issued a statement to the press deploring the deed and stressing that although the terrorists were Jewish their actions did not reflect on Jews as a whole or Judaism. 'We feel that we are no more responsible for acts of terror than are the Christian community of England for the murder of six million Jews by the so-called Christians of Germany . . . We cannot too strongly disassociate ourselves from the act of terrorists who have learned their methods in Hitler's Europe.'[42]

Given the similarity to LEHI's earlier bombing campaign, security around government ministers was tightened up. The increased caution of potential victims gave the police the break they needed. On the morning of 11 May Sir Evelyn Barker's wife took delivery of a cylindrical package mailed from London to their home, Long Orchard, in Cobham. She took it up to her bedroom but as she started peeling away the wrapping paper she noticed a smell resembling the odour of disinfectant. At the same moment she saw wire and black insulating tape. She immediately put down the half-unwrapped parcel and called her husband's office. Barker's aide-de-camp realised at once that it was a bomb. He called the police and within a short time Superintendent Barratt and his team were at the house. Hugh Watts was also summoned. Once he had disarmed the device it was possible to examine it carefully. Several sticks of gelignite were concealed in a cardboard tube, the kind used for posting magazines. The explosive was attached to a battery-operated detonator. As so often in a terrorist investigation an unexploded device provided the breakthrough. It enabled Special Branch to study the bomb maker's modus operandi, identify the source of his materials and obtain fingerprints.[43]

The investigation probably also benefited from leads supplied by MI5. It focused on Monty Harris, an East London Jew who was associated with the Hebrew Legion, the militant Zionist group that had long been under Secret Service surveillance. Harris was twenty-four years old, the son of a Jewish immigrant whose name was Jacob Schiaff until he naturalised and took the maiden name of his wife, Hilda. Monty, also known as Monte or Monti, was educated at a London County Council school in Bethnal Green and the Davenant Foundation School on Whitechapel Road. He left aged fifteen to work in his father's grocery business in Brick Lane. After Jacob Harris died in 1943 Monty took over the shop and relocated to 14 Gravel Lane, off Middlesex Street (Petticoat Lane). It was a small hole-in-the-wall operation, known as a lock-up, but it had a basement and it served his non-commercial purposes very well.[44]

Harris was placed under observation at the beginning of August. Detectives from the CID and Special Branch followed him to and from his shop each working day, and monitored the comings and goings while he was there. They noted men and women arriving with suspicious-looking packages, notably one Nathan Burns who seems to have been known to Special Branch, too. Inquiries also revealed that Harris took mysterious deliveries from an old school friend, Raphael Shovel, who owned a small company making chemicals. On the morning of 15 August 1948, Detective Sergeant Herbert Lawrenson of Special Branch was staking out the lock-up in Gravel Lane when he saw Harris arrive and go down into the basement. An hour later he observed smoke filling the interior of the premises. Suddenly Harris, looking pale and in his shirtsleeves, opened the front door and peered nervously up and down the street. He then went back inside, but left the door ajar so that the abundant bluish smoke could escape. Lawrenson pretended to stroll by so that he could get a closer look and as he did so overheard an elderly man exchange words with Harris. The passer-by asked if there was a fire, to which Harris 'in an agitated voice' replied 'No, no, no. No fire. I was just burning some old paper and sticks and they were wet.' Within a few more days the police were convinced they had uncovered a bomb-making factory. Burt and his lieutenants now organised an elaborate operation to apprehend Harris and Burns. On Saturday 28 August one team of detectives tailed Harris from his home in Southgate while another lay in wait at Gravel Lane. When Harris arrived at the shop Detective Inspector George Smith served him with a search warrant for the premises. Officers swarmed in while others detained Harris. At first he sounded confident and defiant. 'Go on, have a look,' he said. 'You won't find any explosives here.' He even offered to help look. Smith cautioned him and a few moments later officers searching the basement uncovered fuse wire, gun cotton and a variety of chemicals. Harris blustered that he kept an incendiary bomb as 'a souvenir' and then claimed that the material was put there by someone else. When detonators were discovered under an old mattress along with a box containing 365 rounds of .303 ammunition his tone changed. 'I am in the cart and I know it,' he told Inspector Smith. 'This is a political and a national matter. I am caught red-handed and I am not giving you any sob stuff. What about the other things you have found? I do not want you to bring a second charge. I am guilty and only want it all cleared up.'[45]

Realising that he had been caught red-handed, Harris was trying to establish credentials as a political prisoner. He was taken to Bishopsgate police station where he was charged with having in his possession 'certain explosives, in circumstances that gave rise to the reasonable suspicion that his possession of them was not for a lawful purpose'. The police haul included twelve primers, forty-eight feet of safety fuse, four cylinders of gun cotton and two dozen detonators as well as the rifle cartridges. He was arraigned at the Guildhall Court and remanded in custody until 6 September. While this was going on Nathan Burns was arrested in High Road Tottenham by a second team led by Detective Sergeant George Baker, who had started the pursuit at Histons Hill, Codsall. Burns, too, was charged with the illegal possession of explosives. Simultaneous raids were made on other premises in London and at least eleven other Irgun supporters were detained, although no one else was arrested or charged. Ya'acov Heruti remained undetected and slipped back to Palestine.[46]

The raids were widely reported in the press and the coverage was predictably sensational. According to the *Daily Mail* front-page story, 'the secret headquarters in this country of the Jewish terrorist organisation Irgun Zvai Leumi . . . believed to have been responsible for sending letter bombs to notable people has been found by Special Branch officers of Scotland Yard'. The *Daily Mirror* revealed that the arraignment proceedings took place behind specially erected steel shutters. Chastened, perhaps, by the failure to arrest and prosecute anyone Jewish in Britain in the course of previous scares, the *Daily Mirror* and the *Manchester Guardian* refrained from identifying the alleged culprits as Jews.[47]

The evidence against Harris was overwhelming. The Attorney General, Sir Hartley Shawcross, approved prosecution ten days later under Section 4 of the Explosive Substances Act 1883. Committal proceedings were held on 15 and 23 September. In addition to evidence from the investigating police officers the magistrate heard from Horace Mayes, the principal scientific officer to the Home Office explosives department. Mayes testified that the seized aluminium detonators were of a type used in mines and quarries, and also by the military. The fuses were all in working order. Harris had accumulated everything necessary to make a powerful bomb.[48]

Harris and Burns were tried before Mr Justice Sable at the Central Criminal Court, the Old Bailey, on 12–14 October 1948. In reply to a question from the Crown prosecutor, Mr Henry Elam, Mayes stated that with the right preparation the material seized in the Gravel Lane basement 'could do serious damage to a small building, and items could kill quite a number of people'. One of the detectives identified Harris as a leading member of the 'Hebrew Legion' which supported the 'Jewish terrorist organisation Irgun Zvai Leumi'. This was enough to supply a motive for his incendiary activity. Inspector Smith revealed that Harris had acquired a visa for the USA and booked a passage to America on 2 October, which gave the impression that he had planned a getaway. However, the counsel for the defence, Mr Derek Curtis Bennett KC, maintained that Harris was not a member of any 'terrorist organisation'. He did concede, though, that Harris had been persuaded by another, unnamed man to sabotage vehicles intended for export to Iraq where Harris was led to believe they might be used for military purposes against Israel. The jury was certainly unconvinced that Harris was a mere patsy. On the direction of the judge they found Burns not guilty, but they convicted Harris. Mr Justice Sable indicated the gravity of the case and the importance of deterring any repetition by sentencing Harris to seven years in prison. Pronouncing sentence the judge told him: 'You in your blind folly apparently believed that a political cause can be advanced in this nation by the use of explosives and violence. You are wrong. It never has been and it never will be.'[49]

By this time the mandate was history. The British rearguard had departed on 31 June and all that remained was the messy diplomatic aftermath, uncomfortably prolonged by Bevin's stubborn refusal to give official recognition to the state of Israel. The heat had gone out of the Jewish terrorist issue. So, although this time a real Jewish terrorist had been caught, in flagrante delicto, and found guilty, the coverage of the trial was fairly restrained. The *Daily Mail*, true to form, provided the most lurid copy. Its reporter Arthur Tietjen claimed that 'The leading terrorists came to this country eighteen months ago. They set up their intelligence system, financed by blackmail on people known to be supporters of the Israel state.' Tietjen linked the conviction of Monty Harris to the crash of a British airliner over the Atlantic nine months earlier. But there was nothing comparable to the column inches devoted to the terrorist threat in earlier years.[50]

All the same, the trial cast a pall of suspicion over the Hebrew Legion. The following day its former chairman, David de Lange, wrote to the *Daily Telegraph* to reassure its readers that the organisation was 'practically defunct' and that anyway its objective 'was not to stir up terrorist activities here but to explain to people in this country the motives of the Irgun in Palestine.' In a subsequent statement the legion denied that Harris had ever been a member. But MI5 and Special Branch had been watching the Hebrew Legion for years, sending agents to their public meetings, collecting their pronouncements, tapping the telephones of the group's leading lights, and intercepting their mail to and from Tel Aviv. Although it went into steep decline after the establishment of the state of Israel, remnants of the group continued to raise money for right-wing fighters and encourage youngsters in Britain to throw themselves into the struggle.[51]

Monty Harris was released in August 1950 on condition that he renounce his British nationality and emigrate to Israel. This arrangement appears to have been reached in negotiations between the government of Israel and the Foreign Office, which tends to confirm that Harris was engaged in terrorist activity connected with the Jewish underground and suggests that the British authorities were willing to regard him as a political rather than a criminal case. But no one was ever charged with Rex Farran's murder and the file on the investigation remains closed to the public.[52]

Roy was convinced that Harris was the perpetrator. Nothing was known about Heruti's role for years and confusion surrounded the purpose of the killing. In September 1948 two LEHI fighters in Tel Aviv told the *New York Times* reporter Cyrus Sulzberger that the Stern Gang had intended to kill Rex. 'We knew it would hurt Roy Farran more if we killed his brother. It would force him to live with this memory always. We meant to torture him. We knew Roy would be away at that time. Therefore we addressed the package containing the bomb to "R. Farran". In that way his brother was just as likely to open it.' However, many years later Yellin-Mor the former commander of LEHI (he Hebraised his name from Friedman-Yellin) contacted Bernard Fergusson when they both happened to be in Paris and arranged to meet him. Yellin-Mor asked Fergusson to 'Tell Farran that we are satisfied to have had our revenge in this way. Tell him he has nothing to fear from us'.[53]

Heruti, rather like the man he had attempted to kill, found it hard to adapt to peacetime. When he reached Israel he joined the army and fought in the war of independence. Afterwards he resumed his law studies, but he could not give up the habits of the conspirator. During the 1950s he became involved with a right-wing underground group that tried to bomb the Soviet Embassy in Tel Aviv. Heruti was caught and sentenced to several years in prison though he was pardoned and released after just eighteen months. He became a lawyer but remained deeply involved in extreme, nationalist

politics in Israel. In 2005 he admitted to the Israeli journalist Yossi
Melman that he had organised the operation in May 1948 and
confirmed that Rex Farran was killed by accident. 'It is regrettable
that an innocent person was killed. It was not intentional. It is
unfortunate that it happened', he said. But he remained utterly
unrepentant. 'Would I do it again?' he asked rhetorically. 'Yes. It
was a war and in war there are mistakes and there are anomalies.
I am sorry the murderer was not killed.'[54]

After his brother's funeral Roy returned to Scotland to complete
his induction into the world of business. In late August 1948 he travelled to southern Rhodesia to manage the quarrying and construction branch of Keir and Cawdor (Rhodesia) Ltd. In Salisbury he met
Ruth Ardern, a young Canadian from a Calgary ranching family. She
captivated him and before long they agreed to marry.[55] Nevertheless,
he found it difficult to settle. In October 1949 he offered himself to
the Conservative Party as a parliamentary candidate for the
constituency of Dudley and Stourbidge which lay near his family
home. He explained in his application that 'he regarded the British
political situation as sufficiently grave to warrant his entry into public
life in preference to a peaceful existence as a farmer in Rhodesia'. His
proposed candidacy threw the local Conservative Association into
turmoil. Another ex-officer, Major F. G. Goodhart, had put forward
his name some time ago and enjoyed the support of many local Tories.
But a noisy and youthful claque wanted to replace him with Farran.
The dispute attracted national attention when Farran was obliged to
dissociate himself from 'some of his more embarrassing admirers' by
issuing a statement 'disclaiming "fascist or anti-Semitic views"'.[56]

It is not hard to see why the far right was attracted to his banner.
The epilogue to *Winged Dagger* was a bitter lament for lost empire
and a barely disguised attack on the Labour government. He wrote
that he had lost friends in the defence of Britain's Indian empire,
only for the country's leaders to liquidate it with the stroke of a pen,
thereby putting the clock back two hundred years and unleashing
chaos and bloodshed on a scale not seen since the end of the Moguls.
From the days of General Clive, British soldiers had fought to preserve
the jewel of the empire, in which he spent his youth, but just when
Britain was bankrupt it was cast adrift by politicians he considered

little better than demagogues who had never done a thing for the Commonwealth except criticise it. Farran echoed the disillusionment of the 'front generation' that returned from the trenches in 1918, filled with a sense of betrayal and wasted sacrifice, angry with the mainstream political leadership and fearful of the far left. He asked rhetorically if he had really fought in Italy, Germany and France so that Communists could trigger civil war and unrest in these countries. If he had known that, he would have preferred to be a conscientious objector. He wondered why they had defeated Germany only to see Britain turned into a political football kicked between America and Russia. Had they fought on the right side, he asked grimly? He excoriated the government. While the Union Jack still flew over nearly twenty per cent of the world's land surface, how could they say that Britain was bankrupt and a third-rate power? If it was true it was surely the result of gross mismanagement. Farran juxtaposed the solidarity of men in combat to the fractiousness of peacetime, remarking that there was no class conflict on the mountains and in the snow during Operation Tombola. Nor could there have been because there they were British and proud of it. He concluded with a plea to recover the driving force of national pride. Such unvarnished populism, strident nationalism, and his well-publicised altercation with the Jews made him seem a natural recruit to the far right even though he publicly shrugged off their unwanted attention.[57]

Moderate Tories were alarmed by Roy's new-found following and redoubled their efforts to thwart him. However, his supporters refused to let him withdraw and at a noisy meeting of the Dudley and Stourbidge Conservative Association in November rejected Goodhart's nomination. Finally, the executive of the association bowed to pressure and agreed to let his name go forward to a general meeting. On 6 December 1949 he was formally adopted. Such were the passions he generated that his selection was greeted by wild cheering while women 'rushed up and kissed him'.[58]

Even then his nomination was subject to confirmation by Conservative Central Office and they had the jitters after twenty constituency workers had resigned in protest against his adoption. Colin Legum, writing in the *Palestine Post*, speculated that 'Farran's name is not likely to be endorsed, since the Conservative Central

Office is concerned about the manifestations of anti-Semitism that surround his nomination.' Indeed, on the eve of the February 1950 general election *The Times* reported that Farran was obliged to disavow the endorsement of 'the "Free Britain" anti-Jewish organisation whose news-sheet calls on sympathisers to vote only for avowedly anti-Jewish candidates'. Nevertheless, Farran fought the constituency as the official parliamentary candidate for the Conservative Party. His Labour opponent was George Wigg, the outgoing Undersecretary of State for War, who was known to be pro-Zionist as well as a member of the 'Keep Left' group of Labour MPs who espoused a philosophy that Farran reviled. According to one report it was 'the most colourful contest in the Midlands, in which Major Roy Farran's energy in the Conservative cause rouses either the admiration or the astonishment of those in the constituency, according to their political label'. His election address called on his supporters to 'Put on the heat.' They were dubbed the 'Farranites'. None of this energy and enthusiasm sufficed, though. Farran lost to Wigg by 19,825 to 32,856 votes.[59]

Roy retreated to a cattle farm near Malvern in Worcestershire. He still could not settle. Soon after the outbreak of the Korean War he volunteered his services to the War Office because he thought 'his knowledge of guerrilla warfare would be useful'. The War Office was not interested. He later accepted an invitation from Brigadier Mike Calvert, the commander of the SAS, to join a new squadron being formed in Malaya. But Calvert was overruled by his commander-in-chief who thought there were already too many veterans of Palestine in the fray. At the end of August 1950 Roy married Ruth Ardern and emigrated to Canada, settling in her home city of Calgary. He intended to commence dairy farming but, again, proved unable to focus on one thing. He wrote a novel, *Jungle Chase*, based on his experience in East Africa and a history of the Calgary Highlanders Regiment.[60]

In the novel, Farran chewed over his Palestinian experiences albeit in a heavily disguised fashion. *Jungle Chase* concerns a young, naive Englishman called Peter Liddell who meets a tough hunter called Jan Nyholm while prospecting for coal in the Rhodesian bush. Nyholm is on the run after killing his wife's lover. Liddell inadvertently leads the police to Nyholm's hideout and they end up fleeing together into the jungle. During the chase Nyholm falls sick and

Liddell loses a leg in a lion attack. At great risk to himself Nyholm carries the younger man to safety before disappearing back into the wild. He leaves Liddell his two most prized possessions: his rifle and his daughter. Liddell marries the girl and they search for her father. When they find him he is worn out and sick; he expires in his daughter's arms. What makes the story interesting in terms of Farran's own life is the narrative of the chase and the role of the law. On the last page, Liddell reflects on Nyholm's fate in words that could have been Roy talking about his own experiences in Palestine and the tragic aftermath: 'I thought how cruel and harsh were the laws which said that he should atone with his life for a crime committed in a moment's passion. Who could deny that he had suffered more from remorse and from being hounded away from those he loved than he would ever have endured on the gallows?'[61]

If Roy could not forget the years of conflict, neither could the brothers of Alexander Rubowitz. Nor did the Herut Party, the political heir to the Irgun, or the Jewish Agency. Both continued to follow his career and maintained files on his activity. Farran's war memoir was serialised in *Ma'ariv* in 1950 and widely commented on in the Hebrew dailies. The newspaper of the Herut Party returned to his story again and again. In November 1954, Reuven Nochimowski obtained support from the Jewish Agency to launch yet another legal case against Farran. This time Nochimowski travelled to London and obtained the services of a solicitor, Roger Nathan, to apply for an arrest warrant that could be served on Farran anywhere in the British Empire and Commonwealth. Nochimowski also applied for cancellation of the stay of execution of an arrest warrant imposed by the Attorney General of the Palestine government in 1947. This initiative soon foundered; the Rubowitz family did not even know that Farran had emigrated.[62]

Roy meanwhile embarked on a second, much more successful political career. In 1952 he started working for the *Calgary Herald* as a reporter and in 1954 founded his own weekly, the *North Hill News*. Although it was a local paper within a short time it gained a wide reputation for vigorous and entertaining journalism, much of it Roy's personal input. The editorials were resolutely conservative and violently anti-communist. The *North Hill News* was his springboard into politics. By chance, he had landed in the most politically congenial of all Canada's provinces. The Social Credit Party governed Alberta from 1938 to 1971 and was explicitly anti-Jewish for much of this period. Roy had nothing to do with Social Credit and joined the Progressive Conservative Association which trenchantly opposed it. However, the political climate was not such that Roy's conservative views, his colourful past or his clash with the Jews would be a hindrance. In 1961 he was elected a city alderman. Ten years later he was elected to the Alberta Legislature for the Progressive Conservatives. In 1973 he was appointed minister for telephones and utilities and served as Solicitor General from 1975 to 1979. He retired from politics as a much-liked and highly respected elder statesman.[63]

Like Roy, Bernard Fergusson recovered from the debacle in Palestine and went on to enjoy a distinguished career as a soldier, diplomat, and author. Although the Army was not thrilled to have him back in view of his tarnished reputation and appearance in a court martial, General Browning managed to arrange for him to take over the 1st battalion of the Black Watch, which was always his ambition. There was resistance to the appointment within the army hierarchy because of what happened in Palestine, but Browning pushed it through. Fergusson heard him say over the telephone to the Adjutant-General 'Well, after all who sent him there? We did . . . And who gave him Farran? I did!' Fergusson retired from the army as a Brigadier in 1958. In addition to writing several books, including his memoirs, he followed his imperial forebears and served as Governor General of New Zealand from 1962 to 1967. In 1972 he was created a life peer, assuming the title Lord Ballantrae, and in 1974 he was made a Knight of the Thistle, one of Scotland's highest honours. His version of the Farran affair was never challenged in his lifetime. He died in 1980, his reputation unblemished.[64]

The Rubowitz family continued to pursue Farran, although no longer by legal means. Instead, at increasingly infrequent intervals Alexander's brothers and nephews, Zvi and Moshe, tried to contact him for information about the location of Alexander's body. Farran declined to respond and from the 1970s refused even to speak to journalists about the boy's disappearance. Israel never quite forgot him, though, and from time to time the press would carry articles recalling the affair.[65]

Roy was blissfully ignorant of this persistence. In 1979 he took up the chairmanship of the Alberta Racing Commission. This and running the North American Jockeys' Association enabled him to pursue his love of horses. Released from the trammels of party discipline he resumed writing for the *Calgary Herald*. He was also a visiting professor in political science at Alberta University in Edmonton for three years. In his seventies his mind turned to his legacy. He established the Farran Foundation to promote student exchanges between Canada and the Vosges area of France where he had fought in the SAS. In 1994 he returned to Bains-les-Bains to receive the Légion d'honneur in recognition of his wartime exploits. He survived a serious bout of cancer in 1999 that necessitated the removal of his larynx but soon mastered speaking through a voice box. He continued horse riding into his eighties. Roy Farran died in June 2006, a year after his wife. His funeral was a huge event in Calgary. The procession stretched for ten blocks, led by a galaxy of local politicians. Hundreds of admirers crowded into and around the church where the funeral service was held. The Canadian Army arranged an unprecedented artillery salute. Tributes flowed in from all corners. To the *Calgary Herald* he was 'the model citizen'. A friend speaking on CBC News said 'They should write a book about that man.' A colonel in the Canadian Army averred that he was 'a model for all serving men and women in today's armed forces'.[66]

Honours and recognition did not come to members of the Irgun and LEHI until the Herut Party came to power under the leadership of Menachem Begin in 1977. Begin's government initiated a policy of naming streets after the 'dissidents' who died in the underground war against the British, who they regarded as martyrs. One small and rather bleak street in the Jerusalem suburb of East Talpiot, built on land occupied after the 1967 Arab-Israel War, was named after Alexander Rubowitz. Several years later a memorial was erected in his honour on Mount Herzl, the military cemetery in Jerusalem where many of the heroic figures of Zionism have been interred. There is now also a plaque at the exact spot on Ussishkin Street from where he was abducted on the evening of 6 May 1947. But his body still has no resting place.[67]

Epilogue

The abduction and murder of Alexander Rubowitz created a scandal that ate away at British prestige and authority in Palestine, contributing to the demise of the mandate. But the brief history of the special squads had even greater ramifications for the British Empire. To many in the security forces they were a brilliant experiment in counter-insurgency that was sabotaged by a relentless and cunning enemy, though never defeated 'in the field'. They deserved to be emulated wherever the empire was faced by native unrest. So, while the tactical and operational aspects of what became known as the 'counter-gang' or 'pseudo-gang' technique were improved, the ethical and political limitations remained. Wherever the formula was employed it resulted in illegality, extrajudicial execution (that is to say, murder) and scandal. The toxic legacy of the special squads contaminated British colonial policy for decades.

In the short term, the scandal helped to strip away whatever claims Britain had to continue governing Palestine. Of course, the Farran case was only one of many incidents that drove a wedge between the Jewish population of Palestine and the British. It was also mild compared to the brutality with which the British had suppressed the Arab uprising a decade earlier. And Jewish terrorism was far more destructive of human life: at its most extreme it was totally arbitrary. However, the special squads were operating in an unusual political and moral climate. The legitimacy of British rule was under question and the special squads were a tool of the authorities. The Jews enjoyed huge public sympathy as a result of their treatment under the Nazis, so every measure used against them was judged more harshly than it might have merited when seen more objectively. Above all, the timing of the affair gave it disproportionate significance.[1]

This was demonstrated most powerfully by the Jewish Agency's submission to the crucial UNSCOP inquiry in June 1947. The agency painted a picture of government repression combined with loss of control: 'The state of anarchy in this regard was glaringly revealed by an incident that occurred in the Rehavia Quarter of Jerusalem on the evening of 6 May: Alexander Rubovitch [*sic*], a boy of sixteen, was kidnapped from the street by a group of British police in civilian clothes working under the orders of Major Roy Alexander Farran, a former commando officer.' The agency acknowledged that Rubowitz had been distributing 'terrorist leaflets' but this only strengthened the integrity of their case. 'The boy appears to have been taken to an isolated spot outside the city and tortured to death. No trace of the body has been found. The incident created a deep stir.' The agency then told the sorry tale of Farran's flight, pursuit, surrender and second absconding. This example of colonial misrule may have been less spectacular and emotionally shattering for the UNSCOP team than the sight of Jews being dragged off the ship *Exodus* and forcibly re-embarked on ships bound for Europe, but it suggested a malaise that touched a raw nerve amongst the more anti-colonialist members of the committee.[2]

What the UN special commissioners heard and saw with their own eyes was reinforced by the torrent of anti-British propaganda, especially in the United States and even more especially in New York where the UN was based. A prime example of this is an article in the *New York Herald Tribune* by Sumner Welles, a former US Undersecretary of State, in mid August 1947 while UNSCOP was deliberating over its report and prior to the debates at the UN itself. Welles was a prominent ally of the Zionist movement who was highly prized due to his distinguished record in government service. His objective in all his utterances and advice was to drive a nail into the coffin of the British Empire. He admitted that Jewish terrorism, such as the murder of the two sergeants, had done 'infinite harm' to the Zionist cause but he blamed the violence in

Palestine on British policy. He claimed that 'The British military administration in Palestine is shot through from top to bottom with anti-Semitism'. The Rubowitz case 'provided a shocking illustration of existing conditions'. In his version the British police force in Palestine had 'a notorious "strong-arm squad". Last spring a sixteen-year-old boy named Alexander Rubowitz was kidnapped by members of the squad, headed by Major Farran, taken down the deserted Jericho Road, and tortured. He died on the spot.' According to Welles, Farran was 'advised' to flee to Syria and only returned due to 'unexpected publicity'. He was then 'identified by eyewitnesses', imprisoned, 'helped by his fellow officers again to escape' and only surrendered due to the public outcry. 'When we know that the authorities charged with the protection of the inhabitants of Palestine are guilty of such atrocities, and learn of the gross miscarriages of justice that have taken place in the case of the individual officers responsible, it is easier for us to understand why such acts of retaliation as the murder of the British sergeants have been perpetrated.' It was, he concluded, the urgent task of the UN to end British rule over Palestine before there was a worse catastrophe.[3]

The scandal was not just a strategic propaganda gift to the Jewish underground. It hampered the counter-insurgency campaign at a tactical level. In July 1947, the *Palestine Post*, which was no friend of the 'dissidents', explained why the security forces had forfeited significant co-operation in the fight against the Irgun and LEHI. 'The main reason for this is to be sought in the deep-rooted conviction of almost every Jew in this country that the police is an instrument for enabling an unrepresentative government to impose its policy. During the past month, the public's worst suspicions were constantly fed by the gruesome story of the boy Rubowitz, who was kidnapped, by an Englishman, according to eyewitnesses, and never seen again.' In his narrative of events in Palestine while he was GOC, even Lieutenant General MacMillan conceded that the scandal caused significant damage. He decided to include mention of the Farran affair because 'the case caused considerable agitation in the Jewish press, and also some sensation in the world press' and there was 'no doubt that the propaganda in connection with it probably fanned the flames of anti-British feeling among the more extremist sections of the Jewish community'.[4]

Given this woeful catalogue it is extraordinary that the 'special squads' should have acquired a reputation for success and even a certain mystique. Officers who served in Palestine were the first to claim that the squads were on the verge of a breakthrough when they were brought down by false allegations. Farran's memoir *Winged Dagger* was the foundation stone for the myth of a stolen victory. In the 1960s his military admirers, notably Richard Clutterbuck and Colin Mitchell, drew on *Winged Dagger* and their own experiences to create the impression that Fergusson and Farran had opened a glorious chapter in the history of British counter-insurgency warfare. Fergusson's memoir *Trumpet in the Hall*, published in 1970, was an elegant and witty exercise in dissimulation that enhanced the image of Roy as a romantic hero while at the same time admitting the weakness of the scheme.[5]

Within a short time the special squads came to be seen as the inspiration for British counter-insurgency methods in one theatre after another. David Charters, the leading military historian who was first to examine the exploits of the special squads, argued that Fergusson's initiative provided valuable experience for the police and the army that was put to good use fighting communist insurgents in Malaya and the Mau Mau uprising in Kenya. 'The most innovative and potentially most effective counter-insurgency ideas originated with the army officers serving in the police whose wartime experience had been irregular rather than conventional', he wrote. 'Their confidence in the value of covert special operations as a counter-insurgency technique has been borne out by subsequent experience in Malaya, Kenya and Northern Ireland.'[6] In his popular history of the SAS Anthony Kemp states that by the time the SAS became involved in counter-insurgency operations in Malaya 'British forces had a tradition of waging clandestine warfare in plain clothes against terrorists using many techniques that had been developed in Palestine, notably by the redoubtable Roy Farran'.[7]

Similar claims have been made for the origin of undercover units as part of police operations. Georgina Sinclair writes that 'Emergencies required newer forms of policing that brought the traditional paramilitary style into contact with counter-insurgency tactics. The experience of those responsible for policing Palestine shaped the practice of colonial policing. Methods evolved and then were exported throughout the empire by former members of the Palestine police.' In particular the use of counter-gangs or pseudo-gangs modelled on the 'special squads' became characteristic of police methods in Malaya and Kenya. Sinclair also notes that 'Importantly, Palestine became *the* unofficial recruiting ground for senior policemen.' Nicol Gray was appointed commissioner of police in Malaya in September 1948. He brought with him about 500 former members of the Palestine Police Force. They arrived at a crucial moment, when the Malayan Police Force was under-strength and totally lacking in counter-insurgency skills. In short order the Palestinian veterans provided training for existing officers and new recruits, set up special jungle squads, and constructed jungle forts to permanently reclaim territory from the insurgents. Richard Catling was appointed commissioner of police in Kenya in 1954, joining Kenneth Hadingham and other old hands from Palestine. Through them the lessons learned in Palestine were transmitted and instrumentalised. Palestine was not only a source of experienced policemen: it supplied colonial administrators and generals, too. In September 1948 Sir Henry Gurney was appointed the high commissioner in Malaya with a brief to contain the communist insurgency. It was he who brought in Nicol Gray. When General Sir George Erskine arrived in Kenya in May 1953 to command the security forces fighting the Mau Mau rebellion he came with experience of cordon and search operations in Tel Aviv. He used this knowledge to plan Operation Anvil, a major exercise to round up and remove the Kikuyu population of Nairobi suspected of harbouring insurgents.[8]

But was the dissemination of personnel from the Palestine Police Force and the experience of the 'special squads' really beneficial? Charles Townshend, one of the earliest and most perceptive historians of British counter-insurgency, sees the debacle of British rule in Palestine as one in a string of failures: Ireland in 1919–20, Mesapotamia in the 1920s and Palestine in the 1930s. In each case there was a woeful lack of co-ordination between the civil administration and the military. All these weaknesses resurfaced in Palestine in the 1940s when 'the operations of the police showed an ominous slide into illegality'. Townshend was one of the first historians to examine Fergusson's memorandum on the establishment of the 'special squads'. He was scathing. 'Its implication, that only state terrorists could combat dissident terrorists, was indeed alarming. The inevitable disaster was not long in coming . . . As too often before, the attempt at counter-terrorism, albeit disguised in fashionable military jargon – the counter-gang principle – reaped a political whirlwind.'[9]

Indeed, one insightful study of the Palestine Police Force has traced the Farran affair all the way back to the Arab rebellion when a grim pattern was established: 'the absence of support by the population for the aims of the government resulted in a lack of assistance to the police from the population and a refusal of indigenous officers to obey orders. Control could only be maintained by the imposition of an alien body of men, most of whom had no police experience, and a greater willingness to use force.' Lacking manpower, bereft of any intelligence-gathering capacity, without appropriate transport or equipment the police were shoved aside by the army. They began the retreat into fortress-like police stations and armoured car patrols. Hundreds of Arabs suspected of involvement in the insurrection were interned without trial; many were deported by administrative fiat; violence against detainees, even torture, became widespread. The influx of ex-servicemen into the force in the late 1930s further weakened the capacity for routine policing and accelerated the tendency for police morale and discipline to break down under stress. Instead of refining the intelligence arm of the police, the process of militarisation continued during the war. In the fight against LEHI and the Irgun in the early 1940s, the police became heavily dependent on leads provided by the Jewish Agency and the Hagana. When this co-operation stopped after the government announced the perpetuation of the White Paper, the police were virtually helpless. It was almost inevitable, then, that when Montgomery triggered the security-force crackdown in late 1946 it would lead to heavy-handed methods. 'Seen in this light, the Farran case was only a logical extension of what had been created in the earliest days of the mandate.' The Farran affair was 'a fitting conclusion to the history of British policing in Palestine'.[10]

Such damning verdicts warrant a careful re-examination of the influence which Palestine had on colonial policing and counter-insurgency elsewhere. It is true that Gray and the Palestine policemen who poured into Malaya in 1948 provided a quick fix but they also caused a great deal of turbulence. Gray was quickly embroiled in an argument with long-established officers in the Malayan Police Force over the best tactics to pursue. 'Old Malaya hands' cleaved to the model of civil policing, hoping to win the support of the local population by protecting them against disorder and crime. They bridled at the paramilitary methods imported by Gray and swiftly put into effect by the officers bloodied in Palestine. Before long his insistence that the police should lead counter-insurgency operations had split the force into warring factions. There were dozens of resignations at middle and senior levels. Worse, Gray's Palestine veterans soon acquired 'a brutish reputation'. Gurney and Gray presided over a vicious counter-terrorist campaign in which the settlers were given wide latitude to hunt down and kill Chinese who they suspected of communist sympathies. In the course of 1948–9 large-scale sweeps conducted by the army and police on the Palestine model, arbitrary police measures and counter-terrorist operations succeeded only in alienating half a million landless Chinese labourers who provided recruits and succour for the Malayan Communist Party. Gray's insistence on the most rapid possible expansion of the Malayan Police Force and his emphasis on paramilitary training produced a force that was inept at routine police duties, prone to corruption, clumsy when it came to civil relations, and poorly equipped to gain intelligence.[11]

The situation in Malaya was so fraught that when General Sir Gerald Templer was made high commissioner at the start of 1952, following the murder of Sir Henry Gurney by communist guerrillas, he arranged for Gray to be replaced by Colonel Arthur Young from the City of London Police who had been troubleshooting and reforming police forces in the colonies since 1948. Templer also centralised political and military control and overhauled the entire counter-insurgency strategy, putting more emphasis on winning 'hearts and minds'. Arguably, the Palestine model offered nothing significantly useful to the civil administration, the police or the army in Malaya. In the medium term it may even have made things worse.[12]

The same was true in Kenya where the militarisation of the police and the brutalisation of counter-insurgency warfare marched in step. In Kenya, Major Frank Kitson and Eric Holyoakes developed the technique of imitating terrorist gang members in order to extract information from real terrorists or their sympathisers. Before long, Kitson realised that it was more effective to deploy gang members who had been 'turned'. There was not much similarity between this and Farran's method although historians of counter-insurgency continue to see Farran as a way station to Kitson; what they usually fail to observe is the more marked continuation of the nasty side to these covert operations. In Kenya, as in Palestine, the 'pseudo-gangs' soon became associated with cruelty and extra-judicial executions. The familiar tension over command and control also surfaced. Meanwhile, the more conventional use of cordon and search operations followed by mass screenings of the population imitated the techniques used in Palestine, but with a radically different outcome. Operation Anvil in Nairobi led to the detention of thousands of men who were then held without any judicial procedure in camps and subjected to harsh treatment for months or years until they renounced their allegiance to the rebels. These camps, known as the Pipeline, operated in gross violation of every international convention governing human rights.[13]

The descent into arbitrary rule, mass detention, collective punishment, abuse and the profligate use of the gallows points to one of the chief differences between conditions in Kenya and those prevailing a decade earlier in Palestine. Under the mandate the police and the army were hamstrung by the existence of a vibrant local democracy which gave legitimate representation to the Jewish population and enabled them to protest effectively at a local and an international level. The Jews were assisted, and the security forces inhibited, by the presence of the world's press. Police and military actions in Palestine took place under a media spotlight, and the security forces faced a powerful propaganda apparatus that exploited media opportunities to the full. Moreover, Palestine was under constant scrutiny by other governments, the United States in particular, and international organisations, notably the UN, keen to defend human rights in the light of recent horrors under the Nazis. By contrast, as Caroline Elkins demonstrates in her account of Britain's repressive policies in Kenya, the media and the public at home either ignored the insurgency or took the line of the settlers and the authorities. Although human and civil rights abuses were aired in the Houses of Parliament, the UN never intervened.[14]

By a supreme irony Kenneth Hadingham, who was involved in the investigation of Farran's conduct in Palestine, was caught up in a similar affair in Kenya which had a not dissimilar outcome. Hadingham was assistant commissioner of police in Nyeri. In September 1954 he learned of an attempt to block an investigation into the mistreatment of suspected Mau Mau detainees, one of whom had been beaten to death. The inquiry was being obstructed by the district commissioner of Nyeri and the commissioner of the Central Province, backed up by the governor of Kenya himself, Evelyn Baring. Hadingham enlisted the support of Arthur Young, who had transferred from Malaya to Kenya in February 1954, and succeeded in obtaining a small measure of justice in the case. But this was the exception. On the whole, the police, the military and the civil authorities were able to deflect charges of brutality and to defend the arbitrary, often cruel, conduct of the security forces. Elkins observes that Richard Catling, the commissioner of police, was particularly lacklustre in responding to accusations of brutality.[15]

The experience of Malaya and Kenya showed that when the Palestine model of counter-insurgency was repeated in other colonial contexts, with fewer media checks and legal balances, its worst qualities tended to bulk large. If Gray, Fergusson and Farran were pioneers of counter-insurgency this was nothing to applaud, let alone imitate. As Georgina Sinclair observes, 'Emergency situations brought out the more sinister aspects to policing the end of empire, particularly in colonies hosting European settler communities'. Yet the model was repeated, usually with abysmal results. Again, Elkins comments: 'At the start of the century there was the Boer War in

South Africa, and later there were the brutal tactics deployed in Palestine and Malaya. These cases are significant not because they represent other instances where colonial violence was widespread but because each one had an impact, through the sharing of policy or manpower, or both, on the implementation of emergency powers in Kenya. Further, in the history of the transfer of ideas and people around the British Empire, Kenya would later provide models for interrogation and detention used in colonies like Northern Ireland.'[16]

Perhaps the final irony is that Gray's idea, Fergusson's plan and Farran's attempt to execute it were based on a series of fallacies that rendered the special squads totally inappropriate for Palestine in the first place. Farran had never really had experience of covert operations. In Sicily and Italy he led a uniformed commando unit. M. R. D. Foot, the pre-eminent historian of SOE, comments that Farran's exploits in France in 1944 'though romantic, were more cavalry than clandestine warfare'. On his return to Italy, he led irregulars in a guerrilla campaign that bore no resemblance to traditional SAS missions (although it presaged future operations in other theatres). In every one of these actions Farran was alert to tactical intelligence but displayed a casual attitude towards strategic intelligence and, anyway, relied on other agencies to brief him. Crucially, once they were in Palestine Fergusson and Farran, with Gray's connivance, ignored the previous experience of the police force and disparaged its intelligence capability. The result was that the special squads often operated blind, blundering into contact with terrorists rather than executing surgical strikes. It was impossible for them to pass as Jews and blend with the crowd, picking up information or bracketing targets. Even Dick Catling, a friend of Fergusson, lamented their shortcomings. 'Roy hadn't got a hope of succeeding in trailing the pseudo-gang coat.' In an interview for the Imperial War Museum he concluded wearily 'The circumstances were not right, the scene of operations was not right, the enemy was not right, the population was hostile, everything was against its success'.[17]

Ultimately, the lessons learned from the special squads amounted to a list of what not to do. David Charters, while lauding

Fergusson's initiative and Farran's drive, is implicitly condemnatory in his final analysis: 'Special operations by their very nature are conducted in a legal and moral twilight zone; if control or discipline fails, they become merely a guise for counter-terrorism which reduces the government and the security forces to the status of criminals. Secret police methods make bad propaganda – if the cover is "blown", and tactical victories may be squandered by a strategic defeat.' This is exactly what happened and it points to the ultimate significance of the Rubowitz affair.[18]

Given such a catastrophic failure it is remarkable that Fergusson and Farran continue to be so widely admired, at least in military circles. Georgina Sinclair writes that 'It was perhaps fortunate for the Colonial Office that they were able to draw on a pool of former Palestine policemen with experience not only in security and intelligence work, but also in counter-insurgency warfare. They took their experiences to Malaya, Kenya and then to other colonial constabularies as unrest and emergency situations became the normality of end of empire.' It was not so fortunate for suspects gunned down without trial or detainees hanged after dubious judicial proceedings. The final tragedy of Roy Farran's false reputation and glamour is that it helped to justify shoot-to-kill policies on three continents, from Palestine to Northern Ireland. If this is the legacy of the 'special squads' it is hardly one for celebration, let alone emulation. At a time when counter-insurgency warfare is once again at the forefront of military operations by the British Army and NATO, it is perhaps an opportune moment to revisit the events that took place on that balmy evening in Jerusalem sixty years ago as warning of everything that can go wrong when young warriors directed by desperate and unscrupulous politicians wage war on terror.[19]

Notes

PROLOGUE

1 The following account of the abduction of Alexander Rubowitz is mainly based on the official police version: *Report on the Alleged Abduction and Murder of Alexander Rubowitz, And Subsequent Police Investigation*, by K. P. Hadingham, Superintendent of Police, Jerusalem District, 19 June 1947, (Hadingham Report), The National Archives of the UK: Public Record Office, records of the Colonial Office, CO537/2302. To avoid cluttering the notes with abbrevations document collections at The National Archives will be referred to by the department code (CO, FO, HO, LCO, KV, WO, CRIM, MEPO), series and piece number. See Sources and Bibliography to correlate the code with the department. Giora Goodman, 'Who Killed Alexander Rubowitz', *Ha'aretz Weekend Supplement*, 3 September 2004, pp. 14–20, made first use of this new documentation to tell the story in the Hebrew press.

2 For descriptions of Alexander Rubowitz and biographical details, verging on hagiography, see Amos Nebo, 'The Mystery of the Abduction and Murder of Alexander Rubowitz', *Makhaneh Gadna*, 15 May 1971 and 'Alexander Rubowitz' by Ezra Yakim, at http://www.eretzisraelforever.net.il/InTheirOwnWords. Obituary of Yedidya Rubowitz, *Palestine Post*, 21 January 1951. Ya'acov Rubowitz, Alexander's brother, spoke about their

mother's attitude in the interview with Amos Nebo.

3 Nebo, 'The Mystery of the Abduction and Murder of Alexander Rubowitz'; Jon Kimche, *Seven Fallen Pillars: The Middle East 1945–1953* (London, 1953), p. 199; J. Bowyer Bell, *Terror Out of Zion: The Fight for Israeli Independence* (New York, 1996 edn), pp. 108–9; Emmanuel Katz, *Lechi: Fighters for the Freedom of Israel (FFI)* trans. Herzlia Dobkin (Tel Aviv, 1987).

4 Nebo, 'The Mystery of the Abduction and Murder of Alexander Rubowitz'.

5 Expulsions from school, dismissals from places of work and worse were common during the periodic 'hunting seasons' when the Jewish Agency and the Hagana tried to suppress the 'dissidents': see Samuel Katz, *Days of Fire* (London, 1968), pp. 83–5, 182.

6 According to the hagiographic recollection by Ezra Yakim, one of Alexander's comrades, his mother pronounced: 'Each Jew must try to serve his people in his own way. If Haim (Alexander's *nom de guerre*) thinks this is the right one, we have no right to stand in his way.' See Yakim, 'Alexander Rubowitz'.

7 Yakim's recollections of these years are replicated in many memoirs of the Jewish underground, although few from LEHI are accessible in English. See, for instance, Menachem Begin, *The Revolt: The Memoirs of the Commander of the IZL* trans. Samuel Katz, ed. Ivan Greenberg (London, 1951); Doris Katz, *The Lady Was a Terrorist* (New York, 1953); Katz, *Days of Fire*.

8 Yakim, 'Alexander Rubowitz'.

9 The full witness statements and all the other official documents pertaining to the investigation of the disappearance of Alexander Rubowitz were destroyed in spring 1948. However, the local and international press named the witnesses and reported the evidence they gave in public before and during the judicial proceedings connected with the abduction: *HaMashkif*, 18 June 1947; *The Times, New York Herald Tribune, Palestine Post*, 2 October 1947. See also *Yediot Aharanot*, 6 October 1954.

10 *Palestine Post*, 22 May 1947; Hadingham Report, CO357/2302.

11 *Palestine Post*, 18, 21, 30 May 1947. Katz, *Days of Fire*, pp. 83–5, 182.

12 *Ha'aretz*, 9 May 1947.

13 ibid.; *Palestine Post*, 13 May 1947.

14 *HaBoker*, 20 May 1947; *Davar*, 20 May 1947 wrongly stating that the Rubowitz brothers had received a note saying that Alexander was held for a time in a jail in Ramle; *HaMashkif*, 21 May 1947. See trial report, *Palestine Post*, 2 October 1947.

15 Statement by Nehamiah Rubowitz, June 1947, Central Zionist Archives, Jerusalem (hereafter CZA), S25/6200. On Levitsky, see Katz, *Days of Fire*, p. 133.

16 *Palestine Post*, 22 May 1947; *Davar*, 26 May 1947.

17 A copy of the letter has survived in the archives of the Political Department of the Jewish Agency: Anonymous to Mrs Rubowitz, 23 May 1947, CZA, S25/6200.

18 *Palestine Post*, 30 May 1947.

CHAPTER ONE

1 There is a large and contentious literature on this subject. Two of the most reliable and readable studies are Mayir Verité, *From Palmerston to Balfour*, ed. Norman Rose (London, 1992) and Naomi Shepherd, *The Zealous Intruders: The Western Rediscovery of Palestine* (London, 1987).

2 Again, there is a vast and often polemical library of books on the topic. For recent and balanced accounts in addition to the above, see Isaiah Friedman, *The Question of Palestine: Britain, the Jews and the Arabs* (London, 1992 edn); David Vital, *The Origins of Zionism* (Oxford, 1975) and *Zionism: The Crucial Phase* (Oxford, 1987).

3 Naomi Shepherd, *Ploughing Sand: British Rule in Palestine* (London, 1999); Bernard Wasserstein, *The British in Palestine: The Mandatory Government and the Arab-Jewish Conflict, 1917–1929* (Oxford, second edn 1991). The Palestinian side of the story is set out in Illan Pappé, *A History of the Palestinians: One Land, Two Peoples* (Cambridge, 2004), pp.

24–90. See also Neville Mandel, *The Arabs and Zionism Before World War One* (Berkley, 1976) and Yehoshua Porath, *The Emergence of the Palestinian Arab National Movement, 1918–1929* (London, 1974).

4 For the political and diplomatic angles, see Norman Rose, *The Gentile Zionists: A Study in Anglo-Zionist Diplomacy, 1929–1939* (London, 1973), pp. 1–40; Yehoshua Porath, *The Palestinian National Movement: From Riots to Rebellion 1929–1939* (London, 1977).

5 Rose, *The Gentile Zionists*; Michael J. Cohen, *Retreat From the Mandate: The Making of British Policy, 1936–1945* (London, 1978), chapters 1–3; for the economic dimension of the uprising, see Kenneth Stein, *The Land Question in Palestine, 1917–1939* (Chapel Hill, 1984); Baruch Kimmerling and Joel S. Migdal, *The Palestinian People: A History* (Cambridge, Mass., 2003), pp. 102–31. All aspects are covered well in Tom Segev, *One Palestine, Complete: Jews and Arabs Under the British Mandate* (New York, 2000), parts 1–2.

6 Cohen, *Retreat From the Mandate*, chapters 5–9; Yehuda Bauer, *From Diplomacy to Resistance: A History of Jewish Palestine 1939–1945* trans. Alton Winters (New York, 1970), pp. 16–56.

7 Walter Laqueur, *A History of Zionism* (New York, 1978 edn), pp. 270–383; Mitchell Cohen, *Zion and State: Nation, Class and the Shaping of Modern Israel* (New York, 1992); Bowyer Bell, *Terror Out of Zion*, pp. 10–53, 62–100.

8 Joseph Heller, *The Stern Gang: Ideology, Politics and Terror 1940–1949* (London, 1995), especially pp. 45–145.

9 Ronald Zweig, *Britain and Palestine During the Second World War* (London, 1986); Michael Makovsky, *Churchill's Promised Land: Zionism and Statecraft* (New Haven, 2007), especially pp. 140–224; Bauer, *From Diplomacy to Resistance*, pp. 224–72.

10 Michael J. Cohen, *Palestine and the Great Powers 1945–1948* (Princeton, 1982), pp. 16–28; Martin Jones, *Failure in Palestine: British and United States Policy After the Second World War* (London, 1986), pp 39–48.

11 Jones, *Failure in Palestine*, pp. 48–57; cf. Ritchie Ovendale, *Britain, the United States and the End of the Palestine Mandate*

(London, 1989), pp. 77–105; Frank Heinlein, *British Government Policy and Decolonisation 1945–1963: Scrutinising the Official Mind* (London, 2002), pp. 11–18.

12 Jones, *Failure in Palestine*, pp. 57–69.

13 Cohen, *Palestine and the Great Powers*, pp. 68–74.

14 Richard Crossman, *Palestine Mission: A Personal Record* (London, 1947); William Roger Louis, *The British Empire in the Middle East 1945–1951* (Oxford, 1984), pp. 396–419.

15 Cohen, *Palestine and the Great Powers*, pp. 96–115; Jones, *Failure in Palestine*, pp. 70–105; Ovendale, *Britain, the United States and the End of the Palestine Mandate*, pp. 106–40.

16 Cohen, *Palestine and the Great Powers*, pp. 116–34; Jones, *Failure in Palestine*, pp. 105–43; Louis, *The British Empire in the Middle East*, pp. 434–8.

17 Cohen, *Palestine and the Great Powers*, pp. 197–202; Jones, *Failure in Palestine*, pp. 165–70.

18 Cohen, *Palestine and the Great Powers*, pp. 162–70; Jones, *Failure in Palestine*, pp. 170–84; Louis, *The British Empire in the Middle East*, pp. 438–46; Ovendale, *Britain, the United States and the End of the Palestine Mandate*, pp. 141–70.

19 Sir Charles Jeffries, *The Colonial Police* (London, 1952), pp. 157–9; Georgina Sinclair, *At the End of the Line: Colonial Policing and the Imperial Endgame 1945–1980* (Manchester, 2006), p. 22.

20 The sub-units fluctuated with bewildering speed. Gregory Blaxland, *The Regiments Depart: A History of the British Army 1945–1970* (London, 1971), pp. 27–59; David Charters, *The British Army and Jewish Insurgency in Palestine, 1945–1947* (London, 1989), pp. 88–9, 145–8.

21 Charters, *The British Army and Jewish Insurgency in Palestine*, pp. 42–52; Saul Zadka, *Blood in Zion: How the Jewish Guerrillas Drove the British out of Palestine* (London, 1995), pp. 137–9.

22 Charters, *The British Army and Jewish Insurgency in Palestine*, pp. 53–65. See also Appendix III: Insurgent Operations in Palestine, pp. 182–97.

23 Charters, *The British Army and Jewish Insurgency in Palestine*, Appendix III: Insurgent Operations in Palestine, pp. 182–97.

24 Major R. D. 'Dare' Wilson, *Cordon and Search: With 6th Airborne*

Division in Palestine (Aldershot, 1949), pp. 40–8; Charters, *The British Army and Jewish Insurgency in Palestine*, Appendix III: Insurgent Operations in Palestine, pp. 182–97. On the Anglo-American Committee, see Cohen, *Palestine and the Great Powers*, pp. 96–115; Jones, *Failure in Palestine*, pp. 70–105.

25 Charters, *The British Army and Jewish Insurgency in Palestine*, Appendix III: Insurgent Operations in Palestine, pp. 182–97.

26 John Strawson, 'Cunningham, Sir Alan Gordon (1887–1983)', rev. *Oxford Dictionary of National Biography* (Oxford 2004); online edition, January 2006 (http://www.oxforddnb.com/view/article/30991, accessed 21 January 2008). Norman and Helen Bentwich, *Mandate Memories 1918–1948* (London, 1965), p. 171.

27 Sir Alan Cunningham to Secretary of State for the Colonies, 1 and 4 December 1945, Cunningham Papers, Middle East Centre Archive, St Antony's College, Oxford, Box 1, file 1 (hereafter CP, Box 1/1 etc.); Bartley Crum, *Behind the Silken Curtain* (London, 1947), p. 165; Golda Meir, *My Life* (London, 1975), p. 167. William Roger Louis, 'Sir Alan Cunningham and the end of British Rule in Palestine', *The Journal of Imperial and Commonwealth History*, 16(3) 1988, pp. 128–47.

28 Edward Horne, *A Job Well Done: A History of the Palestine Police Force 1920–1948* (Lewes, Sussex, 2003 edn), pp. 35–101. See also Sinclair, *At the End of the Line*, pp. 19–24 and Jeffries, *The Colonial Police*, pp. 152–62.

29 Charles Smith, 'Communal Conflict and Insurrection in Palestine, 1936–1948' in David Anderson and David Killingray, *Policing and Decolonisation: Politics, Nationalism and the Police, 1917–1965* (Manchester, 1992), pp. 62–70.

30 Georgina Sinclair, '"Hard-headed, Hardbitten, Hard-hitting and Courageous Men of Innate Detective Ability . . .": From Criminal Investigation to Political and Security Policing at End of Empire, 1945–1950', in Clive Emsley and Haia Shpayer-Makov eds, *Police Detectives in History 1750–1950* (Aldershot, 2006), pp. 202–3; David Charters, 'British Intelligence in the Palestine Campaign, 1945–1947', *Intelligence and National Security* 6:1 (1991), pp. 115–40.

31 Memoirs of Brigadier John Murray Rymer-Jones, Imperial War Museum Department of Documents, 67/71/1, pp. 123–6; Horne, *A Job Well Done*, pp. 315–37, 463–79, 497–510, 515–25; Sinclair, *At the End of the Line*, pp. 105–17, 109–11; Jeffries, *The Colonial Police*, pp. 157–8; Smith, 'Communal Conflict and Insurrection in Palestine', pp. 71–4.

32 Rymer-Jones, Memoirs, p. 143; Smith, 'Communal Conflict, and Insurrection in Palestine', p. 76; Tim Jones, *Post-war Counter-insurgency and the SAS 1945–1952: A Special Type of Warfare* (London, 2001), pp. 28–9.

33 Cunningham to Sir George Gater, permanent undersecretary at the Home Office, 7 January 1946, CP, Box 1/1; David Twiston Davies ed., *The Daily Telegraph Book of Military Obituaries* (London, 2003), pp. 242–6.

34 *Palestine Post*, 5 March 1946 Bryan Samian, *Commando Men: The Story of a Royal Marine Commando in North-West Europe* (London, 1948), pp. 48–9; John Day, *A Plain Russet-Coated Captain* (London, 1993), pp. 34, 37.

35 Samian, *Commando Men*, pp. 8–30; Peter Barnard, *The Story of 45 Royal Marine Commando 1943–1945* (London, 1945), pp. 12–28; David Young, *Four Five: The Story of 45 Commando, Royal Marines, 1943–1971* (London, 1972), pp. 22–36.

36 Barnard, *The Story of 45 Royal Marine Commando*, pp. 45, 62–7, 74–81; Samian, *Commando Men*, pp. 120–1; Young, *Four Five*, pp. 84–91, 97–108, 123–6.

37 Horne, *A Job Well Done*, pp. 474–5, 523–4, 557–8.

38 ibid., pp. 557–8, 564–5. Sinclair, '"Hard-headed, Hardbitten, Hard-hitting and Courageous Men"', p. 203; Smith, 'Communal Conflict and Insurrection in Palestine', p. 76; cf. Jones, *Post-war Counter-insurgency and the SAS*, pp. 28–9.

39 Cunningham to CO, 1 November 1946; Notes of discussion with IG Palestine Police, 29 November 1946; minute by Attlee, 26 November 1946, CO537/1699; CO to Cunningham, 13 November 1946, CP, Box 1/3; Anthony Kemp, *SAS: The First Secret Wars* (London, 2005), pp. 74–5.

40 Bernard Fergusson, *Travel Warrant* (London, 1979), pp. 19–34.

41 Bernard Fergusson, *The Trumpet in the Hall* (London, 1970), pp. 11–22, 24–5.

42 ibid., pp. 28–52; Charles Townshend, *Britain's Civil Wars: Counter-insurgency in the Twentieth Century* (London, 1986), pp. 118–19 remarks that 'Orde Wingate was dead, but his Chindit right-hand man, Bernard Fergusson, came to Palestine as Assistant Inspector General to establish secret anti-terrorist groups.' See also Thomas Mockaitis, *British Counter-insurgency 1919–1960* (London, 1990), p. 44.

43 Fergusson, *The Trumpet in the Hall*, pp. 61–141 and *Beyond the Chindwin* (London, 1945).

44 Fergusson, *The Trumpet in the Hall*, pp. 192–9; Rymer-Jones, *Memoirs*, pp. 108–46; Horne, *A Job Well Done*, pp. 510, 515–16, 555–6.

45 Fergusson, *The Trumpet in the Hall*, pp. 200–2. Fergusson's memoir is, to put it politely, disinformation intended to confuse anyone trying to trace the origins of the disastrous anti-terrorist initiative that he came to lead.

46 ibid.; report by Sir Charles Wickham to chief secretary Palestine government, 2 December 1946, CO537/2269, hereafter the Wickham Report. The discrepancy was noted by Tim Jones, *SAS: The First Secret Wars* (London, 2005), pp. 74–6, who also speculates on its true purpose.

47 Cunningham to CO, 1 August 1946; CO to Cunningham, 7 August 1947; Wickham to Cunningham, 20 August 1946; Cunningham to Wickham, 5 September 1946, CO537/3847.

48 Wickham Report.

49 ibid.; see also Sinclair, *At the End of the Line*, pp. 108–10.

50 Cunningham to Wickham, 5 September 1946 and Wickham to Cunningham, 4 October 1946, CO537/3847; Horne, *A Job Well Done*, pp. 561–3; minute by W. W. Clark reflecting on the impact which the report had in autumn 1946 on the appointment of seconded army officers, 12 February 1947, CO537/2270.

51 For contrasting views of the Wickham Report, see Smith, 'Communal Conflict and Insurrection in Palestine', pp. 75–6 and Jones, *Post-war Counter-insurgency and the SAS*, pp. 28–9.

Jones speculates that Wickham, thanks to his experiences in Ireland and Greece, helped to cultivate the soil for small-unit anti-terrorist operations. Yet this runs counter to the tenor of his report.

52 Charters, *The British Army and Jewish Insurgency in Palestine*, pp. 85–99, 111–17. 'Action to be Taken Against Jewish Terrorists', issued by 6th Airborne Division General Staff on 14 September 1946 includes patrolling, roadblocks, spot checks on cafes, towns and settlements known to be frequented by suspects, and searches: Papers of General Sir Hugh Stockwell, Liddell Hart Centre for Military Archives, King's College, London, (hereafter Stockwell Papers) 6/1.

53 Harry Sacher, *Israel: The Establishment of a State* (London 1952), p. 48; Cohen, *Palestine and the Great Powers*, pp. 74–8; Joseph Heller, 'Neither Masada – Nor Vichy: Diplomacy and Resistance in Zionist Politics, 1945–1947', *International History Review*, 3:4 (1981), pp. 552–4.

54 Cabinet minutes, 20 June 1946, CM (46) 60 Conclusions, in Bruce Hoffman ed., *The Failure of British Military Strategy Within Palestine 1939–1947* (Bar Ilan University, 1983), pp. 96–102; Charters, *The British Army and Jewish Insurgency in Palestine*, pp. 18–24

55 Obituary of General Sir Evelyn Barker, *The Times*, 25 November 1983; Alun Chalfont, *Montgomery of Alamein* (London 1976), for his early life, military career, *passim*, and appointment as CIGS, p. 278; Nigel Hamilton, *Monty: The Field Marshal, 1944–1976* (London 1986), pp. 641–7.

56 The definitive three-volume biography is Nigel Hamilton, *Monty: The Life of Montgomery of Alemein: The Making of a General 1887–1942; Monty: Master of the Battlefield 1942–1944; Monty: The Field Marshal, 1944–1976*, (London 1981–6).

57 Montgomery briefing to army commanders, 25 July 1946, Papers of Field Marshal Viscount Montgomery of Alamein, Imperial War Museum Department of Documents, BLM175/1 (hereafter BLM/ etc.) BLM175/1; Cohen, *Palestine and the Great Powers*, pp. 34–9; Jones, *Failure in Palestine*, pp. 27–8,

51–2, 85–7, 91–7, 121–4; Charters, *The British Army and Jewish Insurgency in Palestine*, pp. 18–24.

58 Diary of Field Marshal Montgomery, Part 1, 1 May-29 September 1946, chapter 3, BLM.175/1.

59 Montgomery directive to CICMELF, 27 June 1946, BLM211/3.

60 General Sir Richard Gale, *Call To Arms: An Autobiography* (London, 1968), pp. 168–9; Wilson, *Cordon and Search*, pp. 56–62; Charters, *The British Army and Jewish Insurgency in Palestine*, pp. 117–18; Zadka, *Blood in Zion*, pp. 139–41.

61 CIGS to CICMELF, 1 July 1946, BLM211/3. CAB 63 (46), 1 July 1946, BLM211/5; Hoffman ed., *The Failure of British Military Strategy Within Palestine*, p. 22. See also Thurston Clarke, *By Blood and Fire: The Attack on the King David Hotel* (London, 1981).

62 CAB 73 (46), 25 July 1946, BLM211/70; Cabinet minutes, 23 July 1946, CM (46) 72 Conclusions, CAB128/6 in Hoffman ed., *The Failure of British Military Strategy Within Palestine*, pp. 103–9 and Cabinet minutes, 30 July 1946, CM (46) 75 Conclusions, CAB128/6 in Hoffman ed., *The Failure of British Military Strategy Within Palestine*, pp. 112–15.

63 Barker to CO, 22 July 1946, CP, Box 1/1; Dempsey to Montgomery, 24 July 1946, WO216/194, in Hoffman ed., *The Failure of British Military Strategy Within Palestine*, pp. 109–10; Cunningham to CO, 23, 24 and 27 July 1946, CP, Box 1/1; CO to Cunningham, 25, 26 July 1946, CP, Box 1/1. Charters, *The British Army and Jewish Insurgency in Palestine*, pp. 119–20.

64 Cohen, *Palestine and the Great Powers*, pp. 90–3; Charters, *The British Army and Jewish Insurgency in Palestine*, pp. 69–70.

65 ibid. Barker was indubitably and unapologetically anti-Jewish: see Segev, *One Palestine, Complete*, pp. 468–70, 479–80.

66 CO to Cunningham, 29 July 1946, CP, Box 1/1; Montgomery Diary, BLM175/1, chapter 7; Montgomery to Hall, 6 August 1946, BLM211/10.

67 See Monthly Survey of Palestine Affairs sent to the CO, 5 November 1946, CP, Box 1/3; Montgomery Diary, BLM177/1, Pt IV.

68 Cabinet minutes, 30 July 1946, CM (46) 94 Conclusions, BLM211/13; Dempsey to Montgomery, 16 November 1946,

BLM211/12; Dempsey to Cunningham, 19 November 1946, CP, Box 1/3; Cunningham to CO, 19 November, CP, Box 1/3; Mockaitis, *British Counter-insurgency 1919–1960*, pp. 101–7 and Townshend, *Britain's Civil War*, pp. 118–19.

69 Telephone report by Mr Ward to FO, 4 a.m., 31 October 1946, FO371/60786; embassy report to FO, 31 October 1946; Sir Noel Charles to FO, 3 November 1946, CO537/1729. For press reports see *The Times, Daily Telegraph, Manchester Guardian*, 1 November 1946. The full text of the communiqué is in Rome Embassy to FO, 4 November 1946, FO371/60786. The version of the communiqué printed in the British and Jewish press differs in terms of translation and editing. Compare *The Times, Manchester Guardian*, 5 November 1946, the *Jewish Chronicle*, 8 November 1946 and the pro-Irgun *Jewish Standard*, 18 November 1946. See also *Daily Mail*, 13 November 1946.

70 Report by A. J. Kellar, MI5, February 1945; high commission for Palestine to CO, 19 March 1945; Brigadier Sir David Petrie to Sir Alexander Maxwell, HO, 2 April 1945; Lieutenant Colonel P. R. Barry, MI5, to MI11, 23 April 1945, KV5/29. The same file contains reports of conversations between the DSO Palestine and Kollek dated 18 August and 15 September 1945 that were forwarded to London. See Ronen Bergman, 'The Scorpion File', *Seven Days* magazine, *Yediot Aharanot*, 30 March 2007.

71 Liddell to Assistant Deputy Commissioner A. Canning, Special Branch, 15 January 1946 and 14 February 1946, KV5/29. The high commission for Palestine passed the same alert to the CO, 13 February 1946, KV5/29. J. C. Robertson, MI5, to J. D. Bates, CO, 2 January 1946, CO537/1723.

72 CO to high commission for Palestine, 17 August 1946, CO537/1723. A. J. Kellar, MI5 to Trafford Smith, 26 August 1946; Oldfield message, 27 August 1946; J. C. Robertson, MI5, to Burt and Robertson to Trafford Smith, FO, 27 August 1946, KV3/30.

73 'Notes for DGs Meeting with PM', 28 August 1946, KV3/41. Also, warnings to WO against Jewish terrorists entering the

UK as military personnel, J. C. Robertson, MI5, to Trafford Smith, FO, 20 September 1946 and Sir George Gater, permanent undersecretary at the HO, to Sir Edward Bridges, Cabinet Office, 25 September 1946, discussing co-ordination of security for government buildings CO537/1723. J. C. Robertson, MI5, 'Present Trends in Zionism', 2 September 1946, KV3/41.

74 'United Zionist Revisionists – Notes on Activities', 23 September 1946, KV3/41; Bowyer Bell, *Terror Out of Zion*, pp. 128–33, 178–9; Katz, *Days of Fire*, pp. 103–10 and translation of the Hebrew version of his Personal Memoirs posted at http://www.eretzisraelforever.net/katz; *Daily Telegraph*, 10 November 1946.

75 Katz, Personal Memoirs; on Tavin, see also biographical details at http://www.eretzisraelforever.net/InTheir OwnWords.

76 Telephone report by Ward to FO, 4 a.m., 31 October 1946, FO371/60786; embassy report to FO, 31 October 1946; Sir Noel Charles to FO, 3 November 1946, CO537/1729. Report by J. O'Sullivan, Palestine CID, 17 November 1946, CO537/1729. *The Times, Daily Telegraph, Manchester Guardian*, 1 November 1946.

77 Ward to FO, 4.20 a.m., 31 October 1946, FO371/60786; Attlee (via FO) to Rome Embassy, 11 a.m., 31 October 1946, FO371/60786; Carey Foster, British Embassy to CO, 1 November 1946; CO to high commission for Palestine, 1 November 1946, FO371/60786.

78 Sir Noel Charles to FO, 3 November 1946, CO537/1720.

79 Rome Embassy to FO, 4 November 1946, FO371/60786; high commission to CO, 2 November 1946; Report by J. O'Sullivan, 17 November 1946, CO537/1729. *The Times, Daily Telegraph*, 2 November 1946.

80 Rome Embassy to FO, 5 and 9 November 1946, FO to New York, 13 November 1946, FO371/60786. Sir Noel Charles to Foreign Secretary Bevin, 14 January 1947, FO371/67796.

81 Preliminary Report on the Rome Outrage by Richard Catling and J. O'Sullivan, 16 November 1946, CO537/1729; Begin, *The Revolt*, pp. 117, 131–2. Moshe Galili had organised several boatloads of illegal immigrants to Palestine before

the war. He had been a member of BETAR in his youth and studied in Italy so he knew the terrain well: Dalia Ofer, *Escaping the Holocaust* (New York, 1990), pp. 12–13, 71–3.

82 Preliminary Report on the Rome Outrage by Richard Catling and J. O'Sullivan, 16 November 1946; Rome Embassy to FO, 29 November 1946; high commission for Palestine to CO, 18 December 1946; CO to high commission, 23 December 1946, CO537/1729; Rome Embassy to FO, 4 January 1947; Rome Embassy to FO, 22 October 1947; FO to Rome Embassy, 3 December 1947, FO371/67796; Yitshaq Ben-Ami, *Years of Wrath, Days of Glory: Memoirs from the Irgun* (New York, 1983 edn), p. 395; Begin, *The Revolt*, p. 132; Katz, *Personal Memoirs*.

83 J. C. Robertson, MI5, to Telfer Smollet, WO, 9 November 1946, KV5/38; report from CID Jerusalem, 12 November 1946, CO537/1729; note of threat to Montgomery, 6 November 1946, CO537/1723; MI5 to SIME, DSO Palestine, 14 November 1946, KV5/38; J. C. Robertson to A. J. Kellar, November 1946; note by Robertson, 6 November 1946; Robertson exchanges with Kellar, November 1946, KV4/216.

84 *Daily Mail, Daily Telegraph*, 11 November 1946.

85 *Inspector Burt of Scotland Yard by Himself* (London, 1959), p. 118; *The Times, Daily Telegraph*, 11 November 1946.

86 *The Times, Daily Telegraph*, 12 November 1946; *Daily Mail, Daily Telegraph*, 13 November 1946; threatening letter to Christopher Mayhew, undersecretary for foreign affairs, 5 December 1946, FO371/61586. A similar phone threat was made to the colonial secretary, Arthur Creech Jones. See also A. J. Kellar, MI5, to Trafford Smith, FO, 18 December 1946, CO537/1723; death threat to Vansittart, 5 December 1946, KV5/35.

87 'United Zionist Revisionists', 23 September 1946, KV3/41; *Daily Telegraph*, 13 November 1946; Creech Jones to Shawcross, 16 January 1947, FO371/61865.

88 *The Times, Daily Telegraph*, 14 November 1946.

89 *The Times; Daily Telegraph*, 15 November 1946.

90 *The Times*, 14 November 1946; Begin, *The Revolt*, p. 131; Bowyer Bell, *Terror Out of Zion*, p. 181.

91 Defence Committee minutes, 20 November 1946, BLM211/15.
92 B. L. Montgomery, *The Memoirs of the Field Marshal Viscount Montgomery of Alamein* (London, 1958), pp. 467–8; colonial secretary to Cunningham, 21 November 1946, CP, Box 1/3; Montgomery to Dempsey, 21 November 1946, BLM211/16.
93 Minutes of conference held at Government House, Jerusalem, 29 November 1946, BLM177/8; Townshend, *Britain's Civil Wars*, pp. 115–17; Jones, *Counter-insurgency and the SAS*, pp. 26–8.
94 Montgomery Diary, BLM177/1, Pt IV; Montgomery to VCIGS and WO, 2 December 1946, BLM211/21.
95 Cunningham to Creech Jones, 3 December 1946, CP, Box 1/3.
96 Joint WO-CO memorandum prepared in accordance with the view of the Defence Committee 20 November 1946, 19 December 1946, BLM211/22.
97 Wilson, *Cordon and Search*, pp. 85–90; Cohen, *Palestine and the Great Powers*, pp. 177–83, 229–35; Jones, *Failure in Palestine*, pp. 196–8.
98 Defence Committee minutes, 1 January 1947, BLM211/23; Montgomery Diary, 10 November 1946–3 February 1947, chapter 33, BLM178/1.
99 Note of Conference at the CO, 3 January 1947, BLM211/24 reproduced in Hoffman ed., *The Failure of British Military Strategy Within Palestine*, pp. 131–4.
100 Montgomery to Creech Jones, 4 January 1947, BLM210/4; Army Council Secretariat brief for Secretary of State for War, 14 January 1947, BLM211/27; Directive to high commissioner for Palestine on the Employment of the Armed Forces in the Suppression of Terrorism, 7 January 1947, BLM/4. Cunningham informed the CO that at a meeting on 13 January Ben-Gurion seemed 'genuinely worried at the prospect of continued terrorism and the inability of the Jews themselves to stop it': Cunningham to CO, 13 January 1947, CP, Box 1/4.
101 Cabinet minutes, 15 January 1947, CM 6 (47) Conclusions, BLM211/13; Montgomery to Dempsey, 16 January 1947, BLM211/28. For differently weighted accounts of the clash of strategies and personalities, see Hoffman ed., *The Failure*

of British Military Strategy Within Palestine, pp. 23–9; Townshend, *Britain's Civil Wars*, pp. 115–6; Louis, 'Sir Alan Cunningham and the End of the British Rule in Palestine', pp. 130–1; Charters, *The British Army and Jewish Insurgency in Palestine*, pp. 100–7; Jones, *Counter-insurgency and the SAS*, pp. 26–8; John Newsinger, *British Counter-insurgency: From Palestine to Northern Ireland* (Basingstoke, 2002), pp. 20–4.

CHAPTER TWO

1 Order from General Barker, 23 January 1947, CP, Box 1/4, also in Hoffman ed., *The Failure of British Military Strategy Within Palestine*, pp. 135–6; Cunningham to CO, 2 February 1947, CP, Box 1/4; MacMillan, Lieutenant General G. H. A. MacMillan, *Palestine Narrative of events from February 1947 until withdrawal of all British Troops* (1948), pp 2–3, Papers of Lieutenant General G. H. A. MacMillan, IWM Department of Documents, pp. 2–3; Wilson, *Cordon and Search*, pp. 102–3.

2 Townshend, *Britain's Civil Wars*, pp. 116–17; David A. Charters, 'Special Operations in Counter-insurgency: The Farran Case, Palestine 1947', *Journal of the Royal United Services Institute*, 124:2 (1979), p. 58. Jones, *Post-war Counter-insurgency and the SAS*, pp. 35–6 argues that the squads were brought into existence by a clique of senior officers promoting the idea of special forces. Townshend, *Britain's Civil Wars*, pp. 118–19 detects the influence of Wingate on Fergusson: Wingate set up the 'Special Night Squads' in the late 1930s, highly trained small units of Jewish policemen who tracked and hunted down Arab guerrillas. Fergusson, of course, served under Wingate in Burma.

3 Bernard Fergusson to Sir Thomas Lloyd permanent under-secretary, CO, 'Secondment of Army Officers to Palestine Police', 12 February 1946, CO537/2270.

4 Fergusson, 'Secondment of Army Officers to Palestine Police', 12 February 1946, CO537/2270.

5 Rymer-Jones, Memoirs, p. 151; Cunningham to Gray, 5 February 1947; Fergusson to Gray, 6 February 1947,

CO537/2270. Mathieson, CO, to Howe, HO, 22 September 1947, CO537/2302.

6 Sir Eric Speed to Sir Thomas Lloyd, 6 February 1947; Cunningham to CO, 11 February 1947; Martin to Lloyd, 13 February 1947; minute by J. Martin, 13 February 1947; Lloyd to Speed, 13 February 1947, CO537/2270.

7 Fergusson, *Trumpet in the Hall*, pp. 210–11; Cunningham to Martin, CO, 19 January 1947, CP, Box 1/4. Colonel C. R. W. Norman to Mrs Norman, 2 February 1947, Papers of Colonel C. R. W. Norman, IWM Written Archive, 87/57/2. Jones, *Post-war Counter-insurgency and the SAS*, p. 35, maintains that Fergusson drew up a list of possible recruits who had served in SIS (MI6) and SOE using his SAS contacts for information, especially Brigadier Mike Calvert. He states that 'SIS offered the Colonial Office the services of three officers trained in special operations'. However, the basis for this assertion is sketchy. Jones may be more correct in stating that 'by March, all Whitehall's main IS [internal security] agencies accepted the potential value of wartime experience for COIN [counter-insurgency]'. See also Charters, 'Special Operations in Counter-insurgency: The Farran Case', p. 58.

8 Rymer-Jones, Memoirs, p. 151.

9 Fergusson, *Trumpet in the Hall*, pp. 206, 221–2; Horne, *A Job Well Done*, pp. 564–5. This interpretation is followed by Sinclair, '"Hard-headed, Hardbitten, Hard-hitting and Courageous Men"', p. 204. On the supposed differences of emphasis between Cunningham, Gray and Fergusson see Townshend, *Britain's Civil Wars*, pp. 118–19; Charters, 'Special Operations in Counter-insurgency: The Farran Case', pp. 58–9; Smith, 'Communal Conflict and Insurrection', pp. 76–7.

10 Nicholas Bethell, *The Palestine Triangle: The Struggle Between the British, the Jews and the Arabs 1935–1948* (London, 1979), pp. 302–3.

11 Information from the CV Roy Farran submitted to the Progressive Conservative Party in Calgary, Canada: papers of the Alberta Progressive Conservative Party, Glenbow Archive, Calgary, M1744, file 94. For slightly incorrect obituaries see

Daily Telegraph, 5 June 2006, *The Times*, 6 June 2006. Farran certainly liked to give the impression that he was born in India: see Edward Romaine, 'The Charmed Life of Roy Farran', *Weekend Magazine*, vol. 6, no. 50, 1956, p. 6; cf. the *Albertan*, 1 June 1976.

12 History of Bishop Cotton School, http://bishopcottonshimla. com/history.htm. accessed 19 July 2007.

13 Romaine, 'The Charmed Life of Roy Farran', pp. 6–7; Roy Farran, *Winged Dagger: Adventures on Special Service* (London, 1948), p. 174.

14 Trooper R. A. Farran, 6803683, date of enlistment 31 May 1939, joined the RAC Wing OCTU some time in late 1939 and left on 27 April 1940 with a commission in the 3rd Dragoon Guards. Information about Farran at the Royal Military Academy kindly supplied by Dr Peter Thwaite, archivist, RMA. Fergusson, *Trumpet in the Hall*, p. 225.

15 Hector Bolitho, *The Galloping Third: The Story of the 3rd King's Own Hussars* (Aldershot, 1963).

16 Fergusson, *Trumpet in the Hall*, p. 235; Colonel Henry 'Todd' Sweeney, Imperial War Museum Sound Archive, 11133, tape 2; Major Victor Dover, *The Silken Canopy* (London, 1979), p. 45. Farran's candid autobiography, *Winged Dagger*, gives the full flavour of his character with all its contradictions. See also 'The Mystery of Major Farran', *Daily Express*, 6 August 1947.

17 Farran, *Winged Dagger*, pp. 20–32. Jon Latimer, *Alamein* (London, 2002), pp. 11–13; Stephen Bungay, *Alamein* (London, 2002), p. 6.

18 Farran, *Winged Dagger*, pp. 33–84; Major General G. L. Verney, *The Desert Rats: The 7th Armoured Division in World War II* (London, 1954), pp. 36–48.

19 Farran, *Winged Dagger*, pp. 84–91. For a fine account of the battle, using Farran's reminiscences, see Antony Beevor, *Crete: The Battle and the Resistance* (London, 1991).

20 Farran, *Winged Dagger*, pp. 102–6.

21 After the war Filer claimed that he helped Farran, too, but there is nothing in Farran's memoir to confirm this: *Yediot Aharanot*, 19 September 1946.

22 Recommendation for Award of Military Cross, 4 November 1941, WO373/27 and Bar to MC, 26 March 1942, WO373/61; Farran, *Winged Dagger*, pp. 107–36.

23 ibid., pp. 136–40.

24 ibid., pp. 140, 142–51; Verney: *The 7th Armoured Division*, pp. 101, 104–18.

25 ibid., pp. 152–6, 161–2; Anthony Kemp, *The SAS: The Special Air Service Regiment 1941–1945* (London, 1991), p. 97.

26 ibid., pp. 5–97; J. Strawson, *A History of the SAS Regiment* (London, 1984).

27 Farran, *Winged Dagger*, pp. 157–9, 162–3.

28 Shabtai Teveth, *Moshe Dayan* (London, 1972), p. 151–2; Farran, *Winged Dagger*, pp. 164–7, 206–7.

29 Dover, *The Silken Canopy*, pp. 44–5.

30 Kemp, *The SAS*, pp. 103–4; Gavin Mortimer, *Stirling's Men: The Inside History of the SAS in World War II* (London, 2004), pp. 89–94; Farran, *Winged Dagger*, pp. 167–72, 175–85.

31 ibid., pp. 186–98, 201–7; Kemp, *The SAS*, pp. 104–9; Hamish Ross, *Paddy Mayne: Lt Col Blair 'Paddy' Mayne and 1st SAS Regiment* (London, 2003), pp. 117–26.

32 Recommendation for Award of Second Bar to Military Cross, 10 February 1944, WO373/4; Farran, *Winged Dagger*, pp. 187–222; Kemp, *The SAS*, pp. 114–15.

33 Farran, *Winged Dagger*, pp. 223–4, 238–54; recommendation for Award of Distinguished Service Order, 17 January 1945, WO373/53; Mortimer, *Stirling's Men*, pp. 244–55; Kemp, *The SAS*, pp. 173–8, for accounts of Operation Wallace. Farran's Post Operation Report from WO218/197 is reprinted in Kemp, *The SAS*, pp. 237–40.

34 Farran, *Winged Dagger*, pp. 255–62; Kemp, *The SAS*, p. 203; Tim Jones, *SAS: The First Secret Wars: The Unknown Years of Combat and Counter-insurgency* (London, 2005), p. 12 and pp. 13–32 on Greece.

35 Roy Farran, *Operation Tombola* (London, 1960), pp. 6–7, 17–18; Kemp, *The SAS*, pp. 203–5; Mortimer, *Stirling's Men*, pp. 281–4.

36 Farran, *Winged Dagger*, pp. 263–71.

37 ibid., pp. 168, 271; Farran, *Operation Tombola*, pp. 17–18, 19.

38 ibid., pp. 47ff.

39 Kemp, *The SAS*, pp. 208–9.

40 Farran, *Operation Tombola*, pp. 83–114. For other experiences of this campaign, see Mortimer, *Stirling's Men*, pp. 285–90.

41 Farran, *Operation Tombola*, pp. 120–254.

42 Kemp, *The SAS*, pp. 209–11; Farran, *Operation Tombola*, p. 254.

43 Farran, *Winged Dagger*, pp. 341–2.

44 ibid., p. 343. For recollections of the 3rd King's Own Hussars at this time, see R. Hammerton, *Cliff and I (Memories of Army Service from 1944–1948)*, pp. 14–15, Imperial War Museum Department of Documents, 05/45/1.

45 Farran, *Winged Dagger*, pp. 142, 239, 253 and 343–4 for his treatment of a captured Muslim; Farran, *Operation Tombola*, pp. 48, 61.

46 *HaBoker*, 7 July 1947; *Palestine Post*, 9 July 1947.

47 Farran, *Winged Dagger*, pp. 370–2.

48 Wilson, *Cordon and Search*, pp. 40–1; Farran, *Winged Dagger*, pp. 344–5.

49 ibid.

50 ibid., pp. 346–7.

51 Jones, *Post-war Counter-insurgency and the SAS*, pp. 35–6; Jones, *SAS: The First Secret Wars*, pp. 13–74.

52 Ya'acov Eliav, *Wanted* trans. Mordecai Schreiber (New York, 1984), pp. 17–33, 39–41, 61–5, 68–70, 103–95, 203–33.

53 *Daily Express*, 25 August 1948; Eliav, *Wanted*, pp. 235–9. On David Knout and his activity, see Asher Cohen, *Persécution et Sauvetages: Juifs et Français sous l'Occupation et sous Vichy* (Paris, 1993), pp. 378–82, and Renée Poznanski, *Jews in France During World War Two*, (Hanover NH, 2001), pp. 155–7. See also 'What connects Molotov, LEHI underground?' by Yinon Royhman, posted on 11 May 2006, at http://www.ynetnews.com/articles/0,7340,L-3320855,00.html. It is, however, a myth that Molotov was related to the composer Scriabin, and therefore that there was any connection between Betty Knut and the Soviet foreign minister.

54 MI5 briefing, 'Zionist Subversive Activities', 16 March

1948, (probably by A. J. Kellar) KV3/41; Eliav, *Wanted*, pp. 240–2.

55 *The Times, Daily Telegraph, Daily Mail, Manchester Guardian*, 8 March 1947; undated leaflet, LEHI communiqués and posters, 1941–9, LEHI Collection, JI K5–2/1. Whether the communiqué was not noticed by the British press or deliberately ignored it was not reported in London.

56 Eliav, *Wanted*, pp. 243–6; Annie Cohen-Solal, *Sartre: A Life* (London, 1991 edn), pp. 205, 284–5.

57 *The Times*, 17 April 1947; *Palestine Post*, 18 April 1947; Eliav, *Wanted*, p. 243.

58 Burt, *Commander Burt of the Yard*, pp. 126–7.

59 On McGregor's background and recruitment, see Jones, *Post-war Counter-insurgency and the SAS*, p. 36 and Jones, *SAS: The First Secret Wars*, p. 78, Kemp, *The SAS*, pp. 111–14, 185–6.

60 Farran, *Winged Dagger*, p. 348; Fergusson, *Trumpet in the Hall*, pp. 225–6.

61 ibid.; Farran, *Winged Dagger*, pp. 348–50; Sinclair, "'Hardheaded, Hardbitten, Hard-hitting and Courageous Men'", p. 204, fn. 41, names the men in both squads who are listed in a document in the Private Papers of Edward Horne. Five of the names occur in *Winged Dagger*, pp. 374–81. Another, Pilkington, was interviewed in 1996 for the Imperial War Museum Sound Archive, IWM 16854. He mentions Farran but does not refer explicitly to membership of the 'special squads'. It is possible that 'Said' may have been a Jew, W. Abraham, who appears on Horne's list. Farran also refers to a Constable Jones whose name is not recorded by Horne.

62 Horne, *A Job Well Done*, pp. 335, 517; Fergusson, *Trumpet in the Hall*, pp. 227–8; Farran, *Winged Dagger*, p. 349. For critical observations about the abbreviated training regimen, see Jones, *SAS: The First Secret Wars*, pp. 80–1.

63 Fergusson, *Trumpet in the Hall*, pp. 227–8; Farran, *Winged Dagger*, pp. 349–50. At some point they acquired a dog, too, although it may have been a mascot rather than part of their arsenal.

64 Farran, *Winged Dagger*, p. 349.

65 Sir Richard Catling, interview recorded September 1988,

Imperial War Museum Sound Archive, 10392/9. At least one of the sergeants, Murphy, was able to read printed Hebrew. See Farran, *Winged Dagger*, p. 379. On the mistrust and lack of co-ordination between the police and the army, as well as their respective failings, see Charters, 'British Intelligence in the Palestine Campaign, 1945–1947', pp. 123–32 and Smith, 'Communal Conflict and Insurrection', p. 77.

66 Farran, *Winged Dagger*, pp. 370–1. The most exhaustive research by Charters, 'Special Operations in Counter-insurgency: The Farran Case', reveals little more than what Farran and Fergusson disclosed. For exaggerated claims about the efficacy of the special squads see R.L. Clutterbuck, 'Bertrand Stewart Prize Essay, 1960', *Army Quarterly*, 81:2 (June 1961), pp. 161–80. See also Colin Mitchell, *Having Been A Soldier* (London, 1969), pp. 61–2.

67 Fergusson, *Trumpet in the Hall*, p. 227; Mitchell, *Having Been A Soldier*, p. 61, mentions the involvement of the Argyll and Sutherland Highlanders.

68 Farran, *Winged Dagger*, p. 374.

69 ibid., pp. 350, 377–9.

70 Charters, *The British Army and Jewish Insurgency in Palestine*, pp. 59–60; Katz, *Days of Fire*, pp. 91–2. Apart from two operations against British military targets in July and August 1947, after Operation Agatha the Hagana confined itself to carrying out illegal immigration.

71 Farran, *Winged Dagger*, pp. 374–9.

72 ibid., pp. 379–80; Katz, *Days of Fire*, pp. 149–54; Cohen, *Palestine and the Great Powers*, pp. 242–3.

73 Farran, *Winged Dagger*, p. 375.

74 ibid., p. 345; Mitchell, *Having Been A Soldier*, p. 61.

75 Farran, *Winged Dagger*, p. 351; Fergusson, *Trumpet in the Hall*, p. 227.

76 Hadingham Report, CO537/2302 and Gray to Gurney, 20 June 1947, CO357/2302.

77 Hadingham Report, CO537/2302.

78 ibid.

CHAPTER THREE

1 *Report on the Alleged Abduction and Murder of Alexander Rubowitz, And Subsequent Police Investigation*, by K. P. Hadingham, Superintendent of Police, Jerusalem District, 19 June 1947, CO537/2302.

2 Gray to Gurney, 24 June 1947, CO537/2302; Fergusson, *Trumpet in the Hall*, p. 206 on Catling.

3 Gray to Gurney, 24 June 1947, CO537/2302. Gray gave this account to Sir Henry Gurney, the chief secretary of the Paletine government, who replaced Sir John Shaw in August 1946. By explicitly placing Farran in the car Fergusson implicated him yet more deeply in the events of 6 May.

4 Hadingham Report, CO537/2302; *Palestine Post*, 18 and 22 May 1947.

5 Gray to Gurney, 24 June 1947, CO537/2302.

6 Cunningham to CO, 19 June 1947, CO537/2302; Gray to Gurney, 24 June 1947, CO537/2302; Horne, *A Job Well Done*, p. 170; Sir John Gutch, *Colonial Civil Servant* (Padstow, 1987), p. 87 for a sketch of Gurney.

7 Hadingham Report, CO537/2302; *Palestine Post*, 4 and 9 June 1947.

8 Farran, *Winged Dagger*, pp. 352–3; Fergusson, *Trumpet in the Hall*, p. 228.

9 Fergusson, *Trumpet in the Hall*, p. 228, differs from Farran's account in *Winged Dagger*, pp. 353–4. Fergusson says that Farran was interrogated on the morning he fled. Farran mentions that he concocted his cover story with Fergusson, implying that he was at the house that morning.

10 Farran, *Winged Dagger*, pp. 354–60.

11 Fergusson, *Trumpet in the Hall*, pp. 228–9.

12 Hadingham Report, CO537/2302; Fergusson, *Trumpet in the Hall*, pp. 228–9.

13 Farran, *Winged Dagger*, pp. 360–2.

14 Cunningham to CO, 13 June 1947; Hadingham Report, CO537/2302; *Palestine Post*, 9 June 1947. Fergusson, *Trumpet in the Hall*, pp. 231–2.

15 Farran, *Winged Dagger*, pp. 363–6; Fergusson, *Trumpet in the Hall*, pp. 233–4.

16 Farran, *Winged Dagger*, pp. 365–6; Fergusson, *Trumpet in the Hall*, pp. 235–6.

17 Reuters report, 7 June 1947; Hadingham Report, CO537/2302.

18 Scrivener, Damascus, to FO, 9 June 1947, CO537/2302; *Palestine Post*, 17 June 1947.

19 Fergusson, *Trumpet in the Hall*, pp. 236–7; Scrivener, Damascus, to FO, 9 June 1947; Cunningham to CO, 13 June 1947, CO537/2302.

20 PALCOR bulletin, 13 June 1947.

21 Farran, *Winged Dagger*, pp. 366–7; C. A. F. Dundas, British Legation in Damascus to high commissioner, Jerusalem, 15 June 1947, CO537/2302; *Palestine Post*, 17 June 1947.

22 Cunningham to CO, 13 June 1947, CO537/2302.

23 CO to high commissioner, 13 February 1947, CP, Box 1/ File 4. See also Cohen, *Palestine and the Great Powers*, pp. 203–33; Jones, *Failure in Palestine*, pp. 203–28; Louis, *The British Empire in the Middle East*, pp. 451–63; Peter Clark, *The Last Thousand Days of the British Empire* (London, 2007), pp. 476–85.

24 Montgomery Diary, 3 February-21 April 1947, Pt VII, BLM180/1.

25 Cunningham to CO, 18 and 24 February 1947, CP Box 1/ File 4. Weekly Summaries, 3 and 11 March 1947 and Monthly Report, 6 March 1947, CP, Box 1/ File 4; 1st Infantry Division Report on Operation Elephant, Palestine 1947 (April 1947), Stockwell Papers, 6/23; Cabinet minutes, 20 March 1947, CM 30 (47) Conclusions, BLM211/32; Cohen, *Palestine and the Great Powers*, pp. 238–9; Charters, *The British Army and Jewish Insurgency in Palestine*, pp. 121–3; Hoffman ed., *The Failure of British Military Strategy Within Palestine*, pp. 29–32.

26 Montgomery Diary, 3 February-21 April 1947, Pt VII, BLM180/1; Ilan, '"Withdrawal Without Recommendations": Britain's Decision to Relinquish the Palestine Mandate, 1947' in Kedourie and Haim eds, *Zionism and Arabism in Palestine and Israel*, pp. 183–209.

27 Eliav, *Wanted*, pp. 246–8.

28 *Daily Mail, Manchester Guardian*, 5 June 1946; *The Times, Daily Telegraph, Manchester Guardian*, 6 June 1947.

29 *Manchester Guardian*, 6 and 7 June 1947. Not coincidentally, Sir Noel Charles warned the FO of an escalation of Jewish underground activity in Italy on 30 June 1947, FO371/60786. *Daily Telegraph*, 7 June 1947.

30 *Daily Telegraph*, 9 and 11 June 1947; Katz, *Lechi*, pp. 91–2.

31 *Daily Express*, 10 and 11 June 1947; *Inspector Burt of Scotland Yard*, pp. 126–7; Giora Goodman, 'Who Killed Alexander Rubowitz?' p. 20.

32 *Daily Telegraph*, 13 and 21 June 1947; Royhman 'What connects Molotov, LEHI underground?'; Eliav, *Wanted*, pp. 259–64.

33 *Daily Express*, 27 and 28 June 1947; *Manchester Guardian*, 27 June 1947. See also *Daily Telegraph*, 7 June 1947 for evidence of unease in the Jewish community. An MI5 briefing by Alex Kellar on 'Zionist Subversive Activities', 16 March 1947, confirmed that the theft was not connected with any terrorist, KV3/41. Curiously, an MI5-led operation that uncovered an arms cache including twenty-seven stolen grenades and resulted in the deportation of two Jewish terrorists passed without notice although it is recorded in this report.

34 Emphasis in original. LEHI poster, Sivan 1947, LEHI Collection, JI, K5–2/1; Rex Keating Collection, IWM Department of Documents, 86/1/16. See also Eli Tavin and Yohan Alexander, *Psychological Warfare and Propaganda: Irgun Documentation* (Washington, 1982), pp. 169–71.

35 The information came from a Syrian government press conference held the previous day that reported the detention of British officers in Aleppo. *Davar*, 12 June 1947; *Palestine Post*, 12 June 1947; *HaMashkif* and *Davar* 15 June 1947; *Palestine Post*, 13 June 1947; *Ha'aretz*, 15 June 1947.

36 Mathieson minute, 14 June 1947, CO537/2302.

37 *New York Times*, 14 June 1947.

38 *Palestine Post*, 15 June 1947; Attlee to Creech Jones, 16 June 1947; E. R. Edmonds to Cunningham, 17 June 1947,

and E. R. Edmonds (private secretary to Creech Jones) to T. L. Rowen, the prime minister's private secretary, 17 June 1947, CO537/2302.

39 CO to Cunningham, 18 June 1947, CP, Box 2/1.

40 Cunningham to CO, 18 June 1947, CP, Box 2/1.

41 Creech Jones to Cunningham, 19 June 1947, CP, Box 2/1.

42 Cunningham to CO, 20 June 1947, CP, Box 2/ File 1.

43 Attlee to Creech Jones, 19 June 1947, CO537/2302.

44 Minutes by Mathieson and Creech Jones, 19 June 1947, CO537/2302.

45 Summary of Evidence of Court of Inquiry into Escape of Major Roy Farran, 23 June 1947, CO537/2302; Gray to Gurney, 20 June 1947, CO537/2302; Hadingham Report, CO537/2302.

46 Summary of Evidence of Court of Inquiry into Escape of Major Roy Farran, 23 June 1947, CO537/2302.

47 *Palestine Post*, 19 June 1947; *HaMashkif, Davar, Ha'aretz*, 19 June 1947 wrongly reported positive identifications; *Davar, Ha'aretz*, 20 June 1947, corrected the false reports of the previous day; Cunningham to CO, 18 June 1947, CP, Box 2/1; press statement, 19 June 1947, CP, Box 2/ File 1. See also report of Farran's court martial, *Palestine Post*, 2 October 1947.

48 Cunningham to CO, 19 June 1947, CP, Box 2/1.

49 Summary of Evidence of Court of Inquiry into Escape of Major Roy Farran, 23 June 1947; Gray to Gurney, 20 June 1947, CO537/2302.

50 Summary of Evidence of Court of Inquiry into Escape of Major Roy Farran, 23 June 1947, CO537/2302; Farran, *Winged Dagger*, pp. 237–8; Fergusson, *Trumpet in the Hall*, pp. 236–7, 239.

51 ibid., p. 237.

52 Cunningham to CO, 20 June 1947, CP, Box 2/1; Creech Jones to Cunningham, 20 June 1947, CP, Box 2/1; Summary of Evidence of Court of Inquiry into Escape of Major Roy Farran, 23 June 1947, CO537/2302; Cunningham to CO, 25 June 1947, CO537/2302.

53 Montgomery Diary, BLM181/1; *Palestine Post*, 24 June 1947.

54 *Daily Telegraph, News Chronicle, Daily Express, Daily Mail,*

Evening Standard, Star, 20 June 1947; *The Times, Daily Telegraph, Manchester Guardian, Daily Express, Daily Mail*, 21 June 1947. The unofficial briefing was made to the Palestine Telegraphic Agency on 23 June and reported by George Lichtheim, London correspondent of the *Palestine Post*, 24 June 1947.

55 *AP Bulletin*, 20 June 1947; *New York Times*, 21 and 22 June 1947.

56 *Daily Mail*, 22 June 1947; *Manchester Guardian*, 24 June 1947; *Daily Express*, 26 June 1947.

57 Press release, Palestine government, 25 June 1947, CP, Box 2/1; *The Times, Manchester Guardian*, 26 June 1947.

58 *Daily Telegraph*, 26 June 1947; *Daily Graphic*, 27 June 1947.

59 *News of the World*, 29 June 1947.

60 *Hadashot haErev, HaBoker, Ha'aretz*, 22 June 1947; *Ha'aretz*, 23 June 1947.

61 *HaZofeh*, 24 June 1947, *Ha'aretz*, 25 June 1947.

62 *Achduth HaAvodah*, 26 June 1947; Goodman, 'Who Killed Alexander Rubowitz?' p. 17.

63 Goldie Myerson to Sir Henry Gurney, 23 June 1947, CZA, S25/6200. The Jewish Agency had first issued a statement on the affair on 14 June, calling for a purge of the Palestine Police Force, see *New York Times*, 15 June 1947.

64 'The Alexander Rubowitz Case', submission by the Political Department of the Jewish Agency, n. d., CZA, 25/6200.

65 Gurney to Myerson, 25 June 1947, CZA, S25/6200; *Palestine Post*, 25 June 1947; Haganah poster, undated, CZA, S25/6200. See also government of Palestine, Weekly Intelligence Appraisal, item 7, 26 June 1947, CP, Box 2/1: 'References to the Farran case have not begun to appear in the press. So far local comment has been restrained. The Jewish Agency has addressed government giving certain alleged information on the case and has been invited to place any evidence which it has at the disposal of the investigating officer.' Giles wrote to Myerson requesting further information on 25 June 1947, CZA, S25/6200.

66 Cunningham to Creech Jones, 26 June 1947, CP, Box 2/1.

The actual reports were removed from Cunningham's papers. They are in the CO files, CO537/2302.

67 CO to Cunningham, 25 and 26 June 1947; Sir Henry Gurney to CO, 25 June 1947; *Parliamentary Debates (Hansard) Fifth Series*, Vol. 439 [439 H.C. DEB. 5s], 23 June-11 July 1947, Written Question 162, 2 July 1947, and reply, Tom Driberg to Secretary of State for the Colonies, Mr Creech Jones.

68 Cunningham to CO, 1 July 1947, CO537/2302; *Palestine Post*, Ha'aretz, 25 June 1947; *The Times, Manchester Guardian*, 25 June 1947; *Daily Mail*, 2 October 1947. See also *HaBoker, Davar*, 25 June 1947.

69 *HaBoker*, 27 June 1947; *HaMashkif, HaZofeh*, 29 June 1947.

70 *The Times, Daily Telegraph, Daily Express*, 30 June 1947; *New York Times*, 28 and 30 June 1947; MacMillan, *Palestine. Narrative of events*, p. 10; Palestine government Weekly Intelligence Appraisal, 5 July 1947, CP, Box 2/1.

71 Captain W. B. MacDavid, assistant camp commander HQ Palestine, the duty officer, logged Farran's surrender at 11.50 a.m.: *Palestine Post*, 3 October 1947; Cunningham to CO, 29 June 1947, CO537/2302; *Yediot Aharanot*, 29 June 1947; *Daily Telegraph*, 30 June 1947; Farran, *Winged Dagger*, p. 368.

CHAPTER FOUR

1 *Daily Telegraph*, 30 June 1947.

2 *Palestine Post*, 1 July 1947; *The Times*, 3 July 1947. The pre-trial process and procedure for trial by general court martial are lucidly set out in Gerry R. Rubin, *Murder, Mutiny and the Military: British Court Martial Cases, 1940–1966* (London, 2005), pp. 20–31; Farran, *Winged Dagger*, p. 9.

3 *Ha'aretz*, 30 June 1947. Also *Hamashkif, Mishmar, HaBoker, Hadashot HaErev*, for variations on the story, 30 June 1947.

4 John Watson to Mr and Mrs Watson, 30 June 1947, Letters of John Wells Watson, IWM Department of Documents, 94/25/2. See also Philip Brutton, *A Captain's Mandate: Palestine 1946–1948* (London, 1996), pp. 81–2.

5   *New York Times*, 29 June 1947; *Chicago Daily Tribune*, 3 July 1947.

6   Palestine government Weekly Intelligence Appraisal, 5 July 1947, CP, Box 2/1; CO to Cunningham, 30 June 1947, CO537/2302.

7   Mathieson minute, 1 July 1947; Cunningham to CO, 1 July 1947, CO537/2302.

8   Mathieson and others minutes, 1, 4 and 5 July 1947, CO537/2302.

9   Mathieson to Styles, 1 July 1947, CO537/2302; 439 H.C. DEB. 5s, Written Question 162, 2 July 1947, and reply, Tom Driberg to Secretary of State for the Colonies, Mr Creech Jones; PALCOR Bulletin, 2 July 1947; *Palestine Post*, 3 July 1947 also *HaBoker* and *Ha'aretz*, 3 July 1947.

10 Reuven Nochimowski, open letter, *HaMashkif*, 4 July 1947; *Mishmar*, *HaBoker*, 4 July 1947; Lipton to Creech Jones, 9 July 1947, 439 HC DEBS 5s, 2196; *Palestine Post*, 10 July 1947.

11 Fergusson, *Trumpet in the Hall*, p. 237; Mitchell, *Having Been a Soldier*, p. 62; Farran, *Winged Dagger*, p. 9.

12 ibid., p. 10.

13 ibid., p. 382; *Palestine Post*, 10 July 1947; *Ha'aretz*, 10 July 1947; Mortimer, *Stirling's Men*, pp. 185, 351. George [surname illegible] to Maj. Gen. Robert Laycock, 18 July and 10 September 1947, Papers of Maj. Gen Sir Robert Laycock, Liddell Hart Centre for Military Archives, King's College, London, 6/27 [hereafter Laycock Papers, 6/27].

14 Minutes of Security Conference, Jerusalem, 11 July 1947, CP, Box 4/1 File 1. See also 441 H.C. DEB 5s, Written Question 155, 5 August 1947, reply by Ivor Thomas, CO minister, to Tom Driberg, stating that the summary of sworn evidence was taken on 17 and 18 July. *The Times* and *Daily Express*, 2 July 1947 reported that he received counsel a month earlier.

15 Minutes of meeting at the CO, deputy JAG Brigadier Shapcott, Mr Gutch, Mr Mathieson, the Attorney General Sir Hartley Shawcross, and others, 14 July 1947, CO537/2302. For a discussion of the legal issues, see Lord Russell of Liverpool, *Though the Heavens Fall* (London, 1956), pp. 111–27.

16 Gutch minute, 15 July 1947; Sir Thomas Lloyd to Creech Jones, 16 July 1947; CO to Cunningham, 17 July 1947, CO537/2302.

17 Cunningham to CO, 19 July 1947, CO537/2302.

18 *The Times*, 5 August 1947; *Jewish Chronicle*, 8 and 15 August 1947; Cunningham to CO, 5 August 1947, CO537/2302; Tony Kushner, 'Anti-Semitism and austerity: the August 1947 riots in Britain' in Panikos Panayi ed. *Racial Violence in Britain, 1840–1950* (Leicester, 1993), pp. 149–68.

19 Gutch minute of meeting with Mr Bellenger, 8 August 1947; Lloyd to Creech Jones, 11 August 1947; CO to Cunningham, 14 July 1947; WO to commander-in-chief of Middle East Land Forces, 12 August 1947, CO537/2302; Lord Russell of Liverpool, *That Reminds Me* (London, 1958), pp. 160–81, 184–202, 264.

20 Charters, *The British Army and Jewish Insurgency*, p. 67; Lord Inverchapel to FO, 22 June 1946, FO371/52595 and 17 March 1947, FO371/61915; *New York Sun*, 24 June 1946; *Daily Mail*, 26 August 1947; obituary for Baruch Korff (1914–95), JTA, 27 July 1995; *New York Times*, 27 July 1995.

21 *New York Herald Tribune*, 7 September 1947; *The Times, Daily Mail, Daily Herald*, 8 September 1947. Korff's leaflet is reproduced in Bowyer Bell, *Terror Out of Zion*, photospread between pp. 112–13.

22 Katz, *Lechi*, pp. 91–2; 100–1; *The Times, Daily Mail*, 9 September 1947.

23 *Daily Mirror*, 9 September 1947; *Daily Mail*, 9 and 10 September 1947; Katz, *Lechi*, p. 101; Aviva Halamish, *The Exodus Affair* (London, 1998), pp. 108–16 and *passim*. See also Alan Swarc, 'Illegal Immigration to Palestine, 1945–1948: The French Connection', unpublished PhD, University of London, 2006. In 1968 Korff met Richard Nixon and became one of his confidants during Nixon's years in the White House, advising him on Jewish matters. Korff defended the president vehemently during the Watergate scandal and set up the President Nixon Justice Fund and the National Citizens Committee for Fairness for the Presidency. He saw Nixon on

the day he decided to resign and pleaded with him to fight on: *Time* magazine, 29 July 1974.

24 Boris Senior, *New Heavens. My Life as a Fighter Pilot and a Founder of the Israel Air Force* (London, 2005), pp. 87–88; Katz, *Personal Memoirs*. On Kook and Merlin, see Judith Tydor Baumel, *The 'Bergson Boys' and the Origins of Contemprary Zionist Militancy* (Syracuse, 2005), especially pp. 210–31 for their activities in postwar Europe.

25 On Eliyahu Lankin see Begin, *The Revolt*, pp. 62, 64–5 and biography at http://www.knesset.gov.il/mk and Katz, *Personal Memoirs*.

26 Boris Senior, *New Heavens: My Life as a Fighter Pilot and a Founder of the Israel Air Force* (London, 2005), pp. 49–90.

27 Ezer Weizman, *On Eagles' Wings: The Personal History of the Leading Commander of the Israeli Air Force* (New York, 1976), pp. 46–8.

28 Senior, *New Heavens*, pp. 91–2; Security Service surveillance of Senior and Homesky is recorded in 'Zionist Subversive Activities', KV3/41.

29 Senior, *New Heavens*, pp. 93–7; Weizman, *On Eagles' Wings*, pp. 48, 111; Bowyer Bell, *Terror Out of Zion*, pp. 307–8. Ezer Weizman also recounted his misadventures to Nicholas Bethell in *The Palestine Triangle*, p. 307.

30 *Palestine Post*, 16, 18 and 24 July 1947; Laurence Collins and Fearnley-Whittingstall to the Secretary of State for the Colonies, 5 December 1947, Laycock Papers, 6/27. Bickford-Smith also patrolled the press and challenged anything that he considered likely to prejudice his client's chances of a fair trial. At one point he forced Reuters to retract a statement that Farran had been extradited from Syria and issue a correction stressing that he had returned to Palestine voluntarily, Reuters bulletin, 10 August 1947.

31 Yitzhak Ben-Zvi, president Vaad Leumi, to chief secretary, Palestine government, 22 July 1947, CZA, S25/6200.

32 *Palestine Post*, 31 July 1947.

33 Cunningham to CO, 5 August 1947, CO537/2302; *Palestine Post*, 5, 8 and 10 August 1947; *Daily Express*, 5 August 1947,

The Times, 8 and 9 August 1947. R. Nochimowski to the National Committee, Vaad Leumi, 4 August 1947, CZA, S25/6200.

34 *The Times*, 29 August and 2 September 1947; *Palestine Post*, 28 and 29 August 1947, 2 September 1947.

35 *Palestine Post*, 2, 11, 17 and 18 September 1947.

36 Obituary for William Fearnley-Whittingstall, *The Times*, 29 October 1959.

37 Laurence Collins and Fearnley-Whittingstall to the Secretary of State for the Colonies, 29 July 1947, CO537/2302.

38 Mr Dale minute, 5 August 1947; minute by 'B' (probably Beeley), 7 July 1947; Laurence Collins and Fearnley-Whittingstall to the Secretary of State for the Colonies, 7 August 1947; CO to Laurence Collins and Fearnley-Whittingstall, 15 August 1947, CO537/2302.

39 Laurence Collins and Fearnley-Whittingstall to the Secretary of State for the Colonies, 7 August 1947; Secretary of State for the Colonies to WO, 21 August 1947; Palestine (JAG) to CO, 3 September 1947; Trafford-Smith, CO, to Brigadier Shapcott, WO, 9 September 1947; Brigadier Shapcott, WO, to Trafford-Smith, 9 September 1947; CO to high commissioner, 13 September 1947, CO537/2302.

40 Laurence Collins and Fearnley-Whittingstall to Major General Robert Laycock, 16 August 1947; Brian Franks to Robert Laycock n.d. but between 16 and 20 August 1947; Laycock to Franks, 20 August 1947; Laycock to Laurence Collins and Fearnley-Whittingstall, 20 August 1947 and reply, 21 August 1947; Laycock to Laurence Collins and Fearnley-Whittingstall, 24 August 1947; Laycock to Browning, 24 August 1947; Laycock to Franks, 24 August 1947; Browning to Laycock, 9 September 1947, Laycock Papers, 6/27.

41 Mathieson minute, 16 and 19 September 1947; CO to Cunningham, 19 and 24 September 1947, CO537/2302. Scotland Yard was also consulted due to Fergusson's references to the Metropolitan Police Force: Mathieson to Howe, Scotland Yard, 22 September 1947 and reply, 23 September 1947, CO537/2302.

42 Damascus Legation to FO, 14 September 1947; FO to Damascus Legation, 23 September 1947; Damascus Legation to FO, 3 October 1947, CO537/2302.

43 Mathieson to JAG, 22 September 1947; Mathieson to Lord Russell, 22 September 1947, CO537/2302. For the setting of the date, Cunningham to CO, 20 September 1947, CO537/2302.

44 Fergusson, *Trumpet in the Hall*, p. 238.

45 *The Times, Daily Telegraph*, 25 September 1947; *Palestine Post*, 25 September 1947; *Ha'aretz*, 25 September 1947.

46 *New York Herald Tribune*, 2 October 1947; *Palestine Post*, 2 October 1947.

47 *Daily Mail, New York Herald Tribune, Palestine Post*, 3 October 1947.

48 *Palestine Post*, 1 October 1947 for the charge and 2 October 1947 for other details. See also, *The Times, Daily Telegraph, Daily Express*, 2 October 1947.

49 Farran, *Winged Dagger*, p. 382; *Daily Express, Palestine Post*, 2 October 1947.

50 No record of the trial appears to be in The National Archives although a copy existed in 1955 when Lord Russell asked the Lord Chancellor's Office for permission to consult it for a book he was writing. See LCO4/114. This account is taken from the press, primarily *The Times* and *Palestine Post*, 2 and 3 October 1947. Reports of varying quality were also carried by the *Daily Telegraph, Manchester Guardian, Daily Mail, Daily Express*.

51 *The Times, Daily Mail*, 2 October 1947; *Palestine Post*, 2 October 1947.

52 *The Times, Daily Mail, Daily Express*, 2 October 1947; *New York Herald Tribune*, 2 October 1947; *Palestine Post*, 2 and 3 October 1947; Fergusson, *Trumpet in the Hall*, p. 238.

53 *Daily Mail*, 2 October 1947; *Palestine Post*, 2 October 1947.

54 Shapcott to Trafford-Smith, 12 September 1947, CO537/2302; *Palestine Post*, 2 October 1947; *New York Herald Tribune*, 2 October 1947.

55 ibid.; *Daily Mail*, 3 October 1947.

56 *The Times, Daily Telegraph*, 3 October 1947.

57 *The Times, Daily Telegraph, Palestine Post*, 3 October 1947;

New York Herald Tribune, 3 October 1947; Fergusson, *Trumpet in the Hall*, p. 239.

58 *Palestine Post*, 3 October 1947; *Daily Telegraph, Manchester Guardian, Daily Mail, Daily Express, Daily Mirror, Daily Herald*, 3 October 1947; *New York Herald Tribune*, 3 October 1947.

CHAPTER FIVE

1 *Daily Telegraph, Daily Express*, 14 October 1947.
2 *Palestine Post, Daily Telegraph, Daily Express*, 3 October 1947. Exit of Fearnley-Whittingstall courtesy of Mr Sam Sylvester. See also Robert Glenton, 'The Briton Who Faced the Hatred of a Nation', *Sunday Express*, 13 January 1963.
3 *Palestine Post*, 16 October 1947; Fergusson, *Trumpet in the Hall*, p. 239.
4 ibid.; *Palestine Post*, 9 October 1947; Watson to mother, 21 October 1947, IWM Department of Documents, 94/25/1.
5 *Palestine Post*, 3 October 1947; Weekly Intelligence Appreciation, 4 October 1947, CP, Box 2/2.
6 *Palestine Post*, 9 October 1947.
7 *New York Herald Tribune*, 3 October 1947; *New Statesman*, 11 October 1947; *Daily Mail, Daily Express, Daily Mirror, Daily Telegraph*, 3 October 1947.
8 *Palestine Post*, 7 and 8 October 1947.
9 *Guardian, Daily Telegraph, Daily Mail, New York Herald Tribune, Palestine Post* 14 October 1947; Farran, *Winged Dagger*, p. 382.
10 *Daily Express*, 4 August 1947; *The Times*, 5 August 1947; *Jewish Chronicle*, 15 August 1947; Kushner, 'Anti-Semitism and austerity', pp. 149–68.
11 *Manchester Guardian, Daily Telegraph, Daily Mail, Daily Express, Daily Mirror*, 14 October 1947; *Palestine Post*, 15 October 1947.
12 George Thomas to Secretary of State for War, 28 October 1947, 443, H.C. DEB, 5s, 685.
13 *Palestine Post*, 19 and 20 October 1947. The contents of the file on Fugitive Offenders 1947 which passed from the Mandatory authority into the Israel State Archives,

AG8/58704/36, have been destroyed. The Home Office opened a file on the matter, HO45/21445, consisting mainly of press cuttings and a minute explaining why no action was necessary.

14 *Daily Telegraph, Palestine Post*, 23 October 1947; Palestine government to CO, 23 October 1947, CO537/2302. Cunningham to CO, 28 October 1947, CO537/2302; minute, 30 October 1947, HO45/21445.

15 *New York Herald Tribune*, 28 October 1947; *Daily Telegraph, The Times*, 29 October 1947.

16 *Daily Herald*, 23 October 1947; *Palestine Post*, 29 October 1947.

17 *Daily Express, Daily Mail, Daily Herald, Daily Telegraph, Daily Graphic, Daily Sketch, New York Herald Tribune*, 31 October 1947.

18 *Daily Herald, Daily Graphic*, 31 October 1947.

19 Yossi Melman, 'The Heruti Code', *Ha'aretz Magazine*, 14 January 2005. See also Tom Segev, *The Seventh Million* (New York, 1993), pp. 267–8. Bowyer Bell, *Terror Out Of Zion*, pp. 308–9. However, this account is partial and confused. Even more fragmentary and dubious is Avner, *Memoirs of an Assassin: Confessions of a Stern Gang Killer*, trans. Burgo Partridge (New York, 1959), which purports to tell the story of a LEHI agent despatched from France to Britain in June 1948 with a mission to kill Bevin.

20 Melman, 'The Heruti Code'; Doris Katz, *The Lady Was a Terrorist*, p. 54. MI5 reports on the Jewish Legion as the Hebrew Legion was also known, KV5/11; report on Jewish legion propaganda, TNA, KV5/39; 'Zionist Subversive Activities', 16 March 1947, TNA, KV3/41.

21 Katz, *Lechi*, p. 101; Avner, *Memoirs of an Assassin*, pp. 115–46; Goodman, 'Who Killed Alexander Rubowitz?', p. 20; J. C. Robertson, lecture, 2 September 1946, KV3/67; Ilan, '"Withdrawal Without Recommendations": Britain's Decision to Relinquish the Palestine Mandate, 1947', pp. 183–209, argues that Bevin did not make the final decision until several weeks after the announcement of withdrawal, and then only after the persistence of terrorism showed that a military victory was impossible.

22 Cohen, *Palestine and the Great Powers*, pp. 260–78, 292–330; Jones, *Failure in Palestine*, pp. 256–81, 283–96. On Bevin's 'bluff', see Ilan, '"Withdrawal Without Recommendations": Britain's Decision to Relinquish the Palestine Mandate, 1947'.

23 *Daily Express*, 4 December 1947.

24 *Palestine Post*, 7 and 23 December 1947, 12 and 14 January 1948, 11 and 26 February 1948. The *People* was later the subject of a successful legal action by Farran's solicitors, *The Times*, law report, 26 May 1948.

25 Affidavit sworn by Lieutenant Colonel Robert Cowell-Parker, 27 October 1947, enclosed with Laurence Collins and Fearnley-Whittingstall to CO, 6 November 1947; Laurence Collins and Fearnley-Whittingstall to Sir Henry Gurney, 27 November 1947 and Laurence Collins and Fearnley-Whittingstall to CO, 5 December 1947, CO537/2302.

26 Fox-Strangeways to CO, 6 December 1947; CO537/2302 Cunningham to CO, 5 January 1948, CO537/3872.

27 Mathieson minutes, 21, 14 January 1948, CO537/3872; Brigadier Head to Secretary of State for the Colonies, 28 January 1948, 446 H.C. DEB. 5s, 1015–16, 28 January 1948.

28 CO to Cunningham, 2 February 1948; Cunningham to CO, 9 February 1948, CO537/3872.

29 Fearnley-Whittingstall to Secretary of State for the Colonies, 4 March 1947, CO537/2302.

30 Fearnley-Whittingstall to Secretary of State for Foreign Affairs, 2 February 1948; minutes by Clark and Mathieson, 11 March 1948, CO537/3872.

31 M. Martin, CO, to Laurence Collins and Fearnley-Whittingstall, 15 March 1948; CO to Cunningham, 18 March 1948; Cunningham to Laurence Collins and Fearnley-Whittingstall, 9 April 1948; Cunningham to CO, 13 April 1948; Cunningham to CO, 24 April 1948, CO537/3872. On the ending of the Mandate, see Cohen, *Palestine and the Great Powers*, pp. 301–17, 339–41 and Jones, *Failure in Palestine*, pp. 309–23. The evacuation is chronicled in MacMillan, *Palestine. Narrative of Events from February 1947 until withdrawal of all British Troops*.

32 This was perhaps the first and only time in modern history that the reigning monarch shook hands with a murderer. *Palestine Post, New York Times*, 11 February 1948; advertisement, *The Times*, 17 March 1948.

33 Romaine, 'The Charmed Life of Roy Farran', p. 9.

34 Bowyer Bell, *Terror Out of Zion*, pp. 308–9. Goodman, 'Who Killed Alexander Rubowitz?'; Melman, 'The Heruti Code'. In 1977 an Israeli called Yehudah Benari claimed to have joined Heruti's cell. Benari was originally a British Jew or the child of refugees who arrived in Britain before 1939. He said that his family were evacuated close to the Farrans' home in Staffordshire during the war. He claims that he located Farran when he saw that Roy was invited to become a prospective parliamentary candidate for South Kensington. Benari inveigled the Constituency Association into inviting Farran to London for several days on the grounds that he had special information about him that he and they needed to hear. When Farran came to London Heruti's men took over and tailed Farran back to his parents' house. However, the dates and other details in the deposition do not tally with the available facts. Benari may have been involved in some way but his account is not reliable. Yehudah Benari Deposition, Tel Aviv, 14 April 1977, LEHI Collection, JI, K5-5/3/1. Details about Farran's family and home, *Daily Express*, 4 August 1947.

35 The file containing the police investigation into this incident, MEPO 2/8766, is retained by The National Archives. This account is assembled from reports in the press: *The Times, Daily Express, Daily Telegraph*, 4 May 1948. Benari said he purchased the book at Foyles. Heruti said that they chose Shakespeare because the volume was large and heavy enough to accommodate 30–50 grams of explosive without arousing suspicion. The particular edition was very common and would be hard to trace to one shop: Goodman, 'Who Killed Alexander Rubowitz?'

36 *Daily Mail, Daily Mirror*, 4 May 1948.

37 *News Chronicle, Daily Herald, Manchester Guardian*, 4 May 1948. The US press also carried extensive reports: *Chicago Daily Tribune, Los Angeles Times*, 4 May 1948. Heruti said

that the package was mailed from the main post office at Marble Arch by one of the British Jewish volunteers: Goodman, 'Who Killed Alexander Rubowitz?'

38 *Daily Telegraph*, 4 May 1947. Romaine, 'The Charmed Life of Roy Farran', p 8.

39 *Daily Mail, Daily Express, Daily Telegraph*, 8 May 1948. The verdict of the inquest, held on 29 June 1948, was that Rex Farran was 'feloniously killed by person or persons unknown', *The Times*, 30 June 1948.

40 *Daily Mail, Palestine Post, New York Times*, 6 May 1948.

41 *Palestine Post*, 4 May 1948; *The Times, Daily Telegraph*, 5 May 1948.

42 *Palestine Post*, 5 and 6 May 1948; *New York Times*, 6 May 1948.

43 *Daily Mail, Daily Express, Manchester Guardian, New York Times*, 12 May 1948; *Inspector Burt of Scotland Yard*, pp. 129–30.

44 Surveillance of the Hebrew Legion began in January 1946: MI5 reports on the Jewish Legion, 1946–1948, KV5/11; 'Antecedents', *Rex v Harris & anor*, CRIM1/1951.

45 Sworn statements, 15 and 23 September 1948, *Rex v Harris & anor*, CRIM1/1951.

46 *The Times*, 31 August 1948; *Inspector Burt of Scotland Yard*, pp. 129–30.

47 *Daily Mail, Daily Mirror, Daily Express, Manchester Guardian*, 15 October 1948.

48 Sworn statements, 15 and 23 September 1948, *Rex v Harris & anor*, CRIM1/1951.

49 *Rex v Harris & anor*, CRIM1/1951. *The Times, Manchester Guardian, Daily Mail, Daily Telegraph*, 15 October 1948.

50 *Daily Mail*, 15 October 1948.

51 *Daily Telegraph*, 15 October 1948; *The Times*, 18 October 1948; MI5 reports on the Jewish Legion, in particular Sir Percy Sillitoe, director general of MI5, to Major General R. Palmer, commissioner of South African Police, 6 October 1948, KV5/11.

52 *Inspector Burt of Scotland Yard*, p. 130; *Palestine Post*, 18 August 1948. A request under the Freedom of Information Act to access

the file held at The National Archive, MEPO 2/8766 – Murder of Francis Rex Farran by parcel bomb posted by terrorist organisation at Codsall, Staffs 3 May (1948–1953) was rejected by the information commissioner, 22 January 2008. Ironically, the reason given – that 'this record relates to the investigation of a case of murder that remains unsolved to this day and could potentially still achieve prosecution' – applies with equal force to the documents pertaining to the abduction and murder of Alexander Rubowitz, which have been released.

53 *New York Times*, 17 September 1947; Bethell, *The Palestine Triangle*, pp. 347–8.

54 Goodman, 'Who Killed Alexander Rubowitz?'; Melman, 'The Heruti Code'.

55 Romaine, 'The Charmed Life of Roy Farran'; *Palestine Post*, 12 April and 27 August 1948; Farran, *Winged Dagger*, p. 149.

56 *Palestine Post*, 23 October and 3 November 1949. His political career was nearly terminated when his flight to London crash-landed at London Airport on 27 October. Three passengers were killed and ten injured, but Roy walked out of the wreckage with nothing worse than a cut finger.

57 Farran, *Winged Dagger*, pp. 382–4.

58 *The Times*, 2, 10 and 14 November, 3 and 8 December 1949; *Palestine Post*, 3 and 14 November, 4 December 1949.

59 *The Times*, 10, 17, 22 and 24 February 1950; *Palestine Post*, 19 January and 27 February 1950.

60 *Palestine Post*, 7 and 31 August 1950; obituary, *Daily Telegraph*, 5 June 2006 and at www.standardbredcanada.ca/news/royfarran – posted on 12 June 2006.

61 Roy Farran, *Jungle Chase* (London, 1951), p. 254.

62 *Maariv*, 15–19 January 1950; *HaHerut*, 6 February 1949, 2 and 3 May 1950; *Palestine Post*, 13 September 1954; *Yediot Ahranot, Yom Kippur Supplement*, 6 October 1954.

63 Press cuttings on Roy Farran, 1952–2006, Calgary Public Library, Local History Collection; obituary, *The Times*, 5 June 2006; *Jerusalem Post*, 1975; *The Times*, 29 October 1979. Howard Palmer with Tamara Palmer, *Alberta: A New History* (Edmonton, 1990), pp. 221, 290, 322–4; Jewish History Society of Southern

Alberta, *A Joyful Harvest: Celebrating the Jewish Contribution to South Alberta Life 1889–2005* (Calgary 2005), p. 3. See also Janine Stingel, *Social Discredit: Anti-Semitism, Social Credit and the Jewish Response* (Montreal, 2000).

64 Fergusson, *Trumpet in the Hall*, pp. 241–42. His other books included: *The Wild Green Earth* (London, 1946); *The Black Watch* (London, 1950) *Beyond the Chindwin* (London 1951); *Rupert of the Rhine* (London 1952); *The Watery Maze: The Story of Combined Operations* (London, 1961); *Wavell. Portrait of a Soldier* (London, 1961); *Travel Warrant* (London, 1979). He also wrote a novel *The Rare Adventure* (London, 1967) and a volume of poetry.

65 *Davar*, 15 and 16 January 1963; *HaBoker*, 16 January 1963; *Ha Herut*, 18 January 1963; *Makhaneh Gadna*, 15 April 1971; *Yediot Aharanot*, 17 April 1975; *Ha'aretz*, 18 April 1975; *Maariv*, 4 May 1979; Goodman, 'Who Killed Alexander Rubowitz?'

66 Obituary, *Daily Telegraph*, 5 June 2006; *Calgary Herald*, 12 June 2006; CBC News, 12 June 2006; www.standardbred-canada.co/news/royfarran – posting on 12 June 2006.

67 Hillel Fendel, 'Death of British War Hero Recalls Unsolved Jerusalem Murder', 7 June 2006, Arutz Sheva Israel National News at www.israelnationalnews.com/News/News.aspx/106731.

EPILOGUE

1 See, for example, the observations of Arthur Koestler, *Promise and Fulfilment: Palestine 1917–1949* (New York, 1949), pp. 148–9, 171–4.

2 Jewish Agency for Palestine, *The Jewish Plan: Memoranda and Statements presented by the Jewish Agency for Palestine to the United Nations Special Committee on Palestine* (Jerusalem, September 1947), p. 42; Jorge García-Granados, *The Birth of Israel: The Drama as I Saw It* (New York, 1949), pp. 6–17, 48–9, 113; Louis, *The British Empire in the Middle East*, pp. 466–73.

3 *New York Herald Tribune*, 12 August 1947; Louis, *The British Empire in the Middle East*, pp. 487–93.

4 *Palestine Post*, 2 July 1947; MacMillan, *Palestine: Narrative of*

events from February 1947 until withdrawal of all British Forces, p. 7.

5 Farran, *Winged Dagger*; Fergusson, *Trumpet in the Hall*; Richard Clutterbuck, 'Bertrand Stewart Prize Essay, 1960'. *Army Quarterly*, 18:2 (Jan. 1961), pp. 161–80; Mitchell, *Having Been A Soldier*, pp. 61–2.

6 David Charters, 'From Palestine to Northern Ireland: British Adaptations to Low Intensity Operations' in David Charters and Maurice Tugwell eds *Armies in Low Intensity Conflict: A Comparative Analysis* (London, 1989), pp. 169–249, especially pp. 207–12; Charters, *The British Army and Jewish Insurgency in Palestine*, pp. 172–5. David Charters, 'Special Operations in Counter-insurgency: The Farran Case,' pp. 56–61; Mockaitis, *British Counter-insurgency 1919–1960*, pp. 13–14, 45–8, 100–11 is anything but complimentary about the role played by the special squads. Nevertheless he argues that 'The principles developed unevenly and, despite major defeats in Northern Ireland (1919–21), and Palestine (1944–7), coalesced into the highly effective campaign in Malaya (1945–60).' See also Thomas Mockaitis, *British Counter-insurgency in the Post-imperial Era* (Manchester, 1995), pp. 1–11.

7 Kemp, *The SAS*, p. 78; Jones, *Post-war Counter-insurgency and the SAS*, pp. 1–18, 38–74, and *SAS: The First Secret Wars*, pp. 33–60, 85–105, differs in the emphasis he puts on the experience gained by special forces in Greece in 1945–7 as against Palestine. There was a very close relationship between the two theatres so even if Palestine did not show much success in the short term it was not a dead end for strategic and tactical innovation. Several SAS officers who served in Palestine later resurfaced in Greece, notably Roy Farran's companion-in-arms Alistair McGregor.

8 Townshend, *Britain's Civil Wars*, pp. 157–61; Mockaitis, *British Counter-insurgency 1919–1960*, pp. 167–71; Sinclair, *At the End of the Line*, pp. 115, 152–8, 166–9; Caroline Elkins, *Britain's Gulag: The Brutal End of Empire in Kenya* (London, 2005), pp. 52, 121–30, 276–80.

9 Townshend, *Britain's Civil Wars*, pp. 118–19; Mockaitis, *British*

Counter-insurgency 1919–1960, pp. 43–4 is also critical of Fergusson's scheme. 'The special squads functioned outside of the traditional institutions imbued with the principle of minimum force. Like the Black and Tans and Wingate's night squads before them they were neither police nor soldiers. Specifically created to deal with a situation that had got out of hand, they could all easily convince themselves that they were justified in taking any action that they felt necessary to redeem the situation.'

10   Smith, 'Communal Conflict and Insurrection in Palestine, 1936–1948' in Anderson and Killingray, *Policing and Decolonisation: Politics, Nationalism and the Police, 1917–1965*, pp. 62–70, especially pp. 69–70.

11   Townshend, *Britain's Civil Wars*, pp. 157–61; Sinclair, *At the End of the Line*, pp. 72–8; Christopher Bayly and Timothy Harper, *Forgotten Wars: The End of Britain's Asian Empire* (London, 2007), pp. 436–9, 441–3, 479–80; Karl Hack, 'British Intelligence and Counter-insurgency in the Era of Decolonisation: The Example of Malaya', *Intelligence and National Security*, 14:2 (1999), pp. 124–47.

12   Mockaitis, *British Counter-insurgency 1919–1960*, pp. 111–24; Sinclair, *At the End of the Line*, p. 170; Bayly and Harper, *Forgotten Wars*, pp. 479–80.

13   Mockaitis, *British Counter-insurgency 1919–1960*, pp. 45–50; Major Frank Kitson, *Gangs and Counter-gangs* (London, 1960), pp. 62–82, 185–8 and *Bunch of Five* (London, 1977), pp. 3–65; David Anderson, *Histories of the Hanged: Britain's Dirty War in Kenya and the End of Empire* (London, 2005), especially pp. 284–6 on the 'pseudo-gangs' and pp. 200–6 on 'Operation Anvil'.

14   Charters, *The British Army and Jewish Insurgency in Palestine*, pp. 65–80, 164–7; Elkins, *Britain's Gulag*, pp. 46–50, 91–100, 306–9.

15   Elkins, *Britain's Gulag*, pp. 276–80.

16   Mockaitis, *British Counter-insurgency 1919–1960*, pp. 45–6; Sinclair, *At the End of the Line*, p. 160; Elkins, *Britain's Gulag*, p. 306.

17 M. R. D. Foot, *SOE in France: An Account of the Work of British Special Operations* (London, 1984), pp. 356–7; Kemp, *The SAS*, pp. 211–12; Sir Richard Catling interview, IWM Sound Archive, 10392/9. See also Horne, *A Job Well Done*, pp. 566–7.

18 Charters, 'Special Operations in Counter-insurgency: The Farran Case', p. 56.

19 Sinclair, '"Hard-headed, Hardbitten, Hard-hitting and Courageous Men"', p. 214. For a partisan but cogent rejoinder to the adulation of British counter-insurgency, Newsinger, *British Counter-insurgency From Palestine to Northern Ireland.*

Glossary and Abbreviations

AIG	Assistant Inspector General (of police)
AWOL	Absent Without Leave
BETAR	Brit Trumpledor: Revisionist Zionist youth movement
BUF	British Union of Fascists
CIGS	Chief of the Imperial General Staff
CID	Criminal Investigation Department
CICMELF	Commander-in-Chief Middle East Land Forces
CO	Colonial Office, London
CZA	Central Zionist Archive, Jerusalem, Israel
DIG	Deputy Inspector General (of police)
DP	Displaced Person
DPP	Director of Public Prosecutions
DSO	Defence Security Officer
DSP	District Superintendent (of police)
FO	Foreign Office, London
GOC	General Officer Commanding
Hagana	Semi official militia of the Jewish community of Palestine
HO	Home Office, London
IG	Inspector General (of police)
Irgun	Irgun Zvai Leumi: National Military Organisation
IZL	Irgun Zvai Leumi
ISA	Israel State Archives
JAP	Jewish Agency for Palestine

JI	Jabotinsky Institute, Tel Aviv, Israel
JRUSI	*Journal of the Royal United Services Institute*
JTA	Jewish Telegraphic Agency
LEHI	Lohamei HaHerut b'Yisrael: the Fighters for the Freedom of Israel, also known as the Stern Gang
MI5	Military Intelligence, Section 5: the Security Service
MI6	Military Intelligence, Section 6: the Secret Intelligence Service
MI11	Military Intelligence, Section 11
NYT	*New York Times*
PAC	Palestine Action Committee
Palmach	Full time elite force of the Hagana
PMF	Police Mobile Force
PPF	Palestine Police Force
PRO	Public Records Office (in The National Archives, London)
RMC	Royal Marine Commando
SAS	Special Air Service
SIME	Signals Intelligence Middle East
SOE	Special Operations Executive
TNA	The National Archives, London
UN	United Nations
UNRRA	United Nations Relief and Rehabilitation Administration
UNSCOP	United Nations Special Committee on Palestine
WO	War Office, London
Yishuv	The Jewish population of modern Palestine

Sources and Bibliography

1. Unpublished Primary Sources

Calgary Public Library, Local History Collection

Press cuttings on Roy Farran, 1952–2006

Central Zionist Archive, Jerusalem

Records of the Jewish Agency Political Department: File on
the murder of Alexander Rubowitz, CZA, 525/6200
Press cuttings on Alexander Rubowitz, S71/840
Vaad Leumi records concerning Alexander Rubowitz, JI/7307

Glenbow Archive, Calgary

Papers of the Alberta Progressive Conservative Party, M1744

Imperial War Museum Collections Department of Documents

R Hammerton, *Cliff and I (Memories of Army Service from
1944–1948)*
Papers of Lieutenant General G. H. A. MacMillan
Papers of Field Marshal Viscount Montgomery of Alamein
Papers of Colonel C. R. W. Norman
Memoirs of Brigadier John Murray Rymer-Jones
Letters of John Wells Watson

Imperial War Museum, Sound Archives Oral History Interviews

Sir Richard Catling
Edward Parker Horne
William Pilkington
James Robertson
John Murray Rymer-Jones
Terrence Shand
Colonel Henry 'Todd' Sweeney

Israel State Archives

Records of the Government of Palestine, files of the Attorney
General: AG8/58704/36, 11/14, 705/21

Liddell Hart Centre for Military Archives, King's College, London

Papers of Major General Sir Robert Laycock
Papers of General Sir Hugh Stockwell

Jabotinsky Institute Archive, Tel Aviv

LEHI Collection: K5–5/3/1, Personal file of Alexander
Rubowitz; K5–5/3/2, Press Cuttings concerning Alexander
Rubowitz; K5–2/1, LEHI Posters and Propaganda Leaflets

Middle East Centre Archive, St Antony's College, Oxford

Papers of Sir Alan Cunningham
Diary of Sir Henry Gurney, 15 March – 15 May 1948
Sir Henry Gurney, 'Palestine Postscript: A Short Record of
the Last Days of the Mandate

The National Archives: Public Records Office, London

Colonial Office Records: CO537 series: files: 1699, 1720, 1723,
1729, 2302, 2425, 2269, 2270, 3846, 3847, 3854, 3856, 3858,
3859, 3870, 3872, 3932, 3933, 3934, 5384, 5385

Foreign Office Records: FO371 series: files: 52595, 60786, 61586, 61865, 61866, 61915, 67796, 67813, 68630

Home Office Records: HO45/21445

Lord Chancellor's Office Records: LCO4/114

Records of the Security Services: KV3 series: files: 30, 40, 41, 67; KV4 series: files: 216; KV5 series: files: 11, 29, 31, 32, 34, 35, 36, 37, 39, 39

War Office Records: WO216 series: files: 221; WO373 series: files: 4, 27, 30, 53, 61, 148

Records of the Central Criminal Court, Depositions: CRIM1/1951

Metropolitan Police Office Records: MEPO2/8766

2. Published Primary Sources

Jewish Agency for Palestine, *The Jewish Plan: Memoranda and Statements presented by the Jewish Agency for Palestine to the United Nations Special Committee on Palestine* (Jerusalem, September 1947)

Government of Palestine, *Supplementary Memoranda by the Government of Palestine, including Notes on Evidence given to the United Nations Special Committee on Palestine up to 12 July 1947* (Jerusalem, 1947)

Newspapers and Periodicals

Army Quarterly
The Albertan
Associated Press
Calgary Herald
Chicago Daily Tribune
Daily Herald
Daily Express
Daily Graphic
Daily Mail
Daily Sketch
Daily Telegraph
Evening Standard

Jewish Chronicle
Jewish Standard
Jewish Telegraphic Agency
Los Angeles Times
Manchester Guardian
New York Herald Tribune
New York Times
News Chronicle
News of the World
New Statesman
North Hill News
Parade
PALCOR
Palestine Post
Reuters
Star
Time
The Times
Weekend Magazine

Hebrew press

Ha'aretz
Achduth HaAvodah
HaBinah
HaBoker
Davar
Hadashot haErev
HaHerut
HaMashkif
HaZofeh
Maariv
Makhaneh Gadna
Mishmar
Yediot Aharanot

Parliamentary Debates (Hansard) Fifth Series, Vol. 439, 23 June-11 July 1947; Vol. 441, 28 July-20 October 1947; Vol. 443, 21 October-7 November 1947; Vol. 446, 20 January-6 February 1948

Memoirs and Autobiographies

Avner *Memoirs of an Assassin: Confessions of a Stern Gang Killer*, trans. Burgo Partridge (New York, 1959)

Begin, Menachem *The Revolt*, trans. Samuel Katz and edited by Ivan Greenberg (London, 1951)

Ben-Ami, Yitshaq *Years of Wrath, Days of Glory: Memoirs from the Irgun* (New York, 1983 edn)

Bentwich, Norman and Helen Bentwich, *Mandate Memories 1918–1948* (London, 1965)

Brutton, Philip *A Captain's Mandate: Palestine 1946–1948* (London, 1996)

[Burt, Leonard] *Inspector Burt of Scotland Yard by Himself* (London, 1959)

Crossman, Richard *Palestine Mission: A Personal Record* (London, 1947)

Crum, Bartley *Behind The Silken Curtain* (London, 1947)

Day, John *A Plain Russet-Coated Captain* (London, 1993)

Dover, Major Victor *The Silken Canopy* (London, 1979)

Eliav, Ya'acov *Wanted* trans. Mordecai Schreiber (New York, 1984)

Farran, Roy *Operation Tombola* (London, 1960)

Farran, Roy *Winged Dagger: Adventures on Special Service* (London, 1948)

Fergusson, Bernard *The Trumpet in the Hall* (London, 1970)

Fergusson, Bernard *Travel Warrant* (London, 1979)

Gale, General Sir Richard *Call To Arms: An Autobiography* (London, 1968)

Garciá-Granados, Jorge *The Birth of Israel: The Drama as I Saw It* (New York, 1949)

Graves, R. M. *Experiment in Anarchy* (London, 1949)

Gutch, Sir John *Colonial Civil Servant* (Padstow, 1987)

Katz, Doris *The Lady Was a Terrorist* (New York, 1953)

Katz, Samuel *Days of Fire* (London, 1968) first published in Hebrew, 1966; selected translations under the title *Personal Memoirs* posted at http://www.eretzisraelforever.net/katz

Meir, Golda *My Life* (London, 1975)

Mitchell, Colin *Having Been A Soldier* (London, 1969)

Montgomery, B. L. *The Memoirs of the Field Marshal Viscount Montgomery of Alamein* (London, 1958)

Senior, Boris *New Heavens: My Life as a Fighter Pilot and a Founder of the Israel Air Force* (London, 2005)

Shamir, Yitzhak *Summing Up. An Autobiography* (London, 1994)

Weizman, Ezer *On Eagles' Wings. The Personal History of the Leading Commander of the Israeli Air Force* (New York, 1976)

Yakim, Ezra 'Alexander Rubowitz' at http://www.eretzisraelfor ever.net/InTheirOwnWords

Books and Articles

Bauer, Yehuda *From Diplomacy to Resistance. A History of Jewish Palestine 1939–1945* trans. Alton Winters (New York, 1970)

Bayly, Christopher and Timothy Harper, *Forgotten Wars: The End of Britain's Asian Empire* (London, 2007)

Beevor, Antony *Crete: The Battle and the Resistance* (London, 1991)

Bernard, Peter *The Story of 45 Royal Marine Commando* (London, 1945)

Bethell, Nicholas *The Palestine Triangle. The struggle between the British, the Jews and the Arabs 1935–1948* (London, 1979)

Blaxland, Gregory *The Regiments Depart: A History of the British Army 1945–1970* (London, 1971)

Bolitho, Hector *The Galloping Third: The Story of the 3rd King's Own Hussars* (Aldershot, 1963)

Bowyer Bell, J. *Terror Out of Zion: The Fight for Israeli Independence* (New York, 1996 edn)

Brenner, Y. S. 'The "Stern Gang" 1940–1948', *Middle East Studies* 2:1 (1965)

Sources and Bibliography

Bungay, Stephen *Alamein* (London, 2002)

Chalfont, Alun *Montgomery of Alamein* (London 1976)

Charters, David A. 'British Intelligence in the Palestine Campaign, 1945–1947', *Intelligence and National Security* 6:1 (1991)

Charters, David A. 'From Palestine to Northern Ireland: British Adaptations to Low Intensity Operations' in David Charters and Maurice Tugwell eds *Armies in Low Intensity Conflict: A Comparative Analysis* (London, 1989)

Charters, David A. 'Special Operations in Counter-insurgency: The Farran Case, Palestine 1947', *Journal of the Royal United Services Institute*, 124:2 (1979)

Charters, David A. *The British Army and Jewish Insurgency in Palestine, 1945–1947* (London, 1989)

Clark, Peter *The Last Thousand Days of the British Empire* (London, 2007)

Clarke, Thurston *By Blood and Fire: The Attack on the King David Hotel* (London, 1981)

Clutterbuck, R. L. 'Bertrand Stewart Prize Essay, 1960', *Army Quarterly*, 81:2 (June 1961)

Cohen, Asher *Persécution et Sauvetages: Juifs et Français sous l'Occupation et sous Vichy* (Paris, 1993)

Cohen, Michael J. *Palestine and the Great Powers 1945–1948* (Princeton, 1982)

Cohen, Michael J. *Retreat From the Mandate: The Making of British Policy, 1936–1945* (London, 1978)

Cohen, Mitchell *Zion and State: Nation, Class and the Shaping of Modern Israel* (New York, 1992)

Cohen-Solal, Annie *Sartre: A Life* (London, 1991 edn)

David Anderson, *Histories of the Hanged: Britain's Dirty War in Kenya and the End of Empire* (London, 2005)

Elkins, Caroline *Britain's Gulag: The Brutal End of Empire in Kenya* (London, 2005)

Farran, Roy *The History of the Calgary Highlanders, 1921–1945* (Calgary, 1955)

Farran, Roy *Jungle Chase* (London, 1951)

Farran, Roy *Never Had A Chance* (London, 1967)

Farran, Roy *The Search* (London, 1958)

Fendel, Hillel 'Death of British War Hero Recalls Unsolved Jerusalem Murder', 7 June 2006, Arutz Sheva Israel National News at www.israelnationalnews.com/News/News.aspx/-106731

Foot, M. R. D. *SOE in France: An Account of the Work of British Special Operations* (London, 1984)

Friedman, Isaiah *The Question of Palestine: Britain, the Jews and the Arabs* (London, 1992 edn)

Goodman, Giora 'Who Killed Alexander Rubowitz?', *Ha'aretz Weekend Supplement*, 3 September 2004

Hack, Karl 'British Intelligence and Counter-insurgency in the Era of Decolonisation: The Example of Malaya', *Intelligence and National Security*, 14:2 (1999)

Halamish, Aviva *The Exodus Affair* (London, 1998)

Hamilton, Nigel *Monty: The Life of Montgomery of Alamein: The Making of a General 1887–1942; Monty: Master of the Battlefield 1942–1944; Monty: The Field Marshal 1944–1976* (London 1981–86)

Heinlein, Frank *British Government Policy and Decolonisation 1945–1963: Scrutinising the Offical Mind* (London, 2002)

Heller, Joseph 'Neither Masada – Nor Vichy: Diplomacy and Resistance in Zionist Politics, 1945–1947', *International History Review*, 3:4 (1981)

Heller, Joseph *The Stern Gang: Ideology, Politics and Terror 1940–1949* (London, 1995)

History of Bishop Cotton School, http://bishopcottonshimla.com/history.htm 19 July 2007

Hoffman, Bruce ed. *The Failure of British Military Strategy Within Palestine 1939–1947* (Bar Ilan University, 1983)

Horne, Edward *A Job Well Done: A History of the Palestine Police Force 1920–1948* (Lewes, Sussex, 2003 edn)

Hurwitz, J.C. *The Struggle for Palestine* (New York, 1976 edn)

Ilan, Amitzur '"Withdrawal Without Recommendations": Britain's Decision to Relinquish the Palestine Mandate, 1947' in Elie Kedourie and Sylvia Haim eds, *Zionism and Arabism in Palestine and Israel* (London, 1983)

Jeffries, Sir Charles *The Colonial Police* (London, 1952)

Jewish History Society of Southern Alberta, *A Joyful Harvest: Celebrating the Jewish Contribution to South Alberta Life 1889–2005* (Calgary 2005)

Jones, Martin *Failure in Palestine: British and United States Policy after the Second World War* (London, 1986)

Jones, Tim *Post-war Counter-insurgency and the SAS, 1945–1952: A Special Type of Warfare* (London, 2001)

Jones, Tim *SAS: The First Secret Wars. The Unknown Years of Combat and Counter-insurgency* (London, 2005)

Katz, Emmanuel *Lechi: Fighters for the Freedom of Israel (FFI)* trans. Herzlia Dobkin (Tel Aviv, 1987)

Kemp, Anthony *SAS: The First Secret Wars* (London, 2005)

Kemp, Anthony *The SAS: The Special Air Service Regiment 1941–1945* (London, 1991)

Kimche, Jon *Seven Fallen Pillars: The Middle East 1945–1953* (London, 1953)

Kimmerling, Baruch and Joel S. Migdal, *The Palestinian People: A History* (Cambridge, Mass., 2003)

Kitson, Major Frank *Bunch of Five* (London, 1977)

Kitson, Major Frank *Gangs and Counter-gangs* (London, 1960)

Koestler, Arthur *Promise and Fulfilment: Palestine 1917–1949* (New York, 1949)

Kushner, Tony 'Anti-semitism and austerity: the August 1947 riots in Britain' in Panikos, Panayi ed. *Racial Violence in Britain, 1840–1950* (Leicester, 1993)

Laqueur, Walter *A History of Zionism* (New York, 1978 edn)

Latimer, Jon *Alamein* (London, 2002)

Lindsay, Oliver *Once a Grenadier . . . The Grenadier Guards 1945–1995* (London, 1996)

Louis, William Roger *The British Empire in the Middle East 1945–1951* (Oxford, 1984)

Louis, William Roger 'Sir Alan Cunningham and the end of British Rule in Palestine', *The Journal of Imperial and Commonwealth History,* 16:3 (1988)

Louis, William Roger and R. W. Stookey eds, *The End of the Palestine Mandate* (Austin, 1986)

Makovsky, Michael *Churchill's Promised Land. Zionism and Statecraft* (New Haven, 2007)

Mandel, Neville *The Arabs and Zionism Before World War One* (Berkley, 1976)

Marlowe, John *The Seat of Pilate: An Account of the Palestine Mandate* (London, 1959)

Melman, Yossi 'The Heruti Code', *Ha'aretz Magazine*, 14 January 2005

Mockaitis, Thomas *British Counter-insurgency 1919–1960* (London, 1990)

Mockaitis, Thomas *British Counter-insurgency in the Post-imperial Era* (Manchester, 1995)

Monroe, Elizabeth *Britain's Moment in the Middle East 1914–1956* (London, 1961)

Mortimer, Gavin *Stirling's Men: The Inside History of the SAS in World War II* (London, 2004)

Nachmani, Amikam 'Generals at Bay in Post-war Palestine', *Journal of Strategic Studies*, 6:4 (1983)

Nachmani, Amikam *Great Power Discord In Palestine. The Anglo-American Committee of Inquiry into the Problems of European Jewry and Palestine 1945–1946* (London, 1987)

Nebo, Amos 'The Mystery of the Abduction and Murder of Alexander Rubowitz', *Makhaneh Gadna*, 15 May 1971

Neillands, Robin *By Sea and Land: The Story of the Royal Marine Commandos* (London, 1987)

Newsinger, John *British Counter-insurgency From Palestine to Northern Ireland* (Basingstoke, 2002)

Obituary for Roy Farran posted at www.standardbredcanada.co/news/royfarran

Ofer, Dalia *Escaping the Holocaust* (New York, 1990)

Ovendale, Ritchie *Britain, The United States and the End of the Palestine Mandate* (London, 1989)

Pappé, Illan *A History of the Palestinians: One Land, Two Peoples* (Cambridge, 2004)

Porath, Yehoshua *The Emergence of the Palestinian Arab National Movement, 1918–1929* (London, 1974)

Porath, Yehoshua *The Palestinian National Movement: From Riots to Rebellion 1929–1939* (London, 1977)

Poznanski, Renée *Jews in France During World War Two* (Hanover NH, 2001)

Romaine, Edward 'The Charmed Life of Roy Farran', *Weekend Magazine*, vol. 6:50, (1956)

Rose, Norman *The Gentile Zionists. A Study in Anglo-Zionist Diplomacy, 1929–1939* (London, 1973)

Ross, Hamish *Paddy Mayne: Lieutenant Colonel Blair 'Paddy' Mayne and 1st SAS Regiment* (London, 2003)

Royhman, Yinon 'What connects Molotov, LEHI underground?' posted on 11 May 2006, at http://www.ynetnews.com/articles/0,7340,L-3320855,00.html

Rubin, Gerry *Murder, Mutiny and the Military: British Court Martial Cases, 1940–1966* (London, 2005)

Lord Russell of Liverpool, *Though the Heavens Fall* (London, 1956)

Sacher, Harry *Israel: The Establishment of a State* (London 1952)

Samian, Bryan *Commando Men: The Story of a Royal Marine Commando in North-west Europe* (London, 1948)

Segev, Tom *One Palestine, Complete: Jews and Arabs under the British Mandate* (New York and London, 2000)

Segev, Tom *The Seventh Million* (New York, 1993)

Shepherd, Naomi *Ploughing Sand: British Rule in Palestine* (London, 1999)

Shepherd, Naomi *The Zealous Intruders: The Western Rediscovery of Palestine* (London, 1987)

Sherman, A. J. *Mandate Days: British Lives in Palestine 1918–1948* (London, 1997)

Sinclair, Georgina '"Hard-headed, Hardbitten, Hard-hitting and Courageous Men of Innate Detective Ability . . .": From Criminal Investigation to Political and Security Policing at End of Empire, 1945–50', in Clive Emsley and Haia Shpayer-Makov eds, *Police Detectives in History 1750–1950* (Aldershot, 2006)

Sinclair, Georgina *At the End of the Line: Colonial Policing and the Imperial Endgame 1945–1980* (Manchester, 2006)

Smith, Charles 'Communal Conflict and Insurrection in Palestine, 1936–1948' in David Anderson and David Killingray, *Policing and Decolonisation: Politics, Nationalism and the Police, 1917–1965* (Manchester, 1992)

Stein, Kenneth *The Land Question in Palestine, 1917–1939* (Chapel Hill, 1984)

Stingel, Janine *Social Discredit: Anti-Semitism, Social Credit and the Jewish Response* (Montreal, 2000)

Stockwell, A. J. 'Gurney, Sir Henry Lovell Goldsworthy (1898–1951)', rev. *Oxford Dictionary of National Biography* (Oxford 2004); online edition, January 2006, (http://www.oxforddnb.com/ view/article/33611, accessed 21 January 2008)

Strawson, John 'Cunningham, Sir Alan Gordon (1887–1983)', rev. *Oxford Dictionary of National Biography* (Oxford 2004); online edition, January 2006, (http://www.oxforddnb.com/-view/article/30991, accessed 21 January 2008)

Sykes, Christopher *Cross Roads to Israel* (London, 1965)

Tavin, Eli and Yohan Alexander, *Psychological Warfare and Propaganda: Irgun Documentation*, (Washington, 1982)

Teveth, Shabtai *Moshe Dayan* (London, 1972)

Townshend, Charles *Britain's Civil Wars: Counter-insurgency in the Twentieth Century* (London, 1986)

Twiston Davies, David ed. *The Daily Telegraph Book of Military Obituaries* (London, 2003)

Tydor Baumel, Judith *The 'Bergson Boys' and the Origins of Contemporary Zionist Militancy* (Syracuse, 2005)

Verité, Meyer *From Palmerston to Balfour*, edited by Norman Rose (London, 1992)

Verney, Major General G. L. *The Desert Rats. The 7th Armoured Division in World War II* (London, 1954)

Vital, David *The Origins of Zionism* (Oxford, 1975)

Vital, David *Zionism: The Crucial Phase* (Oxford, 1987)

Wasserstein, Bernard *The British in Palestine: The Mandatory Government and the Arab-Jewish Conflict, 1917–1929* (Oxford, 2nd edn 1991)

Wilson, Major R. D. 'Dare' *Cordon and Search: With 6th Airborne Division in Palestine* (Aldershot, 1949)

Young, David *Four Five* (London, 1972)

Zadka, Saul *Blood in Zion: How the Jewish Guerrillas drove the British out of Palestine* (London, 1995)

Zweig, Ronald *Britain and Palestine During the Second World War* (London, 1986)

3. Unpublished Secondary Sources

Jones, Timothy Llewellyn 'The development of British counter-insurgency policies and doctrine, 1945–1952', PhD thesis, University of London, 1991

Swarc, Alan 'Illegal Immigration to Palestine, 1945–1948: The French Connection', PhD thesis, University of London, 2006

Picture Credits

Grateful acknowledgement is made to the following for permission to reprint photographs:

Portrait of Alexander Rubowitz and missing person description from Hebrew Press

Ussishkin Street, Jerusalem © David Cesarani

Plaque commemorating the abduction © David Cesarani

Roy Farran in the SAS, leaning against a jeep, at Stavanger airport, Norway, May 1945 © John Tonkin

Bernard Fergusson, photographed while leading a Chindit column in the Burmese jungle in 1943 © Bernard Fergusson, *Trumpet in the Hall*

Nicol Gray as Inspector General of Palestine Police Force,1946 courtesy of Edward Horne

British Embassy in Rome damaged by Irgun bomb, 31 October 1947 reproduced by permission of *Guardian* and *Observer* Syndication; picture source unknown

LEHI Communiqué, issued in Paris, March 1947 courtesy of the Jabotinsky Archive

Daily Express, front page, 2 October 1947, reporting Farran's court martial and Fergusson's refusal to testify reproduced by permission of Express Group Newspapers

Roy Farran being decorated by Gen Clayton Bissell with the US Medal of Honour in London, October 1947 © Getty Images

Yaakov Heruti in 1955 © *LEHI People*, reproduced *Ha'aretz* magazine, 14 January 2005

Daily Express, front page about bombing at Farran's home in Codsall reproduced by permission of Express Group Newspapers

Roy Farran with his surviving brothers and parents at his brother Rex's funeral in Codsall on 7 May 1948 © Getty Images

Street in the Jerusalem suburb of East Talpiot © David Cesarani

Street sign commemorating Rubowitz © David Cesarani

Acknowledgments

The research for this book would not have been possible without the expertise, patience, and kindness of archivists in several countries. In Britain I would like to thank the staff at The National Archives at Kew, London, and pay tribute to the technological innovations over which they have presided; the staff at the Imperial War Museum Department of Documents and the Sound Archives, London; the British Library Newspaper Collection at Colindale, London; Debbie Usher at the Middle East Centre Archive, St Antony's College, Oxford; Dr Peter Thwaites, Sandhurst Collection, Royal Military Academy. I would also like to thank Dr Lynette Nusbacher, Royal Military Academy, Sandhurst, who pointed me in the right direction. In Israel I want to thank Masha Zolotarevsky and the staff of the Jabotinsky Institute Archive, Tel Aviv; the staff of the Central Zionist Archive, Jerusalem; and the staff of the Israel State Archives, Jerusalem. In Canada my thanks go to John Wright, Military and Strategic Studies Librarian, University of Calgary Library Archives and Special Collections; Suzanne Daly, Calgary Military Museums Society; the staffs of the Glenbow Archives, Calgary and the Calgary Public Library Local History Archive. The London Library is the best library of its kind in the world and I am indebted to its wonderful staff.

Many dear friends have contributed to this book in various ways. Yvonne Lipman expertly translated acres of miniscule print from the Hebrew press while Jonathan Lipman took me on 'field trips' with and without the company of the Carmel Mountain Bike Club. I also want to thank them for all the hospitality they have shown to me and my family during many visits to Haifa. I would like to thank Daniel and Barbara Eilon for the loan of their flat in Jerusalem, in a block on the site of the Allenby Barracks and ten minutes walk from the Israel State Archives. I must also thank Dr Rob Rozett, director of the Library at Yad Vashem, Shoshi Rozett and their children for providing a refuge in Jerusalem on another, wintry visit. Antony Metzer read the manuscript with an eye to the legal aspects, made excellent suggestions and saved me from many errors. I would specially like to thank his father-in-law, Sam Sylvester, for helping to fuel my interest in the Farran affair and for plying me with anecdotes. Dr Dave Lawrence and Bob Abbott, amongst my father's oldest friends, enriched my understanding of the period with their reminiscences about military service in the Middle East. I also benefited from conversations with Edward Horne, Malvyn Benjamin, Professor Avi Shlaim, and Dr Nicholas de Lange. I regret that members of Roy Farran's family did not respond to my efforts to speak with them. Dr Lawrence Goldman, a fellow history student at Cambridge in the 1970s and now editor of the *Oxford Dictionary of National Biography*, came across an early edition of Farran's *Winged Dagger* and sent it to me with the admonition to use it well. For copyright reasons it was not possible to quote directly from Roy Farran's memoir.

The writing was completed while on leave from the Department of History, Royal Holloway, University of London, where I have the privilege to be a research professor. I would like to thank the Principal, Professor Stephen Hill, for his unwavering commitment to fostering research; Professor Adam Tickell, the Dean of the Faculty of History and Social Sciences, for the interest he has taken in my work; and above all Professor Justin Champion who is a superb head of department. I presented a paper which drew on the research for this book to the departmental research seminar and I would like to thank my colleagues who gave their comments, especially Professor Vanessa Martin. An earlier version was delivered at the Jewish Museum, Cape Town, under the auspices of the Kaplan Centre for Jewish Studies at the University of Cape Town and I would like to thank the centre's director, Professor Milton Shain, for arranging the event and inviting me to be a visiting fellow. I

Acknowledgments

am indebted to my friend Alan Elsner, a hugely experienced writer in several genres, who read the manuscript and instantly saw how it could be improved. I am grateful to Jason Arthur, at Random House, for his gentle insistence that it could be better, David Milner, for his skilful editing, Laurie Ip Fung Chun for her assistance and Martin Lubikowski for his cartography. Jonny Geller, at Curtis Brown, made sure that everyone was happy with the results. Dawn, Daniel, and Hannah know the true price of a book and I can never repay them enough.

This book is dedicated to the memory of my father, Henry Cesarani. Amongst my most treasured possessions are the books he purchased at Steimatsky's in Tel Aviv during trips he made to Palestine while on leave from the British Army in 1944–6, when he was based at Qassasin near the Suez Canal. He followed the progress of *Major Farran's Hat* with the loving enthusiasm he showed for all my publishing ventures, but died before it was completed. I miss him terribly.

Index

Index

Index

Saving
Shiloh

Phyllis Reynolds
Naylor

Thorndike Press • Waterville, Maine

Text copyright © 1997 by Phyllis Reynolds Naylor

PUB 4/23/02 22 L

Sequel to Shiloh Season

Published in 2002 by arrangement with Simon & Schuster Children's Publishing Division.

Thorndike Press Large Print Juvenile Series.

The tree indicium is a trademark of Thorndike Press.

The text of this Large Print edition is unabridged.
Other aspects of the book may vary from the original edition.

Set in 16 pt. Plantin by Christina S. Huff.

Printed in the United States on permanent paper.

Library of Congress Cataloging-in-Publication Data

Naylor, Phyllis Reynolds.
    Saving Shiloh / by Phyllis Reynolds Naylor.
       p. cm.
    Sequel to: Shiloh season.
    Summary: Sixth-grader Marty and his family try to help their rough neighbor, Judd Travers, change his mean ways, even though their West Virginia community continues to expect the worst of him.
    ISBN 0-7862-3713-9 (lg. print : hc : alk. paper)
    1. Large type books. [1. Dogs — Fiction. 2. Family life — West Virginia — Fiction. 3. West Virginia — Fiction. 4. Prejudices — Fiction. 5. Large type books.] I. Title.
PZ7.N24 Sav 2002
    [Fic]—dc21   2001044590

To anyone who ever
tried to make a difference

Thanks to our friends,
the Maddens,
of Friendly, West Virginia

One

There's one last thing to say about Shiloh before the story's over. I guess a dog's story ain't
— isn't — ever over, even after he dies, 'cause
if you lose a pet, you still go on loving him.
But I couldn't bring myself to tell this part
until now; of all the stuff that's happened, this
was the scariest, and just thinking on it starts
my hands to sweat.

When I first tried to get Shiloh from Judd
Travers, who was treating that dog meaner
than mud, at least there was a chance that if
I couldn't have him for my own, Judd would
let him live.

And even after Judd turns his beagle over
to me, then starts drinkin' and talkin' ugly,
there's hope he never meant it. But sometimes hope seems out of human hands
entirely, and when the third thing happened . . . well, here's all that's left to tell.

Next to Christmas, I guess, Halloween is
big in West Virginia — out where we live,

anyway, which is the little community of Shiloh, up the winding road from Friendly there on the Ohio River. It's because I first saw the little dog here in Shiloh that I named him what I did.

To get to our house, you go through this place called Little — you'll know it by the church — and you keep going along Middle Island Creek, wide as a river, till you see this old falling-down gristmill. It's right by this rusty bridge, and just over the bridge, you'll see the old Shiloh schoolhouse. SHILOH SCHOOL — 1920–1957, reads a sign above the door, like a gravestone or something. I seen plenty of buildings got the date on them when they were built, but I never seen a building got the date when it died.

We live on the side of the creek near the mill, up the lane in a two-bedroom house. You sit out on the steps of an evening, don't move even your little finger, and pretty soon a buck will step out of the trees, a doe or two behind him, and parade across your field just as grand as you please. Now you tell me how many sixth-grade boys in the United States of America got somethin' like that to look on!

"What you going to be for Halloween next year, Marty?" asks Dara Lynn at supper. Halloween is over and gone, see, and already my skinny seven-year-old sister is thinkin' about the next. With her there's never no question. She dresses up like a witch every single year just so Ma can paint her fingernails black.

"I don't know," I tell her. "A ghoul, maybe."

"What's a ghoul?" asks Becky, who's three.

"Halfway between a ghost and a zombie," I say.

"Like a vampire?" asks Dara Lynn. Dara Lynn's big on vampires.

"Naw. Its skin is green, and it don't suck blood," I say.

"Marty!" Ma scolds, nodding toward my littlest sister.

We're having biscuits with sausage gravy for dinner, and there's nothing in the world I love more than sausage gravy. Except Shiloh, of course. And Shiloh loves that gravy, too, 'cause all through supper he's sittin' beside my chair with his muzzle on my leg, just waiting for me to finish up and pass that plate down to him so's he can lick up every last bit.

"I'm going to be a bunny," says Becky.

"Bunnies don't scare no one!" says Dara Lynn. "Why don't you be a pirate or something?"

"I don't *want* to scare no one," says Becky.

I guess there are *two* things I love more

11

than sausage gravy: Shiloh and Becky.

Dad's washing up at the sink. We wait for him if we can, but sometimes his mail route takes longer than he thinks, and Becky gets hungry, so we eat.

"Passed by Sweeneys' house on the way home, and two of those straw men they rigged up on their porch have fallen over and been dragged out in the yard by their dogs," Dad says, sitting down at the table. "Look like a couple of drunks keeled over on the grass."

"Those straw men in overalls don't scare nobody," says Dara Lynn. "I want a dead man on our porch next Halloween with a face as white as flour."

"What's Shiloh going to be?" chirps Becky.

"He ain't going to be anything but his own self," I tell her. "Nobody messing with my dog."

"All this talk of Halloween, when Thanksgiving's right around the corner!" says Ma.

I guess there isn't that much to holler about where we live, so when a special day comes along, you want to hang on to it — keep Halloween stuff around till Christmas, and Christmas lights goin' till Easter. I'm thinking how Ma wouldn't let us go trick-or-treating this year, though — not by ourselves.

"Houses too far apart for you kids to be

12

walking out on the road," she'd said.

Well, the houses weren't any farther apart this year than last, and Dara Lynn and me went out then. But this time Dad drove us to the Halloween parade in Sistersville, and we had to do all our trick-or-treating there. I knew Ma was thinking of Judd Travers and the accident he'd had a month ago out on the road, drunk as he was. Knew she didn't want some other drunk to run his car into one of us.

Dara Lynn must have guessed what I'm thinking, 'cause she jokes, "We could always stuff Judd Travers and put him up on our porch. He'd scare off anybody."

"Hush," scolds Ma.

"There's enough talk going around about Judd Travers without you adding your two cents' worth," says Dad.

My ears prick up right quick. "What kind of talk?"

"None that makes one bit of sense," Dad tells me. "The man paid his fine for drunk driving, he busted up his leg and his truck besides, and as far as I can tell, he's trying to turn himself around. You'd think folks would want to help."

"I thought they were," I say. "Whelan's Garage fixed his truck up for him; people were takin' him groceries. . . ."

"That was when he was flat on his back, when he was really down. Now that he's on his feet again, there's the feeling around here that he got off way too easy. Heard Ed Sholt say as much down at the hardware store last week. Said we ought to keep Judd on the hot seat, let him know his kind wasn't wanted around here, and maybe he'd move somewhere else."

That sure would solve a lot of problems, I'm thinking. Ma wouldn't be so afraid for us kids out on the road, Dad wouldn't have to worry about Judd hunting up in our woods where a stray bullet could find its way down to our place, and I could rest easy that Judd wouldn't look for excuses to take Shiloh back; that he wouldn't hurt my dog out of spite, he ever got the chance. I think maybe I like the idea just fine.

"But what if he *doesn't* move?" says Ma. "What if everybody starts treatin' him worse'n dirt, and he stays right where he is?"

And suddenly I see a meaner Judd Travers than we ever saw before. Madder, too. I think how he used to kick Shiloh — even took a shot at the log where Shiloh and me were sitting once. A meaner Judd than that?

"Way I look at it," Dad goes on, "is that Judd's doing fine so far, and we ought to wait and see what happens."

Dara Lynn's got a mouth on her, though. "Ha! He's still got his leg in a cast," she says. "Get that cast off, and he'll be just as bad as before."

"Well, I believe in giving a man a second chance," Dad tells her.

"Beginning now," says Ma, fixing her eyes on us. "Your dad and I have talked about it, and we're inviting Judd here for Thanksgiving dinner."

Dara Lynn rolls her eyes and falls back in her chair. "Good-bye turkey!" she says, meaning she won't have no appetite come the fourth Thursday in November. As for me, I lose my appetite that very minute and set my plate on the floor.

Two

On the school bus next day, I tell David Howard who's coming to our house for Thanksgiving.

"Judd *Travers?*" he yells, and David's got a mouth bigger than Dara Lynn's. Every last person on that bus takes notice. *"Why?"*

" 'Cause he don't have no other place to go," I mumble. All the kids are looking at me now.

"He'll probably show up drunk and drive right into your porch," says Fred Niles.

"He'll bring his gun and shoot your dog," says Sarah Peters.

Michael Sholt says, "If it was us, *my* dad wouldn't let him in the house! Judd was the one who knocked over our mailbox when he was drinking. And it was Dad who caught his black-and-white dog when somebody turned Judd's loose. Said it was almost as mean as Judd."

"He's just coming for dinner," I say. "It

ain't like he's movin' in." I wish I'd never said anything. David Howard's my best friend, but he sure is loud.

In school, we're learning far more about Pilgrims than I ever wanted to know. All our spelling words for the last two weeks have had something to do with Pilgrims, so I have to learn words like "treaty," "colonist," "religious," and "celebration."

What I do like, though, is learning about the two Indians, Samoset and Squanto, who taught the Pilgrims how to plant corn. And how, except for the Indians, every single person who lives in the United States is either an immigrant himself or his great-granddaddy, maybe, came from a foreign country. Us Prestons are mostly English, a little Scotch and Irish thrown in. Miss Talbot says a lot of the early colonists were convicts, people who had been in jail in England, and were deported to America. I'll bet you anything Judd's great-great-great-great-granddaddy was somebody who'd been in jail.

Thanksgiving morning, I can smell the turkey roasting before I even open my eyes. We got a sixteen-pounder on sale, so Ma gets it in the oven early. I guess being hunkered down on a warm sofa, which is where

I sleep, smelling turkey and knowing I don't have to go to school is about as close to heaven as I can get. Shiloh must think so, too. He's asleep against my feet, and every so often I can feel his paws twitch, like he's dreamin' of chasing rabbits.

Once Becky's awake, though, I don't sleep anymore, 'cause she'll come right over to the couch and stand with her face two inches from mine. She knows she's not supposed to wake me, so what she does is just stand there, her hot breath warming my eyelids. If I don't wake up right off, she'll start blowin' real soft — short little puffs — and then I know that whatever sleep I ain't had yet, I'm not gonna get.

I scoot over to one side so Becky can climb up and watch cartoons on TV. This morning, though, she's not content just to blow, her breath smelling of Cheerios and sleep; she's got to tap me on the cheek with the edge of the cardboard Pilgrim Dara Lynn brought home. I'm beginning to wish I'd never heard of Thanksgiving or Pilgrims, either one.

My job is to crack the bag of walnuts somebody give us so Ma can make a walnut pie — we always have us a walnut pie and pumpkin both. As soon as I'm dressed and get some cinnamon toast in me, I begin.

Dara Lynn's settin' the table, putting little toothpick and marshmallow turkeys she's made by each plate. Dad slides the extra leaf in the table so there's room for Judd, and Shiloh just hangs around the kitchen, smelling that turkey. He don't know who's coming for dinner, and it's just as well.

Usually Ma sings when she's feeling good, but I notice she's not singing today. There's a frown-line that shows up on her forehead, and she bites her bottom lip as she tests the pie.

About two o'clock Dad says, "Well, I better drive over there and pick up Judd. Marty, why don't you come along?"

There's no reason I can think of why I should, but when Dad says that, it's 'cause he's got something to say to me. So I get my jacket.

I climb in the back of the Jeep. Judd, with his left leg in a cast, is going to need room up front to stretch himself out. As soon as we start down the lane, Dad says, "Now Marty, you being the oldest, Dara Lynn and Becky are going to take their cue from you. You treat Judd with respect, your sisters will learn a little something."

What's he think? I'm gonna start some kind of argument right there at the table? I don't respect Judd, but I can be polite.

19

"What I mean is," Dad goes on, "if he says something about Shiloh, don't go getting hot under the collar. Let's see if we can't get through this meal at least being good neighbors."

I want just as bad as anyone else to make peace with Judd, but there's one condition: "Long as you don't let him borrow Shiloh to go hunting," I say.

"Judd won't be doing any hunting this season, you can bet," says Dad. "He's got even more injuries besides that leg to heal up."

We reach the road, turn right a few yards, go around the big pothole that sent Judd's pickup truck rolling down the bank last month, then cross the bridge by the old mill. We turn right again and keep going till we get to the brown-and-white trailer where Judd lives.

He's already out in the yard, hobbling about on his cast and crutches. He's got brown hair, eyes that look smaller than they are on account of being so close together, and a mouth that don't seem to open as wide as it should, the words sliding out the corners when he speaks. Judd comes down the board walkway holding a gunnysack in one hand.

"Brought the missus a little somethin',"

he says, sliding in after Dad leans over and opens the passenger door. He eases himself onto the seat — I'm wondering should I get out and help him — then pulls his crutches in after him, and rests the bag on his lap. Black walnuts, I figure.

"You seem to be getting around a little better," says Dad, making a U-turn and heading back toward the bridge.

"Doin' okay, but I'm still mighty sore," says Judd.

"How long you got to wear that cast?" I ask.

"Another month, I'm lucky. Longer, if I'm not."

I sure am glad to hear that — that he'll have that cast on all through deer season. There's only 'bout a week and a half of it left.

Middle Island Creek is on the other side of us now. Dad and Judd are talking about Judd's work at Whelan's Garage where he's a mechanic, and how wasn't it a good thing Whelan kept his job open for Judd while his bones heal — kept his job open and fixed up his truck, both. Then we're heading up the lane toward our house, and there's Shiloh standing out by the porch, tail going back and forth, his rear end doing this little welcoming dance.

But suddenly his dancing stops, tail goes between his legs, and he's up on the porch, whining to get in. Don't take no genius to know he's got a whiff or a look or both of Judd Travers, and is scared the man's come to take him back. I wouldn't let that dog go to save my life.

Ma opens the door for Shiloh, then comes out herself. "Happy Thanksgiving, Judd," she says, and when she smiles, she's got this dimple in one cheek. "I got dinner on the table. Hope you're hungry."

Judd thunks up the steps and hands Ma the gunnysack. "Brought you somethin'," he says.

Becky and Dara Lynn are hangin' back by the door, but they get wind there's a present, they're right out there, tryin' to see in the bag.

"Why, thank you, Judd," says Ma. She opens the sack and starts to put one hand in, then draws it out real quick.

"Eeeuuu!" cries Dara Lynn, getting herself a look. "What is it?"

"Squirrel," says Judd, mighty proud of himself. "They're already bled. Woulda skinned 'em, too, if I'd had the time, but I shot 'em not long before Ray come over."

I see now where the blood's stained one side of the gunnysack.

"Those'll make a fine-tasting stew," says Dad, and he takes the bag himself and sets it on the porch. "I'll skin these after dinner." And then, "Didn't know you could hunt with that leg like it is."

Judd laughs. "Not much hunting to it. I just picked those squirrels off while I was sittin' on my front steps." And he follows my folks inside.

I'm feeling sick at my stomach. I'm remembering how David Howard and me were over at Judd's once, before the accident, and saw him shoot a squirrel just for the pure mean joy of it. Didn't even cook it, just threw it to his dogs.

"Well," says Ma. "Guess we can all sit down at the table, if you're ready."

Becky takes the long way around the kitchen so she don't have to get within four feet of Judd. Shiloh's nowhere to be found; usually he'd have his nose right at the edge of the table, waiting for a piece of that turkey to stand up and walk his way.

It sure ain't — isn't — what you'd call a comfortable Thanksgiving. About the way the Pilgrims must have felt with Indians there. Or maybe the way Samoset and Squanto felt with the Pilgrims — everybody a little too polite.

Ma usually has us do somethin' special on

23

Thanksgiving. Like last year, we each had to think up three things we were thankful for, and the year before that, we had to say something nice about the person on our right, except that Becky couldn't talk yet, and the person on *my* right was Dara Lynn. Only nice thing I could think to say about her was that she didn't look too bad with three teeth missin'.

This year, though, with Judd there, Dad offers the prayer he usually prays on Sundays. He thanks God for the food before us and says, "Bless it to nourish our good. Amen." Dara Lynn don't even bow her head, she's so afraid somebody's going to get the drumstick she's set her eye on.

Everyone smiles when the prayin's over, and Ma says, "Now Judd, you just help yourself to whatever you see before you, and we'll start the platters around. I've sliced some white meat and dark meat both." And the eatin' begins.

With all that food coming at me, I almost forget for a time that we got Judd to look at across the table, but once we get a little in our bellies, I can see the conversation isn't going very far.

First off, Judd's embarrassed. I think he likes the food, all right, but he don't especially like being at our table. It's like he owes

24

us somethin' for finding him after his accident, and Judd don't like to owe nobody nothing. Guess he figured if he was to refuse our invitation, though, it'd be like a slap in the face. And bad as he is, even he's got a limit to rudeness. I look across at him, shoveling that food in like the sooner he gets it down the sooner he can leave, and I'm tryin' to think of a question to ask that'll give everybody a chance to say somethin'.

But right that minute Becky says, "What was the turkey's name?"

We all look at her.

"Only pet turkeys have names, Becky," Dad says. "We bought this turkey at the store."

That gives Judd something to talk about. "I got me a fine wild turkey last year. Bought one of those turkey callers, and after I got the hang of it, I bagged a thirteen-pounder."

Dara Lynn's thinkin' that over. "You make a call like a turkey, and when a real one shows up, you blow its head off?"

"That's about it," says Judd.

Ma never looks up — just goes on cutting her meat, her cheeks pink — but Becky stops chewing her turkey wing and she is glaring at Judd something awful. Boy, you get a three-year-old girl lookin' at you that way, she's got a scowl would stop a clock.

I'm just about to ask Ma to pass the sweet potatoes when I hear Becky say, "We'll blow *your* head off!" and suddenly there is quiet around that table you wouldn't believe.

Three

Well, Thanksgiving sure went downhill after that. You wouldn't think a three-year-old could say anything that would cause much trouble, but it just seemed to put into words the feeling we had about Judd Travers.

Judd looks over at Becky and says, a little sharp-like, "Hey, little gal, you ain't havin' much trouble eatin' that turkey, I see. Somebody had to kill that."

Becky looks at the turkey wing and slowly lowers it onto her plate, then turns her scowl toward Judd again, her bottom lip stickin' out so far you could hang a bucket on it.

Everybody starts talkin' at once. Ma asks wouldn't Judd like some more gravy, and Dad wants to know if he's going to watch the football game that afternoon, but their voices seem too loud and high. By the time Ma cuts the pie, we don't have much taste for it. I don't, anyway. Judd eats one piece of pumpkin, and Ma says she'll send a piece of the walnut home with him. Then her cheeks turn pink again, 'cause it sounds like maybe she can't wait for him to go, and she says, "But of course you're staying to watch the game, aren't you?"

Judd don't say yes or no, but when Dad turns on the TV, the picture's fuzzy on account of we don't have us a satellite dish. Judd's got one in his yard that's bigger'n his trailer, almost. And that gives him a real fine excuse to say no, he thinks he'll go on home, prop up his leg, and watch the game there.

Now that he's leavin', we're all smiles and politeness, standing around waiting for Judd to get his jacket on.

"Where's that dog of yours?" Judd says to me, pulling his sleeve down over the cuff of his shirt. That's about the first time he ever admitted that Shiloh was really mine.

I decide Shiloh's gonna say good-bye if I have to drag him out, and I do. I go behind the couch where he's lyin', about as far back in the corner as he can get, and I have to take two of his paws and tug. He's shaking already, but I hold him tight so he'll know he belongs to me.

Judd looks him over. "Shyest dog I ever seen," he says. But again, just like he did when we went to visit him after the accident, Judd puts out his hand and strokes Shiloh

28

on the head. He's still awkward about it, but he's learnin'. It was Shiloh who barked when Judd's pickup rolled down the bank, really Shiloh who saved his life, and Judd knows that. And once more, Shiloh licks his hand. It's a feeble sort of lick, but Judd likes it, I can tell. I figure Judd's a person who don't get no kisses and hugs from anyone.

After Dad and Judd get in the Jeep, Ma moves about the kitchen, her lips pressed together like she's seen better Thanksgivings, so Becky and Dara Lynn make themselves scarce. They go in the next room and gather up all the Thanksgiving cutouts Dara Lynn brought home from school. They make like they're paper dolls, the Pilgrims riding around on the big cardboard turkey, and the Indians sittin' on this pumpkin.

When Dad gets back, though, he takes out after me! I can't believe it!

"Marty, you didn't say more'n five words to Judd the whole time he was here."

I bet I said fifty, maybe, but I'll admit, I didn't say a whole lot. "What're you yellin' at me for?" I ask. "It's Becky you should be scolding for sayin' too much."

He knows it and I know it, but truth is, you can't hardly scold a three-year-old girl for anything, and Dad would rather cut off his thumb than make Becky cry.

Then Ma chimes in: "Marty's right, Ray. Don't take it out on him."

Dad turns on her then: "Why do you always side with Marty? We have a guest for dinner, I expect everyone to pitch in and be sociable. Can't me be doing all the talking."

I know he's not really mad at Ma, either. He just wishes the day had gone better — we was all so stiff.

But that's enough to set Ma off. "Well, if you want to stand out here in the kitchen and do all the cooking next time, *I'll* sit in the other room and talk. How about that?"

Oh boy, this is the worst Thanksgiving I can remember. Dad turns on the TV to watch the game, then turns it off again, picture's so bad. Becky's leaning over a sofa cushion, sucking her thumb and twisting a lock of hair — ready for a nap.

And then I realize that not a single word's been aimed at Dara Lynn. If *she* had opened her mouth, no telling *what* would've come out; she can sass the ears off a mule. How come *she* got through Thanksgiving without even a look? I find myself gettin' all churned up inside, and when she comes out of the kitchen with the wishbone — the Thanksgiving turkey *wish*bone — and asks Becky to pull it with her, it's all I can do not to reach out and sock her arm.

"Make a wish, Becky, then pull," she says.

This ain't no fair contest, 'cause Dara Lynn's holding that wishbone right close to the top, and Becky's little hand hardly has a grip on it. Guess who wins.

"I got the center, so now you got to tell your wish," Dara Lynn crows.

Becky stands there looking at the broken wishbone in her hand and starts to cry.

"It's *supposed* to break, Becky!" Dara Lynn says, but Becky goes on bawling, and finally Dad snaps at Dara Lynn. Nicest thing that's happened all day.

I hate it when Ma and Dad aren't talking, though — feel all tight inside. Shiloh feels the same say, I can tell. Lies down on his belly with his head on his paws, his big brown eyes travelin' back and forth from Ma to Dad. Every so often, when their voices get extra sharp, his ears will twitch. But that evening, after we have us some turkey sandwiches, Dad says to Ma, "Why don't you go put your feet up, and Marty and I will make stew out of that squirrel meat."

Last thing in this world I want to do, but I put on my jacket and go out on the porch with Dad. He shows me how you skin a squirrel by cutting a ring around the back legs at the feet, then around the top of the base of the tail. He lays the squirrel on its back, puts his foot on its tail, grabs its back legs and pulls, and the skin comes off like a jacket, right up to the neck. I think I am going to throw up.

"You get the other two done, you call me," I say, and go back inside. Why Judd Travers would bring over three dead squirrels as a present to my ma, I don't have a clue. But the thing is, Dad's a hunter, too, so I got to be real careful what I say. When he comes back in, he's cut off the heads, the back feet, and the tails of those squirrels, he's gutted them, and now we got to soak them. I fill a pan with water.

It's later, after Ma's put Becky to bed and is reading a story to Dara Lynn, that Dad and me cut up the squirrel meat. I feel like a murderer.

"I don't think I want any of this after it's cooked," I say finally.

"Nobody's going to make you eat it," says Dad.

"Bet I could be a vegetarian," I say. "I could live just fine on corn and beans and potatoes."

"For about a week, maybe," Dad tells me. "You'd be first to complain."

"Would not!" I say. "I just can't see going hunting. I can't see how you can shoot a deer or a rabbit or anything." I sure am getting smart in the mouth, I know that.

Dad's voice has an edge to it. "You like fried chicken, don't you? Like a good piece of pot roast now and then?"

I think about all I'd have to give up if I gave up meat. Forgot about fried chicken.

"Judd was right about one thing," Dad goes on. "Just because we didn't kill the meat we get from the store don't mean it died a natural death. The hamburger you eat was once a steer, don't forget. Somebody had to raise that steer, send it to market, and someone else had to slaughter it — just so's you could have a hamburger."

I'd have to give up hamburgers, too? I'm quiet a long time trying to figure things out. "Well, if I wanted to be a vegetarian, could I?"

Dad thinks on this awhile as he drops the meat in a pot of water he's got boiling on the back of the stove. "Suppose you could. But of course you'd have to get rid of that cowboy hat I bought you at the rodeo. Your belt, too."

"Why?" I say.

"They're leather; it's only fair. You don't want animals killed for their meat, then I figure you don't want 'em killed for their hide, either. And you know those boots you had your eye on over in Middlebourne? You

33

can forget those, too. Same as that vest you got last year at Christmas, the suede one with the fringe around the bottom."

Man oh man, life is more complicated than I thought. One decision after another, and no matter which way you lean, there's an argument against it. What it comes down to is that I like to eat meat if I don't have to know how the animal died. And I sure don't want to give up my rodeo hat.

"Well, one thing I know," I tell my dad as we set to work cutting up the potatoes and carrots, "I don't want Shiloh turned into a hunting dog."

Dad don't answer right off, but I can tell by the way he's chopping that I struck a nerve. "He was already a hunting dog before you got him," he says. "I was hoping I could take him coon hunting with me some night."

"He's not going to be no hunting dog!" I say louder.

"Well, he belongs to you, Marty. You got the right to say no, I guess." And then, after we put the vegetables in the fridge, waiting to go in the pot when the meat's tender, Dad says, "Tomorrow, I want you to take some of this stew over to Judd, and thank him for the squirrels."

I figure this is my punishment, and maybe I had it coming.

Four

When I get up next morning, Ma's got this big waffle sittin' on my plate, a sausage alongside it, little pools of yellow margarine melting in the squares. Syrup's hot, too.

Still, a waffle can't make up for the fact that on a day off school, wind blowin' like crazy, I got to hike over to Judd's place and give him the remains of what I wish he hadn't shot in the first place.

To make things worse, Dara Lynn's sittin' across from me in her Minnie Mouse pajamas and, knowin' I got to go to Judd's, crows, "I'm not gonna go outside alllll day! I'm just gonna sit in this warm house and play with my paper dolls." And when that don't get a rise out of me, she adds, "*Alllll* day! I don't have to go nowhere."

I asked Ma once if Dara Lynn had been born into our family by accident or on purpose, and she said that wasn't the kind of question you should ask about anyone. Ac-

35

cident, I'm thinkin', looking at her now. Nobody'd have a daughter like that on purpose.

Shiloh starts dancin' around when I put on my jacket and cap. He thinks we're going to take a run down to Doc Murphy's or somethin', but I know that as soon as I turn right at the end of the lane, he'll start to whine and go back. Surprises me, though. This time he goes halfway across the bridge before he stops. I finish the rest of the trip alone.

I'm thinkin' how when a man wrecks his truck and his leg both, and almost loses his job — his life, even — he's sunk about as low as he can get. Dad says either he'll hate himself so much he'll decide to change, or he'll hate the way other folks feel about him, and turn that hating onto them. Sure hope he don't turn his hating onto me.

I'm passing by the house of one of Judd's neighbors, the family that took two of his dogs to care for till Judd's better. I see the smaller one at their window now, barkin' at me, but his tail's wagging. Never saw any of Judd's dogs wag their tails before.

I get to Judd's and have to knock three times before he comes to the door, and then I see I woke him up.

"What you doin' out this early?" he asks,

hair hangin' down over his face, his pants pulled on over a pair of boxer shorts bunched up above his waistband.

"Dad wanted me to bring over this squirrel stew," I tell him, handing him the jar. "Thought you ought to have a share of it."

That pleases him then — as much as you can please a man you just woke up. "Can get some more squirrels where those come from — pick 'em right off the tree," he says, and laughs.

It's then I know this is one big mistake.

"Well," I say, "actually, we don't eat all that much meat. But Ma didn't want the stew to go to waste." Trying to be polite and honest at the same time is hard work.

Judd quits smilin'. "She *didn't* like it then, so you're giving it to me?"

Uh-oh. "No! She likes it fine. Just wanted you to have some." Right this minute I am wondering what the difference is between a fib and a lie. Last summer, when Shiloh run away from Judd and come to me, and I hid him up in our woods, I told Judd Travers I hadn't seen his dog. Didn't tell my folks I had Shiloh, neither, and they claim I lied. What am I doing now? I'd like to know. Ma don't appreciate those dead squirrels any more than I do. If I stand here and tell Judd

Travers the naked truth, though, I'll get my britches warmed pretty quick when I get home, you can bet.

"Well, you tell your ma that anytime she wants some more, let me know. I can't hunt nothing else, I can at least shoot squirrel."

"I'll tell her," I say. And I head back home.

There's somethin' good waiting for me when I get there. Ma says David Howard called and wants to know can I spend the day at his place. His ma will be picking me up about eleven.

"Ya-hoo!" I say, throwing my jacket in the air, and Shiloh dances around, too; if there's any happiness going on, he's a part of it.

"Change your shirt and comb your hair," says Ma.

I go into the girls' bedroom where I got a bureau in the corner, all my clothes in it. I get out a sweatshirt with BLACKWATER FALLS on it, and put it on.

Dara Lynn's still in her pajamas — she and Becky. Got their paper dolls spread all over the bed.

"Where *you* goin'?" Dara Lynn asks.

"Over to David's," I say. And then, not even looking at her, "Can't wait to have lunch at David Howard's: chicken salad with pineapple in it, pickles and potato chips, and a big old fudge brownie covered with coffee ice cream and chocolate sauce." Truth is, I don't know what we're havin' for lunch, but figure that's close.

Now I done it. Dara Lynn slides off the bed and goes hollerin' out to the kitchen to ask why don't we never have fudge brownies and chocolate sauce, and I get away just in time.

David's in the car with his mother when they pull in. For the second time that day, Shiloh thinks he's going somewhere, but don't even get out of the house. I give him a hug and tell him we'll have a run when I get home, and then I slide in the backseat beside David. Since we usually play up in David's room, his ma don't appreciate a dog runnin' around inside the house.

"How was Thanksgiving, Marty?" she asks. Mrs. Howard's got blond hair, and she's wearin' a heavy white sweater. She teaches high school. David's dad works for the *Tyler Star–News*.

"Yeah," says David. "How was dinner with Judd?"

"Nothing special," I say. "It was okay."

"Was he drunk?"

" 'Course not, but he's still banged up pretty bad. He'll be wearing that cast another month, at least."

39

"Do you see any change in him, Marty?" asks Mrs. Howard, and I can tell by her voice she don't expect much.

"Not a lot, but Dad says he's tryin'," I answer.

David and me each tell what all we ate on Thanksgiving — how many rolls and helpings of stuffing, and after the car goes back down the winding road, through Little, and past the post office in Friendly, we get to David's house, which is two stories high (four, counting the attic and basement), and has a porch that wraps around three sides of it.

David whispers he has a secret but won't tell me till we're in his room, so while his mom gets lunch, we go upstairs. David's room has a map of the universe on one wall and a globe on his bookcase. Except for the bunk beds, David Howard's bedroom looks like a school. Got his own desk and chair, bulletin board, and encyclopedias.

As soon as we're alone, he closes the door. "Guess what? You know that fight Judd Travers was in, back before his accident?"

"Yeah?" I say. "With the guy from Bens Run?"

"Yes," says David. "Well, the man's missing. It's going to be in the newspaper this week."

40

"So?" I say. "What's Judd got to do with it? He's been laid up for weeks now with that broken leg."

David's eyes gleam like two small penlights. "The man's been missing since *before* Judd's accident. His family just now reported it. What do you bet Judd killed him?"

"*What?*"

"I think Judd was trying to wreck the evidence along with his truck."

"Go on!" I say. "And maybe kill himself in the bargain? You're nuts!"

"Marty, we've got to check it out! I'll bet we'd find blood on the seat or something." David gets excited about somethin', he almost shoots off sparks.

"If there's blood on the seat, it's Judd's," I tell him.

David shakes his head. "Here's how I figure: Judd and the man from Bens Run had another fight, and Judd kills him. Maybe he didn't mean to, but he did. Throws the body into the cab of his pickup to hide it, then buries it and tries to rig up an accident so any blood in the truck will look like his own."

David's imagination has got us in trouble before, and I know what would happen if Judd catches us snooping around his truck.

"Nope," I say. "Whelan's Garage fixed

that truck up for him after the accident. Cleaned the inside and everything. If there was any evidence, it's long gone. Besides, he wouldn't stuff a body in the cab. He'd put it in the back."

David sighs. He don't like to give up a good idea. "Judd could've buried that body down by the creek!" he says.

"Well, the fella from Bens Run must not have been too popular if nobody reported him missing for a month!" I say.

"His family thought he'd gone to visit a cousin in Cincinnati. That's why they didn't report him missing before now," David tells me.

Must be nice, I'm thinking, to have a reporter for a dad — learn all the news before it comes out in the paper.

"There's nothing to say we can't take a look around the bank where Judd's truck went down," David goes on.

"I suppose we can do that," I answer.

Mrs. Howard calls us to lunch then, and this time it's turkey sandwiches with turkey soup. I think I've seen enough turkey to last me awhile, but the real disappointment is there's leftover mince pie for dessert. Just about the time I'm wondering if she invited me to help eat up leftovers, though, David's mom says, "Now if you'd rather have chocolate chunk cookies, Marty, I've got those, too."

"I'd rather have the cookies," says David.

"Me, too," I tell her.

She smiles and takes the pie away and comes back with a plate of homemade cookies and two bowls of mint chocolate-chip ice cream.

Only thing I don't like about being at David's house is I got to watch how I talk. Mrs. Howard don't — doesn't — correct me the way Miss Talbot does at school, but she'll repeat my words using the right ones, and then I know I made a mistake.

"Well, deer hunting season began last Monday," she says as she removes a tea bag from her cup. "At least Judd Travers won't be out there shooting. I suppose your dad will go hunting this weekend?"

"Maybe," I say. "He don't hunt as much as some folks."

"He doesn't?" she says, and I know I got to say it over.

"No, ma'am, he doesn't," I tell her. David grins.

Miss Talbot tells me I'm smart enough to be almost anything I want if I just work on my grammar, so I'm trying.

After lunch we fool around up in David's room. He's got this revolving light, and if you close all the shades and turn it on, it sends sparkles of light, like snowflakes, swirling over the walls and ceiling.

It's time to go home before I'm ready — we're having a really good time — but when Mr. Howard pulls up, David's mom says he's driving me home. David gets his coat and goes along.

"They find out any more about that man from Bens Run?" David asks his dad.

"I haven't heard anything. Only that the cousin in Cincinnati says he never showed up there."

"Is the sheriff investigating?" asks David.

"He's asking around," says his dad.

Just before I get out of the car, David whispers, "Remember! Next time I come over, we check out the creek bank."

Five

Saturday mornings I work for John Collins, the veterinarian down in St. Marys. Dad drops me off early and I change the paper in the pens, scrub the floor, clean the dog run, refill the water and food bowls, and answer the phone. Sometimes, if his assistant's busy, I'll put on the thick gloves Doc Collins keeps around and help get a balky cat out of a cage or something.

I got to know Doc Collins when we took Shiloh in for his shots, and it was him who told me how to get a dog settled down and trusting again after Judd's other three dogs were set loose once. Never did find out who did it, but could have been anyone. Michael Sholt's dad said he might of thought of it himself just to get even with Judd for all he did when he was drinking. Judd sure made a lot of enemies. The talk is that it was the man down in Bens Run who'd had a fight with Judd that did it. Now, of course, the man from Bens Run is missing.

The longer I work for John Collins, the more I want to be a vet. A vet's assistant, anyway. This morning I'm counting sacks of dog and cat food in the supply room so we'll know how much to order.

John Collins is so busy he hardly knows what to tackle first. No sooner get a dog vaccinated or a rabbit patched up than here come a parrot or a snake. The way I see it, a vet has to know a whole lot more than a people doctor, 'cause what's a parrot and a snake got in common? I'd like to know.

Eleven o'clock and John Collins pours himself a cup of coffee.

"Doc Collins," I say, "a few more weeks and Judd Travers is going to get his three dogs back. I was wondering how he could keep them from turning mean again, now that somebody's been kind to 'em."

"Well, just like people, you can't always predict what they'll do," he says. "Some folks who grow up in the worst kind of homes manage to make something of themselves, and others lash out — want to treat everybody the way they were treated. Same with a dog."

"So what should Judd do?"

"For starters, I'd fence my yard so I wouldn't have to chain them up again. You chain a dog, he knows he's not free to fight if he's attacked, so he tries to appear as ferocious as he can. And Judd should certainly stop kicking them around the way he used to, beating on them with a stick. That's just common sense."

Dad picks me up at noon in his Jeep and drives me home along his mail route. Takes about ten times as long to get home this way as if we just drove it straight — Sellers Road, Dancers Lane, Cow House Run Road — but I don't complain. He hands me the mail to put in the boxes, and I turn up the little red flag on the box to let folks know there's something in it, so they don't have to come all the way down their driveway if there's not. Out where we live, the houses are little, but the land is big.

You feel real bad for people who don't get any mail at all. Some folks are tickled just to get a catalog. What I like, though, is finding something in the box for Dad — a piece of pie, maybe. This morning Mrs. Harris leaves a paper plate with five chocolate cupcakes on it. She waves to us from her window up on the hill, and we wave back. I eat my cupcake right away.

"Judd's going to be getting his dogs back soon," I say, wiping my hands on my jeans, and I tell Dad what John Collins says about how chaining a dog makes it mean.

Dad gives a sigh. "Marty, don't you never quit? You're makin' an old man of me, I swear it. You couldn't rest till you got Shiloh for your own, and now you're worrying about those other three dogs."

"But they've settled down some, Dad. Be a shame to chain 'em all over again."

"Maybe so," says Dad, "but I know better than to tell a man how he should be raising his dogs. And I got a whole lot of other things to think on besides that."

I got other things to think about, too, and soon's I get home, I stretch out on the floor, my head on Shiloh, and put my mind to Christmas. He makes the best backrest! I got eighteen dollars saved so far from working for John Collins. Work for Doc Murphy, too, only he takes my pay off the bill I owe him. It was him who stitched up Shiloh after the German shepherd tore him up last summer. At Doc's I'd trim the grass around his fence. He don't mind the mowing, but hates the trimming. With winter coming on, though, he finds other jobs for me to do.

I'm trying to think what to get Dara Lynn. Got the other gifts decided on. Becky's was easy — a tiny yellow bear, the kind you hang on a tree, fluffy as a new mitten, holdin' a box with two Whitman's chocolates in it. Got Ma a cassette tape of her favorite country singer, and for Dad, a giant-sized coffee mug.

Dara Lynn's gift, though, is giving me fits because the pure truth of the matter is I don't want to waste a nickel on her. Far back as I can remember, she's envied every nice thing that ever happened to me and rejoiced in the bad. Like the time I found a dollar bill at the county fair, and she was mad as hornets it wasn't her that saw it first. And then, when I lost it on the Ferris wheel — it blows right out of my hand and goes floating down over the crowd — she almost falls out of the seat laughing.

Nothing makes her smile as wide as when I got to go outside in the cold to do a job I don't like, and she gets to stay indoors eating buttered popcorn. Don't know why the feeling grew up between us like it did, but lately it's been worse than ever.

Dara Lynn's my sister, though, and I got to get her something, so I settle on a cocoa sampler I seen in Sistersville, three different flavors in a little wooden box.

I don't offer up one word about inviting Judd Travers to our house for Christmas, and at dinner that night, I'm glad to hear Ma say that Doc Murphy told her Judd was going off to visit friends at Christmas. Only Doc don't believe him, because as far as anyone knows, Judd don't have hardly any friends. Not the kind to invite you for Christmas, anyway.

"What I think," says Ma, "is that Judd made the story up so nobody would feel sorry for him. One thing he can't stand is people feeling sorry."

I got one hand under the table giving Shiloh a bite of my chicken, feelin' how glad I am he belongs to me and not to Judd. Do you know how lucky you are, dog? I'm thinkin'. You know how hard I had to work to make you mine? But just when I'm most grateful that Judd won't ruin this holiday, I find out it's going to be ruined anyway.

"We're going to have a different kind of Christmas this year," Dad tells us. "Going to drive to Clarksburg on Christmas Day and have dinner with your Aunt Hettie, then go see Grandma Preston in the nursing home."

There is nothing I can say, because I know it's kind and good to go, but there is not one small inch of me that wants to visit a nursing home on Christmas. I don't say a word because I know Dara Lynn will do it for me. She sets up such a howling you'd think she caught her finger in the door.

"Not the whole daaaay!" she wails. "I don't wanna sit in a nursing home with an old woman who goes around stealing false teeth!"

Grandma Preston's got quite a reputation in that nursing home for takin' things from other people's rooms.

"Dara Lynn, your grandma wouldn't do half of what she does if she had her mind back," says Dad. "She might not even know who we are, but it's not fair that Hettie has to spend all her holidays alone with Mother. We're going to do what we can."

"Good-bye, Christmas!" Dara Lynn sings out, and it's a miracle to me she don't get a slap on the mouth.

It snows on Sunday — first big snow of the season. Not some little half-inch job where you can still see sticks and stones underneath, but four or five inches of stuff so white you got to squint your eyes when the sun's on it. Wind blows it high against the shed.

Ma hates to see snow ruined by footprints, but she knows we got to go try it out. She helps Becky on with her boots and jacket, and when we find our caps and mittens, she turns us loose.

We spend the first five minutes just laughing at Shiloh — the way he leaps up

51

over the snow, disappearing down into a snowbank, then makin' another leap and another. He looks like a porpoise. Ma and Dad come out on the porch to watch.

A big clump of snow falls off a tree and lands on Shiloh's head. We throw snowballs at him then, and he tries to catch them in his mouth. He's running and barking and chasing and skidding, and by the time Dad gets out our sled, there are dog-crazy tracks all over the place.

Dara Lynn drags the sled to the top of our hill and I haul up Becky. I settle myself on the sled, Becky between my knees, heels dug deep in the snow. The plan is that Dara Lynn'll give us a push, then jump on behind me, but when I lift my feet and Dara Lynn pushes, she goes down on her knees and the sled takes off without her, Dara Lynn screechin' bloody murder.

I take Becky and the sled back up and this time Dara Lynn gets in the middle and I crawl on behind. We are flying down that hill, coming to a stop between the henhouse and the shed. We've just started back up for a third time when the crack of a rifle sings out, then another. Way up at the top of our hill, we see a buck go leaping across the field.

"Marty!" Dad yells from the doorway.

"You kids get in here! Now!"

We leave the sled where it is, and run for the house. We know it's not Judd Travers up there, but even though we got the woods posted, there are always other hunters, other rifles.

"I wish this season was over," says Ma, closing the door behind us.

Six

It stays cold and windy, so David Howard don't come to check out the creek bank like he'd said. We decide we'll wait till after Christmas.

Usually our family cuts our own pine tree to bring inside, but this year — with us driving to Clarksburg and all — Dad says why don't we just string lights on the cedar outside the window? No need to do all that decorating when we won't be here on Christmas Day.

Becky hasn't had enough Decembers yet to care, but Dara Lynn sets up a bellow could've attracted a moose.

"We have to sit outside and open our presents in the snow?" she wails.

But there's new snow come Christmas Eve, and the lights of the tree shine on the ice and make a prettier tree than we ever had inside.

So we just sit at the living room window

54

Christmas morning, eating our pancakes and opening our gifts. Ma loves the cassette I give her, Dad uses my mug for his coffee, Becky eats her Whitman's chocolates, and Dara Lynn even likes the cocoa. I bought a box of doggie treats for Shiloh, and we hide them under all the wrapping paper. He goes nuts trying to trace the smell. Paper and ribbon all over the place. He finds the box and I toss the treats up in the air, one at a time — make him snap at them. Whew! That dog's breath is somethin'!

Ma and Dad give me a new pair of jeans, a Western shirt, and a Pittsburgh Steelers watch.

We change our clothes to go to Aunt Hettie's and, leavin' Shiloh behind, climb in the Jeep. He don't like it one bit when we go off without him; follows the Jeep right down to the road, like any minute we're going to realize we left the most important thing and whistle for him to climb in. When we don't, he trots back up to the house, tail between his legs. I sure do wish dogs could understand English, you could explain things to 'em.

I don't like Shiloh bein' left outside during hunting season, but Ma says it's good to have a dog guarding your house when you're away. Anybody come up our drive with the wrong idea in mind, he might think twice if a barking dog comes out to meet him.

We're only a couple miles down the road when Dara Lynn's got to go to the toilet.

"For heaven's sake," Ma scolds. "If it was Becky, I could understand, but you're almost eight now, Dara Lynn!"

"It's not like I planned it," she shoots back, and we got to stop at Sweeneys' house, ask if we can use their bathroom. Ma takes Becky in, too, for good measure, and I stay in the car with Dad, my faced turned toward Middle Island Creek, embarrassed.

We start off again, Becky's car seat in the middle of the back so's to separate me and Dara Lynn. But she'll stretch her body from one side of the Jeep to the other just to rile me. I'm sitting here minding my own business, and I can feel Dara Lynn's shoe kickin' my leg. She's wriggled down so far that her seat belt's up under her armpits.

"Get on over there where you belong," I say, giving her leg a punch.

Dara Lynn sits up, but this time she spreads her arm across the back of the seat behind Becky so that she's rapping me on the side of my head.

"Stop it, Dara Lynn!" I say, punching her

arm, but my elbow bonks Becky, who gives a squeal.

"Marty, keep it down back there. I can't drive and be referee, too," yells Dad. Ma turns and gives us a look.

It's always me gets the blame 'cause I'm the oldest. I wish Dara Lynn could be the oldest for one whole day. I'd get her in so much trouble she'd beg to be let off.

In Clarksburg, Aunt Hettie's waiting at the door, and she don't look anything like Dad, which makes me feel better, 'cause I sure don't want to look like Dara Lynn when I'm grown. Don't want anyone to know we're related. Hettie's wide about the hips, and her arms are round, but she's got Dad's smile, all right. When she hugs you, you know you been hugged.

"You just get on over here and see what's under the tree," she says.

Mostly it's candy, the homemade kind — lollipops for Becky, fudge for me, and peanut brittle for Dara Lynn. Dara Lynn hates peanut brittle, and her mouth turns down so at the corners Ma has to give her a nudge. But Aunt Hettie has dinner waiting with roast beef so juicy I wish Shiloh was there so I could share mine with him.

"Now you've got to be prepared for that nursing home," says Aunt Hettie as we finish her caramel spice cake. "It's not the finest in the world, but the nurses do the best they can."

We go see Grandma right after we eat, before Becky turns cranky, needing her nap. I guess what hits you when you walk in a nursing home — this one, anyway — is that it don't — doesn't — smell so good. Like the bathroom needs cleaning and the food's overcooked. There's eight or ten people in a room with a television in it, all of 'em watching a boys' choir singing "O Holy Night." Two of the women are asleep, and one old lady, tied to her wheelchair with a bedsheet, is tapping on her tray with a spoon.

We sign in at the desk, and a young woman in a red Santa Claus cap says that Grandma's around somewhere, and then here she comes, flyin' down the hall in her wheelchair, banging her gums together 'cause she hasn't put her teeth in yet, asking everyone did they see her snow shovel.

Dad goes over and stops the wheelchair before she can run into the artificial tree.

"Merry Christmas, Mother," he says, kissing her cheek. "I brought the family to see you."

"It was right outside my door," says Grandma, not making any sense.

"What was, Mother?" asks Dad.

"My brand-new snow shovel, right outside my door," she says, and fastens her eyes on me. "You take my shovel?"

"No, ma'am," I say.

Becky's backing away, trying to squeeze behind Ma's legs, but Dara Lynn's just staring, her eyes bugging out like a frog's.

"We brought you a present, Grandma," says Ma, putting a box in her lap.

Grandma tears away at that wrapping paper, got fingers like claws, almost, nobody to cut her nails except Hettie, and Ma leans down to help get the ribbon off. Grandma pulls out a robe, a rose-colored robe with a flower on each pocket.

"It's got to have pockets," says Grandma, handing it back to her, "I don't want a robe without pockets." Ma tries to show her the pockets, but Grandma's talkin' about somethin' else now. It pains Ma, I can tell.

The nurse comes over and suggests we wheel Grandma around the nursing home so she can see the decorations in the dining room and parlor. It gives us something to do. Ma and Aunt Hettie stay in the reception room to talk, but Dad pushes Grandma's wheelchair, and us kids troop along.

Becky's got the idea that we come to see

Santa, and now she spots some old man with a beard sitting at his window.

"There's Santa!" she yells excitedly. The man turns and laughs.

"Come here, sweetheart," he says, holding out his arms, and I take Becky inside his room to say hello. She sits on his lap and tells him what all she got for Christmas, and he's so tickled. Becky don't even notice he only has one leg.

But Grandma wants to go. "That man is *no good!*" she says to Dara Lynn. "He stole my change purse."

"Mother, your change purse is right there in your pocket," Dad tells her as we start off again, and Becky waves to the man with the beard.

But Grandma goes on about how she lives in a den of thieves and liars, and how if Dad really loved her, he'd get her out of this place.

It hurts Dad, 'cause it was more than Aunt Hettie could manage to care for Grandma at home, and it'd be even worse for Ma, with a family to look after, too.

"I ever get old and crazy, just shoot me," murmurs Dara Lynn.

After we tour the whole building and take Grandma back to her room, we read the Bible together and then we all sing "Silent

Night." For the first time, Grandma gets real quiet — studies us hard while we're singin' — and I see tears in her eyes, like maybe for the first time she remembers who we are.

But by the time we get our coats, she wants to roam around in her wheelchair again. She's got her new robe over her shoulders like a cape now, won't let nobody touch it, and says she's got to go see the man with the beard and get her change purse back.

The attendant winks at us. "You go on," she says. "I'll handle this."

So we go back out to the Jeep, and spend the rest of the day at Aunt Hettie's. Becky takes a nap on her bed, and Dara Lynn and me put together a jigsaw puzzle of a pepperoni pizza, and I'm thinking how Dara Lynn and me are getting along fine right now, why can't we get along like this all the time? I wonder does it have anything to do with Shiloh being my dog, when all the while what Dara Lynn really wanted was a kitten?

We have a light supper before we leave — cold roast beef sandwiches — and then we set out. Sky's almost dark, but the snow gives off light so it don't seem as late as it is. Starts to snow some more, too.

Ma says, "It's always hard to visit Grandma and it's always hard to leave." Her own ma died a few years back, so Dad's is the only ma she's got.

We see we left the lights shining on our outdoor Christmas tree when we pull in the drive, and it's a welcome sight, but I'm lookin' around for Shiloh. Usually he'd be dancin' down the drive by now, head goin' one way, tail the other.

"Where's Shiloh?" Becky asks, missing him, too.

"Probably running around with that black Labrador, I'll bet," says Ma. "Nice that he's got a friend."

I'm thinking, though, that it's not often our whole family's gone the way we were today. Usually Ma's home while Dad's at work and we're in school. But this time we've been gone from almost eleven in the morning to eight at night, time enough for a dog to wonder if you're ever comin' back. Go lookin' for you, maybe.

We walk inside and turn on the TV to get the last of the Christmas music we'll hear all year, and when my Steelers watch says ten o'clock and Shiloh's still not back, I put on my boots and jacket and go out on the porch.

First I just stand on the steps and whistle.

Never did learn to whistle like Dad can, though. Mine's a puny little noise that don't travel much beyond the cedar tree.

"Shiloh!" I call, and my voice echoes against the hills. "Here, boy! Shiloh! Come on, boy!"

Nothin' stirs but the bushes, branches blowin'.

I clump down to the end of the drive, hands in my pockets, shoulders hunched.

"Shiloh!" I yell, loud as my lungs will let me. "Shi . . . loh! Shi . . . loh!" Air's so still I figure that dog should be able to hear me a half mile off.

Then I stand real still and listen. Used to be I could hear his feet scurrying through the field or down the path from the meadow, but I know that with all the snow, that dog could be right behind me and I wouldn't hear a thing 'cept his collar jingling.

I walk to the bridge and yell some more, then go left and follow the road in the other direction, bellowing like a new calf.

Nothin' answers but the wind.

Seven

It's hard to sleep that night. Our sofa's got more lumps than bean soup, and every time I turn over, I pull out the blanket from the bottom.

I get up about two in the morning and stand at the window. Moon's almost full, and the snow sparkles like diamonds. I'm not lookin' for moonlight or snowlight, though — only Shiloh. We keep the shed door open on nights like this so he can go in there and sleep if he comes back late. But I know my dog; he'd make at least one detour up on the porch first to see if somebody was awake to let him in. Not a fresh paw print anywhere.

I'm thinking of the hunters we heard up in our woods. Deer season's over now, but there's possum and coon to hunt; rabbit and groundhog, too. What if a hunter took it in his head to steal Shiloh? You ride along and see notices posted on trees about a dog missing, and most of the time someone's made off with it — someone who wants a good hunting dog, or a watchdog, or both.

I get this sick feeling — what if I never see Shiloh again? What if somebody's got him chained, beatin' on him like Judd used to do? All I got to remember him by are yesterday's paw prints, most of 'em half covered now by new snow. I lay back down and fall asleep out of sheer sadness.

Don't have to go to school till the second of January, so Ma lets us sleep in next day. Can't believe I sleep till nine thirty, and I only wake then because I hear dogs yipping out in the yard. I sit straight up.

"Shiloh's back!" says Ma from the kitchen. "My stars, what's that dog got now?"

I leap off the couch and run to the door. There's Shiloh and the black Lab. Shiloh's got a piece of orange rag in his mouth, and they're playin' and tuggin' at it. Thing about dogs, they can get enjoyment out of the most common ordinary object you could ever imagine. I'm so happy to see him I pull on my jeans, push my feet in my shoes, and grab my jacket. I run outside and wade through the snow to where Shiloh and the Labrador are chasing each other around and barking.

Rag looks like a piece of vest a traffic cop

wears. I'm hoping those dogs didn't get in somebody's clothes basket or, worse yet, run off with somethin' belonging to the sheriff. I stick the rag in my jacket pocket and reach down to hug my dog. "You're weird," I tell him. "You and your friend both." He gives me the wettest kiss this side the Mississippi.

When I go in the house, Shiloh follows for his breakfast, and the Labrador trots off, lookin' for some other mischief. Becky's up, wantin' me to play Candy Land with her — most boring game in the whole world, but I do.

Ma's feeling good this morning, I can tell. Shiloh's back, Christmas is over, she's done her duty by Grandma Preston, and she's in the kitchen making cinnamon rolls. She sings along with the cassette I give her:

"The roughest road in the valley,
Longest I ever did roam,
But the sweetest path in the country,
Because it leads me home."

I tell Dara Lynn it's her turn to play Candy Land with Becky, and I call up David Howard. After I hear what he got for Christmas, my presents don't sound all that much. He got two computer games, a pair of

Nike Air Gridstar crosstrainers, a basketball, a sleeping bag, four books, a Chicago Bulls T-shirt, and a horn for his bike. And that was just from his folks. He still has presents coming from his grandparents.

"Why don't I come over to your house tomorrow, and we'll check out the creek bank where Judd had his accident?" says David.

"Okay with me," I tell him.

Dad's got the *Tyler Star–News* with him when he comes home, and while he sits in the kitchen talking to Ma, I take the paper in on the sofa and look through it, see if there's anything more about the missing man from Bens Run. Don't find anything of interest except a story about a car crash up in Wheeling, an escape from the county jail, a robbery up in Sistersville, and a hunter who shot a man over in Marion County by mistake. Nothing about nobody from Bens Run.

David Howard's mom drives him over the next morning, and it's the kind of gray winter day that can't decide if it's going to rain or snow. We plan to head out for Middle Island Creek soon as we eat lunch. Becky, of course, goes and asks David to play Candy Land with her, but he don't have little sisters, and don't know you got to let Becky win. When it's him doing the winning, Becky slides down off the chair and runs in the bedroom, then comes back out later with a towel over her head so no one can see she's been cryin'. David must think I got the strangest family!

Ma says lunch is ready. It's only hot dogs and soup, but there's cinnamon rolls for dessert, the frosting still warm.

"You boys playing in or out this afternoon?" Ma asks.

"Out," I tell her. "Maybe do some hiking."

We put on our jackets and head down to the bridge, Shiloh trotting along behind. I point out the place the pickup went over, and we crawl down the bank, our feet turned sideways.

"Nothing to see!" I say to David. "Everything's covered with snow."

But David keeps going. The thing about David Howard is he don't let real life get in the way of his imagination. If he wants to find clues that Judd Travers murdered the man from Bens Run, then David'll find plenty; just won't happen to be the right clues, that's all.

Shiloh's comin' down the hill after us, glad to be doin' whatever we are, though he's no idea in the world what that is.

David turns and points at Shiloh. "Sniff!" he says.

Shiloh wags his tail.

"What you doing, David?"

"I'm telling him to sniff. If there was a dead body buried down here, I'll bet a dog could find it."

I laugh. "Shiloh don't even know the word 'sniff,' " I tell him. So David says it again, and gets down on all fours, trying to show my dog what to do. I fall down in the snow laughing my head off, and Shiloh falls on top of me, joinin' in the fun.

We're rolling around on the bank, havin' a wrestling match, when all of a sudden my knee hits somethin' hard.

"Ow!" I yell, and push David off me.

Shiloh comes runnin' over like a snow-plow, pushin' up snow with his nose, and before you can blink, he's dug up a man's boot, frozen hard as cement.

Eight

David and I sit on our knees in the snow, turning that boot over and over.

"Evidence!" says David, his eyes snappin'. "This could put Judd Travers behind bars for life."

That's the way folks feel about Judd, see. They remember how he was — and maybe still is, far as I know. His meanness to dogs and people, the way he cheated and lied. When you've done all the things Judd did, how do you get folks to start trusting you? It's true he might be tryin' to change, but the tryin' part still needed a lot of work.

"David, you don't even know whose boot that is!" I say. David Howard's case against Judd is as stupid as flypaper in winter. "Even if it *does* belong to that man from Bens Run, and even if Judd *did* murder him, just 'cause he wrecked his truck here don't mean that's where the man is buried. The one don't have a single thing to do with the other."

Even Shiloh's laughin'. Sittin' there in the snow with his mouth open. Sure looks like a grin to me.

But David says, "You know how a criminal always returns to the scene of the crime? He just can't help himself! Same with Judd Travers. Maybe his conscience drove him here."

If I was a teacher and this was homework, I'd give David a failing grade. One thing sure, he's never going to let himself be bored, and that's what I like about David Howard: He don't have enough excitement, he'll make it up.

We walk upcreek for a spell, watching a flock of ducks fly low over the water. Probably going to light down on one of the islands out in the middle. A little farther on, we can make out Judd's trailer across Middle Island Creek.

"Who named this a creek instead of a river? Paul Bunyan?" says David. "Sure looks like a river to me."

"We walk far enough, we'd get up to Michael Sholt's cousin's house," I tell him. Michael lives down toward Friendly, but his cousin lives way upcreek and takes a different bus to school.

"If we walk far enough we'll get to the North Pole!" says David. Think he's getting a little tired of all this hiking. Getting cold, leastways. Probably got his mind on Ma's cinnamon rolls.

"Want to go back?" I ask.

"Yeah," he says. "But keep the boot."

I don't know what I'm going to do with a frozen shoe, but I throw it under the porch steps when we get home, and we eat a plate of cinnamon rolls.

On Sunday, Ma's listening to Brother Jonas preach on TV and Dad's cleaning his razor. Dara Lynn and Becky have pulled bedsheets over a couple chairs in their room to make a tent, and they're pretending that Shiloh's a bear, tryin' to get in. The more they squeal, the more Shiloh wiggles about, tryin' to get his nose under the edge of the sheet, tail going ninety miles an hour. If that dog had wings, he'd fly, except his propeller would be on the wrong end.

"I'm going over to visit Judd — see how he's doing," I tell Dad.

Dad don't look at me, just frowns a little at his razor. "You could always pick up the phone," he says, not too sure, I guess, about me goin' over alone to visit a man like Judd, no matter how many chances he'd give him.

"I might could give him a hand with somethin', help him out," I say.

"Well, don't stay too long," says Dad.

Outside, I pull that boot out from under the steps, tuck it under my arm, and start off.

I cross the bridge, Shiloh beside me, and watch to see if he'll come ahead or turn back. This time he goes a few steps beyond the other side, then sits down in the snow and whimpers. I walk on about fifty yards and look back over my shoulder. Shiloh's trottin' back across the bridge. Guess he's decided not to freeze his bottom waiting for me.

Sky is bright, but cold. Sun don't seem to warm me at all. The thing about West Virginia is it takes so long for the sun to come up over those hills on one side of the creek that it don't seem any time at all before it's sliding down behind the hills on the other. Boy, you live in Kansas, flat as an ironing board, I'll bet the sun comes up in the morning before you even open your eyes. You go to bed, it's still got a way to go before it's down.

Then I realize I'm not cold from the weather, I'm cold from fear. The goose bumps I can feel popping out on my arms under my jacket don't have nothing to do with the snow. Shiloh had the right idea turning back. What I am fixing to do is walk right up to Judd Travers holding the one piece of evidence he just might kill for to get.

Could be he's thinkin' on digging around over on that bank himself as soon as his leg gets better, and here I am, showing him what I got, what David and me know.

I got this far, though, I got to go on. If Judd's looking out of his trailer now, he's already seen me comin', knows what I got. I wonder if there's a rifle pointed at me right this very minute.

Climb the steps to his trailer and knock, but I don't hear any sound at all from inside — no TV, no radio. Can hear my teeth chattering. I hug my arms tight around my body, the boot still tucked under my arm, and knock again. Then I hear this engine. I turn around, and here come Judd's pickup. He gets out, hauling his left leg down first, then his crutches. The cast is a dirty white, but nobody's wrote his name on it or anything, the way they'd do at school. He don't have his gun with him, and that cheers me right quick.

"Hey!" I call. "You're driving now!"

"I can get where I want to go, that's about it," Judd says. He unfolds himself like an old man. Got a paper sack in his hand, and I hope it's not whiskey.

I knew that as soon as Judd could start driving again, he would, because he loves his truck almost more than anything else in this world. Washes it every weekend, and finds any excuse he can to drive to Friendly and back, just ridin' around, listenin' to his radio. Last summer, on the Saturdays he wasn't working, wouldn't be anything at all to see Judd passing three or four times out on the road, goin' nowhere in particular.

He's comin' slow up his board walk, cast and crutches tapping a rhythm like old Peg Leg the Pirate. "What you doin' over this way?" he wants to know.

"Just came to say hello, see how you're doin'."

"Well, I'm alive," he tells me.

Judd goes in first, leaves the door open behind him, and I figure that's all the invitation I'm gonna get, so I go in, too. Close the door. I guess what I plan to do is show him the boot and ask does he know who it belongs to. I figure I can tell by the look on his face if it belongs to that man from Bens Run, and if Judd's the reason he disappeared. With Judd hobbling about on that leg of his, I can be out the door and in the bushes if he gets mad.

Judd puts the sack on his table, then reaches inside and pulls out a half gallon of milk, some bread, and a tin of sardines.

"What you got there?" Judd asks, nodding toward the boot.

I swallow. "Oh, just somethin' I wonder if you'd recognize," I say, and hold it up. Wonder if I'm sounding smart-mouth.

Judd's jaw drops and he stares at it for a moment. "Where'd you find it?"

"Over by the creek." I study his face, my heart thumpin' hard. "Know who it belongs to?"

"Of course," says Judd. "It's mine."

Talk about feelin' stupid! I don't tell him what David Howard figured.

"Never thought I'd see *that* again! Couldn't wear it anyway, it's soaked up so much rain and snow. Most of my clothes, they just cut them off, you know. In the emergency room, they don't fool around." He takes the boot and throws it back into his bedroom.

"Didn't you miss it when you dressed to come home from the hospital?"

"Missed it before then, so a guy from work brought me a pair of his old sneakers to get home in. You want a pop or somethin'?" Judd asks me.

"Okay." I sit down on Judd's couch, remembering how only a few months past, he had me workin' out there in the summer sun in order to earn his dog, and then, when I'm about done, tells me I can't have Shiloh after all — that nobody witnessed our agreement, and I'm a fool to do all that work. Guess I'd have to say it was the worst day of my life. No — the worst hadn't happened yet; I'm gettin' to that — but it was a time I'll never forget.

Judd gets me a 7Up from his refrigerator and pours himself a mug of leftover coffee. Then he sits down, his jacket still on, 'cause he keeps his trailer cold. Holds the cup under his chin, lettin' the steam warm his face.

"So how's things?" he asks.

"Okay," I tell him. "I been working for that vet down in St. Marys on Saturday mornings. Learnin' a lot about dogs."

"Yeah?" says Judd.

"We see a lot of dogs that have been chained up, and most of 'em are mean as nails. John Collins — he's the vet — says it's because they feel trapped that way. If something came along to attack 'em, they'd be in a tough spot 'cause they can't fight free, so they act real fierce to scare you off."

"That a fact?" says Judd, and I'm tryin' to read his face as he takes another drink of coffee. "Well," he says at last, "I sure know how it is to feel cornered. Know what it's like to feel trapped."

I don't say nothing. I'm remembering what Doc Murphy told me about how he

77

knew the Traverses when Judd was a little kid, and how the father used to whip those kids with the buckle end of a belt.

Judd stares out the window beyond my head like he don't hardly see me at all. And suddenly he stands up and says, "Well, I'm goin' to take a nap, Marty." That's a good-bye if I ever heard one, so I set my empty pop can on the floor.

"Okay," I say. "See you around."

I'm halfway across his yard when I realize what I've done. My hands feel all clammy. Why do I think I can believe Judd Travers? If David Howard *was* right, and Judd done something to that man from Bens Run, and if that boot belonged to him, you can bet Judd'll burn it faster than a dog can pee. Why didn't I ask to see that other boot — see if it matched? I can't believe how stupid I am — just handed the evidence right over!

Figure I got to steal a look in the back of his pickup as I walk by, see if there're any clues in there. Judd keeps all sorts of stuff in there, but he's got a tarp over it now, and the tarp's covered with snow. I manage to lift a corner and peer underneath. Piece of plywood, a coil of rope, truck battery, tires, roofing shingles, iron pipe, canvas. . . .

And then I see Judd Travers watchin' me from his window. I drop that tarp right quick, give him a wave, and head on home. Feel like the worst kind of fool.

But I feel even worse later. Walk in the house and Ma says, "David called, Marty. Wants you to call him back right away."

I go out in the kitchen and dial David's number.

"Marty!" he says. "Guess what?"

I kid around. "They found the guy from Bens Run with a bullet in his head?"

There's silence from the other end. Then, "There wasn't any bullet, but they found him. And he's dead."

Nine

I don't see David again till we go back to school after New Year's. By then I'm ready for vacation to be over. Becky's come down with chicken pox, and Dara Lynn's stepped on my Steelers watch and broke the glass. Now we got to send it all the way to the factory for a new face cover, which means I can't wear it on the first day back to school.

Big news is that the man from Bens Run died of a blow to the head, says the *Tyler Star-News*, and David and I been on the phone to each other most every day about it. Body was found down along the Ohio River by a highway maintenance crew, but the man's shoes were missing. Murder weapon's missing, too, and David's sure Judd's the one who done it. I'm not so sure about the shoes — they could have come off and floated most anywhere. I'm thinking about the murder weapon. What I'm remembering, and wish I wasn't, is that piece of iron pipe in the back of Judd's pickup.

School bus comes up our road as far as the bridge, then turns around. Anybody living on the other side has to walk over here or catch another bus somewhere else. I think it's because that old bridge might not hold a bus full of kids. Fire truck come up once makin' a safety run, and had to empty its tank before it crossed, then fill up again from the other side of the creek.

Driver picks up anybody who's ready on the way up, and everybody else on the way back, so that kids who live along this route got two chances to catch the bus.

"Happy New Year, Marty," says Mrs. Sims, the driver. "How you doin', Dara Lynn?"

Dara Lynn never smiles at nobody before nine o'clock in the morning, and she don't say nothing, but I wish Mrs. Sims a Happy New Year, too, and go sit across from Michael Sholt. Out the window I can see Shiloh trotting back up the lane to the house. Ma says that sometimes after we're gone in the mornings, she picks that dog up and rocks him like a baby. Don't many dogs have a grown woman who'll do that, I'll bet.

"Heard the news?" Michael crows as soon as I step on the bus. "The man from Bens

81

Run was found murdered, and they think Judd did it."

"*Who* thinks?" I say.

"*Everybody!*" says Fred Niles. "Everyone's talking that it's Judd!"

Sarah Peters is up on her knees on the seat so she can see around the whole bus. "The sheriff's questioning a whole lot of people, and one of 'em's Judd. It was on the news this morning." I see pretty quick that whether Judd done it or not, the feelin's going against him.

"Just because they questioned him don't mean he did it," I say.

"How come you're stickin' up for Judd, Marty?" asks Sarah. "Thought you used to hate him worse'n poison."

"Maybe he's tryin' to change. You ever think of that?" I ask her. But I don't even know that myself.

One by one, other kids climb on, and everyone's wearin' a little something they got for Christmas — a jacket or sneakers or cap. By the time David gets on, the other kids are looking at Michael Sholt's baseball cards and telling what all they got for Christmas. David sits down beside me.

"Anything new?" I ask.

"Judd was called in for questioning, but the sheriff released him," David says.

"Doesn't mean he's innocent. It just means they haven't charged him with anything yet."

"Do they know where he was when the guy was murdered?" I ask.

"They don't even know the exact day. It was about the time of Judd's accident, but it could have been a week before or a week after." He looks at me. "I think we better turn that boot over to the sheriff."

I swallow. "I don't have it," I say.

"Where *is* it?"

I'm so miserable, my stomach hurts. "Judd said it was his, so I gave it to him."

David slides down in the seat, can hardly believe it. "We could've been on the witness stand, Marty!" he says. "Maybe we could have solved the case!"

"Just be quiet about it," I say. I'm feeling low enough as it is.

David don't tell the other kids what I did, but he is sure disgusted.

At school, Miss Talbot's wearin' something new she got for Christmas, too. It's a diamond ring, and all the girls got to gather round her desk and make her turn her hand this way and that, see the diamond sparkle. She's engaged to a high school teacher over in Middlebourne.

Soon as the kids start talking about Judd

Travers being guilty, though, she puts a stop to it. "This class is not a courtroom," she says, and we know that — ring or no ring — she means business.

At home, Dad won't let us talk about Judd being the murderer, either.

"That Ed Sholt!" he says. "Shootin' off his mouth . . . !" Dad kicks off his shoes and sinks down on the sofa. "Saw him at lunch today in Sistersville, and he's worked out the whole thing in his head — all the different ways the man could have been killed, and he's got Judd doing the killing in every one of 'em. 'Pipe down, Ed,' I tell him. 'A man's innocent till proven guilty, you know. He's a right to his day in court, it ever gets to that.' But he says, 'You're the one who should worry, Ray. You live closer to Judd than the rest of us. If it were me, I'd get a good strong lock for my door and keep a gun handy.' "

I swallow. "You talk to the sheriff yet?"

"Yes, and he's guessing Judd's not the one. They can't tell when the man was killed exactly, not when a body's been dead this long, but they figure he probably died sometime after Judd's accident; somebody thinks he may have seen him later than that, anyway."

I'm wondering what it's like to have everybody suspecting you of a crime you didn't do — just when you're tryin' to be better. Maybe you think, what's the use? If everybody figures you're bad, might as well go ahead and be bad. But if Judd gives up now, those dogs of his, when he gets 'em back, are going to have a worse time of it than before. Judd'll hate everything and everybody, includin' his dogs. On the other hand, what if he *did* do it? What if he really is a killer?

I try not to let myself think on that. The only thing I can see to do — for Judd's dogs, anyway — is to get Judd Travers a fence. Once I do something for *all* Judd's dogs, I can stop feelin' so guilty about saving only the one. So I say to Dad, "You know anybody got some old chicken wire stuck away that we could use to fence in Judd's yard for his dogs?"

Dad turns the TV down and looks at me. "*Chicken* wire? You got to have somethin' stronger than that, Marty! You need regular fencing wire and metal posts, and nobody I know has a whole fence just sittin' around, I can tell you."

Seem like everything I think of to do has got a hitch to it.

All week the weather stays mild, and the snow's disappearin' fast. "January thaw," Ma says. Tells us that for a few days most

Januarys, it seems, there's a mild spell to give us a promise of spring before the next big snowfall.

The sun shines on into the weekend, and Saturday afternoon, after I get back from the vet, I decide that I'm going about this fence idea all wrong. If nobody's going to keep an old fence around after they take it down, then I got to find somebody with the fence still up that he'd just as soon wasn't there.

I walk over to Doc Murphy's, Shiloh frisking alongside me, tryin' to get me to run. I'm thinking how last September, when I was helpin' Doc in his yard, he'd said now that his wife wasn't there to garden anymore, he wished he didn't have a fence around that vegetable plot, just a nuisance when he mowed.

Doc's got a couple of men patching his roof and cleaning his gutters, and he's out there scattering grass seed on all the bare patches of lawn. Shiloh goes right over and waits for Doc to pet him. I wonder if in his little dog brain he remembers that Doc saved his life after the fight with the German shepherd.

"Hello there, Marty," he says, scratchin' Shiloh behind the ears. "I'm getting a jump on old man winter. Figure if I can get this seed in the ground before the next snow, it'll be the first grass up come spring."

"Too bad that fence is still there, or you could plant right over the postholes," I tell him.

"I was thinking the same thing," says Doc. He lets Shiloh go, and scoops up another handful of seed from his bag.

"I could maybe take it down for you," I offer.

He gives this little laugh. "That's not a job for a kid. Lot of wire there, and those posts are heavy."

"I bet I could. Would haul it away for you, too."

Doc studies me over the rim of his glasses. "Your dad wants this fence?"

"It's for Judd Travers. To keep his dogs happy when he gets 'em back. He won't let 'em run loose, 'cause they're his hunting dogs, but John Collins says they wouldn't be half as mean if they weren't chained — if they had a yard to play in."

Doc Murphy don't say anything for a minute. Just turns his back on me and goes on scattering that seed. Finally he says, "Tell you what: I'll have Joe and Earl there" — and he nods toward the men on the roof — "take that fence down if you can have it off my property by tomorrow. I don't want a pile of fencing sitting around here. Then I can get the whole place seeded in this warm spell. Deal?"

"Deal," I say. "Dad and me'll come pick it up in the morning."

I don't even have time to be happy, because I realize Judd Travers don't know a single solitary thing about any of this. You don't just show up at a man's house and start fencing his yard.

Only thing I can think of to do is walk on over to Judd's and ask. I'm not real eager to go over there by myself, though. I mean, what if that boot we found *did* belong to the dead man, and Judd knows that I know what it looked like? Where it was found? 'Course, why would Judd kill a man, leave his body by the river, but bury his boots someplace else? That don't make a whole lot of sense, either.

I walk back up the road and my mind's goin' around and around, first how Judd must have done it for sure and then how he didn't, like to drive me crazy. I cross the bridge, but when I head for the brown-and-white trailer, Shiloh turns back. I get to Judd's about the time he's sittin' down to lunch.

Any other man would ask me to come back later or invite me to share his food. Judd Travers invites me in to watch him eat,

I guess, 'cause I sit at his table and he only offers me a pop. And right off he says:

"What you want? Everybody else seems to think I killed a man. That what you come to say?"

"No," I tell him. " 'Course not." Already my heart's knockin' around beneath my jacket.

"Then what were you doin' snoopin' in the back of my truck last time you were here?"

My breath seems to freeze right up inside my chest. One thing about Judd Travers, he don't forget. I decide to tell it straight. "Trying to figure where that other boot of yours was," I tell him. "To match the one I found."

"Why should you care?" asks Judd, his narrow eyes on me.

I shrug. "No particular reason. Just wondering, that's all."

"Well, I threw it out," Judd says. "When you think you've seen the last of one, not much use for the other."

Wonder just how far Judd trusts me; about as far as I trust him, I guess. I talk about somethin' else: "When do you suppose you'll get your dogs back?"

"Soon's I can get around without this cast," he says. "Doc's taking it off next

Wednesday. I'll still be hobblin' around on crutches, but I figure I can at least tend to my dogs."

"You know," I say, "the way I hear it, the happiest dogs make the best hunters."

"Don't know about that," says Judd. "My pa always said to keep 'em lean and mean."

Can't help myself. "Maybe your pa wasn't always right," I say.

Judd pauses, a piece of macaroni on his fork. He looks at me for a minute, then puts the fork to his mouth, don't say nothing. I figure that don't get me no points.

"All I know is what I learn from Doc Collins, that chainin' up dogs is one of the worst things you can do," I say.

"Well, that's just a pity, because I don't have no money for a fence," Judd tells me, and takes a big swallow of water, wipes his hand across his mouth, and hunches over his plate again, like his macaroni and beef is a chore he's got to wade through.

"What I come to tell you is that Doc Murphy's having his garden fence took down this afternoon, wants if off his property by tomorrow. First come, first get. I asked him not to give it to nobody till I'd talked to you." I pray Jesus this isn't a true lie, just a social conversation.

"What's the catch?" asks Judd.

"Nothin'. He wants to plant grass seed over the postholes during this warm spell."

"Well, I got the strength of a ninety-year-old man right now, and Doc knows that. I can't be fooling with a fence."

"Dad and me can bring it by. Put it up for you."

Judd gives this half smile and a "*Huh!* Nobody does nothing for free," he says.

"We're not askin' anything, Judd! Just see a chance to do a little something for those dogs."

"Why? They're not your dogs. You got Shiloh. You got an eye on them, too?"

"No! What you talkin' about? We're just bein' neighborly, that's all."

"Well, my dogs'll get along fine without you," says Judd, and goes on eating, and my stomach does a flip-flop.

I stand up. "If you don't want it, I know folks who do. What's the name of that man with all those hunting dogs over in Little — those really *fine* dogs? He knows they need a place to run, and he'd like that fence, I'll bet." I am stretching the truth so far I can almost hear it snap. Don't even know a man in Little.

I wait for two . . . three seconds, but Judd don't say a thing. I push my chair in and head out the door.

Ten

All the way home I am chewin' myself out. What am I, some kind of fool? Judd Travers don't care about his dogs any more than I care about mushrooms. Couldn't get that man to change if you was to hold his feet to the fire.

And now I feel a rage buildin' up in my chest that's almost too much for me to handle. All I am trying in this world to do is make life a little easier for Judd Travers's dogs, and what do I get? Trouble up one side and down the other. Bet he *did* kill that man from Bens Run. Judd's got enough meanness in him to do most anything.

Right this very minute Doc's got those men takin' down his fence. I cross the bridge and can look way down the road, see where one is digging up those posts, and the other is winding up that wire. And tomorrow morning my dad, who don't even know it yet, is to drive his Jeep over and pick up a whole yard of fence that Judd Travers don't want in the first place.

I am too mad to go inside our house. Too mad to look myself in the mirror. Shiloh comes out to meet me and I don't even say hello. Just march on by and head up the path to the far hill, Shiloh running on ahead, bouncing with pure joy.

"It's all because of you," I tell him, knowing all the while I'd do it again, even so. It's true, though. If it weren't for Shiloh, Judd Travers would be just somebody to stay away from when we could, say your howdys to when you couldn't. But because I got Shiloh, I am smack in the middle of all Judd's problems.

I'm remembering it was up here I saw that gray fox last summer with the reddish head. Suppose somebody's shot it by now, with all the meanness around. Every minute of every day there are folks like Judd Travers bein' born; every minute of every day they are thinkin' up ways to be worse than they were the day before.

What do I care what happens to Judd? I ask myself. What do I care what happens to his dogs? I am turnin' myself inside out to be nice to a man who hasn't an ounce of kindness in his whole body, and who's probably a killer, too.

All afternoon I stomp and storm around our woods and meadow, pickin' up every limb I can find and whackin' it so hard against a stump I send splinters every which way. Every log becomes a Judd Travers I got to kick and whack, till my feet and arms are tired.

Finally, when I been gone so long I know Ma will worry, when even Shiloh's laid down to rest himself, I turn around and start back. I get home about the time Dad's coming up the drive in his Jeep.

"You look like you been hiking some," Dad says as I follow him into the house where Dara Lynn and Becky are watching TV.

"*Wondered* where you were, Marty," Ma calls from the kitchen.

I throw my jacket on the floor. "I don't want to have anything more to do with Judd Travers the whole rest of my life!" I say.

Now Dad's lookin' at me. "Marty, I don't think I want you going over there alone," he says. "Didn't have a fight with him, did you?"

"No, I didn't have no fight!" I say, a little too loud, and grab a box of cheese crackers from the cupboard like they was out to get me. Lean against the counter and stuff 'em in my mouth, hardly even tasting. I think again how that fence is waiting over there at

Doc Murphy's, and figure I'm not just mad, I'm crazy. Whatever Grandma Preston's got wrong with her mind, I got it, too.

But Dad's been delivering the JC Penney spring catalog, and he's too tired to take on my worries. "You'd think it was Christmas all over again, the way folks were waiting for 'em," he says. And then, "Ooof," as he sits down at the table and pulls off his boots. "I don't ever want to get up again. Think I'll spend the night right here in this chair."

Ma laughs and rubs his shoulders.

"I am going to stretch out on that couch and not move except to eat," he tells her.

Telephone rings, and I answer.

It's Judd.

"What kind of fence did you say it was?" he asks.

I blink. Swallow. "Green yard fencing, the wire kind," I tell him, and swallow again. The cheese crackers are dry in my mouth.

"Well, I don't want no gate. Don't want anybody sneakin' in, lettin' my dogs loose again."

I stare at the clock above the sink. "What time you want us to come over tomorrow?" I ask.

"Not before nine, that's for sure."

"See you tomorrow, then," I say, and hang up.

I am suddenly so quiet my hand freezes there in the box of crackers. Dad is telling Ma about the deliveries he made that day, and I slip the crackers back on the shelf. Go stare out the window. Now how in the world am I going to tell my dad I volunteered him to put up fencing at Judd's?

"Ground's softening up," I say finally. "Good time to work in the yard."

Dad gives me a sideways glance. "You want to work in the yard, Marty, you got my blessing." He reaches for the mug of coffee Ma pours for him, warm him up a little.

I try again. "Dad, what if you was to find that tomorrow's your one good day to do a really fine deed for a person? And what if I said I'd help out?"

Dad slowly slides that coffee mug back on the table, turns to me, and says, "What in the world have you done now?"

I tell him about Doc Murphy's fence, and what a good thing this would be for Judd's dogs.

"Marty, just two seconds ago you even mention Judd's name, you're spittin' nails!" Ma says.

"Well, a person's got a right to change, hasn't he?" I plead, lookin' at Dad. "Didn't you say you believe in second chances?"

Dad gives such a long, drawn-out sigh

96

you'd think there couldn't be that much air in a human lung.

"We'll see how I feel tomorrow," he says.

Tired as I am, I don't sleep so good. What if Judd changes his mind? What if we haul all those posts over to Judd's tomorrow and, out of sheer spite and meanness, he says to get 'em off his property, he don't want 'em there? Worse yet, what if after all this work, Judd does turn out to be the one who murdered the man from Bens Run, and I'm doin' all this work to please the devil?

Next day Dad says he feels better. Not good, but better. The sun helps, so he wants to start early, get it over with, and we drive to Doc's to load that fencing in the Jeep, then make trips back and forth to Judd's till it's all there. I know there's a hundred other things my dad would rather be doing, but when he's got a chance to do what's right or to do what's easy, he can work the legs off most any man in Tyler County.

Judd comes outside, and if he's not exactly friendly, he's helpful. But I never knew that putting up a fence could take so long or be so hard. First thing we do is measure to see just how much of it we can use, bringing it right up to Judd's trailer so's he can step out his back door and into the dog run. Then we lay those posts where they're going to go, and Dad and I take turns with the shovel, digging the holes and packing the dirt in around the posts till they're rock solid. Judd can't do any digging, but he helps uncoil the fencing and fasten it in place. We put the extra behind his shed.

It's well into afternoon before the job's done, and when Dad and me get home, we both stretch out on the living room rug and don't wake up till dinner.

"Judd was about as pleasant today as I've seen him," Dad says to Ma, helpin' himself to the black-eyed peas and ham.

"Maybe so, but I'm still uneasy about him," she answers.

I'm thinking that the sheriff's guess is right. Judd may have had a fight once with the man from Bens Run, but he probably wasn't the one who killed him. 'Course, they could have had a second fight, and Judd killed him not meaning to. That's another way it could have happened.

That don't keep me from going over to Judd's on Wednesday after school to see the neighbor on one side of Judd bring the two dogs he's been keepin', and the folks on the other side bring over the one. Those dogs don't know which to smell first, the new fence or each other. They get to yippin' and runnin' around in wider and wider circles like they can't believe their freedom. We laugh at their craziness. I reach out every time a dog comes by, like I'm tryin' to grab him, and he just runs all the harder — knows I'm playin'.

"Look at the exercise their legs are getting, Judd," I say. "That'll make 'em all the stronger; they'll go up hills like nobody's business."

He points to his own leg, out of the cast now, but still weak. "Maybe I should get in there with 'em," he jokes.

Not no accident that each of his neighbors has a little something to say to Judd, things like: "Well, we're returning your black and white better-tempered than it was before," and, "Think we put a little meat on their bones; they look better fattened up some, don't you think?" and, "You treat these dogs right, Judd, you'll get many years of good hunting from them."

I wish they'd just leave; Judd don't need no sermon right now. But I know he figures he owes 'em something, so he just nods, and after a time they go home. Then Judd and me sit on his back steps watching those dogs enjoyin' themselves, and I sure do feel good. Still, can't help glancin' at Judd's hands now and then and wondering, Those the hands of a killer? He the one who done it?

When I get home and tell Dad about Judd getting his dogs back, I can see he's feeling good, too. Glad to be on neighborly terms with Judd Travers again, no hard feelings between them.

Ma's not feeling too good, though.

"Tooth is actin' up again," she says.

"You ought to go have it looked at," Dad tells her.

"Well, the pain comes and goes. I got some oil of clove on it now," she says.

One thing about Ma, she sure hates to go to the dentist. Dad says he don't know how a woman who can stand giving birth to three children is so afraid of the dentist, but Ma says there's no comparison. Children you ask for; toothaches you don't.

What I'm thinkin' is that Ma's been hurting since yesterday — I could see it in her eyes, but didn't say nothing. I give more time to Judd Travers, who, if he's not ninety-nine percent evil is sixty percent at least, and paid no mind to her at all.

"I'll read to Becky tonight," I tell her, when Becky's beggin' for a story. Ma nods and hands me the book. So Becky, still scratchin' her pox, crawls up on my lap, Shiloh beside us. When Becky leans her head back against me and sits real quiet, one hand resting on mine as I turn the page, I can understand why Ma would go through pain to have children and still not like the dentist. Of course, she give birth to Dara Lynn, too, but that's somethin' else entirely.

Becky and Dara Lynn go off to take a bath together, and Ma gets out the quilt she's makin' and settles down in front of the TV with Dad. I finish my homework at the table. We give up on Pilgrims, and we're studying about Alaska now; I'm reading how it gets as cold as seventy-six degrees below in winter.

I try to figure how cold seventy-six degrees below is. Wonder if you spit, would it freeze before it hit the ground? After the lights are out and I crawl under my blanket on the couch, all that coldness gets to me. When I hear Shiloh's toenails clickin' about on the porch, I feel my way to the door in the dark to let him in; he makes one fine back-warmer.

As I close the door again, I see this little beam of light movin' way off in the direction of Middle Island Creek. Can't place where it is exactly, but it's there sure as I got eyes in my head. It's sort of bobbing around, like somebody's holding a flashlight. I watch for fifteen, twenty seconds, maybe, and then the light goes out.

Eleven

It's the next day on the school bus I tell David about the light. And even though it probably don't mean spit, David Howard can work up one heck of a story with it, I know.

"Like a signal or something?" he asks, eager.

"Well, it could have been," I say.

He's cautious, though. "How do you know it wasn't just somebody with a flash-light out jogging after dark?"

"It was movin' too slow for that. And didn't stay on more'n fifteen seconds."

"Like somebody looking for something?" asks David.

"Maybe."

"The other boot!" whispers David. "We found one, and now Judd wants to find the other."

"David, that don't make any sense at all!" I tell him. "Why would the killer leave a body out in plain sight, but go hide the shoes somewhere else?"

"The murder weapon, then," says David. "Maybe Judd buried it somewhere along Middle Island Creek, and now that the police are looking for it, he wants to be sure it stays buried."

I lean back against the seat and stare out the window, wondering if David could be right. The sheriff hasn't found enough evidence to arrest Judd, but everybody from here to Wheeling is ready to string him up, it seems. Maybe they got good reason.

"Besides," says David, lookin' over at me, "if somebody's looking for something, why would they go out at *night?*"

"That's what I'm *tellin'* you! We got a mystery on our hands. But it don't mean it's anything to do with Judd," I say. Deep inside, though, I'm thinkin' maybe it does.

What's fun is sitting in Miss Talbot's class, me and David, and having this secret. During math, we pass these notes back and forth.

How high off the ground was the light? writes David.

How in the world would I know that? I wonder. It was dark — couldn't even tell where the ground was. But I write back, *Three feet, maybe four.*

Then it was a man holding the flashlight, answers David. *If it had been a kid, it'd be more like two or three feet from the ground.* I tell you, he can find clues in almost anything.

"Marty?" says Miss Talbot.

"Three," I say, staring at the blackboard where she's pointing. I don't even know what the question is.

Somebody snickers.

"What I'm asking," says the teacher, "is whether you would multiply or divide."

"Multiply," I tell her, making a guess.

"Correct," she says, and I let out my breath real slow.

On the bus going home, David says he'll ask his ma if he can stay at my house this weekend. That way we can take turns watching for the light. So when I get home with Dara Lynn, and Shiloh comes dancin' and wigglin' down the drive to meet us, I'm not surprised to hear the phone ringing soon as I step inside.

"Mom says it's your turn to come to our house," David tells me. "I can't sleep over there till you come here."

I ask Ma can I spend the night at David's.

"I think it's his turn to come here," she says.

"He was just here!" I say.

"Not to spend the night," she says. Nothin' is ever simple with mothers.

"Well, I can't go down there till you sleep here," I tell David.

Finally Ma says I can go to David's house for an overnight if David will sleep over the weekend after that. And on Friday morning, I put my toothbrush and pajamas and some clean underpants in my book bag before I leave for school.

"You be polite at the Howards' now," Ma says as she hands me a plate of fried cornmeal mush, cut in slices, crisp around the edges. I slather on the margarine and then the hot syrup.

"Why don't anybody ever invite me to sleep over?" gripes Dara Lynn, glaring down at her fried mush.

" 'Cause you're a sourpuss, that's why," I tell her.

On the way to the bus stop, Dara Lynn says to me, "I wish you'd get run over and your eyes pecked out by crows."

"I wish you'd fall down a hole and pull the dirt in after you," I say.

If Shiloh hears the meanness in our voices he sure don't show it. Happy as can be trottin' along beside us till he sees that school bus comin' to take us away.

"See you tomorrow, boy," I tell him, give him a hug.

Somebody on the school bus is passing

out Gummi Bears, though, and Dara Lynn revives in a hurry. Sitting there beside a girl in third grade, eating Gummi Bears and swinging her legs, Dara Lynn don't look like such a poor neglected child to me.

Fred Niles gets on, and he's got a story to tell. Seems that somebody walked right into their house the day before and stole two jackets and a shotgun.

"Just walked right in while you were home?" asks Sarah.

"Ma was only gone two minutes," says Fred. "She walked down to the road to check the mailbox, and later we discovered what all was missing. We're locking our doors and windows from now on. Never had to do it before."

"Wouldn't surprise me if Judd Travers had something to do with it," says Michael Sholt. "Heard he got his cast off this week. Bet he's making up for lost time."

I got this feeling Michael may be right. But I say, "Could have been anyone at all."

"You know anybody else around here who would walk in a neighbor's house and steal from him?" Michael asks.

At school, we are so deep in Alaska I don't see we can ever get out. We're buying and feeding imaginary sled dogs for math, figuring how many pounds of food per day they're going to eat, and how many pounds they can pull. We're studying Eskimo paintings in art, and listening to Eskimo folktales, and for spelling I got to memorize words like "tundra," "Aleutian," "glacier," "petroleum," and "permafrost." Now I *know* I never want to feel what seventy-six degrees below zero is like.

I get off at David's house after school. David has his own key. His ma gets home a half hour after he does, and she's got a pile of papers to grade.

"Hi, Marty," she says. "There's chocolate pudding in the refrigerator if you boys want a snack."

"We already found it," David tells her.

I guess maybe everybody feels more comfortable at his own table in his own house. I know I feel a little awkward at David's. First off, there's always a tablecloth. I can't imagine a cloth on our table at home. Becky would drop spinach on it first off, and Dara Lynn would spill her milk. The Howards have napkins, too. Cloth napkins. And everything's in bowls that you pass around. Ma just sets a pan right from the stove on our table; it keeps the food hot, you want some more.

David's folks are nice, though. David and I tell his dad how we're studying Alaska, and he tells us about this dogsled race they hold up there every year called the Iditarod, and how you have to travel a thousand miles and sleep out in the snow and be careful your dogs don't drop off the ice and I don't know what all.

"You see much of Judd Travers these days?" Mr. Howard asks me finally when David's ma brings out the dessert.

"Some," I tell him.

"Wonder how he takes to all this talk of the murder."

"Don't take to it at all, same as you or me," I tell him.

Mr. Howard grows quiet after that.

Later we're lyin' on our backs on the top bunk in David's room, trying to make out the constellations on his ceiling. David and his dad got a package of those stick-on stars and planets, and they put them in just the right places so that the ceiling looks something like the sky would look if you stepped outside at night a certain time of the year.

"That's Orion, the Hunter," says David, pointing. "See those two bright stars there in the middle, and then the three bright stars below? Well, the two stars are supposed to be his shoulders, and the three stars are his belt."

Now who figured that out, do you suppose? How do they get a whole man out of five little stars? Why couldn't those two stars on top be the eyes of a wolf or something, and the three below be his mouth? Makes as much sense to me as a hunter.

And then, because we're talking about hunters, maybe, David says, "I'll bet it *was* Judd Travers who stole those jackets and that shotgun from Fred's house."

I roll over on my side, trying to see his face in the dark.

"How come whatever happens has to be Judd's fault?" I ask. "How come it all goes back to him?"

David thinks about that a minute. "I guess it's because anything that happened around here before was usually Judd's fault. The way he'd cheat Mr. Wallace over at the store. We've both seen him do that. Give him a ten-dollar bill, then get to talking, and when he got his change back, say he gave Wallace a twenty. Driving drunk and knocking over people's mailboxes. Kicking his dogs. Other people have done one of those things maybe once in their lives, but Judd can do all those things in a single month!"

"Yeah, but what if he's changed?" I say.

David thinks about that, too. "Maybe," he says. "But once you get a reputation, it follows you around like your shadow. That's what Mom says, anyway." He's quiet a moment. Then he tells me, "Mom said I can't come to your house anymore unless we promise not to go anywhere near Judd's."

Right then I see how I got connected in people's minds with Judd Travers.

"You haven't gone with me to his house since last fall," I tell David. "We can keep on not going there together. I don't care."

"I just wanted you to know," says David.

Next thing they'll suspect *me* of murder!

"You know, Marty, if he *did* have anything to do with killing that man, he could go to jail for a long time and you probably wouldn't have to worry about him ever again," David says.

I think about that awhile. Why *don't* I wish Judd would be found guilty? Why don't I wish he'd get sent to jail? David's right. It sure would solve a lot of problems, just like that. I wonder why I been trying so hard to take his side?

Because I think I know how Judd got to be the way he is, that's why. Once you know what happened to someone as a little kid, it's hard to think of him as one hundred percent evil. If Judd's the way he is because of what his dad done to him, though, maybe his *dad* was that way on account of what *his* dad done, and maybe the grandpa was that way because *his* father. . . . When's it going to end?

Dad picks me up early the next day before he starts his mail route and takes me down to the vet's in St. Marys. I'm stacking twenty-pound bags of cat box litter when John Collins comes in to scrub his hands, getting ready to operate on a collie that was hit by a car. The vet scrubs with a brush, even under his fingernails.

"What's happening up in Shiloh these days, Marty?" he asks me. "I've had two customers come in this week telling me that their homes have been broken into. Walk-ins, more like it. Somebody coming in when they weren't home, and helping themselves to whatever they want."

"You must be talking about Fred Niles's family," I say. "They got a shotgun and some jackets missing."

"No, hadn't heard about them. But one family's missing two twenty-dollar bills they kept on a shelf in their kitchen, and a woman tells me she came home to find half the food in her refrigerator gone. Drove her husband to work, she says, and came back to find a whole roast chicken, half a cake, and a pan of scalloped potatoes missing."

"Who do they figure took it?" I ask.

"Nobody knows. There's talk about Judd

Travers doing it. Of course, as I said to Mrs. Bates, it could be more than one person. Could be a whole ring of housebreakers. I sure don't like to hear about that shotgun, though. Walking in a house when no one's there and helping yourself to a chicken is one thing; walking in with a gun, if they start using that shotgun, is something else."

Doc Collins puts on his surgical gown and then his gloves, and goes into the operating room. I go on with my stacking. Maybe it's me who's got his head in the sand, I'm thinking. Maybe I just don't want to face the fact it could be Judd. How long's he had that cast off now? Three days? And when did the robberies begin? Three days ago, exactly.

Twelve

David's got an idea about the light I saw over near the bridge. If Judd didn't murder the man from Bens Run, he says, maybe someone's trying to murder Judd.

He slips this note to me during history:

1. Let's say Judd didn't murder anyone, but suppose he knows who did?

2. What if the light you saw was the real killer's flashlight? I'll bet you he knows Judd could squeal on him, and he's setting a trap for Judd down by the creek.

I turn over my spelling paper and send a note back to David:

1. I think you're nuts.

2. I think that whoever the killer is, Judd or anyone else, he threw his murder weapon down the creek bank, and now he's trying to find it before the police do.

113

I remember how David says he wants to be either a forest ranger or a biologist. I write a P.S.:

P.S. I don't think you're going to be a biologist or forest ranger either one. I think you are going to write detective stories. Bad ones.

David reads my note and laughs.

"David," says Miss Talbot. "May I see that note, please?"

I don't move. I can feel the color rise to my face. David don't move, neither. He sure don't want Michael Sholt and the whole sixth-grade class knowing about that light I saw and snooping around the creek themselves.

"I . . . I can't," he says. "It's . . . it's not my note to give."

"Who wrote it?" asks the teacher.

Now the whole class is watching.

"I did," I say.

"Then may I see the note, please, Marty?"

I swallow and shake my head. Everyone's staring.

"It's . . . private," I tell her. This is a real good secret David and I have going, and Miss Talbot just might pin it up on the bulletin board, the way she did Jenny Boggs's note last week.

"I see," says Miss Talbot. "And is this class a private place?"

"No, ma'am," I say.

"Then, because you were taking school time for private business, I suggest you stay in after lunch and use some of your personal recess time for your studies," she says.

That's fair enough, I guess. I see David stick the note in his pocket. So while the other kids are playing kick-ball out on the playground, I've got to make a list of Alaska's natural resources and David's got to list the mountain ranges. Why do we have to study Alaska in January? I wonder. Why couldn't it be Hawaii? The only thing we've got to look forward to is the next weekend, first of February, when David gets to stay overnight at my place.

That night when I go to the door to let Shiloh in, I see the light again. Feel so cold inside my body it's like I had ice cubes for supper. Now I know this mystery's real, not just something David Howard and me put together to have some fun. Somebody's out there in the night doing something he don't want nobody to see. Looking for something he don't want nobody else to find, I'll bet. Maybe even studying our house like I'm studying the light from our window, standing in the dark. Is it the killer? Is it Judd?

I stay at the window watching till the light disappears, trying to figure just where it's coming from, but when there's nothing but blackness outside your window, you got nothing to pin it to. The old gristmill seems the most likely place.

Turns out David can't come for a sleep-over that weekend, though, on account of we're not home. We got to go to Clarksburg for Grandma Preston's funeral on Saturday.

"It was pneumonia," Aunt Hettie cries over the phone. Can hear her voice all over the kitchen. "It happened so fast! One day she had a cold, and the next thing we know it's pneumonia, and then she's gone — just like that. I should have been with her. I could have taken off work, and gone to that nursing home and stayed right by her bed. . . ." She cries some more.

"Now Hettie, don't you go blaming yourself for something you couldn't help in a million years," says Dad. "You did the best you could for Mother, and no one's faulting you now. We'll be there Friday evening, soon as I can get away."

"What about Shiloh?" I ask when my dad hangs up. Grandma Preston's dead, see, and first words out of my mouth are about my dog.

"I'll ask Mrs. Sweeney to come by and feed him," says Ma.

"But the whole family's never been gone overnight before," I say. "Shiloh might figure we're not coming back." All I can think of is that a lot can happen to a dog in twenty-four hours.

"Marty, that dog of yours is rompin' all over creation with that Labrador, and he won't even miss you," says Dad.

"Couldn't we just put him in the house?" I beg.

"And ask Mrs. Sweeney to let him out every few hours for a run?" says Ma. "What if he doesn't come back when she calls him, and her with that bad knee? It's enough she's asked to feed him."

There's not much to say after that.

Ma spends the rest of the week cooking food for the funeral dinner. "Here's one thing I can do for Hettie," she says, wrapping up a ham and a dish of sweet potatoes.

Dad tells the post office why he won't be in on Saturday, and I call Doc Collins. By five o'clock Friday evening, we're on our way to Clarksburg, and Ma's in the front seat, trying to answer our questions.

Dara Lynn's just told Becky we aren't going to see Grandma Preston ever again.

"Not ever, ever, ever, ever, ever," she says.

"Why?" asks Becky.

" 'Cause she's dead," says Dara Lynn.

"What's dead?"

"It's when your body gets as cold and stiff as an icicle and somebody could put a red-hot iron on your leg and you wouldn't feel nothing," Dara Lynn says.

"Dara Lynn, shut up," I tell her.

Becky asks if she's ever going to die, and Dara Lynn says yes, and Becky starts cryin', says she don't want nobody putting a red-hot iron on her leg.

"Becky," Ma says from the front seat, "your grandma's gone to be with the angels, and there won't be anymore sickness or pain for her ever again. We can rejoice in God's love."

"She won't be stealin' nobody's false teeth anymore, neither," says Dara Lynn, and we can't help ourselves. Have to laugh. We all feel better after that.

We sit up late that night talking to all the people who drop by Aunt Hettie's to remember Grandma Preston, and we sit real quiet through the service at the church next day. Dara Lynn keeps her hands to herself and Becky hardly makes a peep. I'm beginning to think Dara Lynn's not gonna be too bad a sister after all, but when we get to the

118

cemetery, I wish she'd never been born.

She's standin' there beside me at the grave while the preacher reads from the Bible, the coffin resting on one side of the hole, waiting to go in. But when the preacher asks us to bow our heads and begins his prayer, Dara Lynn inches right over to that hole and peers down inside. I can't believe it!

"Dara Lynn, get back here!" I hiss.

Just then the dirt gives way, her being so close to the edge. Dara Lynn's arms start goin' around like a windmill, and somehow, though one leg went over the side, she lands on her knees and keeps from goin' in. She just don't have any sense at all when it comes to danger.

Ma reaches out and grabs that girl and yanks her back beside us — Dara Lynn's white socks all dirty now and mud on both hands. I'm thinkin' what I said about how I wish she'd dig herself a hole and fall in, but my mind don't stop there. I'm thinking how what if nobody saw her, and what if she really did fall in, a whole pile of dirt on top of her, and then the coffin goes in and Dara Lynn's buried alive.

It's such an awful thought I can feel the sweat trickle down my back. Sometimes a thought comes to you that you just can't help, but you don't go to jail for *thinking!*

And then we're all back at Aunt Hettie's, and it's like a picnic supper. Everybody's bringin' more food — sliced cheese and a turkey, and little rolls to fold the meat up in. There's potato salad and cherry pie and burnt sugar cake and marshmallow Jell-O. Can't tell if this is a party or a funeral.

It's near ten o'clock when we get home that night. First thing I look for is my dog, but this time I can hear him before we even turn up the drive. He is barking his head off, and when we get out of the Jeep, he don't even come over — just stands back there by the henhouse, his nose toward the woods, his body jerking with every bark he makes.

"Shiloh!" I say, and he comes over to give me a lick, then goes right back to barking again. Even after we take him inside, he's jumpy. Goes from one window to the next.

"What in the world has got into that dog?" asks Ma.

She checks out the house. Our TV is still there — the money box, Dad's shotgun. Nobody's made off with the toaster or the radio or anything else that we can see.

"I'm going to get my lantern and have a look outside," Dad says. He takes a flashlight, puts his coat on again, and goes to the shed.

But a few minutes later he's back. "The

lantern's gone," he says. "Somebody took my shears and my knife, too. If it weren't for Shiloh, that thief probably would have broken into the house."

I had goose bumps on my arms before, and now even the goose bumps have goose bumps. Was it because of Shiloh's barking that the thief didn't come in, or was it that we turned up the drive just about then? And if we *hadn't* come home when we did, would the robber have made off with Shiloh, too?

"Oh, Ray!" says Ma, and sits down hard on a kitchen chair. They stare at each other. "It's like someone knew we were gone."

"Well, I didn't go around telling everybody — just my supervisor at the P.O.," says Dad.

"I only told Mrs. Sweeney so she'd feed the dog," says Ma. "And Marty called the vet and David Howard, but that's all."

They stare at each other some more, and Dad don't even blink. "Only other person who saw us leave was Judd Travers," he says at last. "We passed his pickup just after we pulled out of the drive."

Thirteen

And then the blizzard comes. We go back to school on Monday, the TV talking three inches of snow, but by the time the bus lets us off that afternoon, it's five or six, and still comin' down.

"We gonna be snowed in!" Dara Lynn crows happily, dropping her coat on the floor.

Becky looks worried, but Dara Lynn grabs her hands and dances her round and round the kitchen, tellin' her how we might not have to go to school for a whole week. Then Shiloh gets into the act, skidding around the linoleum, his toenails clickin' and scratchin'.

"Well, I sure wish I'd got extra milk," says Ma. "I can always make bread, and I've got beans and salt pork enough for an army, but there's not much substitute for milk."

"We can always put snow on our cereal!" says Dara Lynn, laughing.

Ma decides to get in the spirit of things,

too, so she gets out her valentine cookie cutter, and she and the girls make cookies while I carry in wood for the little potbellied stove in the living room. Our house has a furnace, but it don't work if the electricity goes out, so a couple years back Dad put in the potbellied stove.

"Next best thing to a fireplace," Ma says.

I know if I don't bring in the wood now and stack some more on the porch, I'm not going to be able to find the woodpile in another couple hours.

Shiloh goes out with me, and tries to tunnel through the snow with his nose. I stack wood on the porch first, then stamp the snow off my boots and make another couple trips from the porch to the stove inside. By this time Shiloh's had his fill of snow and comes when I call. He plops down close to that potbellied stove, giving out big contented sighs, his eyes closin'. He wore himself out.

Every time there's another report on TV about the blizzard nobody knew was comin', the weather bureau moves the number of inches up. Twelve to fifteen inches of snow, one of the weathermen says now, and, a half hour later, he's talkin' two feet.

Dad finally gets home about eight, and can hardly make it up the drive. He's got snow tires on the Jeep and four-wheel drive, but the wind's blowin' the snow in drifts across the road. I can tell by the look on Ma's face when she hears that Jeep that it's about the best music in the whole world to her.

Dad's real pleased to see all the wood I brung in.

"Good for you, Marty," he says. "Last I heard, we're goin' to need every stick of it. They're talking thirty inches now."

Dara Lynn squeals some more.

I wake up next morning and look out the window in sheer wonder. Dad's stomping back in the house to say that he can't move the Jeep one inch — he'd have to shovel all the way down to the road, and then couldn't go anywhere. Plow hadn't been down there, either.

"Well, Dara Lynn, looks like you got your wish," Ma says, turning the French toast over in the skillet.

It's only the second time in all the years Dad's worked for the post office, though, that he hasn't been able to get his Jeep through, and he worries about people who are waiting for their pension checks.

"Even if the checks got through, nobody could get to a bank to cash them," says Ma.

David calls, of course, and tells me they

haven't been plowed out yet down in Friendly, either, and his dad is still trying to get to the newspaper office. Then Ma calls Aunt Hettie in Clarksburg to make sure she's okay, and finally there's nothin' else to do but give in to being snowbound.

Snow finally stops about noon, and Dad goes out with a yardstick to measure where it's flat in the yard. Thirty-one and a half inches, not counting six or seven feet along the side of the house and shed where it's drifted. We shovel a path to the henhouse to get some feed to the chickens.

Us kids have to go out in it, of course. I take a shovel and dig a path from our porch to a tree, just so Shiloh can do his business. Dara Lynn and Becky, fat as clowns in their snowsuits, scarfs wrapped around their faces, only their eyes peeking out, set to work diggin' a cave at one side of my path, but Becky no sooner sits down inside it than the roof falls in on her. She's squallin', looks like she got hit in the face with a cream pie, and I got to carry her into the house. I sure wish David Howard was here. We'd dig a tunnel all the way down to the road.

We have a fine time — go out and come in so many times that Ma just puts our caps and mittens beneath the potbellied stove to dry out, so they'll be ready again when we are. House smells like wet wool and Ma's home-baked bread. Dara Lynn's cheeks are red as apples, her nose, too. She wouldn't be half bad-lookin' if she'd just keep her mouth shut.

By middle of the afternoon, though, Dad's gettin' calls sayin' that trees are down, and power lines as well. The snow's wet and heavy, like pudding, and plows can't get through till the trees are cleared off the roads. They got a substitute mail carrier deliverin' what mail he can down in Friendly, and I know Dad wants in the worst way to be doin' his own route. A matter of pride.

Ma's cheerful, though. Says we can toast marshmallows in the woodstove after supper, and then we watch a *National Geographic* special on alligators. But fifteen minutes from the end, the TV goes out along with the lights.

"Hey!" yells Dara Lynn. "What happened?"

"What do you suppose?" I say. "The electricity went off."

"Ray . . . ?" says Ma.

Dad makes his way into the kitchen to get the flashlight. "Well," he says, "I imagine a transformer went out somewhere. Guess we're lucky it waited till we had our supper."

We hang round the stove till the fire dies down. Dad don't want to put in any more wood, in case the power's off a long time, and we need every bit of wood we can find.

"Why don't we go to bed early to stay warm, and maybe the electricity will come back on in the night," says Ma, and she gets out some candles to make an adventure of it. The girls go to bed without their baths, because we all got wells out this way, and the electric pump won't bring up the water if the power's off. The only water we got for drinking and cooking is what's left in the water heater right now.

Shiloh and me are lucky. Because the woodstove's in the living room, and we're sleepin' on the couch, we got the warmest place of all. But when we get up the next morning, the house is cold as an ice chest. Dad's got his coat on over his pajamas, and he's bringing in wood from the porch to feed the stove.

Ma tells me to dress without washing up, and nobody's to flush a toilet. Dara Lynn immediately sets up a howl.

"It's gonna stink in there!" she cries. "I ain't going to use no toilet that stinks!"

Ma turns on her suddenly. "Dara Lynn, I can think of a hundred worse things that could happen to you, and I don't want to hear another word. You don't want to use the bathroom, you can potty in the snow."

That shuts Dara Lynn up in a hurry. I smile; can't help myself — just thinking of Dara Lynn with her backside in a snowdrift. But I can see right off that today's not goin' to be near as much fun as yesterday. The woodstove's got a round top on it, not made for cookin', so Ma puts a pot over it upside down, and grills our toast on its flat bottom. Everything takes twice as long to make, though, and finally, cold as we are, we settle for Cheerios and the last of the milk. It's right about then we hear the sound of an engine grinding out on the road somewhere.

"Snowplow!" sings out Dara Lynn, looking toward the window.

No sight of anything, though. Don't look like there's any plow comin' along the country road. And then we see Judd's pickup, a plow blade in front, turnin' right up our driveway.

Slowly, his wheels spinning, Judd pushes his way through the snowdrifts till he can't go no more, then backs up and makes another run at it. We all go to the window to watch, and Dad steps out on the porch and waves.

The pickup keeps comin', huge mounds of snow moving ahead of it. Every so often,

Judd turns the wheel, ramming into the snowbanks with the plow to get rid of his load. The snow sure isn't doin' his truck any good, but Judd keeps at it, pushin' a little bit farther each time before he backs off and makes another run. Finally he gets up as far as our porch.

"Judd, I sure do appreciate this," Dad calls.

Judd rolls down his window. "Thought you might need to get out."

"Won't you come in and warm up?" Ma calls.

"Couple more folks I got to help out," Judd yells. "Thanks, anyway." And he makes a wide sweep to turn himself around, then heads off down the driveway, pushing more snow in front of him.

If people would just give him a chance! I'm thinking. See how much he's changed! But at the same time, I'm wondering is that a new jacket he's wearin'? And is that shotgun I see resting above the back window in the truck really his?

Fourteen

By next day, the electricity's still off, and we all sleep on the floor in the living room around the stove. Dad brings in a pail of snow and sets it by the toilet to flush it, but the bathroom's so cold the snow don't thaw. Now we got buckets of snow settin' all around the stove, coaxin' it to melt. Only good thing we've had to eat is hot dogs, 'cause you can put 'em on a stick and shove 'em right in the fire.

Dad gets out his Jeep to see how far he can go, but this time he's stopped by a tree that's down. Trees and wires all the way between here and Little, and when he tries to go the other way, across the bridge and on past Judd's, he come to the place where even Judd quit plowin'. Big wall of snow blocking the whole road. Drifts clear up over Dad's head.

"Sure am glad I'm not expectin' a baby in a blizzard like this," says Ma. I see her hand go up to her jaw and figure she's thinking a toothache would be even worse.

The bad part is we can't get no news on the TV or radio, neither, and with the sky that sick color again, like it's going to throw up more snow, we don't much feel like rompin' around outside. Takes too long to warm up afterwards. Even Shiloh hangs back when we open the door.

And then things slide from bad to worse. Our phone line goes out.

I know Ma's thinkin' that if one of us had an accident or something, there'd be no way to call for help. No way for anyone to get in with an ambulance, either. Last year down in Mingo County, a man got hurt during a snowstorm and they had to send a helicopter to pick him up. Almost worth knockin' Dara Lynn off the roof just to see a helicopter set down in our field. I smile to myself, but you sure can't say a joke like that out loud.

Everybody's tired of snow. We're tired of eatin' cold food, tired of settin' on a cold toilet seat, and of everybody crowded together at night on the living room floor just to stay warm, gettin' on each others' nerves. Dad's the only one half cheery. He says just pretend we're campin' out, but I can tell he's itchin' to get to work, and Ma just plain wants out of the house. And as if that ain't enough, it starts snowin' once more.

But then, fast as things got worse, they get better. The power comes on during the night. We're all sound asleep when suddenly the TV starts blarin' and the lights come on. We sit up and cheer. Hear the furnace click. By morning the phone's workin', too, and about nine, we hear chain saws goin' out on the road, crews workin' to remove trees that are down, and then the low grinding sound of the snowplow.

Dad gets to work about noon. Weatherman on TV says the four more inches of snow we got is all it will be for a while, and suddenly the world looks good again.

Weren't all the roads in the county cleared, though, so the schools stay closed till Friday. Then everyone's got stories to tell of just how bad the blizzard was at his place, and I make a point of telling how Judd Travers come and plowed us out; plowed out some other driveways, too. To hear me tell it, Judd was part Paul Bunyan and part Jesus Christ, doin' all kinds of hero and wonderful things. No one says a bad word against him this time, but I don't hear no kind word for him, neither.

And then that evening, I see the light again over near Middle Island Creek. I stand at the window in the dark watching, and get the feeling like something real bad is out there. Why's it staying right across from where we live? Why don't it go somewhere else? How do I know that after I go to sleep at night, that light won't come floating and bobbing right up our driveway and around our place? I'm glad David Howard's comin' to sleep over the next day. Sometimes I feel we got us a mystery I'd just as soon not have.

I go to my job at the vet's Saturday morning, and when Dad picks me up at noon, we stop by David Howard's and get him. As soon as we finish our lunch, we're going to explore the gristmill, where I figure that light's got to be.

This time, though, Dara Lynn wants to go with us.

"No way," I tell her.

"Why not?" she says.

" 'Cause we're doing our own stuff. You go do yours."

"I'll just watch," says Dara Lynn.

"You will not!" I yell, as she follows us to the door.

Ma comes out of the bedroom. "Dara Lynn, you got things to play with in here," she says. "I'll mix up some flour paste, and you and Becky can cut pictures out of magazines, make a scrapbook."

"I don't want to make no scrapbook! I can play out in my own yard if I want!" Dara Lynn says.

David and I go out, but leave Shiloh inside so he won't give us away when we give Dara Lynn the slip. We're tryin' to beat her to the bridge, but we get halfway down the drive and here she comes, clomping along in her boots, not even buckled. So we have to make like we're going hiking along the creek in the other direction, hide behind some trees, then head back the other way using the same footprints in the snow to confuse her.

By now the thirty-one inches have sunk down to twenty or so, and melting all the time, but every step we take is still a high one. Finally we see Dara Lynn headin' back up toward the house, so we make our way toward the bridge, down the bank, and push our way through the tangle of bushes and trees and snow to the cinder block supports of the old mill.

The old white-shingled building is propped up on a dozen or so columns to keep it out of the water in flood season, and one whole side of it's been burned or collapsed out of sheer misery, can't tell which. Dad won't let us climb up in there — too dangerous — but we take a good look below.

We hold on to each other, 'cause we know that the ground slants toward the creek, and it's full of ruts and gullies. One wrong step, and we're in a snowbank over our heads. Can't even tell where the bank stops and the creek begins. You get thirty-one inches of snow falling down in this place, plus the four or five inches more, plus all the snow that blows off the road or was pushed down here by the plow, why . . . a person could get buried, and nobody find him till spring.

I take this old dead limb and dig out a path in front of us. Even without snow, it's hard to see just what's here. Imagine the waterwheel was on the side next to the creek, but we sure can't make out anything.

"Know what?" David says at last. "If anybody had been down here, either we'd find his footprints or he's buried at the bottom of this snow."

I stop and think. Without moving my feet, I twist my body all around, lookin' in every direction, and I don't see any footprints here at all, not around the gristmill nor the bank nor the path leading up to the road — only the tracks we made ourselves.

"Shoot!" I say, disappointed.

"If we dig, though, we might find a body under the snow," says David.

"Yeah," I say, not all that eager. We don't

even know what we're lookin' for anymore — just talkin' nonsense. We both know we're not about to go back to my place, carry a shovel all the way down here, and start digging.

We claw our way back up the bank, same place we come down, and make a whole pile of snowballs — line 'em up on the bridge. Then we take turns seeing if we can hit a stick far out there on the ice.

We do a couple of throws, and I've just picked up my third snowball when suddenly there's this loud *whomp!*, like a whole house has rose up in the air and set down again.

David and I turn, starin' in the direction of the noise, just in time to see snow slidin' off the roof of the old Shiloh schoolhouse. We run over and wade through the school yard, and there's half the roof caved in, settin' there like it's been that way forever.

"Wow!" I say.

"It went just like that!" says David. "All that snow!"

"Let's check it out!" I tell him, and we go over and try the door. Locked, of course. Paint flecks scattered all about. Through the dusty window I can see an old refrigerator, a flowered armchair that the mice have nested in, some children's desks, a table. . . . We go around back to where the outhouse is. And then we stop dead still and stare, because there's a fresh path in the snow between the outhouse and a cellar window.

"Marty!" David whispers, his eyes half popped from his head.

We know what we're going to do. We check out the outhouse first, and my heart's like to jump out of my skin. The snow's been cleared away where the door's ajar, and I figure if anybody's in there hearing us talk, he'd probably pull the door to. But I know if we get up to that door and peer around it and see somebody sittin' inside, I will die on the spot.

We're lifting our feet so high with each step it looks like we're marching, and David gets to the door first.

Ready? he mouths to me. I nod. He hooks one finger around the edge of that door and slowly, slowly pulls it open.

Creeeaaak! it goes, just like in the movies.

"Whew!" I say, when I see the seat's empty.

Together, we turn and look at the school, knowing that somebody could be watching us that very minute. At the same time, we know as sure as we got teeth in our mouth that we're going to climb in there and take a look. You can see by that open window where somebody's been crawlin' in and out.

"Who's gonna go first?" asks David,

meaning that he was the one who checked out the outhouse, and now it's my turn.

I get down on my knees, stick one leg inside, and back in. See that somebody's put an old bench below the window to step down on, and soon as both my legs are in, and then my back and head, I look around.

"What do you see?" David whispers.

"Junk," I tell him. "Broken-down chairs. An old blackboard. Rats' nests — pigeon poop." But I don't see a living soul. Don't hear a single sound except the creak of some boards where the wind blows through.

"Come on in," I say to David, and he climbs in, too. The floor above us is sagging, so we hug the wall wherever we can. Have to crawl over a ton of stuff to get to the stairs, and then we stick to the sides in case they give.

When we get to the top, we see where the roof's come down, spilling snow onto what's left of a classroom.

"David!" I say, and point. There is my dad's lantern, sittin' right on the floor beside a blanket. I'd know it anywhere — got a piece of tape at the back to hold the batteries in. We look around, and there's a shotgun, too. And some chicken bones and a box of crackers. Any minute now, I'm thinking, I'll feel a gun in my back.

I walk over to pick up Dad's lantern, but then my heart almost gives out and my legs start to buckle. All I can do is grab David's sleeve and point, 'cause there, sticking out from under one of the fallen rafters, with snow and shingles on top, are the curled fingers of a man's glove. And on down the pile of rubble, about where his foot would be, is half a man's boot showing.

Fifteen

Forget Dad's lantern. David and me tumble back down those steps, scrambling over junk in the basement, sure that any minute someone's goin' to snatch us by the ankles, pull us back. We get outside, and go floppin' and falling through the snow till we reach the road, then tear across the bridge and on up the drive, our breath comin' in steamy puffs.

We reach the house, scramble up on the porch, and we're both trying to squeeze through that door at once, falling over Dara Lynn's boots she's left right there on the rug.

"Marty, what . . . ?" asks Ma, lookin' up from her sewing.

"Over in the schoolhouse . . ." I point. "The roof caved in from all the snow and there's a dead man under the rafters." I collapse on a chair, my chest heaving.

Ma rises from the sofa, her scissors sliding to the floor. "You sure 'bout this, Marty?"

"Sure as Christmas," says David, and we wait, starin' at each other while Ma makes the call to the sheriff.

Dara Lynn says she will never forgive us, not takin' her along.

"I never seen a dead person in my whole life!" she cries.

"You have too. You seen Grandma Preston," I tell her.

"I never seen one that got a roof caved in on him," she wails.

I am actually thinking of taking Dara Lynn over there and showing it to her, but Ma says David and me are not to go back till the sheriff gets here, and Dara Lynn's not to go at all. Not somethin' for a little girl to see. So we watch from the window, and when the sheriff's car shows up out on the road later, David and me go on over. They got a police dog with 'em.

Sheriff rolls down his window. "You the boys who found a body? Your ma called?"

I nod. I point to the schoolhouse.

Car moves on slow across the bridge, and David and me follow. We show 'em the path in the snow from the basement window to the outhouse, and one of the deputies points out another path leading off into the woods. David and I didn't notice that one at all.

"Okay, now," the sheriff says. "I want you

boys to stay outside with Frank here while Pete and I go take a look." Frank's the man with the police dog, I guess.

David and I stand there watching, wondering how in the world Pete, the fat one, is going to get himself through that basement window — jacket, gun, belly, and all — but he does.

Frank lets us pet his dog while we wait. We can hear the other men talking inside, but can't make out the words. Now and then a board creaks, something else giving way, I guess. Footsteps going back and forth across the floor.

After a while the men come out again, Sheriff crawling out first through that basement window, Pete behind him, dragging a leaf bag filled with stuff. I can see the shotgun sticking out of the bag. I tell 'em Dad's lantern is in there, but they say they've got to keep all the evidence for a while.

"So what you got?" Frank asks the others.

Sheriff grins at us. "Well, there was a glove and a boot, all right, but nobody in 'em. I'll admit, it sure looked like there was a body under there, but it was just some clothes."

But before David and I have a chance to feel really stupid, Sheriff says, "But look what else we found, Frank," and holds up a pair of bright orange pants.

Frank whistles, then smiles.

"Know what this is?" the sheriff asks David and me. "The uniform over at the county jail. We've been lookin' for those two escapees, and it appears this is where they've been."

My hand moves into my jacket pocket and deep down in one corner where I'd forgotten all about it, I find this piece of orange cloth that Shiloh and the Lab were playing with.

"There you go!" says the sheriff when he sees it. "Piece of the shirt! Where'd you find that?"

"My dog brought it home," I say, as David stares.

"Surprised they got this far," says Pete. "Probably dropped their clothes as soon as they could steal something else to put on their backs."

"Well, we figured they'd show up sooner or later, weather like this," says the sheriff, taking the piece of shirt in my hand and sticking it in the bag, too. "What I can't figure, though, is why two men, who only had thirty days to serve for disorderly conduct, would pull something like this. Walk off that work detail. Now they've got to serve even more time when we catch 'em."

"Heck," says Pete. "I'd choose jail just to

stay nice and warm. Three square meals, a bunk and blanket . . . who knows what they were eating here!"

I'm wondering the same thing. I've been up to Middlebourne before with my dad, and the jail actually don't look too bad. Sort of like a castle snuggled there next to the courthouse, with the words, COUNTY JAIL in bright red letters. You put a wreath on the door, it'd look right cheery.

"But where are they now?" I ask.

"That's what Sergeant here is going to find out," Sheriff says, and he gives that dog a good healthy sniff of the jail clothes.

David and I watch as that dog buries his nose in the uniform, like he's drinking in the scent, and then he starts running around, nose to the snow. Pretty soon he's on the path to the outhouse and, after that, the path through the woods.

The story makes the next edition of the *Tyler Star–News*. There's a picture of the old Shiloh schoolhouse with its roof caved in, and the story says how two boys found the hideout. And then it tells how those men, who'd been arrested for disorderly conduct, turned out to be the chief suspects in the murder of the man from Bens Run. David was right about that much, anyway. They'd figured that the longer they were in jail, the better chance the sheriff had of connecting them to the killing, so they got away when they saw the chance. Seems they'd been gambling with the man from Bens Run, who owed them a pile of money, and when he said he couldn't pay them, they got in a fight. Whether they meant to kill him or not, the court, I guess, will decide.

The story says that the police dog found them a couple miles away, coming back through the woods with some more blankets and half a roast beef. Photographer wanted to come and take our picture, but Mr. Howard wouldn't let him. Dad wouldn't even let the newspaper use our names. Said he didn't especially want the men to know who the boys were who found the hideout, and where they lived.

But it felt pretty good to be a hero for a day — me and David both. Tell the truth, I'd forgot about those men escaping from the county jail, and never dreamed they'd got clear over to Shiloh lookin' for a place to hide.

The kids on the bus Monday morning want to hear all about it — don't take them long to figure out who the two boys were.

"It *was* you and David, wasn't it?" squeals Sarah Peters.

"You see 'em go in the schoolhouse, or what?" asks Fred Niles.

"They pull a gun on you?" Michael Sholt wants to know.

Tell the story all over again, but I guess I skim the truth a little by leavin' things out — like how David and me run like roosters when we saw that glove sticking out from under the rafter. But if I leave things out, David puts things in, and after he gets on the bus, each of us giving our account in our own way, we have a story rolling like you wouldn't believe.

One kid tells another, and he tells somebody else, each of 'em tacking on a little something, so that by the time the bus gets to school and the story reaches Miss Talbot, it seems David and me had trapped the vicious killers in the old Shiloh schoolhouse, and then we climbed up on the roof and tramped around so that it fell down, burying the men in snow up to their armpits.

But wouldn't you know, Miss Talbot made a lesson of it? She can make a lesson out of anything. First it's Pilgrims, then Alaska, and now we got to find out all about prisons — how many in the state of West Virginia, how you get there by doin' what, and how long you got to stay. Don't ever tell your teacher somethin' she don't need to know, or she'll make homework out of it quicker'n you can say, "My dog Shiloh."

Each time we tell the story, though, I say, "See? It wasn't Judd, after all! You had him all wrong. He's changin'! You should see all he's done for his dogs."

But the worst was right around the corner, and maybe, if I'd known what was comin' next, I wouldn't have said nothing at all.

Sixteen

Valentine's Day, and David and me get more valentines than any other boys in our class — most of 'em from girls. In sixth grade, we don't go much for valentines — just the gross and crazy kind — but here are all these hearts with our names on 'em. I even got a valentine from Sarah Peters with a stick of spearmint gum stuck to the front, and the words VALENTINE, I CHEWS YOU! Sarah Peters never give any boy a valentine before, namely 'cause she's so stuck on herself, and all because she can swim. On a swim team or something. But here's this big valentine with her name on it. Embarrassing is what it is, especially since I didn't give out any valentines at all.

On the way home, after David Howard gets off the bus, Dara Lynn comes and sits beside me. She's showin' me all her valentines, and then she reaches in her coat pocket and pulls out the one from her teacher. Got a whole Milky Way bar with a ribbon around it.

I can't believe her teacher gave everybody a big candy bar like that. Dara Lynn, of course, starts peelin' the wrapper off that chocolate real slow like, wavin' it around in front of my nose till I think I hate my sister worse'n spinach.

And then, all of a sudden, she breaks that candy in half and hands a piece to me. "Here," she says.

I look at the candy. Look at Dara Lynn. "That half got poison in it?" I say.

"No," she tells me, jiggling it a little. "Go on. You can have it."

I take the candy and look it over good. Seems fine to me. Take a bite. The purest, sweetest chocolate you ever did taste. Dara Lynn settles back in her seat, swingin' her legs and eatin' that chocolate bar, and I eat my piece, too, and think how if I live to be a hundred, I will never understand my sister.

Kids still talkin' about the men from the county jail hidin' out in the old Shiloh schoolhouse. All the stuff that they'd stolen was returned, and Fred Niles's dad got his shotgun and two jackets back.

"See?" I say to Fred. "You were accusing Judd for nothing."

"I'll bet he's taken stuff we don't even

know of, though," Fred says.

I turn halfway round in my seat. "Why are you always tryin' to blame Judd for every little thing that happens?" I ask, angry.

But Sarah says, "The way he used to treat Shiloh, Marty, I'd think you and Judd would be enemies. Tell me one good thing he's done."

"He plowed us out after the blizzard. Plowed out a few more besides," I say, and try hard to think of something else. Judd wasn't drinkin' anymore that I knew of. Wasn't knocking down anybody's mailbox. Wasn't going around stealing all the stuff people thought he had. Then I see that all I'm doing is thinking of things he *wasn't* doing. I was short on things he did.

"You know what I think?" says Michael Sholt, maybe jealous of all the attention David and me got that day. "I think you and your dad are afraid of him. No matter what he does, you say a good word. He's got you scared!"

Now I'm really mad. "Has not! I wasn't too scared to stand up to him and take Shiloh!" I say. "Dad wasn't scared to go tell him not to hunt on our land!"

"Well, *my* dad says the Traverses have been trouble ever since they been here — my granddad knew his granddad — and they are bad news, the whole lot of them! If a man goes driving around drunk, destroying people's property, you don't reward him by fixing up his truck and taking him food."

"But it worked, didn't it?" I say. "He's not driving drunk anymore! He didn't kill that man or rob those houses. What else do you want him to do?"

"Move to Missouri, as far from here as he can get," says Michael, and laughs. Sarah and Fred laugh, too.

At dinner that night, I tell Dad what Michael said.

"Well, Marty," he says, "a person's got to make up his mind: Does he want someone to change for the better or does he want to get even? And if you want to get even with somebody, you'll get back at him, he'll get back at you, and there's no stopping it."

"But I wish there was some way we could make people like Judd better," I tell him.

Dad don't answer for a moment. Puts a square of margarine on his mashed potatoes and covers it all with pepper. "You can't *make* folks like you, Marty, and you especially can't make folks like somebody else."

I lay on the living room floor after supper over by the woodstove and wrestle with Shiloh. He had his head on my leg all through dinner, his big brown eyes watchin' every morsel of food that travels between my plate and my mouth, like why don't something make a detour down his way? And sometimes, when Ma ain't lookin', I'd slip him a piece of fat off my pork chop.

But now we both been fed, and Shiloh sure loves to romp after a good dinner. I lay down on the floor and hide my face in my arms, and that dog goes nuts. Tries every which way to roll me over, and finally he'll run his nose up under my arm and all down my side, and get to tickling me so I laugh and have to turn over, and then he's happy.

Ma's watching from over in her chair and smiling. "Maybe he thinks you're not breathing, Marty, lyin' so still. Maybe he's got to see you're still alive," she says.

Hard to tell sometimes if that dog's playin' or workin', but we roll around till we're both wore out, and then I lay still on my back and let him put his head on my chest. Stroke his ears and think how I must be one of the luckiest people in the whole state of West Virginia.

February turns to March, and every now and then we get a little taste of spring. Wind feels just a bit warmer. You walk outside and everywhere you hear the sound of running water. Snow sliding off the roof, ice melting on the shed, and all the extra water makes the creek run higher and faster, so the sound's louder than it was. Every day the heaps of dirty snow that the plow left at the side of the road get smaller and smaller, and now and then there's a good hard rain that almost melts it down while you watch.

In between the rains, the sun shines warmer and brighter, and all the water in the ditches and gullies shines back at you. Ma sees her crocuses starting to come up, and goes out to count them.

Judd works at Whelan's Garage every other Saturday, meanin' that every other week he's got the weekend off. Once in a while I hang around his place — help him wash his truck, maybe.

Can't say I see a huge change in the way he treats his dogs, but I see some. He don't cuss at 'em like he used to, and I don't see him kick 'em. Now and then he'll reach out to pet one of 'em, but they always shy away a little when he does that. Guess it's the same with animals as it is with people — takes them a long time to win back trust.

"I think your dogs are happier now that they got a yard to run in, don't have a chain around their necks," I tell him as I wipe the hubcaps on his pickup.

"Seem happy," Judd says. "Neighbors say they don't bark as much."

"Well, that's good, then," I tell him. "Fence holding up okay?"

"Yeah, but I wish I'd put a gate in it after all. When I'm in the backyard and want to go round front, I got to go in through the trailer first," Judd says.

"Well, we got the extra fencing behind your shed," I say. "Want me to help you put the gate on?"

"I'm going over to Middlebourne today, but you can come by tomorrow, you want to," Judd says.

"Sure," I tell him.

Sunday's on the cold side, but when the sun comes out from behind a cloud, the air takes on a different feel. Something about a March sun on the back of your neck, you know spring's not far off. Shiloh's out with the black Labrador somewhere, and I'm glad, 'cause we both seem to feel guilty when I head for Judd's — Shiloh, for not comin' with me, and me, 'cause I'm goin' somewhere without him. But today he don't have to watch me leave, and I tell Dad I'll be back soon as I help Judd put on that gate.

When I get to the trailer, Judd's dogs are having a fine time out in the yard. He's thrown 'em an old sock with a knot in it, and they are just chewin' it to pieces, growlin' and tugging and shakin' their heads back and forth, holding on with their teeth for dear life. Keeps 'em busy while we work on the fence. Judd's got pliers and a hammer, and he unhooks the wire from one of the poles. We roll it up and haul his gate into place. Got to move another pole over closer, and fasten some hinges on it.

It ain't as easy as it first seemed. I'm holdin' the gate upright and Judd's tryin' to hammer a pin down inside a hinge. His dogs are still at work on that sock, tumbling around and makin' like they're all so fierce. John Collins says that tug-o'-war's a game you shouldn't play with your dogs — makes 'em aggressive; turns 'em mean. But we done enough preaching already, and I'm not about to tell Judd how his dogs should *play*.

Suddenly — it happens so fast I almost miss it — Judd steps backward to test the gate, and the heel of his boot comes down hard on the left front paw of the black-and-white dog. Dog gives this loud yelp, Judd turns, lookin' to see what's happened, and next thing we know, the black and white's sunk his teeth deep in Judd's leg.

Judd's bellowing in pain, I'm trying to call his dog off, the other dogs are barking, and a

155

neighbor down the way opens her back door to see what's going on.

All the noise just seems to put the black-and-white dog in a frenzy. He's the biggest one of the lot, and he's tuggin' at Judd's leg like a piece of meat, growlin' something terrible. It's as though all the anger and meanness that dog's felt for Judd all these years is right now comin' up out of his mouth. Judd groans, swears, bellows again, tryin' to swing himself around, get the leg free, but he can't.

I'm about to run inside for a pail of water to throw on that dog when Judd lifts the hammer, hangs back a moment, then brings it down on the black and white's head.

The dog's legs give out from under him, his jaw goes slack, then he slumps to the ground and lays still.

Seventeen

I can't hardly breathe. Don't know who to head for, Judd or the dog, so I don't move at all.

"Clyde!" comes the neighbor's voice. "Judd Travers just killed that dog!"

That gets my feet moving. I go over to the black and white and put my hand on his chest to see if the heart's beating. Then I feel for the pulse on the inside of his hind leg, the way John Collins taught me. Nothing at all.

I look over at Judd. He's sittin' on the ground, arms on his knees, head on his arms. His pant leg's soaked with blood. The other two dogs have crept off to a far corner, just watching. Don't make a sound.

"Judd," I say, "you sit tight. I'm callin' Doc Murphy." And I run to the back door of his trailer.

"What's happened over there?" calls the neighbor's husband.

"Dog attacked Judd," I call back, but all the while I'm wondering, did he have to *kill* him? Judd's leg looks bad, though. Not the same leg that was broke, either. The other one. Now he's got *two* bum legs.

Doc Murphy says he's just about to walk out the door, going to visit his brother down in Parkersburg, and I say, "Doc, Judd's been hurt by one of his dogs and he's bleedin' pretty bad."

"Where you calling from, Marty?"

"Here at Judd's," I tell him. "He's out back."

I go out the door again. Judd is in the same position I left him, but he suddenly rears back and socks the fist of his right hand into the palm of his left just about as hard as a man can hit, cussing hisself out. Then he slumps again, and don't lift his head.

"Anything we can do?" the neighbor woman calls.

"Doc's on his way over," I yell back.

I sit down beside Judd. He's shakin' his head back and forth, back and forth, his shoulders twitching once or twice like he's about to hit himself again.

"My best hunting dog," he says. "Now I've lost two." I know he's counting Shiloh.

"This one ever do anything like that before?" I ask.

"Was always chained before. Don't know what got into him this time. I never meant to step on his paw."

"I know you didn't," I say.

He eases up his pant leg, and that is some bite. Big flap of skin just hanging there.

We hear a car coming down the road from the bridge, and it's not long before Doc Murphy makes a U-turn in front of Judd's and pulls his car off the pavement. Comes hurrying around to the back and walks through the opening in the fence. Judd's other two dogs don't even bark. One of 'em's lying down now, head on his paws. Look like they're both too scared to move. They can tell something's happened to the black and white.

Doc Murphy grunts and sets his bag on the ground, then bends over Judd's leg and gives a whistle. His eye falls on the dead dog, blood oozing out one corner of his mouth, eyes fogged over. Sees the hammer, too, and shakes his head.

"You provoke that dog, Judd?"

"No, he didn't," I say, answering for him. "I seen the whole thing. Judd accidentally stepped on his paw. The dog bit him and wouldn't let go."

Doc sighs. "Well, we got trouble enough right here," he says. "Come in the house,

159

Judd, where I can sew you up. Don't like to stitch up a dog bite if I can help it. Better to keep the wound open, keep it clean, but this one's going to take a whole bunch of stitches, I can tell you."

Seems like Judd just got through limpin' on one leg, and now he's limpin' on the other. I unwind that roll of wire fence back again and stretch it over the opening where the gate was to be so the other two dogs won't get out, and I fasten it good. Then I go inside. Soon as the yard's empty, I see the other dogs come over and sniff the black and white. One of 'em makes a whining sound in his throat. Don't tell me dogs don't cry!

I sit off to one side while Doc works on Judd. Got him sitting up on the table, leg stretched out on a towel where Doc can reach it. I get some more towels, and some hot water, scrub up good, and hand Doc things as he needs them.

"Okay, now, Judd," Doc says at last. "Don't want you to get that bandage wet. You come by in a couple of days, let me take a look at it, and we'll take the stitches out in two weeks or so. I got to pump you full of antibiotics now before I leave." He writes out a prescription, too. "And I got to take that dog with me; it's the law. Check him for rabies."

"Tell 'em I want him back," says Judd, real soft.

Doc turns around. "What you say?"

"I want the body back when they're done with it."

"Sure, Judd," Doc says. "I'll tell them."

I find an old box out back. Roll the dog's body into the box, and set it on the floor of Doc's car.

When he's gone, I go inside to wash up, see if Judd wants me to stay. He don't. He's on the couch, staring straight ahead.

Finally I tell him, "I'm sure sorry today turned out like it did."

But he don't answer, and I leave.

I tell my family what happened. Everyone's looking real sorry, even Dara Lynn.

Ma sighs. "Some people just seem to attract trouble," she says at last.

And Dad says, "Does seem like there should have been some other way to make that dog let go, but I don't know what. A dog get his teeth in you like that, he can tear you up mighty quick."

One good thing about bein' an animal is you don't have to know all the bad things happening around you. When Dara Lynn and me walk down to the school bus stop on Monday, Shiloh goes dancin' along beside us, frisky as you please. Don't even know one of his own kind was killed. But I see that all the sorry's gone out of Dara Lynn's eyes, too, and there's pure eagerness in its place.

"Listen here," I say. "I don't want you tellin' anybody that Judd killed one of his dogs. Hear?"

"You can't make me not tell!" she says.

"If you tell what Judd did, I'll tell the whole bus how you threw up on your new shoes last summer," I say.

Dara Lynn's mad as hornets. "Okay!" she shouts. "I won't say he killed a dog!"

The bus comes and we get on, and the first thing out of her mouth is worse: "Judd Travers killed something yesterday!" And then, to me, "I didn't say *what*, did I?"

Fact is, couple of the kids had already heard, so the whole bus already knew.

"Just picked up a hammer and hit his own dog over the head. That's what his neighbor said," Fred Niles tells the rest.

"Listen!" I say. "I saw it happen. That dog was tearing up his leg. If Judd hadn't hit him when he did, he might not be walking now."

"Yeah, but why do his dogs hate him so much? Ask him that!" says Michael Sholt.

I worry a lot about Judd after that. Doc Murphy says he come by to have his stitches out, and the wound's healing nicely. The black and white didn't have rabies, the test showed, and as far as Doc knows, Judd's going to work every day. But when Judd's out in his truck and passes me on the road, it's like he don't even see me.

I go over once to ask if he wants to finish putting that gate on yet, 'cause the wire fencing's right where I left it, the gate swingin' in the breeze with no opening there at all. Judd's truck's out in front, but when I knock, nobody answers. I call, but nobody comes.

I go around in back to see if Judd's there. His two dogs are inside the fence, but beyond that, out past his satellite dish, even, I see a little mound of fresh dirt at the edge of Judd's property. I walk back, hands in my pockets, and look down. There's a horse-shoe stake driven in the ground at the head of this little grave, and around the stake is a dog's leather collar.

Eighteen

Seems like maybe we're back where we started with Judd Travers. Can't tell what's going on in his mind, 'cause he don't ever stop to talk to me. Saturdays I'll see him pass by out there on the road two, three times, but if I'm out there he don't even wave. Either he's mad at me, I figure, for bringin' that fence by in the first place, or he's grievin' for his dog.

Maybe all my work to be friendly and to give his dogs a better life is going to backfire, and when he looks at me, what he'll think about is how two of his dogs are gone.

"Just you stay away from him for a while," says Dad. "You got to give a man time to sort things through."

Closer it gets to April, the more it rains. Not a bit of snow left. Everything's mud, and just when you think there's not a drop of water could be left in the sky, it rains some more.

When it rains hard enough and long

164

enough, Middle Island Creek overflows its banks and we get stranded. Being up the hill a ways from the road, our house don't get wet, but there's a stretch of road near the church in Little that floods when the creek is really high. "The Narrows," we call it, and Dad'll have to get to work another way. What we do is count the layers of stones in the supports that hold up the bridge here in Shiloh. If we can only see nine stones between the bottom of the bridge and the top of the water, we know the road down at Little will be flooded. More than nine, we're probably okay.

On Saturday when I go to the vet's, there's a litter of kittens somebody found along the creek. A mama cat had gone in one of those school bus shelters, no bigger than a phone booth, and had her babies, and the water was threatening to carry them off. She was meowing and somebody heard and brought 'em to John Collins. Hadn't even got their eyes opened yet.

I'm making sure each of those babies gets a turn at the mother's milk, and thinking how Dara Lynn wanted a kitten even before I wanted Shiloh. Can't believe I'm thinking what I am, but I say, "I'll take one of those kittens, Doc Collins."

"You get your pick, Marty," he says. "But

you'll have to wait till they're eight weeks old. You don't want to take them from their mother too early."

Dara Lynn's got a birthday in May, and that'll be just about the right time to surprise her. But knowing my sister, she'll probably say something ugly — like how come she didn't get to choose it herself, or I got the wrong color. Sometimes you just have to take chances.

Somebody brings in a dog that morning to be checked over 'cause he's tearing up the furniture. The man says that every time he comes home from work in the evening, the dog's destroyed something else.

I scratch the retriever's ears while John Collins talks to the owner — explains that dogs, like people, want a little more out of life than just hanging round waiting for somebody to come home, pay them some attention. They got to feel needed.

"Let your dog know that when you come home, it's his time, and you expect things of him," Doc says, "even if it's only to bring in the paper or chase the squirrels away from the bird feeder. Your dog wants to know he has a purpose."

The last Saturday in March, Dad picks me up after my job at the vet's and then we pick up David. Been raining all week, off and on, and the water's right high, lapping at the side of the road through the Narrows. When we get to the Shiloh bridge, we see there're only ten layers of stones showing on the supports between the floor of the bridge and the top of the water.

"It's close," Dad says.

He drops us off at the driveway and goes on to deliver the rest of his mail, and David and I run up to the house where Ma's got grilled cheese sandwiches and tomato soup waiting.

"Da-vid!" sings out Becky, all smiles, when she sees him. Girls always like to show off for David.

"Hi, Popcorn," says David.

Then Dara Lynn has to be her usual nuisance, and keeps kickin' us under the table and pretending it was Becky did it.

"Dara Lynn, will you stop it?" I snap, almost sorry I'm savin' that kitten for her.

"Dara Lynn, I'm not tellin' you again! Behave!" says Ma, and I notice she's holding her cheek. "I got no patience with you today." And then she gives this little half smile to David and says, "Sorry I'm not more cheery, but I got a toothache that is making my whole face sore."

I take a good look at Ma. "It's swelling up some, too," I say.

She feels with her hand, then goes and looks in the mirror. "Guess I ought to have gone to the dentist like your dad said," she tells me.

She goes back in the bedroom and lies down, and we try to keep it quiet in the living room. We spread out my Monopoly set on the floor and let Dara Lynn play, but when you get down on the rug like that, Shiloh thinks it's playtime, and he wiggles and rolls and tries to lick our faces, and soon the houses on Park Place are all over the board. Becky thinks it's funny, but Dara Lynn gets mad.

"Stupid old dog!" she yells, and hits at him hard. Shiloh gives this little yelp and comes around behind me. I swoop all Dara Lynn's houses and money off the board, and tell her the game's over. "Don't you ever, never, hit my dog!" I say.

"Oh, who wants to play Monopoly, anyway? Come on, Becky," she says, and the girls go off to their bedroom, get down the box of old jewelry Grandma Preston give them once, and try on all the pieces.

It's raining lightly outside, and David and me are waiting for it to stop. Then we're going back to the old Shiloh schoolhouse to see if we can find any more stuff those men left behind — keep it for a souvenir.

We horse around a little, try to teach Shiloh to help David take his jacket off, make himself useful. But Shiloh yanks too hard on one sleeve and a seam pulls out at the shoulder.

Ma comes out of the bedroom and makes some calls in the kitchen, then comes over to me.

"Marty, I've called the dentist and he says if I can get down there right now, he'll take me today. This toothache's gettin' worse and worse. I called Mrs. Sweeney, and she said she and her daughter are going to Sistersville and they think they can squeeze me in the cab of their pickup, too. Mrs. Ellison is going to come up here and watch you kids till I get back."

"We don't need a sitter!" I say, embarrassed.

"Maybe not, but the girls do, and I want you to behave for her now. Hear?"

She goes in the bathroom to brush her teeth, and by the time she's got her coat on, we can see Mrs. Sweeney's pickup coming up the drive. Ma goes out and gets in.

Great! I'm thinking. David comes for an overnight, and we get a baby-sitter! Mrs. Ellison's nice, though. Always leaves a little something in her mailbox for Dad when she bakes, and I'm thinking she might show up with a chocolate cake. At least Dara Lynn and Becky are having a fine time in their bedroom, and are leaving David and me alone for a change. We open a pop and watch a basketball game on TV.

Fifteen minutes go by, though, and Mrs. Ellison still hasn't come. Phone rings and she says, "Marty, your ma still there?" I tell her she's gone, and Mrs. Ellison says, "Well, the water here in Little is higher than I thought, and I'm afraid if I get over to your place in our Buick, I might not make it back again. Sam's on his way home right now, and he's going to drive me to your house in the four by four. Everything okay there?"

"Everything's fine," I tell her.

No sooner hang up than it rings again, and this time it's Michael Sholt.

"Marty!" he says. "I'm up at my cousin's, and there's a dead man floating down the creek! He just went by! Should be by your place in five minutes. Go see who he is!"

Nineteen

I drop that phone and David and me grab our jackets and run outside, Shiloh at our heels. The rain's tapered off, but there's mud everywhere. We don't care, though. We run up on the bridge and wait right in the middle, looking upstream. That is one wild-looking creek!

"You suppose dead men float on their backs or their stomachs?" I ask David.

"Stomachs," he says. "That's the way they do in the movies, anyway."

Who could it be? I wonder. Bet someone's called the sheriff already and there'll be men waiting down at the bend where the water slows — see if they can snag him, pull him in. Wouldn't it be something if David and me could find out who he is, and be the first to call the paper? And then the thought come to me: What if it's Judd Travers? Don't know what made me think that, but it just crossed my mind.

We stand out there on the bridge watching that muddy water come rushing at us and disappear under our feet. No one in the *world* would think Middle Island Creek was anything but a river now.

"You figure five minutes are up?" I ask David.

"Probably ten," he says. "What if Michael was kidding? Be just like him, you know. Get us standing out here on the bridge waiting to see a dead man, and him and his cousin laughing their heads off."

We stare some more at the water. You look at a river long enough, it makes you dizzy.

"There's something!" David yells suddenly, and I look hard where he's pointing. Sure enough, bobbing around the curve ahead is something about the size of a man. When it bumps a rock, we see an arm fly up.

"Jiminy!" breathes David.

We run to the far side of the bridge where it looks like the body is heading. Can't tell what color his hair is — can't even see his hair, just the shape of his head, and then his feet, tossing about on the current like the feet of Becky's rag doll.

"Here he comes!" yells David, just as I see Dara Lynn and Becky cross the road.

"Go on back!" I yell. "We're comin' right up." I turn toward the water again, and next

I know, the body's coming smack toward us, sliding under the bridge, and we see it's no dead man at all, it's one of those dummies left over from Halloween.

"Ah, shoot!" says David, as we turn and watch it pop out from under the bridge on the other side, its straw-stuffed legs flopping this way and that. Even Shiloh's been fooled — runs across to the other side and barks.

"What was *that?*" Dara Lynn demands, hurrying over. She and Becky got their shoes on, but the laces are flopping, and Becky's jacket's inside out.

"It wasn't nothing — just somebody's Halloween dummy," I say. "Go on back to the house, I said!"

"Don't have to!" says Dara Lynn, sticking out her chin. "Ma didn't say I couldn't come down here. I can walk on the bridge same as you."

"We're all goin' back," I tell her.

But David's mad at Michael Sholt. "Bet he knew it was a dummy all along," he's grumbling. "Maybe he and his cousin dropped it in the creek themselves!"

Becky goes over to the edge of the bridge where the railing makes a diamond pattern. She's lookin' at a spiderweb strung in one of those openings. It glistens silver from the rain. I'm thinking that this water is rising faster than I ever seen it before, as though a couple more creeks have suddenly emptied into it up the way, and it's all of them together rushing under the bridge now.

"Come on," I say again, stopping to tie Becky's shoes for her. "We're goin' up to the house. Mrs. Ellison'll be along, wonder where we went."

Becky starts off again, Shiloh trotting ahead of her, and David catches up with me, talking about what he's going to do if Michael starts a story around that he saw a dead man in Middle Island Creek.

"Look at me!" sings out Dara Lynn behind us. I turn and see she's worked her head through one of those diamond openings in the railing, acting like she's a bird, going to sail out over the creek. Her big puffy jacket on one side of the opening, her head on the other, she looks more like a turtle. Girl can't stand not having all the attention on her.

"Dara Lynn, you cut that out and come on," I say. "Get on up to the house."

She just laughs. I grab her by the arm and pull her back through the railing just as the Ellisons' four by four turns in our drive and moves on up to the house.

"I got it!" says David. "If Michael says there was a dead man in the creek, we'll say we saw him, too. Only we'll make it different. Say it was a man with red hair and a blue shirt on."

I laugh. "His face all swole up. . . ."

"And he looked like he'd been shot in the heart!" says David. We both laugh out loud, thinking of Michael's face if we turn that trick around.

" 'What'd I miss?' he'll be thinking," I say, "and . . ."

"Who-eeee!" I hear Dara Lynn whoop. I turn around and my heart shoots up to my mouth, 'cause right at our end of the bridge, Dara Lynn's climbed up on the railing, her skinny legs straddling it, one foot locked behind a metal bar to keep her balance. Both her arms are in the air, like kids do on a roller-coaster.

"Dara Lynn," I bellow, my voice cracking. "Get off there!"

She laughs, and in her hurry to climb up where I can't reach her, wobbles, grabs at the rail to steady herself, but misses. There's this short little scream, and then . . . then she's in the water.

"Dara *Lynn!*"

Stomach feels like I'm on a roller-coaster myself. Can't even swallow. I'm hanging over the rail, but Dara Lynn's too far down to reach. She's lookin' up at me with the wildest, whitest eyes I ever seen, her arms straight out at the sides like the cold of the water has paralyzed her. And then, just like the straw man, she disappears beneath the bridge.

David's shouting something, I don't know what, and Becky's run screaming up our driveway, then turns around and screams some more. I can see Mr. and Mrs. Ellison running down the drive toward her. David is running over to the railing on the other side of the bridge, his face as white as cream.

"Where is she?" he asks, turning to me. "She didn't come back out."

I am running around the end of the bridge, slipping and sliding down the bank toward the high water.

"What happened?" Mrs. Ellison calls.

"Dara Lynn fell in," I yell, and it's more like a sob.

"Oh, Lord, no!" cries Mrs. Ellison in the background, offering up a prayer for all of us.

All I can think of is havin' to tell Ma that Dara Lynn drowned. Of having to remember every last awful thing I ever said to her, like wishin' she'd fall in a hole and pull the dirt in after her. I am praying to Jesus that if he will save my sister I will never say a mean thing to her as long as I live, even while I know it's not humanly possible. "Just don't let her die, please, please!" I whisper. She'll drown without ever knowin' I gave her a kitten.

I squat down, lookin' under the bridge. I see that Dara Lynn's been snagged by the small trees and bushes sticking out of the water near the first support. At that moment she feels herself caught, and her arms come alive, floppin' and flailin' to turn herself around, and finally she's holding on, screamin' herself crazy.

Mr. Ellison's beside me now, and he's shouting instructions to Dara Lynn to pull herself hand over hand toward the bank, to grab on to the next branch and the next, and not let go on any account, while he wades out into that swirling water as far as he can to meet her.

It's when Dara Lynn pulls herself close enough for us to grab her that I think maybe the thumpin' in my chest won't kill me after all. But then it seems my heart stops altogether, for I see Shiloh out there in the water, the current carrying him farther and farther away. I know right off he jumped in to save Dara Lynn, and now he's got to save himself.

Twenty

All I hear is my scream.

We're haulin' Dara Lynn out, her clothes making a sucking sound as she leaves the water, but I can see my dog trying to paddle toward us; the current's against him, and he can't even keep himself in one place.

Most times Shiloh could throw himself into Middle Island Creek, chasing a stick I'd tossed, and come right out where he'd gone in, the water moves that slow. But when the rains are heavy and the creek swells fast, the water just tumbles around the bend, and Shiloh's never been in nothing like this before. He keeps tryin' to turn himself around in the water and get back to us.

"Shiloh!" I'm yellin', while behind me, back up on the road, Becky sets up a wail of despair.

"Oh, Lord Jesus, that little dog!" cries Mrs. Ellison, praying again, while her husband takes off his coat and wraps it around

Dara Lynn. Dara Lynn's crying, too — huge sobs.

Is God puttin' me to some kind of test, I wonder — saving my sister and drowning my dog? Did I trade one for the other? Lord knows I can't swim. Oh, Jesus, why didn't you make me go to the park in Sistersville and take lessons with Sarah Peters? Why'd I get to sixth grade and not even know how to float?

My mouth don't seem connected to my head. Can still hear it screaming. "Shiloh! Shiloh!"

All he's doin' is tirin' himself out tryin' to swim back to us.

I slide farther down the bank, one foot in the water.

"Don't you try to go in there, Marty," Mr. Ellison shouts.

I claw my way back up the bank, eyes stretched wide, thinkin' how I can make better time up on the road, maybe get myself down to the place where the creek narrows, and Shiloh might be close enough I can reach out to him somehow.

David's running beside me. I know I'm cryin' but I don't care. One foot squishes every time my shoe hits the pavement. Run as fast as we can.

And then I see this pickup comin' up the

road from Friendly, and I'm like to get myself run over.

Judd Travers stops and leans out the window. "You want to get yourself killed?" he calls, right angry. And then, "What's the matter, Marty?" Sees Mr. Ellison comin' up the road behind me, thinks he's chasin' me, maybe. He gets out of the truck.

I'm gasping. Point to the creek.

"Shiloh! He's in the water, and we can't reach him!"

"Marty, that dog will have to get himself out!" Mrs. Ellison calls from far behind us. "Don't you try to go after him, now."

But Judd crashes through the trees and brush, half sliding down the muddy bank, and I point to the head of my beagle back upstream, out there bobbing around in the current. Once, it looks like he goes under. Now David's cryin', too, squeaky little gasps.

Judd don't say a word. He's scramblin' up the bank again and grabs that rope in his pickup. Hobbles down the road, fast as his two bum legs will carry him, goin' even farther downstream, me and David at his heels. Then he ties one end of that rope to a tree at the edge of the water, the other end around his waist, taking his time to make a proper square knot, and I'm thinkin', Don't worry about knots, Judd — just go!

180

He's plunging into that cold water — all but his boots, which he leaves by the tree. I see now why he went so far downstream, 'cause if we were back closer to the bridge, Shiloh would have gone past us by now.

Another car stops up on the road. I hear voices.

"What happened?"

"Who's out there?"

And Mr. Ellison's giving the answers: "Judd Travers is going after Marty Preston's dog."

Mrs. Ellison and the girls have reached the spot now. Dara Lynn is dripping water, but she won't hear of going home. Every muscle in my body is straining to keep me as close to the water as I can get, my eyes trained on that muddy yellow surface, looking for Shiloh. Maybe this was a mistake. Maybe I should have stayed back where we saw him last, kept my eye on where he went. What if he's pulled under? What if his strength just gave out, and he can't paddle no more?

David gives a shout. We can see Shiloh now. Looks for a time like he's found something to crawl up on out there in that water, a tree limb or something, but while we watch, he's swept away again.

Judd's treading water out in the center of

Middle Island Creek, fighting the current himself, and Shiloh's about twenty feet upstream from him. But then — as I stare — I see him turning away from Judd! I wonder if my dog knows how much danger he's in. Wonder if he figures that between the water and Judd Travers, he'll take the water.

"Here, Shiloh! Come here, boy!" Judd calls, his hair all matted down over his eyes.

Shiloh seems spooked. He's lookin' straight ahead, neither to the right nor left. I see his eyes close again, the way he looks lyin' by the stove at night when he's about to fall asleep.

Judd's working his way out farther and farther, trying to get out in the middle of the creek before Shiloh goes by. He's got his head down now, his arms slicing through the water, but it seems like for every three strokes he takes forward, the creek carries him one stroke sideways.

"Don't give up, Shiloh!" I breathe. And then I begin yelling his name. "Come on, Shiloh! Go to Judd. Come on, boy! Come on!"

I wonder if Judd can make it in time. What if Shiloh's too far out and sails on by? What if the rope's not long enough for Judd to reach him? My breath's coming out all shaky.

Judd's out now about as far as he can go, and that rope is stretched taut. One hand is reaching way out, but seems like Shiloh's still trying to paddle away.

"No, Shiloh!" I plead.

Just then Judd gives this whistle. I know that when Shiloh was his, he was taught to come when Judd whistled. Come or else.

I see my dog start to turn. I see Judd's hand go out, and I hear Judd sayin', "Come on, boy. Come on, Shiloh. Ain't going to hurt you none."

And then . . . then my dog's in his arms, and Judd's shoulders go easy. He is just letting that current swing him on downstream and back to the bank. The rope is holding, and Judd don't have to work much — just let the creek do all the carrying.

I slosh along the bank down to where I can see Judd is headed. The Ellisons are going there, too, and a couple of men up on the road.

"Anybody got a blanket?" I hear someone say.

"I got one in my trunk," a man answers.

Arms are reaching out, hands ready. Somebody puts an old blanket around Judd's shoulders soon as he climbs out.

And now Shiloh's against my chest, his rough tongue licking me up one side of my face and down the other, his little body shaking. With Shiloh in one arm, I reach out and put my other around Judd.

"Thanks," I say, my voice all husky. "Thank you, Judd." I'd say more if I could, but I'm all choked up. I just give him a hug with my one free arm, and strangest of all, Judd hugs me back. It's a sort of jerky, awkward hug, like he hadn't had much practice, but it's a start.

I won't repeat what-all my folks said to us later. Dad does the yelling, Ma the crying, and David's got to sit and listen to the whole thing. That me and David went down to that swollen creek in the first place! That we left the girls alone! That Dara Lynn was reckless enough to climb up on that bridge railing. . . .

"Isn't it enough I have the worst toothache of my life without having to come home and find one of my daughters almost drowned?" weeps Ma.

I keep sayin', "I'm sorry" — David, too — but Dad tells us "sorry" wouldn't bring a dead girl back to life. Neither of 'em says anything about Shiloh. That ain't their worry right now.

Dara Lynn hangs her head like the starch has been knocked out of her. Just sits all quiet by the potbellied stove, arms wrapped around her middle. Becky's on the couch, suckin' her thumb. We are the sorriest-looking family right now, but my dog's safe in my arms, and I can't ask for more. Every time he wriggles to get down, I just hold him tighter, and finally he gives up and lays still, knowin' my arms'll get tired by and by.

Next day, though, after Mr. Howard comes for David, my folks are quiet. Seem like every time they walk by one of us, they squeeze a shoulder or pat a head or stroke somebody's hair.

That night after Becky's had her bath and has gone around givin' everyone her butterfly kiss, battin' her lashes against their cheeks, I go out in the kitchen where Dara Lynn's having her graham crackers and milk, and say, "Well, pretty soon you're goin' to have to be sharing that milk with someone else, you know."

She looks at me suspicious-like. "Why?" she says.

" 'Cause we're gettin' another member of the family, that's why."

Dara Lynn's eyes open wide. "Ma's having another baby?"

I laugh. "Not this kind of baby, she ain't. It's gonna be your birthday present from me, Dara Lynn. Somebody brought in a litter of kittens to Doc Collins. You want to come with me some Saturday and pick one out, it's yours."

Dara Lynn leaps off her chair and, with graham cracker crumbs on her fingers, hugs me hard. I hug back — a little jerky and awkward, but it's a start.

Everybody's talkin' about Judd Travers. Michael Sholt thought he was going to have the best story of all — that Halloween dummy he and his cousin dumped in the creek to fool us — but it's Judd everyone wants to hear about.

After David told his dad what had happened, Mr. Howard drove up to Judd's a few days later to write a story about him for the paper. But then, everyone from here to Friendly could tell it — how Dara Lynn fell in the creek, how Shiloh jumped in to save her, and Judd went in for Shiloh.

Asked what he was thinking about out there in that rushing water, Judd said, "Well, I guess I was worried some but I was more scared of not saving Shiloh, on account of that dog once saved me."

Once that newspaper story come out, someone even asked Judd if he'd like to be a volunteer for the Rescue Squad down in Sistersville. He's thinking on it.

We talk about it some in school — how dangerous a flood can get — and on the way home one afternoon, sittin' there beside David Howard, I say, "If you'd asked me last summer if Judd Travers would be a hero, I would have bet my cowboy hat it couldn't happen."

"I'd have bet my new Nikes," says David.

"Not in a million years," I say.

I eat the snack Ma's put out for me, and then — with Dara Lynn and Becky playin' out on the bag swing — I head over to Judd Travers' place. His pickup's not there — he's still at work — but I got a hammer stickin' out of one pocket, pliers and wire clippers out of the other.

His dogs bark like crazy when they see me comin' around the trailer, but they know me now, and I let them sniff my fingers before I unhook that wire fencing and start to work on the gate. Me and Judd almost had it done. I see how he got one of the hinges around that pole, and I set to work on the other. What'll it be like, I'm wondering, not to have to worry anymore about Judd Travers hurting my beagle? To visit him and not have to worry is he drunk? Pretty nice, I reckon.

Gettin' the gate to swing right ain't — isn't — as easy as it seems. You got to get the hinges on straight up and down, or the gate will hang crooked. I see I got the pin shafts turned to one side so the gate's tipped. Got to loosen the bolts and start all over again. But finally, when I give the gate a push, it opens in and it opens out, just the way Judd needs it to do.

I clip off the extra fencing, put it back behind Judd's shed. And then, makin' sure that gate's latched the way it's supposed to be, I go back up the road to where Shiloh's still waiting for me at the bridge. I scoop him up in my arms and let him wash my face good — beagle breath and all.

I'm thinking that someday, maybe, when I cross that bridge and head down this road to Judd's trailer, Shiloh might come along, sure that he's mine forever and nothing's going to change that.

Don't know if a dog — or a man, either — ever gets to the place where he can forget as well as forgive, but enough miracles have come my way lately to make me think that this could happen, too.

The employees of Thorndike Press hope you have enjoyed this Large Print book. All our Large Print titles are designed for easy reading, and all our books are made to last. Other Thorndike Press Large Print books are available at your library, through selected bookstores, or directly from us.

For information about titles, please call:

(800) 223-1244
(800) 223-6121

To share your comments, please write:

Publisher
Thorndike Press
295 Kennedy Memorial Drive
Waterville, ME 04901